THE HISTORY OF HENRY FIELDING

Henry Fielding.
From a Photograph of the Bust in Shire Hall, Taunton

A.W. Elson & Co., Boston

THE HISTORY

OF

HENRY FIELDING

BY

WILBUR L. CROSS

AUTHOR OF

THE DEVELOPMENT OF THE ENGLISH NOVEL
THE LIFE AND TIMES OF LAURENCE STERNE

VOLUME TWO

NEW HAVEN

YALE UNIVERSITY PRESS

LONDON · HUMPHREY MILFORD · OXFORD UNIVERSITY PRESS

MDCCCCXVIII

COPYRIGHT, 1918, BY
YALE UNIVERSITY PRESS

FIRST PUBLISHED, SEPTEMBER, 1918

CONTENTS

VOLUME TWO

ILLUSTRATIONS

VOLUME TWO

THE HISTORY OF HENRY FIELDING

CHAPTER XV

THE TRUE PATRIOT

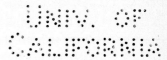

I

The publication of the "Miscellanies" was followed by a period of silence extending over two years and a half, except for one occasion midway when Fielding explained why he was writing no more. Near the close of his preface to the "Miscellanies," he had declared that he would never again publish a book or pamphlet without setting his name to it. Subsequent to this promise, he evidently determined to employ his pen no longer in fiction and political pamphlets, whether anonymous or not. With his "Miscellanies," containing such stray pieces as he wished to preserve, his literary career was to end. Thereafter he would devote himself wholly to the law. If he wrote anything more, it should be on legal subjects. This, if I understand Fielding rightly, was his resolution. He was then only thirty-six years old, and there was yet time for a solid reputation in the law, towards which numerous friends, as seen by the array of legal names among the subscribers to his "Miscellanies," were encouraging him. The decision to cut loose from literature and to rely wholly upon the law for a livelihood meant an heroic struggle. His wife was in declining health, his gout was increasing; nevertheless he took the plunge.

So far as his gout would permit, Fielding was constant, says Murphy, in his appearance at Westminster Hall during term time, and regularly attended every March and August the Assizes on the Western Circuit, which included

1

Winchester, Salisbury, Dorchester, Exeter, Taunton, Wells, and other towns, where he had lived and tramped in his youth. Among his companions on the Western Circuit were his cousin Henry Gould, subsequently a judge of the Court of Common Pleas, and the two future Lord Chancellors whom I have already mentioned—Robert Henley and Charles Pratt. But one searches in vain for the name of Fielding along with theirs in connection with the important trials of the period. The inference is that his practice was confined to small cases, of which he may have had few or many. A story got into the "Annual Register" of 1762 that after attending the judges on the Western Circuit for two or three years without success, he then published proposals for a new law book, which raised him in so high favour among the country people that he was for a time "loaded with briefs at every town." But, it is added, "his practice, thus suddenly increased, almost as suddenly declined."* The law book of the anecdote was probably the "Miscellanies," the only book that Fielding ever published by subscription. Proposals for its publication, if circulated at the Assizes in 1742, may well have prepared the way for more business during the next two years. But Fielding's wide acquaintance in the West and his full devotion to the law, now that he had abandoned politics and literature, must also be reckoned with. He was making extraordinary efforts to succeed.

His delight in the law, despite the hard labour, is apparent in "Joseph Andrews," which draws much of its humour from the administration of country justice and legal anecdotes. There is the justice, in from a fox-chase, before whom Parson Adams was brought on a charge of robbery, whose custom it was never to commit a gentleman, whatever the offence; and Justice Frolic who condemned Joseph and Fanny to Bridewell at the request of Lady Booby on

* "Annual Register," 1762, under "Characters," p. 18.

the charge of cutting a hazel twig while passing through the fields of Lawyer Scout, and afterwards as quickly released them when he discovered who they really were. The dishonesty of pettifoggers Fielding often denounced, and was amused by legal casuistry such as whether the defendant was mad or not. While waiting for briefs at Westminster Hall, he liked to listen, he says, to the arguments between Serjeant Bramble and Serjeant Puzzle. "Now Bramble throws in an argument; and Puzzle's scale strikes the beam; again, Bramble shares the like fate, overpowered by the weight of Puzzle. Here Bramble hits, there Puzzle strikes; here one has you, there t'other has you; 'till at last all becomes one scene of confusion in the tortured minds of the hearers." Another humorous complaint against lawyers was that they were inclined to talk too much about their profession on all occasions, and so spoil many times good company by keeping the conversation from general topics. Perhaps he once met Sir Francis Page, who died in 1741,—a coarse and brutal judge remembered on the Western Circuit, over which he presided during the summer Assizes of 1737 and 1739. At least Fielding relates of him an incident which actually occurred at Salisbury.* As told by Partridge in "Tom Jones," a horse-stealer, who was tried before "Lord Justice Page," set up the defence that he had *found* the horse. "Ay!" retorted the judge, "thou art a lucky fellow; I have travelled the circuit these fifty years, and never found a horse in my life; but I'll tell thee what, friend, thou wast more lucky than thou didst know of: For thou didst not only find a horse, but a halter too, I promise thee." Yet beneath all Fielding's banter of his brethren was a most severe application to the law. Lean as his purse sometimes was, he collected a law library numbering more than three hundred volumes, the majority of which were in folio.

* Mr. J. Paul de Castro, "Notes and Queries," 11 S. X, 253 (Sept. 26, 1914).

These books were studied and annotated in some cases as a preparation for treatises of his own. Fielding was in training for the Bench.

Circumstances, however, checked his immediate ambitions. The Ministry that had been patched up after the fall of Walpole was held in contempt by the politicians of both the Whig factions from which it had been formed. Consequently it had to face a torrent of abuse from the friends of Walpole, who wished to paralyze it, and from the members of the old Opposition, who were angry because their real leaders were left out. In an anonymous "Letter to a Friend in the Country," which appeared in April, 1743, the author declared that at no time in his memory had there ever been afloat so many scurrilous libels, lampoons, and ballads violating all truth and decency. Much of this scandal was laid to Fielding, notwithstanding his solemn promise in the preface to the "Miscellanies" that nothing should ever again come from his pen without his name. Probably he was not greatly troubled because his "Journey from this World to the Next" was quickly followed by an anonymous Lucianic vision, half religious, half political, entitled "A Particular Account of Cardinal Fleury's Journey to the other World, and his Tryal at the Tribunal of Minos. . . . With a curious Description of the Infernal Regions and their Inhabitants. By Don Quevedo, Junior, Secretary to Aeacus." Although Fielding had nothing to do with this pamphlet, it was subsequently advertised as his.

Within a few weeks, came a long verse satire on the legal profession, supposed also to have been written by Fielding —"The Causidicade. A Panegyri-Satiri-Serio-Comic-Dramatical Poem. On the Strange Resignation, and Stranger-Promotion. By Porcupinus Pelagius." Who the real author of this Grub Street production was, is not quite certain. "The Gentleman's Magazine" ascribed it, erroneously I think, to a Mr. Hughes, who died a few months later.* The expressive pseudonym was used afterwards by William Kenrick, one of Fielding's bitter enemies, and apparently by other facetious writers. In 1743, Kenrick, then only a boy, was too young to have been the author. The Porcupine of that year was probably Macnamara Morgan,† an Irish pettifogger, who later wrote poor plays and seems to have relied upon the newspapers for a living. He knew just enough of the London bar to abuse it. His poem derived its title and substance from the resignation of Sir John Strange, the Solicitor-General, and the appointment of William Murray, afterwards Lord Mansfield, in his place. Both the retirement of Strange and the selection of Murray for his office puzzled the general public; for the former, though appointed by the Walpole Government, had taken a stand in favour of the new administration, while the latter, being a Scotsman, was suspected of Jacobite principles. Porcupinus Pelagius undertook to lay bare the political transaction. Under a thin allegorical disguise, the "Inquisitor-General" summons his court, announces his resignation, and calls upon the candidates for his office to plead their claims. One after another, ten or twelve well-known London lawyers of the several Inns, their names partially concealed by the dash, pronounce eloquent eulogies upon themselves, "from the zenith of B—tle to the nadir of W–ll–r"; but in vain, for Murray, in addition to all his qualifications—or rather disqualifications—has the support of the Court and the King. Though so free a use of their names must have been hotly resented by the younger members of the bar, the most offensive passage was levelled at Chief Justice Willes, who is described as having the "weak voice" of a "poor old woman." This "lawless libel" encountered a sharp reply in "Causticks applied to

* "The Gentleman's Magazine," Nov., 1743, p. 569.
† "Notes and Queries," 2 S. I, 94 (Aug. 1, 1857).

the Causidicade . . . by B. Flavius Flap-Bugg of Barnard's Inn.'' Still it ran on through no less than four editions before the year was over. To have one or both of these wretched satires on his own profession and friends ascribed to him gave Fielding great pain. A few weeks before, "Thomas Bootle, Esq; Chancellor to His Royal Highness," and "George Weller, Esq; of the Middle Temple," and scores of other lawyers had subscribed to his "Miscellanies," and now in return they were being subjected to gross ridicule by a brother whom they had aided and supposed to be a gentleman at least. So it was made to appear to the public.

This trading on Fielding's literary reputation continued for a full year, until a book appeared that compelled him, in justice to the real author, to break silence. It happened in this way. While he was out of town in the spring of 1744, his sister Sarah published a novel entitled "The Adventures of David Simple: Containing An Account of his Travels Through the Cities of London and Westminster, In the Search of A Real Friend." Like her hero, Miss Fielding felt that she had no friend among her acquaintances who could help her; and in an "Advertisement to the Reader," appealed as a last resort to the public for support in her undertaking. The first edition of "David Simple" with its cry for help is a very rare book, unknown to all who have written of the novel. The "Advertisement" doubtless reflects in a measure Fielding's distressful circumstances in 1744 as well as his sister's. For this reason it is here quoted in full:

"THE following Moral Romance (or whatever Title the Reader shall please to give it) is the Work of a Woman, and her first Essay; which, to the good-natured and candid Reader will, it is hoped, be a sufficient Apology for the many Inaccuracies he will find in the Style, and other Faults of the Composition.

6

THE TRUE PATRIOT

"Perhaps the best Excuse that can be made for a Woman's venturing to write at all, is that which really produced this Book; Distress in her Circumstances: which she could not so well remove by any other Means in her Power.

"If it should meet with Success, it will be the only Good Fortune she ever has known; but as she is very sensible, That must chiefly depend upon the Entertainment the World will find in the Book itself, and not upon what she can say in the Preface, either to move their Compassion or bespeak their Good-will, she will detain them from it no longer."

The novel runs gently on friendship and good nature, with ingratitude as a foil to these virtues of the heart. Like the Heartfrees in "Jonathan Wild," David is "simple" because he is kind, honest, and generous. Miss Fielding kept her name off the title-page; the novel was written by "a Lady"; and bore the imprint of Fielding's publisher, Andrew Millar. Moreover, "David Simple" resembled "Joseph Andrews" in format—two handsome duodecimo volumes; the chapters were grouped in four books with facetious headings; and there were conversations in a stagecoach, on the road up to London, between a clergyman and an atheist, and Cynthia and a Butterfly. Altogether the novel was a rather pale yet delicate reflection of the master, just such a book as should come from the sister of Henry Fielding, who had lived with him, listened to his wonderful conversation, and read the books he thought not too hard for her. But people, not knowing that Fielding had such a sister, could not be blamed for ascribing "David" to him. Fielding had no good reason for being surprised on his return to London, to find himself the reputed author of an anonymous novel.

It was a curious situation. Fielding felt that his honour was at stake, for he had promised to put forth no more anonymous books or pamphlets; his sister wished to keep her authorship concealed; and Millar, of course, equally wished to retain the shadowy influence of Fielding's name on the sales. The knot was untied by their bringing out another impression of the novel with a title-page enlarged to include "The Second Edition, Revised and Corrected. With a Preface by Henry Fielding Esq." Suppressing his sister's Advertisement, Fielding informed the public in his preface that the author was "a young woman . . . nearly and dearly allied to me, in the highest friendship as well as relation," who needed in the composition of a novel no assistance from him or from anyone else. It appears, however, though his statement is vague, that he did render her considerable aid in the matter of details and the general conduct of the story; and for the second impression he certainly reread much of the novel, correcting "grammatical and other errors in style," and occasionally inserting a piquant phrase, especially in the chapter headings. But all the original lapses of his sister in diction, he declared, amounted to little when set against the beauties of the book and its noble thoughts. His love for his sister is ample excuse for his opinion that "the merit of this work consists in a vast penetration into human nature, a deep and profound discernment of all the mazes, windings and labyrinths, which perplex the heart of man to such a degree, that he is himself often incapable of seeing through them." In this high estimate of Sarah's novel, Richardson for once agreed with his rival. After Fielding's death, Richardson wrote to her, in line with a remark of Dr. Johnson's, that her late brother's knowledge of the human heart was but as "the knowledge of the outside of a clock-work machine," while hers was "that of all the finer springs and movements of the inside."* To be suspected as the author of "David Simple," said Fielding, was an honour that

* Barbauld, "Correspondence," II, 104.

should displease no one. What grieved him was that the public refused to take him at his word, really accused him of duplicity, in breaking a promise which he had solemnly made in print the previous year and had so far strictly kept, "of never publishing, even a pamphlet, without setting my name to it." The honour thrust upon him involved grave dishonour.

"David Simple" aside, Fielding believed that his enemies were engaged in a conspiracy to smirch his good name; they would disgrace him both as a lawyer and as a man of letters. With great vehemence, he denounced them and their "Causidicade," revoked his promise, and bade farewell to literature:

"A second Reason which induces me to refute this Untruth [his writing 'David Simple'], is, that it may have a Tendency to injure me in a Profession, to which I have applied with so arduous and intent a Diligence, that I have had no Leisure, if I had Inclination, to compose any thing of this kind. Indeed I am very far from entertaining such an Inclination; I know the Value of the Reward, which Fame confers on Authors, too well, to endeavour any longer to obtain it; nor was the World ever more unwilling to bestow the glorious, envied Prize of the Laurel or Bays, than I should now be to receive any such Garland or Fool's Cap. There is not, I believe, (and it is bold to affirm) a single Free Briton in this Kingdom, who hates his Wife more heartily than I detest the Muses. They have indeed behaved to me like the most infamous Harlots, and have laid many a spurious, as well as deformed Production at my Door: In all which, my good Friends the Critics have, in their profound Discernment, discovered some Resemblance of the Parent; and thus I have been reputed and reported the Author of half the Scurrility, Bawdy, Treason and Blasphemy, which these few last Years have produced.

.   .   .   .   .

9

THE HISTORY OF HENRY FIELDING

"Among all the Scurrilities with which I have been accused, (tho' equally and totally innocent of every one) none ever raised my Indignation so much as the Causidicade; this accused me not only of being a bad Writer, and a bad Man, but with downright Idiotism, in flying in the Face of the greatest Men of my Profession. I take therefore this Opportunity to protest, that I never saw that infamous, paultry Libel, till long after it had been in Print; nor can any Man hold it in greater Contempt and Abhorrence than myself.

"The Reader will pardon my dwelling so long on this Subject, as I have suffered so cruelly by these Aspersions in my own Ease, in my Reputation, and in my Interest. I shall however henceforth treat such Censure with the Contempt it deserves; and do here revoke the Promise I formerly made; so that I shall now look upon myself at full Liberty to publish an anonymous Work, without any Breach of Faith. For tho' probably I shall never make any use of this Liberty, there is no reason why I should be under a Restraint, for which I have not enjoyed the purposed Recompence."

This passage, so lacking in sanity, came from a mind distraught. Fielding's practice doubtless was not increasing as rapidly as he hoped, and "The Causidicade," so long as it was considered his, must have cooled his legal brethren towards him; but above all else he saw approaching the greatest affliction of his life. Since the death of their first daughter, Mrs. Fielding had never recovered from her illness and grief. The Bath waters would not do their work. "To see her daily languishing and wearing away before his eyes," says Murphy, "was too much for a man of his strong sensations; the fortitude of mind, with which he met all the other calamities of life, deserted him on this most trying occasion." In 1744, Fielding took her to Bath for the last time. Few details are known of the final scene.

10

Mrs. Fielding caught a fever, it is said, and died there in her husband's arms. Her body was brought to London and buried, on November 14, 1744, in the chancel vault at St. Martin's in the Fields by the side of her daughter Charlotte. An account of the last honours paid to her may be read in the sexton's book, along with the expenses, amounting to eleven pounds, seventeen shillings, and twopence for the tolling of the great bell, for lighted candles, for blacks, and for all the ceremonial accorded to noble families. This fine and beautiful spirit that broke under hardships and misfortunes which could not be averted, was to win certain immortality in the memorial that her husband raised for her under the names of Sophia Western and Amelia Booth.

Fielding's grief at the loss of his wife was so vehement, says Murphy, that his friends thought him "in danger of losing his reason." But "when the first emotions of his sorrow were abated, philosophy administered her aid; his resolution returned, and he began again to struggle with his fortune." In the same tenor wrote Lady Louisa Stuart, who repeated what she had heard said by her mother, the daughter of Fielding's cousin, Lady Mary Wortley Montagu. This period of intense grief, which at first "approached to frenzy,"[*] lasted for nearly a year, during which we have no public utterance from or about Fielding.

But soon after the death of his wife, he took a house, Mr. de Castro has discovered, in Old Boswell Court, lying between Carey Street and Butcher Row and now forming a part of the site of the Royal Courts of Justice. Within easy reach of all the great Inns, it was a favourite place of residence for lawyers. Of Fielding's neighbours, Mr. Justice Wright and Serjeant Wynne (whose house was next to his) had subscribed to his "Miscellanies," Serjeant Leeds enjoyed a large practice, and Mr. Thomas Lane, whom Fielding afterwards mentioned in a letter, was Chair-

* "Letters and Works of Lady Mary Wortley Montagu," 1861, I, 106.

man of the Middlesex Quarter Sessions. As revealed by the account of the overseers of the parish of St. Clement Danes, Fielding regularly paid the rates levied against the house he occupied in Old Boswell Court, from the last quarter of 1744 to the end of the third quarter in 1747.*

During this period his sister Sarah probably lived with him; there was a daughter Harriot; and his wife's maid, Mary Daniel, stayed on as housekeeper. The little group, as time went on, was perhaps augmented by the presence of Miss Margaret Collier of Salisbury, coming for long visits. Miss Collier was a daughter of Arthur Collier, the metaphysician, who like Berkeley demonstrated the non-existence of an external world. He died in poverty, leaving two daughters, Jane and Margaret, at the mercy of this non-existent world. The Collier and Fielding children had grown up together at Salisbury. Jane later collaborated with Sarah on "The Cry"; but it was Margaret who eventually became almost a member of the new Fielding household. That there was room for them all may be inferred from the fact that Fielding's parochial taxes amounted, on the average, to six pounds and fifteen shillings a year, next to the largest sum paid by any tenant in Old Boswell Court. As ever, we find him living here, not in the traditional garret, but in a commodious house such as was expected of a gentleman.

Fielding clearly chose his residence in accordance with his previous determination to give undivided attention to the law. But again affairs, public and private, would not permit him to live the life which he had planned. He broke silence in the autumn of 1745, on the invasion of England by Charles Edward, the young Stuart Pretender. The year before, the Ministry which had been formed after the defeat of Walpole went to pieces, and was succeeded by the Broad

* Mr. J. Paul de Castro, "Notes and Queries," 12 S. I, 264-265 (April 1, 1916).

Bottom Administration, so called because it aimed to include every political leader, whether Whig or Tory, whose influence was dangerous. It was a method devised by Lord Chesterfield and others to get rid of an Opposition. With this end in view, they had established in 1743 a newspaper called "Old England, or the Constitutional Journal," for which Chesterfield wrote under the name of Geffery Broadbottom. Henry Pelham, who had been First Lord of the Treasury and Chancellor of the Exchequer for the last year in the previous Ministry, now became virtually Prime Minister, though he was outranked in the Cabinet by his brother, the Duke of Newcastle. Lord Hardwicke retained the Great Seal; Lord Chesterfield, who had led the Opposition in the House of Lords, was appeased by a diplomatic mission to The Hague, and the appointment as Lord Lieutenant of Ireland. Lyttelton, hitherto secretary to the Prince of Wales, became a Lord of the Treasury. Dodington was made Treasurer of the Navy, and Winnington held over as Paymaster of the Forces. Of all the old Patriots, none escaped some sort of office, except Pitt, who wanted a secretaryship in the Cabinet, but had to feed for two years on promises, owing to the King's dislike of him. The new Ministry, thus containing many of the politicians for whom Fielding had fought in "The Champion" when they were in opposition to Walpole, was immediately confronted with the crisis of 1745. On July 24 of that year, Charles Edward landed with seven friends in the Hebrides, and on August 19 unfurled his silk banner of white, blue, and red at Glenfinnan. After collecting a small army of Highlanders, he marched to Perth, where he rested for reinforcements and to discipline his troops. He then proceeded to Edinburgh, and met the English under the command of Sir John Cope at Preston Pans on September 21, rushing upon them with a yell through the mists of morning and cutting them utterly to pieces. Then it was that Fielding, long silent, spoke out for the King and the Government.

People in the south, long accustomed to domestic peace, did not realize the grave danger until war was at hand and the Prince began his march towards the English border. Nor was the national spirit very strong. Although the Jacobites were most numerous in Scotland, they might be found anywhere in England, especially in the northern and midland counties; and the people as a whole had little enthusiasm for the House of Hanover. It was the task of the Whig leaders in church and state to arouse the nation out of its lethargy. The movement began at York late in September, when Archbishop Herring organized the nobility, clergy, and gentry of the diocese into an Association for "the security of his Majesty's Person and Government and for the Defence of the County of York." Fielding, perhaps urged by the Government as well as by his own patriotism, performed his part in this work nobly.

In October,* he sounded the alarm in "A Serious Address to the People of Great Britain. In which the Certain Consequences of the Present Rebellion, Are fully demonstrated. Necessary to be perused by every Lover of his Country, at this Juncture." "The Rebellion," Fielding warns the people, "lately begun in Scotland, under the banner of a Popish Pretender, advised and assisted with the counsels and arms of France and Spain, is no longer an object of your derision. The progress of these rebels is such, as should awaken your apprehensions at least, and no longer suffer you to neglect the proper methods for your defence." As a staunch Whig, Fielding takes his stand squarely with the Revolution of 1688, shows how calamities were brought upon the country by James the Second, a cruel and arbitrary ruler, and expresses doubts concerning the legitimacy of both the Stuart Pretenders. By way of climax he draws

* "The Gentleman's Magazine," Oct., 1745, p. 560.

A SERIOUS ADDRESS

TO THE

People of GREAT BRITAIN.

In which the

CERTAIN CONSEQUENCES

OF THE

PRESENT REBELLION,

Are fully demonstrated.

Necessary to be perused by every LOVER
of his Country, at this Juncture.

---

*Per Deos Immortales, vos ego appello, qui semper Domos,
Villas, Signa, Tabulas vestras, pluris, quam rempublicam
fecistis: si ista cujuscumque modi sint, quæ amplexemini,
retinere; si voluptatibus vestris otium præbere, vultis:
expergiscimini aliquando, & capessite rempublicam. Non
nunc agitur de vectigalibus, non de Sociorum Injuriis;
Libertas & anima nostra in dubio est.*

SAL. BEL. CATALIN.

LONDON:

Printed for M. COOPER, at the *Globe* in *Pater-noster-
Row.* MDCCXLV.

[Price One Shilling.]

a graphic picture of French slavery under the old régime, depicts the horrors of the Inquisition, referring his readers for more bloody details to Philip van Limborch's "Historia Inquisitionis," and ends with a ringing appeal for action: "Let us therefore unite in Associations; let us call forth the old English spirit in this truly English cause; let neither fear nor indolence prevail on one man to refuse doing his duty in the defence of his country, against an invader by whom his property, his family, his liberty, his life and his religion are threatened with immediate destruction."

Within a month "A Serious Address" went into a second edition, with some curtailments and the important addition of "A Calm Address to all Parties in Religion, whether Protestant or Catholic, on the Score of the Present Rebellion; being a brief and dispassionate Enquiry, whether the Reign of the Pretender would be advantageous to the Civil Interest and Commerce of Great Britain, supposing that he was to succeed in his present Attempts, and allowing that he afterwards would conduct himself according to the Principles of Honour and Honesty." The conclusion was that England, should the Pretender succeed, would become a dependency of France, and so have to admit, for instance, wines free of duty; that England would lose Cape Breton and other possessions to France, that Gibraltar would go to Spain as a debt of gratitude in return for aid to the House of Stuart. "Suppose him *good* or *bad,* by principle or disposition, we have nothing to expect from him, no other prospect before us, but misery and ruin to us and our posterity."

Along with the second edition of "A Serious Address," Fielding put out "A Dialogue between the Devil, the Pope, and the Pretender,"* which is a bitter denunciation of the Church of Rome. "Have I not," declares the Pope, "un-

* "The True Patriot," Nov. 5, 1745.

veiled the only religion in the world, which hath ever taught the doctrines of benevolence, peace and charity, to be the foundation of hatred, war, and massacres? Have I not propagated ambition, with the doctrine of humility? . . . Doth not the Book say, Do unto all men, that which you would have them do unto you? And have I not made them, in mere obedience to this law, do unto all men every thing, which they would most fear to have others do unto themselves?'' The Pretender is represented as being instigated by the Pope, who in turn is in league with the Devil, and has become worse than his master. As Fielding conducts the dialogue, the Devil appears before the Pope, who proposes to him the establishment of the Inquisition in England; but the Devil stares at the proposal as beyond anything he had ever had in mind. Thereupon the Pretender enters, and the conversation proceeds between the three, the Devil having disguised himself, at the Pope's suggestion, in the robes of Cardinal Alberoni, that his cloven foot may be concealed from the young gentleman. The Pope bids the Pretender godspeed, and promises him 100,000 indulgences and 200,000 curses for his use; but when the Pretender asks that his chaplain be made Archbishop of Canterbury, the Pope becomes very angry, and compels him to submit wholly to the church in all ecclesiastical appointments.

Before they have done with him, the Pretender accepts the divine right of kings as explained by the Devil, and promises to regard England as a fief held at will from the Pope, to restore the abbey lands, and to massacre all the heretics. As soon as the Pretender leaves, the Devil laughs at the Pope for his impossible project of subduing England to the Church of Rome and refuses to grant so great a bungler a further leave of five years' power. ''Was not Alexander the Great,'' says the Devil, ''contented, that I suffered him to live but half your age? Did not he say, he had lived enough to glory, that is, in other words, he had done mischief enough? whereas you know what a large lease I granted you, and yet you are not satisfied. . . . None of your wild projects for me; shew me you can do any real service to my cause, which another will not execute as well, and I will give you as much time as is necessary to complete it; otherwise, as soon as your lease is expired, I shall expect you below according to Articles: And so I kiss your toe . . ." The Pope angered at the want of respect, exclaims as the Devil passes out: "Impudent rascal! but I will have my terms of him yet, or I'll blow up his church, and send his Inquisition back to the place from whence it came."

Both of these shilling pamphlets appeared anonymously. "A Serious Address" has been mentioned once or twice by writers on Fielding, for he afterwards referred to it as his own in a note to "A Proper Answer to a Late Scurrilous Libel," but it has hitherto existed as a mere title; it seemed to have been lost. "A Dialogue between the Devil, the Pope, and the Pretender," which is really supplementary to "A Serious Address," has so far escaped all notice, but it is certainly from Fielding's pen; he advertised the two pamphlets together in "The True Patriot" of November 26, 1745, as by "the same author." Both may be found in the catalogue of the British Museum—the one under "Great Britain," the other under the "Devil." While their literary merits are not of the highest order, they represent good pamphleteering, and are interesting as preliminary to Fielding's return to political journalism.

II

The Pretender, having become master of most of Scotland, began his march south near the first of November, and took Carlisle on the fourteenth. Thence, outwitting the English army, now under the general command of the

King's youngest son, the Duke of Cumberland, he proceeded south to Derby, which was reached on December 4, and saw the way open to London, where he hoped to eat his Christmas dinner. But he was never to traverse that hundred and fifty miles of road. Few English Jacobites dared join him; the French, who had been counted on to invade southern England, held aloof; and so the disappointed Prince was forced, in order to escape annihilation, to turn backwards, with the Duke of Cumberland in hot pursuit. At the beginning of the triumphal progress south, when no one could foretell what the result would be, Fielding launched, on November 5, 1745, "The True Patriot: and The History of Our Own Times," a weekly newspaper to appear on every Tuesday. It was printed for "M. Cooper, at the Globe in Pater-Noster-Row," who had published Fielding's two pamphlets; and at his bookshop were to be left all advertisements and "letters to the author," of which the latter were to be carefully addressed that Mrs. Cooper, who managed the business, might not open them by mistake, thinking they were intended for her. Subsequently the editor had another and more convenient office at the shop of George Woodfall, "near Craig's Court, Charing-Cross." Other places where the newspaper might be had, were the shops of Andrew Millar in the Strand, Mrs. A. Dodd without Temple Bar, and Henry Chappelle in Grosvenor Street, of whom the last had been a partner in "The Champion." Though Smollett later charged Fielding with being in the pay of the Government, there is no basis for the insinuation. That Fielding was encouraged by his friends in the Ministry, that they gave him access to trustworthy political news, is clear enough; it is probable, too, that they purchased a certain number of copies for free distribution; but there are no indications that he was directly employed by them. "The True Patriot," on the face of it, appears to have been an enterprise of a book-

18

seller—perhaps of a group of them—as strongly anti-Jacobite as the editor, with both of whom patriotism counted much, and money somewhat less at just that time. Their pamphlets had sold, and the next step was a periodical.

Fielding's first leader is a pleasant essay on the changing fashions in dress, amusements, and literature, working itself out into a statement of his design in establishing "The True Patriot." Left solely to his own inclinations, he would hardly have taken to journalism for the display of his literary genius; but as his bookseller, "a man of great sagacity in his business," has informed him that "no body at present reads any thing but newspapers," it is the part of wisdom for an author to conform to "the reigning taste." By neglecting this golden rule, Milton, says Fielding, lived long in obscurity, and the world "nearly lost the best poem which perhaps it hath ever seen"; whereas by adhering to it, "Tom Durfey, whose name is almost forgot, and many others who are quite forgotten, flourished most notably in their respective ages, and eat and were read very plentifully by their cotemporaries." Though not the highest literary ambition, it is probably worth while, Fielding thinks, to set a better standard for the London newspapers, now in the hands of "the journeymen of booksellers," who, having no regard for truth, fill their columns with scandal and nonsense, or at best with trivial paragraphs wholly lacking in human interest, to say nothing of a style so wretched that one wonders whether it is English. Of course an honest newspaper, conducted by "a gentleman" instead of a Grub Street writer, will cost rather more than the other weeklies, which sell at twopence; but a reader should consider that by paying an extra penny he will "gain six times the knowledge and amusement"; in fact that threepence a week will give him all the news besides much entertainment. Just as no man will drink "cider-water" if he can get champagne, so Fielding expects that hereafter no one will read any newspaper but "The True Patriot."

Who the author or editor is, must be left, says Fielding, to the conjecture of the curious, though he is quite willing to give a few hints to the "sagacious guesser." It is clear that he is the "gentleman" he professes to be, for the first number contains nothing scurrilous; and furthermore, that he is of no party, for there is no abuse of Whig or Tory. The editor's style and knowledge of politics incline one to believe—if I may fill out Fielding's stars and dashes—that he is my Lord Bolingbroke; his zeal for the Protestant religion looks as if he were perhaps Dr. Hoadly of Winchester; while his wit and humour make it probable that he is none other than Lord Chesterfield himself. For these and other reasons, he may be Mr. Winnington, Mr. Dodington, Mr. Lyttelton, Mr. Fielding, or Mr. Thomson the poet; "or indeed any other person who hath ever distinguished himself in the republic of letters." At any rate, it is certain that he is "a true patriot," convinced (to take a phrase from the second leader) that "the preserving the present Royal Family on the throne, is the only way to preserve the very being of this nation." So far as this, Fielding lent his hearty support to the Government, some distinguished members of which, he led the public to think, would contribute a share of their ability to an enterprise in which "no person, how great soever, need be ashamed of being imagined to have a part"; for "The True Patriot" will never publish anything "inconsistent with decency, or the religion and true civil interest of my country."

Besides the leader, a typical number of "The True Patriot" had a résumé of foreign news under the heading "The Present History of Europe," dealing mostly with Continental politics and the varying fortunes of England and her allies in the war with France; and a longer account of the movements of the armies in the North, labelled "The Present History of Great Britain." Fielding's observations on the rebellion, running through the first numbers, were especially commended at the time for their moderation. His point of attack was not the Scottish people, whom he loved and honoured, but that band of "outlaws, robbers, and cut-throats" which the Pretender collected for an invasion of England. These banditti, he maintained, were not representative of Scotland. The Scottish nation as a whole—her nobility, her gentry, her clergy, the common people of the Lowlands—remained, he averred, loyal to the House of Hanover. It might have been expected that the initial success of the rebellion would have swept vast numbers into the ranks of the Highlanders; but such had not been the case. "Except outlaws, and one or two profligate younger brothers, there is not," said Fielding, "a single man of any name in the Kingdom, who hath given sanction to the Pretender's cause." All this redounded to the glory of Scotland. The politics of the first number were enlivened by ridicule of the Pretender and his master the Pope, and by "A Loyal Song" to the tune of Lillibullero, "proper to be sung at all merry meetings." A few announcements from the booksellers completed an issue. To Fielding's credit were excluded all those accounts of nostrums by quack doctors—of those pills, drops, and tinctures which disgraced eighteenth-century journalism. In place of them, an advertisement, written by himself and for which he received no pay, does the man the greatest honour. In the ninth number we may read in italics:

A *NY Person who hath enough of real Christianity to preserve a large Family from Destruction by advancing the Sum of Two hundred Pounds, on a reasonable Prospect of its being repaid, may hear further Particulars, by applying to Mr.* Millar, *Bookseller, opposite* Katharine Street *in the* Strand.

Fielding dealt little in the general news, political or other, of the ordinary newspaper except to burlesque it. Such news as he regarded of genuine interest usually formed a part of "The Present History of Great Britain." It was his practice to gather from the newspapers of the week about a page of the more absurd paragraphs and to reprint them with comment beneath the headlines: "APOCRYPHA. *Being a curious Collection of certain true and important* WE HEARS *from the News-Papers.*" He liked to show how one newspaper contradicted another, or how an item was rendered valueless by the vagueness of the rumour upon which it was based. On observing two "we hears" in a single paragraph of "The General Advertiser" he remarks: "As two negatives make an affirmative, two 'we hears,' I am afraid, amount to a negative." The same newspaper announced that the Duke of Richmond's regiment was at Lichfield; and Fielding, in printing the news, adds: "The Duke hath no regiment." The public was informed that yesterday the saddles for the Duke of Bedford's Regiment of Horse set out from town; whereupon Fielding comments: "As the Duke of Bedford hath only a regiment of foot, it is probable these saddles will shortly *set out* on their way home again." "The Daily Advertiser" said, "We hear that the Rebels are much afflicted with the bloody flux"; to which Fielding replies that "it is a distemper which may probably increase, if General Hawley should be able to come up with them." Two men were committed to prison—Patrick Hand as a sneak thief, and Thomas Sutton for stealing old iron. The former, Fielding thinks, made "an ill use of his name"; while the latter "will probably experience the danger Hudibras asserts there is in meddling with that commodity," if the lines be true—

> Ay me! what perils do environ
> The man that meddles with cold iron!

Week by week, "The True Patriot" went on with these "ingenious conceits," as they were called, to the exasperation of the other newspapers, fixing a fashion since revived and continued by "Punch," the wittiest of all periodicals.

A paragraph of the Apocrypha described the "ghosts" of the week, by which Fielding meant false news, puffs, and advertisements that appeared in the other newspapers. There were ghosts of Grub Street poets, lottery-mongers, Jacobite pamphleteers, messengers from the North, and one of a large black man—Orator Henley—suspected of being a Jacobite—who appeared on Sunday evenings at the Papist chapel near Clare Market and "talked for a whole hour what none of his hearers understood." The rendezvous of these apparitions was "The Daily Advertiser" and some other enterprising newspapers, which kept people up all night to wait for "extraordinary" issues—"extras" we now call them for short—bearing fresh tidings from Scotland, afterwards to be found untrue or mere repetitions of what had been published earlier in the day. Though Fielding has his fun with these "extraordinary ghosts," he looked with some favour, he said, on the ghosts of advertisers, and referred them to the business office of "The True Patriot." "Mrs. Cooper, the publisher of this paper," he told them, "is provided with several walking licences for ghosts, by our authority; which she issues forth to the said ghosts at various prices, from three shillings to half a guinea, according to the length and breadth of the respective ghosts; and all shadows which for the future shall venture to *appear* abroad in the shape of puffs or advertisements, without such licence, shall be instantly lay'd in this paper." The facetious paragraph, however, brought very few advertisements to "The True Patriot."

Humorous comment overflowed into the lists of the married and the dead. Almost every woman who married was described by the newspapers as "beautiful" or "agreeable" or possessed of "a considerable fortune." Everybody who died was "eminent." There were eminent booksellers, eminent grocers, eminent apothecaries, eminent brewers, and eminent tobacconists, many of whom were "wealthy" as well as "eminent," and wrote "Esquire" after their names. These lists Fielding made up every week from the other newspapers, with here and there a remark printed in italics to distinguish his own property from that of Grub Street. A pun, I suppose, was intended in addressing the fortunate young man of the following marriage notice:

"Mr. John Rayner, a Quaker, to Miss Cowper, with a handsome Fortune, and every Accomplishment which can render a Lady agreeable. *Friend Rayner, thou hast chosen well.*"

That year a cattle distemper, to which the newspapers gave much space, was raging throughout England. Fielding mingled cows with obscure people in his groups of the dead:

"Mrs. Mary Tyrrington; she was the last of her Name. *She is the first of it I have ever heard of.*

"Rev. Mr. Wicket; he had a Living in Kent. He was well known at the polite End of the Town; *but I have often heard it doubted whether the last Letter of his name was d or t.*

"*Tuesday.* Mr. Tillcock an eminent Stocking Presser in Grub-street. *Wednesday,* Mr. Tillcock is not dead but in perfect Health. *It is unpardonable in these Historians to mistake in Matters of such Consequence, especially in their own Neighbourhood.*

"Upwards of 40 Cows belonging to one at Tottenham Court, *universally lamented by all their Acquaintance.*

"N.B. If great Men and Cattle die so fast, we shall scarce have room to bury them in our Paper."

Sometimes Fielding made merry over old men who take young wives, and over widows who quickly recover from their grief. One story he tells of a woman who lost her husband in the summer, married another in the autumn, and on his death in the winter, died herself. Their friends took up the corpse of the first husband, dug the grave deeper, and put all three in together.

These jests on the dead and the living were not everywhere relished, for we find Fielding making an apology for them in the tenth number of his periodical. "To prevent," he says there, "giving offence to the many eminent dead persons, as well as to several young ladies of great beauty, merit and fortune, we shall for the future register all marriages and deaths as they come to hand, and leave all distinction to the public; after having premised that every word printed in italics is our own, and of these, and these only we will be answerable for the truth."

When someone died whom he knew for his good qualities, or whom the world esteemed, the comment became serious and unconventional in phrase. The death of that old miser, Peter Walter, Esq., Fielding passed by with the remark that he was "worth upwards of £200,000." An Edward Syderham, Esq., was "a gentleman whose heart and hands were ever ready to relieve the wants of mankind." William Avery, Esq., of Bath was "one of a triumvirate of beaus, who have flourished there these fifty years." Richard Witherston, Esq., "a barrister at law, aged 44, by an early application to the most polite and no less useful parts of literature, greatly improved those abilities nature had so liberally bestowed on him." Mr. John Robinson, son of Mr. Robinson of Bath, was "a young man, who had given very early proofs of a great genius in his profession of portrait painting." Of Lord Wyndham, formerly "Lord Chancellor of the Kingdom of Ireland," who had retired to Salisbury when his health broke, and had since come to

London for medical advice, Fielding could say: "He was a good natured and honest man. In public he always pre-served his integrity, and in private life an inoffensive cheerfulness, which made him an amiable companion." When Fielding, the Eton boy, visited his grandmother Gould at Salisbury, this Thomas Wyndham was recorder of Sarum. He subscribed to the "Miscellanies." Of the Rev. Dr. William Broome, who died at Bath, it was recorded: "This gentleman was not unknown in the learned world, tho' perhaps he had less reputation in it than he deserved. He read over the whole comment of Eustathius in Greek, in order to furnish Mr. Pope with notes to his Iliad and Odyssey. Nay perhaps he had some share in the translating, at least in the *construing* those poems, if we may believe Mr. Pope himself." Finally, on Swift there was a paragraph in which Fielding left his most direct estimate of his brother humorist as a man as well as a writer:

"A few Days since died in Ireland, Dr. Jonathan Swift, Dean of St. Patrick's in Dublin. A Genius who deserves to be ranked among the first whom the World ever saw. He possessed the Talents of a Lucian, a Rabelais, and a Cervantes, and in his Works exceeded them all. He employed his Wit to the noblest Purposes, in ridiculing as well Superstition in Religion as Infidelity, and the several Errors and Immoralities which sprung up from time to time in his Age; and lastly, in the Defence of his Country, against several pernicious Schemes of Wicked Politicians. Nor was he only a Genius and a Patriot; he was in private Life a good and charitable Man, and frequently lent Sums of Money without Interest to the Poor and Industrious; by which Means many Families were preserved from Destruction. The Loss of so excellent a Person would have been more to be lamented, had not a Disease that affected his Understanding, long since deprived him of the Enjoy-

ment of Life, and his Country of the Benefit of his great
Talents; But we hope this short and hasty Character will
not be the last Piece of Gratitude paid by his Cotemporaries to such eminent Merit.''

Fielding's leaders also assumed a serious tone as the
danger from the invading army increased on every day's
march further southward. When news reached London
that the Highlanders were at Derby, the capital was struck,
says Fielding, ''with a terror scarce to be credited.'' A
day of fast and humiliation was appointed for December
18. The Bishop of St. Asaph preached before the Lords
at St. Peter's, Westminster, and the Rector of St. Mary-le-
Bow before the Commons at St. Margaret's. Both took
the same text: ''Remember therefore whence thou art
fallen, and repent.'' Never before, according to the newspapers, had there been so great an attendance of Lords
and Commons. The day preceding the fast, Fielding revived Parson Adams for a sermon addressed to the town,
on a text taken from Pythagoras: ''Go upon the work,
having first prayed to the Gods for success.'' Much, I
daresay, as the Bishop of St. Asaph, Parson Adams
attributed ''the unparallel'd success'' of the rebellion to
''the just judgment of God against an offending people.''
During the three or four years that he had ''tarried in the
great city,'' he had seen everywhere ''monstrous impieties
and iniquities,'' far surpassing in wickedness anything recorded of ancient Sodom. Nothing could save a town
void of charity and given over wholly to lying and luxury,
but ''a total amendment of life, a total change of manners.''
Subsequently Parson Adams had another discourse on the
divine wrath that was overtaking a nation bent upon its
own destruction; wherein he imputed all the ills that Great
Britain was suffering under, to ''the notorious want of
care in parents in the education of youth,'' who are no
longer, either in the city or in the country, instructed in the

principles of religion, virtue, morality, and patriotism. The only ambition of a young man, so far as he has observed, is to become a member of the society of *bowes,* a word, if that be the correct spelling, whose etymology and import, the Parson says, he cannot understand, "as it hath never once occurred in any lexicon or dictionary which I have yet perused."

One night, after the rebels had captured Carlisle, Fielding represents himself as having a dream or vision of the Highlanders entering London and massacring the inhabitants. While writing in his study, his children playing about him, he was arrested by a gang of ruffians on the charge of high treason, dragged through streets piled high with the slaughtered, and thrown into a prisoners' pen with the Archbishop of York and the Bishop of Winchester. He was put through a form of trial before a judge who addressed him "in broken English" and only stared when he asserted "that the life of no man was worth preserving longer than it was to be defended by the known laws of his country." The judge immediately gave him over to the executioner; but just as the rope was being put round his neck, his little daughter entered his bedchamber and put an end to the dream, by pulling open his eyes, and telling him that his tailor had just brought him a new suit of clothes for his Majesty's birthday. Not only would worthy citizens of London like himself, said Fielding in another paper, fall into "utter misery and desolation," should a Popish Prince gain the throne, but all those unpatriotic gentlemen discontented with the present order in church and state should pause and reflect on the fate awaiting them. He inquires of the freethinkers who spend their time in ridiculing parsons for "the useless services of praying, preaching, catechising and instructing the people," how they would like to be forced into "auricular confession, pennance, fasting, and all the tiresome forms and ceremonies exacted by the Church of Rome!" Again, he asks those politicians who make it their profession to sell themselves to one party or another, what hope they can have under an absolute Prince. "A freeman," remarks Fielding ironically, "may justly sell himself, but a slave cannot." There is no necessity of purchasing a slave, for he is already owned. The only persons who will be permitted to pillage the country will be "hungry Highlanders" and "hungry priests."

These two papers were subsequently elaborated into "a waking dream," in which are depicted the actual events that would have occurred had the Pretender, instead of retracing his steps from Derby, gone on and taken London. It is an imaginary journal kept by "an honest tradesman living in the busy part of the city" for two or three months after the massacre of Christmas week. In abbreviated form, these are some of the events recorded by the Londoner:

"*January* 1, 1746. This Day the supposed Conqueror was proclaimed at Stocks Market, amidst the loud Acclamations of Highlanders and Friars.

"*Jan.* 2. A Proclamation issued for a *free* Parliament (according to the Declaration) to meet the 20th Instant. The twelve Judges removed, and twelve new ones appointed, some of whom had scarce ever been in Westminster-Hall before.

"*Jan.* 3. Queen Anne's Statue in St. Paul's Church Yard taken away, and a large Crucifix erected in its Room.

"*Jan.* 10. Three Anabaptists committed to Newgate, for pulling down the Crucifix in Paul's Church Yard.

"*Jan.* 20. The *free* Parliament opened—the Speech and Addresses filled with Sentiments of *civil* and *religious* Liberty.

"*Jan.* 22. Three Members, to wit, Mr. D[odingto]n, Mr.

P[it]t, Mr. L[yttelto]n, were seized in their Houses, and sent to the Tower, by a Warrant from a Secretary of State.

"*Jan.* 26. This Day the *Gazette* informs us, that Portsmouth, Berwick, and Plymouth, were delivered into the Hands of French Commissaries, as Cautionary Towns.

"*Jan.* 28. A Bill brought into the Commons, and twice read the same Day, to repeal the Act of Habeas Corpus.

"*Feb.* 3. Father Poignardini, an Italian Jesuit, made Privy-Seal.

"*Feb.* 13. Four Heretics burnt in Smithfield—Mr. *Mac-henly* [Orator Henley] attended them, assisted on this extraordinary Occasion by Father O-Blaze, the Dominican.

"*Feb.* 19. Father Mac-dagger made President of Magdalen College in Oxford.

"*Feb.* 21. The Deanry of Christ Church given to Father Poignardini, and the Bishoprics of Winchester and Ely, to the General of the Jesuits Order, resident in Italy.

"*March* 1. The French Ambassador made a Duke, with Precedence.

"*March* 4. An eminent Physician fined 200 Marks in the King's Bench, for an innuendo at Batson's, that Bath Water was preferable to Holy Water.

"*March* 7. The Pope's Nuncio makes his Public Entry— met at the Royal Exchange by my Lord Mayor (a Frenchman).

"*March* 9. My little Boy Jacky taken ill of the Itch. He had been on the Parade with his Godfather the Day before, to see the Life-Guards, and had just touched one of their Plaids.

"*March* 16. Lord C[hief] J[ustice] W[il]les, and Admiral V[erno]n, hang'd at Tyburn.

"*March* 17. Fresh Rumours of a Plot—a Riot in the City—a Rising in the North—a Descent in the West—Confusions, Uproars, Commitments, Hangings, Burnings, &c. &c."

This is what might have been; but the tradesman's son did not catch the itch from a Highland plaid; nor did holy water become a substitute for the Bath wells. In order to prevent the direful events that Fielding saw in his imagination, "the whole body of the law," says Horace Walpole, "formed themselves into a little army, under the command of Lord Chief Justice Willes, and were to have done duty at St. James's, to guard the royal family in the King's absence."* This remark of Walpole's has led to the assertion that Fielding probably joined with his brethren of the Bar and learned to use a sword as well as a pen. But Walpole's statement is not quite accurate; and the conjecture that Fielding, afflicted with the gout, enlisted in a volunteer corps, is preposterous. All that happened is told by Fielding himself in "The True Patriot." "The young lawyers and students of the Temple," he says in number five, "being willing to defend as well as practice the laws of their country, have lately applied themselves to the study of the laws of arms, in which exercise they are daily attended in the several Inns of Court by serjeants." The news is given with the punning query: "Whether these be serjeants at law, or of the army?" Though Fielding himself was unable to bear arms, he took an active interest in the measures for the defence of the kingdom. Perhaps he wrote that "Loyal Song" beginning—

> O Brother Sawney, hear you the news,
>   Twang 'em, we'll bang 'em, and hang 'em up all.
> An army's just coming without any shoes,
>   Twang 'em, we'll bang 'em, and hang 'em up all.
>   To arms, to arms——

which appeared in the first number of "The True Patriot"; and for weeks he appealed in a series of letters from "a person of great property, as well as great abilities," to the

* "Letters of Horace Walpole," edited by Toynbee, II, 160; and Lawrence, "Life of Fielding," 209.

people everywhere to organize themselves into a militia to supplement the regular army in face of the threatened invasion from France. Without any expense to the Government, volunteer forces were to be raised in every county and city throughout England against "the attempts of our most implacable enemies, now supporting the most atrocious rebellion."

Fielding also lent his aid to the theatres, which often, especially through December, 1745, gave their entire profits to patriotic associations. Old anti-Papal plays were revived, such as Lee's "Massacre of Paris" depicting St. Bartholomew's Day, Ford's "Perkin Warbeck," and Cibber's "Nonjuror." On the same stage were performed Cibber's "Papal Tyranny, or King John" and Fielding's "The Debauchees: or, the Jesuit Caught." Fielding wrote no new play, but was probably the author of "An Epilogue, Design'd to be spoken by Mrs. Woffington, in the Character of a Volunteer."* Mrs. Woffington, "a bold, smart . . . Volunteer," enters "reading a Gazette" and cursing all cowards. The epilogue was used many times at Drury Lane, once with "Three Hours after Marriage." While praising the English actors for their patriotism, Fielding kept up an almost continuous fire at the Italian singers, who had been brought over as usual for the season. Hard pressed by competition with the legitimate drama, "Giovani Cantilena" is represented as appealing to the editor of "The True Patriot" to "rite sumting to recomend de opera, or begar me sal be oblige to go back to Italy like one fool as me did cum"; and the letter becomes the occasion for a mock defence of the opera as the most fitting diversion amid public calamities. It was by music that Nero calmed and composed the agonies of his mind while Rome was in flames; Socrates learned to sing in his old age; and

---

* "The True Patriot," Feb., 18-25, 1746; reprinted, with minor alterations, in "A Foundling Hospital for Wit," June, 1746, pp. 24-25.

Pythagoras held that virtue, peace, health, and all other good things were but harmony. To those who fear that Italian music may enervate the minds of a nation, Fielding replies that it is so much the better for that; if England wishes to be safe from the attack of hostile neighbours, there is no surer way than the employment of every means for weakening the character and morals of the people, so that she will not be worth conquering. Before the season was far advanced, the Italian opera, however, vied with the English theatres in patriotic appeals, extolling the Duke of Cumberland and abusing the Pretender. Thereupon Fielding inserted in his periodical a letter purporting to come from Rome to the effect that the Pope shed tears on hearing the news, and excommunicated all the Roman Catholics in the troupe of Italian singers; and that the Pretender, crying out "Et tu, Lady," fell into a swoon, from which he recovered only to see that his cause was now forever lost.

As soon as Prince Charles was well out of England, an Opposition began to show its head in and out of Parliament. The Government was criticised for ever letting the Highlanders get so far south as Derby, for its conduct of the war with France, for the stagnation in trade, and for the heavy taxes. In reply Fielding declared that, but for the energy of the Government in bringing over troops from Flanders, the Pretender would have long since been in possession of London, and that the foreign war which interfered with shipping and made necessary unusual taxation, was a legacy from the Walpole Administration. And when the Duke of Cumberland shattered the Highland army at Culloden, Fielding proclaimed loudly the complete triumph of his friends and their cause. There had been, he said, able Ministries before, but none ever equalled the one headed by the Pelhams. For the first time were at the helm statesmen good as well as great; for the first time in England's history, "patriot" and "courtier" had become words compatible and necessarily conjoined. The Administration was now in the hands of "a glorious body of men who have shewn that the highest dignity and property in this kingdom are accompany'd with the highest honour; . . . who esteem power and preferment of no value any longer than they can be preferred with a strict adherence to the true interest of their country." The Duke of Cumberland—"that fulmen belli"—was placed among the great military commanders, and his father the King among the ideal princes—just, merciful, benevolent, and happy in the love of his family and subjects.

With those who still remained disaffected, Fielding had good sport. Some of them were "idiots"; others were mischief-makers who for the good of the country ought to give themselves over to Jack Ketch the hangman. Twice, in large type advertisements, Fielding warned these men against attempts to suppress "The True Patriot" by bribing hawkers and booksellers to have nothing to do with it; and, continuing the jest of the hangman, he set a day for their dissection, in lieu of hanging, in "The True Patriot"; but relented on receiving a "humble petition from the people calling themselves the Opposition," who promised to submit to "his Highness, the Great Sole *True Patriot of Great Britain,*" and in particular to subscribe to his newspaper. They pleaded in their own behalf their faulty education, their mean abilities, their inconsiderable number, and their impotency to do harm. "Their actions (or rather their words)," they said, "proceeded from two motives, the one of which hath been always thought noble and laudable, and the latter hath been held almost a justification of any act whatever. These are ambition and necessity. If the Government will please to satisfy these, it is very well known they are ready to become its humble servants at any time. They have no quarrel either with men or measures; but can never agree that their country is taken care of, whilst they themselves, who are that part of their country which they love best, are neglected. They have no more hatred of power than a pack of hounds have of a hare, who bellow after her only because she runs away from them, and they cannot overtake her. Places are what they desire, and many of them very moderate ones." As no malice but only human weakness lay behind the fruitless endeavours of the Opposition, Fielding thought a reprieve should be granted them, though, unless they kept quiet, it might be necessary to proceed against them again and let Jack Ketch have them after all. Later he claimed that the Opposition wholly died out; that England was blessed as never before in his lifetime with "the utter extinction of parties."

As everyone was now a true patriot, said Fielding with a touch of irony, he saw no reason for continuing a newspaper by that name. Accordingly the last number of "The True Patriot"—it is the thirty-third—appeared on June 17, 1746. That last number may have been lost; it is not in the file, otherwise complete, at the British Museum; it has never been described, nor has any reference ever been made to it by Fielding's biographers. Fortunately "the substance" of it was reprinted in "The London Magazine" for June, 1746. Fielding's last leader was a farewell to the public, conceived in the finest spirit of patriotism. "The True Patriot," he told his readers, was undertaken at a time when the rebellion was "attended with an appearance of success that struck the whole nation with a general panick." If he had been in the earlier numbers vehement in his attacks on the Pretender and his followers, it was because he believed that the religion and liberties of his country were then in the gravest danger. Without claiming "any extraordinary merit" from his undertaking, he had merely discharged his "duty as an Englishman, and as a loyal subject to his present Majesty." On the whole, Fielding could say justly that he had shown unusual moderation in his political papers, that his sole aim had been against men in active rebellion. He bore no ill will, he declared, against the Jacobites, but rather lamented their "mistaken tenets" which "had flattered the invader with too great hopes of final success." "I did my utmost," to quote directly, "to dissuade the well-meaning but rash part of my countrymen from general and violent attacks on whole bodies of men, even on the Roman Catholicks themselves, while they retained the duty of their allegiance, and preserved that peace which the law requires. I endeavoured likewise to obviate, as far as I was able, that disinclination which was arising among too many against the whole Scottish nation, which I thought was at once unjust and dangerous to the common cause."

To say the truth, Fielding several times drew a sharp line—sharper than was warranted—between the Scots as a nation and that band of Highlanders which descended upon England; and once praised the Government for releasing from custody a Roman Catholic gentleman of Dorsetshire—a Mr. Weld—for whose good character and loyalty he was ready to bear witness. Had Fielding known that Charles Edward himself would sometime become interested in his novels, perhaps he would have been more kindly disposed to the Prince also. From his seclusion somewhere in France, the exile wrote, on May 18, 1750, to Mademoiselle Ferrand at Paris, requesting her to send him "Joseph Andrews" in English and "Tom Jones" in French.* Had someone told the Prince that a landlady of the latter novel had mistaken Sophia Western for Jenny Cameron—the girl he left behind him? And what would have been Fielding's emotions if he had by chance seen a letter which Lady Mary Wortley Montagu wrote to her

* Andrew Lang, "Prince Charles Edward," 1900, p. 240.

husband, saying that the Prince, whom she met in 1741, was "really not unlike Mr. Lyttelton in shape and air"— not unlike the very man to whom "Tom Jones" was to be dedicated?*

The most personal touch in Fielding's last paper is his reference to the horrible executions of the rebels, from which his whole nature revolted. Though a lord convicted of high treason might merely have his head cut off, many of those proved guilty were hanged until they were partially dead, then cut down, that their bowels might be taken out while they were still alive and burnt before their faces, as a preliminary to chopping off their heads and cutting their bodies into quarters. While many other newspapers and magazines described these scenes in full detail, Fielding, though giving half-hearted support to the severity of the Government, never published a paragraph on them in "The True Patriot." And he tells why in a noble if undeserved tribute to Lord Hardwicke, the Lord High Chancellor. "Whoever knows me at all," says Fielding, "must know that cruelty is most foreign from my own disposition; I have therefore left these unhappy men to that mercy, which I am sure they will find, as far as the prudence of policy, and the insolence of their abettors will allow it to be extended. This they may expect from that great and glorious man, who is at the head of our law, and whose goodness of heart is no less conspicuous than those great parts, which, both in the character of a statesman and a lawyer, are at once the honour and the protection of his country." Because of his moderate temper, Fielding did not quite satisfy the Government, which expected his support through thick and thin. But he placed self-approval above the approval of his party. "Whatever may be my fate," were his final words, "as I have discharged my duty to my King and country, and have, at the same time, preserved even a

* Andrew Lang, "Prince Charles Edward," 1900, p. 28.

decency to those who have (erroneously, I hope) embraced a cause in opposition to both, I shall now retire with the secret satisfaction which attends right actions, tho' they fail of any great reward from the one, and are prosecuted with curses and vengeance from the other.''

The demise of ''The True Patriot'' came suddenly, without previous announcement, though there had been forewarnings of the end three months before. The fact seems to be that Fielding, who began his newspaper under a noble patriotic impulse, found the undertaking too heavy a burden to carry along with the practice of the law. Who were his assistants, we do not know. In advertising the first number of the paper in ''The London Evening Post'' for November 5, 1745, Cooper the publisher spoke of ''the authors'' of the periodical as if more than one writer were to be employed upon it; while Fielding, on the contrary, implied in his first leader that there was only one author or editor, who might be ''Mr. F——g.'' In a sense, both were right. Like other newspapers, ''The True Patriot'' published letters from correspondents on a variety of subjects, all of which the editor promised to print or acknowledge the receipt of. On one occasion he was chagrined that a letter from ''Cato Britannicus'' had been mislaid so that he must ask the British Cato for another copy. There were also occasional letters from foreign parts on the state of European politics, and ''persons of distinction'' supplied Fielding with news from the North. His miscellaneous items called ''Apocrypha'' were gathered from the London newspapers. The series of articles that he ran on the organization of a volunteer army was taken from a book that Millar was publishing under the title of ''A Plan for Establishing and Disciplining a National Militia,'' of unknown authorship though ascribed to a Colonel Martin. But nearly everything that went into ''The True Patriot'' seems to have been more or less edited and sometimes re-worked. Even the extracts from Colonel Martin's book were not printed without "some few variations." All these editorial details involved labour in which Fielding must have received aid from a literary hack. Was the hack his sister Sarah or Parson Young or someone else in the employ of Cooper?

Most surprising nevertheless is the extent to which Fielding's own hand is visible in this journalistic work. While the paragraphs on foreign affairs, cast in the vague newspaper style of the period, were probably put together by another, the war news as it came by post from the North was clearly for the most part reshaped by Fielding himself into connected essays; and no one but him, of course, could have written that humorous comment on marriages, deaths, and trivial items reprinted as "Apocrypha" from his newspaper brethren. Just as certainly he often inserted phrases of his own in the letters which he printed; and in some cases letters signed by fanciful names could have been written only by himself. When, for example, "Rusticus" remarks that the direction—"kill the cattle as soon as they fall sick," if you wish to put an end to the cow distemper—is as if a physician should knock a patient on the head in order to cure him of a cold, we have the Fielding touch. Again, when "Oliver Oldcoat" of Gloucestershire remonstrates with the editor for his praise of the Ministry and hopes to see his "d—d newspaper" burnt by the common hangman, that is Fielding beyond doubt, even down to the phrasing which he had used elsewhere. Likewise a letter from "Heliogabalus" commending "The True Patriot," must have been Fielding's entirely. It was here that Fielding first elaborated his famous comparison, known to all readers of "Tom Jones," between a good newspaper or novel and a well-ordered feast, where in both cases one should begin with the plain dishes and proceed by the proper stages to the highly seasoned ragouts. Heliogabalus, to quote a few of his sentences, wrote to the author of "The True Patriot":

"This Evening at Eight, as our Company had finished their Dinner, to which we seldom allow more than four Hours, a Gentleman pulled your last Paper out of his Pocket, and read it aloud to us; and greatly, I assure you, to the Satisfaction of us all; for we have some Taste besides that which is seated in the Palate, and are capable of *relishing* Wit as well as any Dainty.

"It was observed, that you had cooked up the Entertainment you *serve* to the Public with much Propriety: You give us first a Dish of substantial Food, when our Appetites are brisk and keen; you then *serve up* several *petit Plats* from the News Papers; and lastly, send us away with a *Bon Bouche* of your own.

"A Gentleman of great Delicacy of Taste declared, that you had a most excellent Way of *ragooing* these several Articles which you take from the Historians, as you are pleased to term them; and tho' this is the second Time of Dressing, the *Italic* Sauce which you add by way of Remark, gives a *delicious Flavour* to what was at first *flat* and *insipid*. . . .

"Farewell, I love you as much as I do any thing which I can't eat. . . ."

Finally, nearly all the thirty-three leading articles—what Heliogabalus calls the dishes of substantial food—were from Fielding's pen. Only two of them can be regarded as of doubtful authorship. Number twenty-one, giving the pathetic story of a gentleman who attempted to force his daughter to marry a man she did not love, sounds more like Sarah than Henry Fielding. Number twenty-five, a letter signed "Philander" on true and false patriotism, bears none of the marks of Fielding's style and is altogether too dull for him; whereas number twenty-eight, a letter from "Tom Skipton," a footman in a great family, relating how a man of his own order—one Matthew Henderson*—came to the gallows by imitating the vices of gentlemen, could have been written by no footman that ever lived. Only Fielding would quote "The Beggar's Opera" to the effect that "if little men will have their vices, as well as the great, they will be punished for them." Except, then, in perhaps two instances, Fielding wrote a leader for "The True Patriot" every week, besides doing a large amount of other editorial work such as has been here outlined. It was an immense labour.

The first signs of relaxing energy occurred in the issue of March 4, when Fielding complained of "many malicious and base endeavours" to hinder the sale of his newspaper. This was his explanation—how far justified, no one knows —of a dwindling circulation, due mainly to a decrease in the demand for news of the war. At that time the "Apocrypha" disappeared from "The True Patriot" and was never again resumed. Several good leading articles—particularly one on hanging—were yet to be written; but only the last of them equalled the earlier ones either in point or humour; and in these closing numbers are those two doubtful papers to which attention has been called. It can hardly be a mere coincidence that the Lent Assizes in the West— Justices Dennison and Foster presiding—opened at Southampton on March 4, and continued through the month at Salisbury, Dorchester, Exeter, and Taunton. The law still being of prime importance with Fielding, it is probable that he attended the justices as was his custom on the Western Circuit. If this be so, it accounts for the very general topics discussed in the leaders and essays on politics during March—all of which might easily have been written some time in advance of publication,—and for the termination of the comment on the apocryphal news of the week—those little delicately flavoured dishes which Heliogabalus rel-

* "The Gentleman's Magazine," 1746, pp. 174-175, 218, 220.

41

ished, but which Fielding could not serve up when out of London. Then came in April the sittings of the King's Bench in London and Westminster, which would demand Fielding's presence.

His grip on "The True Patriot," once loosened, was never regained. After April 22, not a single advertisement appeared in the newspaper, none even by the publisher or by Fielding's friend Andrew Millar. "The True Patriot," having served its purpose, ceased to interest the public as well as the editor. Thereupon Fielding closed his books in time for another journey into the West for the summer Assizes. Viewed thus from the narrow personal standpoint, "The True Patriot" was a newspaper which Fielding conducted with vigour during his leisure between the sittings of the courts where he practised, and which he managed to keep alive, with the help of others, during term time. There is no doubt of the editor's exalted patriotism nor of his desire to put money into a depleted purse. His desire was probably not fulfilled to the extent he anticipated; but it is indisputable that he performed important public services during a national crisis—a time of confusion, said Fielding, which he hoped God would "never suffer to have its equal in this kingdom."

His own private affairs, it has recently been shown by Mr. J. Paul de Castro, were also in great confusion. As the legal adviser of a friend, Fielding became his surety and was compelled to pay. The case was this. The Collier sisters had a brother Arthur, who was then practising as an advocate at Doctors' Commons. His name appears among the subscribers to Fielding's "Miscellanies" as "the Worshipful Dr. Collier, L.L.D." Born in the same year, the two men had probably known each other ever since they were boys together at Salisbury. Though a lawyer of some ability, Dr. Collier was rather eccentric and quite untrustworthy in matters of business. Many years before, he had borrowed £400 of Tristram Walton of Salisbury, presumably to help him towards his education in the law, and had very properly acknowledged the debt in "a certain writing obligatory" which he signed and sealed at Salisbury as far back as September 22, 1739. But he declined to pay the debt, although he was often requested to do so, and he flatly refused to admit damages to the amount of £40 which Tristram Walton claimed. Determined to have his money, Walton brought suit against Collier in the Court of the King's Bench on June 14, 1745, and secured from the Court an order for "special bail." Thereupon, according to the record of the proceedings as given by Mr. de Castro:

"James Harris of the City of New Sarum in the County of Wilts Esquire and Henry Fielding of Boswell Court in the parsh of St. Clement Danes in the County of Middlesex Esquire come into the Court of our Lord the King before the King himself at Westminster in their proper persons and become Pledges and each of them by himself did become Pledge for the said Arthur that if it should happen that the said Arthur should be condemned in the plea aforesaid then the said Pledges did grant and each of them for himself did grant that as well the said Debt as all such damages costs and charges as should be adjudged to the said Tristram in that behalf should be made of their and each of their lands and chattels and be levyed to the use of the said Tristram if it should happen that the said Arthur should not pay the said debt and damages costs and charges to the said Tristram or render himself on that occasion to the Prison of the Marshal of the Marshalsea of our Lord the King before the King himself."

The case, being duly tried, was decided in favour of the plaintiff; but Fielding immediately entered a demurrer for his client, which the Court overruled on November 12, 1745, and at the same time awarded the plaintiff further damages to the amount of £8 10s. As a last resort, Fielding then appealed, on November 19, from the Exchequer Court to the Exchequer Chamber on a writ of error. The Chamber, after hearing the appeal on June 4, 1746, ordered:

"That the judgment should be in all things affirmed and should stand in full force and effect notwithstanding the said causes and matters assigned for Error by Arthur Collier. And it was also at the same time considered by the Court that Tristram Walton should recover against Arthur Collier eleven pounds and eleven shillings for his damages costs and charges which he had sustained by reason of the delay of execution of the said judgment on pretence of prosecuting the said Writ of Error."

The fatal day which Fielding had put off for months had at length arrived. Nothing could be collected from Harris, whose goods and chattels were far away in Salisbury. Accordingly an execution for £400 or more was taken out against Fielding. Beyond this we do not know the details. Probably Harris eventually paid his share of the obligation; but Dr. Collier stood by without much concern and let the law take its course. It may not be a mere coincidence that Fielding at once gave a quietus to the moribund "True Patriot," which he had conducted while the shadow of an ungrateful friend hung over him.*

* For the suit, see Mr. J. Paul de Castro, "Notes and Queries," 12 S. II, 104-106 (Aug. 5, 1916); where for Walton *vs.* Collier is cited King's Bench Plea Roll, Trinity Term, 18-19 George II, Roll 210, membrane 741 (Public Record Office).

CHAPTER XVI

THE JACOBITE'S JOURNAL

I

Again there was silence before the time came for another outburst of political journalism. Meanwhile Fielding and his sister continued to live in Old Boswell Court, where we have a casual view of them on an evening when they receive two visitors who call to pay their respects much as people nowadays seek out famous authors. The one who tells the story was Joseph Warton, a son of Thomas Warton, late professor of poetry at Oxford. Joseph was then but a young man recently in orders—not yet the Master of Winchester, and editor and critic of Pope. Of the reception he wrote, on October 29, 1746, to his brother Tom, a student at Oxford: "I wish you had been with me last week, when I spent two evenings with Fielding and his sister, who wrote David Simple, and you may guess I was very well entertained. The lady indeed retir'd pretty soon, but Russell and I sat up with the Poet [meaning Fielding, to whom the title was given by virtue of his plays] till one or two in the morning, and were inexpressibly diverted. I find he values, as he justly may, his Joseph Andrews above all his writings: he was extremely civil to me, I fancy, on my Father's account."* This is the real Fielding in his most delightful humour; but it is not to be inferred, as has

* J. Wool, "Biographical Memoirs of Joseph Warton," 1806, p. 215. In 1728, Fielding made a visit to Upton Grey, a few miles from Basingstoke, where the elder Thomas Warton, having resigned his Oxford professorship, resided as Vicar of the parish. It is probable that the two men were acquainted.

been often done by readers who pay no attention to dates, that he placed his "Joseph Andrews" above "Tom Jones" —a novel of which only a part had yet been written. He merely meant that "Joseph Andrews" was better than his plays, essays, and minor fictions.

While he was conducting "The True Patriot," his sister had been preparing, we know further, to publish by subscription a continuation of her "David Simple," to be called "Familiar Letters between the Principal Characters in David Simple, and Some Others." This was in line with the fashion set by Richardson, who added a second part to "Pamela" after the story had been concluded; for the characters were so real that people were willing to pay half a guinea more to learn how they thrived in the married state. Miss Fielding, owing to the success of her first venture, straightway began her sequel, with the intention, as may be seen in an advertisement in "The True Patriot" for February 18, 1746, of having it ready by the spring of that year; but she deferred publication—naming the next January as the probable date—because "her friends were totally prevented by the late public confusion, to favour her with their interest, as they kindly intended; nor could she herself think it decent to solicit a private subscription, in a time of such public danger." In the meantime Henry Woodfall printed for her, on November 23, 1746, five hundred subscription blanks,* that the work might proceed now the war was over. Some delay intervening, "The Familiar Letters," in two volumes, were not brought out until April, 1747.† It was an enterprise very like her brother's "Miscellanies." The volumes were printed for the author; Millar acted as the agent; and the price was put high—ten shillings a set for ordinary paper and a guinea for royal paper. The public responded nobly.

* "Notes and Queries," 1 S. XI, 419 (June 2, 1855).
† "The Gentleman's Magazine," April, 1747, p. 204.

Among the subscribers, numbering more than five hundred, were the Duchess of Bedford, the Countess of Orford, Mrs. Pitt, Lady Mary Wortley Montagu, Henry Fox, Thomas Winnington, Ralph Allen (who took five sets), the author's cousin, Henry Gould—and "Mr. Richardson," who, needless to say, had not lent the prestige of his name to her brother's "Miscellanies."

The sequel to "David Simple" is a rather dull performance of the moral kind, pieced out with many letters remotely connected with the original novel, the fragment of a fairy tale, a vision elaborated from an allegory of life which Sarah had read in "The Tatler," and two dialogues, called "Much Ado" and "Fashion," which were "a kind present" from an unnamed acquaintance. According to Dr. Johnson, the donor was James Harris, the friend from Salisbury, who was doubtless glad to find a place for the publication of his dialogues.* But what gives the book interest here is the fact that her brother Henry beyond doubt contributed the preface "written by a friend of the author," and the last five letters of the collection, which were introduced by a note in protest against the indirect attacks of Grub Street upon his character and reputation. "The following five letters," it is said in the note, "were given me by the author of the preface. I should have thought this hint unnecessary, had not much nonsense and scurrility been unjustly imputed to him by the good-judgment or good-nature of the age. They can know but little of his writings, who want to have them pointed out; but they know much less of him, who impute any such base and scandalous productions to his pen."

In his preface Fielding writes pleasantly on the different kinds of letters, real and imaginary, that have entertained his own and former times, condemning the inanity

* "Diary and Letters of Madame D'Arblay," edited by Charlotte Barrett, 1904, I, 86.

and conversational style of many French letters and English imitations of them. It is a hit at Richardson—is it not?—when he says: "And sure no one will contend, that the epistolary style is in general the most proper to a novelist, or that it hath been used by the best writers of this kind." Most of all, Fielding admired Lyttelton's "Persian Letters" descriptive of English manners and institutions, supposed to have been written by a Persian travelling in England, and sent to a friend at Ispahan. If novels were to be cast in letter form, he preferred that they should be confined to a letter or two, like some that Lyttelton introduced into this imaginary correspondence. He professed also to like letters such as his sister was writing, wherein is disregarded, to the reader's ease, the regular beginning and conclusion required of a novel; and in pointing out her feminine touches which would be the despair of any man, he quotes "a lady of very high rank, whose quality is however less an honour to her than her understanding"—perhaps Lady Mary Wortley Montagu—on his sister's first novel. "So far," said she, "from doubting David Simple to be the performance of a woman, I am well convinced, it could not have been written by a man." Recommending the new book to the public, Fielding added: "I hope, for the sake of my fair country-women, that these excellent pictures of virtue and vice, which, to my knowledge, the author hath bestowed such pains in drawing, will not be thrown away on the world, but that much more advantage may accrue to the reader, than the good-nature and sensibility of the age have, to their immortal honour, bestowed on the author." If he meant the last clause, like a similar phrase in his sister's note to the five letters, to be taken in irony, it was an ungenerous insinuation, in view of twenty-odd pages filled with subscribers' names.

It is nevertheless an agreeable picture in which we see brother and sister collaborating and each speaking out for the other. Of Henry's five letters, one, hardly rising above the talent of Sarah, is on love as the sweetest passion of life and a nobler incentive to labour than avarice or ambition. A pair of letters between Miss Prudentia Flutter and Miss Lucy Rural contrast the amusements of the town with those of the country during the Christmas holidays. It is a little novel in embryo such as Addison had written and such as in the author's opinion lent itself naturally to the letter form. Stories running to any length in this style Fielding found tiresome. In another letter a Frenchman records for the benefit of a friend at home his observations on a journey by boat up the Thames, from Whitehall Stairs to Putney, along the Surrey side and back by the Middlesex shore. This was an experiment in the humorous manner of Lyttelton, or rather his master, Montesquieu, but rendered lighter by numerous puns in explaining the names of places. Thus of Putney on the south bank and of Fulham directly across the river, it is said: "These two towns were founded by two sisters; and they received their names from the following occasion. These ladies being on the Surry shore, called for a boat to convey them across the water. The watermen being somewhat lazy, and not coming near enough to the land, the lady who had founded the town which stands in Surry, bid them *put nigh;* upon which her sister immediately cried out, 'A good omen; let Putnigh be the name of the place.' When they came to the other side, she who had founded the other town, ordered the watermen to push the boat *full home;* her sister then returned the favour, and gave the name of *Full home* to the place."

The most intimate of these five letters is the one that Fielding put first in his series—from Valentine in London to his friend David Simple in the country. It is a brief survey which Fielding took, early in 1747, of the state of the nation with reference to morals, literature, and politics.

His general proposition was that the moral and literary standards of a people depend upon the character of the leaders. At the present time "there is," he asserts, "no one patron of true genius, nor the least encouragement left for it in this kingdom." Despite this fact, a few writers of real talent manage to survive, but they are like plants growing in "a poor hungry soil." He is reminded, he says, of the answer that a gardener made to a covetous gentleman who was angry because there were no cucumbers in his garden. "How should you have cucumbers, Sir," retorted the gardener, "when you know you would not afford a hot-bed to raise them in?" There being no true standard of taste, literature has run, to the corruption of public morals, into profanity, indecency, slander, and dulness. Nowhere is a firm hand more needed than at the theatres. True, England now has several very great actors; but at Covent Garden, where Garrick and Quin and Mrs. Cibber were playing, the manager has given them rôles all this last winter in fustian tragedies; while the excellent comedians at Drury Lane, instead of treating the public to a lighter kind of "dramatical food," have attempted "to emulate the best actors of Covent-Garden in their best parts; and have vainly endeavoured to rival one [Garrick] who never had, nor, I believe, ever will have an equal." Beyond these tragedies, false and unnatural, the theatres have nothing to offer except "French and Italian buffoonry" and "operas, in which Mr. Handel is totally silent." For himself Fielding solved the problem by seldom visiting either theatre. Perhaps he forgot that his own "Miser" had been admirably cast that very winter at Drury Lane, and both "The Miser" and "The Lottery" at Covent Garden. But the complaint about the theatres was in general well founded. Garrick and Quin played Rowe's "Fair Penitent" many times during the season, and "Jane Shore" almost continually through January.

Outwardly the church seemed to Fielding to be in a flourishing condition; but "with regard to morality, which may be considered as the internal part," he said, "I freely own, I believe no age or nation was ever sunk to a more deplorable state." Everywhere he saw "a total disregard to all true honour and honesty, . . . every kind of corruption and prostitution, no man being ashamed of any thing but the appearance of poverty." Rarely did Fielding fall into so pessimistic a mood. No light could he throw on the dark picture until he came to politics. Then he said: "The administration of our public affairs is, in my opinion, at present in the hands of the very men, whom you, and every honest person would wish to be intrusted with it. Amongst those, tho' there is no absolute Prime Minister, yet there is one, whose genius must always make him the superior in every society, as he hath joined to the most penetrating wit, the clearest judgment both in men and things, and the profoundest knowledge of them, of any man, whom, perhaps the world ever saw." The unnamed minister to whom Fielding pays this fine tribute was probably not Henry Pelham, the brains of the Government, but Lord Chesterfield, who, as Lord-Lieutenant of Ireland, had kept that country tranquil during the late rebellion in Scotland, and had recently been appointed a Secretary of State, in consequence of his discreet management of an impetuous people.

An examination of the fugitive literature of the time reveals the fact that Fielding, after the suspension of "The True Patriot," put forth a number of anonymous pamphlets. Perhaps the first of them was a brief account, costing only sixpence, of a notorious incident sufficiently explained by the title: "The Female Husband; or, the Surprising History of Mrs. *Mary* alias Mr. *George Hamilton,* convicted for marrying a young Woman of *Wells.*" The trifle was advertised by Cooper the bookseller in "The

London Magazine'' and elsewhere in November, 1746; and
Andrew Millar, in giving a list of Fielding's works on a
flyleaf of his sister's ''Lives of Cleopatra and Octavia''
(second edition, 1758), credited it to the author of ''Tom
Jones.'' All further trace of this piece of hack-work, which
may have come from the pen of Fielding, is lost, except
for an allusion to it in the next pamphlet of the series:
''Ovid's Art of Love Paraphrased, and Adapted to the
Present Times.'' The paraphrase of Ovid, which was announced in ''The Gentleman's Magazine'' for February,
1747, was printed for Millar, and placed on sale also at
the shops of Cooper, Dodd, and George Woodfall. Its
price was two shillings. Though no copy of the second
pamphlet in its original form has yet come to light, it was
reprinted at Dublin in 1759, with the title: ''The Lover's
Assistant, or, New Year's Gift; being, a New Art of Love,
Adapted to the Present Times. Translated from the Latin,
with Notes, By the late Ingenious Henry Fielding of Facetious Memory.'' The authorship is perfectly certain. Its
sale not being very brisk, Fielding advertised the pamphlet
a year later (March 12, 1748) in ''The Jacobite's Journal,''
and recommended it there to his readers. Millar also included it among Fielding's works advertised in the first
separate edition of ''Jonathan Wild'' (1754), and again in
Sarah Fielding's ''Lives of Cleopatra and Octavia.'' As
Fielding had a copy of this edition of ''Jonathan Wild'' in
his library, he was aware of the advertisement in that
volume. Equally convincing is the internal evidence. The
little book has all of Fielding's technical peculiarities of
style, and contains allusions and expressions exactly
parallel to several in ''The True Patriot,'' and in the novel
which he was then writing. For example, he reproduces the
praise of the Duke of Cumberland which had appeared in
his newspaper, and makes similar facetious remarks as in
''Tom Jones'' on ''The Gardener's Dictionary,'' an enter-

taining as well as instructive book by Philip Miller of the Chelsea Gardens.

As reprinted in Dublin, the pamphlet is an octavo volume, having a preface of six pages (based upon Fielding's original preface), and eighty-seven pages of text. In the fashion of the time, the original Latin and the paraphrase face each other on opposite pages, while humorous comment runs along beneath the so-called translation. Fielding never got beyond 772 lines of the first book of the "Ars Amatoria," but promised to go on in the same manner not only with Ovid but with other Latin poets, provided he were "properly encouraged." A long quotation in the preface from the defence of Ovid prefixed to Dryden's translation of the first book of the "Ars Amatoria" concluded with the assurance from Fielding that the paraphrase herewith submitted to the public contained "nothing capable of offending the nicest ear," a phrase with which we are now familiar from its appearance, slightly altered, in the dedication to "Tom Jones." "One of the most learned men of this age," it was added, remarked, after "perusing" the book, "that he thought it would serve better to explain the meaning of Ovid to a learner, than any other translation, or all his numerous commentators." The learned man, if Fielding is serious, should be either Chesterfield or Lyttelton.

It is quite evident from Fielding's phrasing that, though he had the Latin before him, he kept his eye close to Dryden's free translation, a copy of which was at hand among his books. What he did with Ovid was to modernize him much as he had done with Juvenal in his youth; only he now chose prose instead of verse as more suitable to a light theme. Rome and its places of amusement become London, Vauxhall, Ranelagh, the Mall, and the theatres, while Baiae is easily converted into Bath, where the springs are equally "sulphurous," and where "Master Dapperwit, bringing home the wounds made by fair eyes in his bosom, cries out, on his return, 'The waters are not so wholesome as they are reported; I have received more harm than good at this place.'" For Ovid's "bunches of grapes in Methymna" and "ears of corn in Gargara," we have "apples in Herefordshire" and "grains of wheat in Hampshire." In the same way Ovid's characters, real and mythical, are transformed into well-known men and women of Fielding's day. The unnatural passion of Pasiphaë has its modern instance in the story of "Mrs. Mary Hamilton," who fell in love with a beautiful girl. Roman augury and divination are displaced by Parson Whitefield's "inspiration"; and "the lying Cretans" make way for the free-thinkers, who "believe nothing which they cannot see and account for." A distinct political colour was given to the paraphrase by turning Augustus Caesar into "our mighty George" meditating "new triumphs" in France, and by identifying the Emperor's grandson with the Duke of Cumberland, whose "matchless labours" were begun at Dettingen and completed at Culloden. "The true English reader," Fielding remarks in a footnote, "will be . . . delighted to see Ovid introduced as singing forth the praises of the British hero."

Again, there appeared, in the same month* as "The Familiar Letters," a shilling volume which, though Fielding's name has, I think, never been associated with it, should probably be assigned to him as author or editor. It is nothing less than "A Compleat and Authentick History of the Rise, Progress, and Extinction of the Late Rebellion, And of the Proceedings against the Principal Persons concerned therein," to give only the opening phrases of a long title-page concluding with "The whole compos'd with the greatest Accuracy possible in regard to Facts and Dates, and free from all Mixture of fictitious Circum-

* "The Gentleman's Magazine," April, 1747, p. 204.

stances, or ill-grounded Conjectures.'' The booklet, extending to 155 octavo pages, bears the imprint of Cooper, the publisher of ''The True Patriot.'' Following the title-page is a chart giving the plan of action at Preston Pans, designed for the Earl of Marchmont by an engineer who was present at the battle. With the additions necessary to complete the story, the pamphlet is based upon the detailed account of the rebellion which Fielding had published piecemeal in ''The True Patriot'' week by week. At times the narrative follows ''The True Patriot'' verbatim, but generally rather in the way of summary with rephrasing in the interest of unity and compactness. Nothing of importance, however, is omitted by the compiler, while much is perforce added, especially towards the close, with reference to the fate that overtook the leaders of the insurrection.

That Fielding himself pieced together this history of the rebellion there can be no reasonable doubt. Of course it may be argued that the work was done by some hack in the employ of Cooper; indeed, the compiler's use of *has* instead of *hath* would at first sight point to a hand other than Fielding's—to the conclusion that Fielding's only connection with the history was that of being the half-editor, half-author of the original narrative which ran through his periodical. But other considerations point directly to Fielding as the man who prepared the pamphlet for Cooper. A reason for Fielding's dropping his favourite *hath* is patent in the opening sentences which take the reader into the author's confidence. ''The merit of a performance,'' it is said there, ''does not at all depend upon its subject; for the lightest may be raised by an able, the most lofty may be injured by a weak and injudicious pen. This that I have undertaken is not so much the result of choice, as of necessity; I thought a succinct History of the Rebellion equally fit for the perusal of the present age, and of posterity.'' In short, Fielding purposely disguised his hand, so far as he could, in doing a piece of journeyman's work to which the hazards of life had driven him. Still, the patriotic aim emerges. At a time when numerous untrustworthy accounts of the rebellion were spread broadcast, the author would relate for his contemporaries and their descendants what really happened. With this purpose clearly stated, the little book began, and so it closed. ''Thus we have brought,'' runs the concluding paragraph, ''this history down from the first contrivance of the rebellion abroad to the death of the last person who suffered for it, with all the clearness, candour, and exactness in our power . . . ; and we shall conclude it with a hearty wish, that nothing of the like kind may happen for the future; but that the British nation may live in the quiet possession of their laws, liberties, and properties, under the auspicious Government of the Royal Family, till time shall be no more; with a continual increase of peace, plenty and prosperity at home, and of respect and glory abroad.''

No one needs to be told that this paragraph was written by the hand that wrote the last leader of ''The True Patriot.'' Fielding overestimated the value that posterity would place upon his history of the rebellion; owing to its anonymity, probably few copies of it—I have seen only one—longer exist; but it is of interest in that it shows Fielding's care for exact dates and other minor details in writing history. Facts aside, the history is not so ''impartial'' as it claimed to be; boldly Hanoverian in tone, it has the appearance of being put out as a political pamphlet to offset the influence of the Jacobite historians.*

* With this pamphlet may be involved another. Late in October, 1745, Cooper published a pamphlet called ''The History of the Present Rebellion in Scotland'' (''Gentleman's Magazine,'' Oct., 1745, p. 560). On a flyleaf of the second edition of Sarah Fielding's ''Lives of Cleopatra and Octavia'' (1758), Millar advertised the ''History of the Rebellion in Scotland, 1745,'' among

The Ministry soon had more pressing need of Fielding's pen. On June 18, 1747, Parliament was suddenly dissolved. Since the Battle of Culloden, opposition to the Government had been gathering strength. People revolted at the carnage in the days succeeding the battle and at the hideous executions of the following summer. Many Englishmen fully sympathized with the indignation that Smollett expressed in "The Tears of Scotland." When, for example, it was proposed to give the Duke of Cumberland the freedom of one of the London Companies, an alderman cried out, "Then let it be of the Butchers," and the Duke was thenceforth known as "Billy the Butcher." Subsequently certain Acts of Parliament aimed at those who had been in rebellion were severely criticised. The wearing of Highland dress was made punishable with imprisonment for a first and with transportation for a second offence. As a blow to the feudal rights of the Highland chieftains, all "heritable jurisdictions" in Scotland were abolished, though provision was made in the statute for partial compensation. An Act of grace was not quite what it claimed to be; for "the King's most gracious, general, and free pardon" specifically excluded by name eighty persons. Withal, people were tired of a foreign war which continued to drift on with no end in sight. In these circumstances, the Ministry, having put through Parliament its measures consequent upon the rebellion, appealed to the country, to the surprise of the Opposition, who were not

books written by Henry Fielding. The presumption is that the two pamphlets, each costing a shilling, were one and the same, and that Fielding was the author. I have been unable to discover a copy of this pamphlet, though perhaps one was formerly in the library of Col. W. F. Prideaux ("Notes and Queries," Jan. 7, 1888, p. 1). In "The True Patriot," Fielding began his account of the insurrection under the title, "Observations on the Present Rebellion," which he soon altered to "The Present History of Great Britain." Thus "A Compleat and Authentick History," whether compiled and elaborated by Fielding or by another hand, appears to have behind it not only the articles in "The True Patriot," but also the pamphlet of 1745.

expecting the action until the next year, when this Parliament would by law come to an end.

Fielding, however, was in the secret. Immediately after the dissolution, he issued anonymously an electioneering pamphlet of nearly a hundred pages,* entitled "A Dialogue between a Gentleman of London, Agent for two Court Candidates, and an Honest Alderman of the Country Party. Wherein the Grievances under which the Nation at present *groans* are fairly and impartially laid open and considered. Earnestly address'd to the Electors of Great-Britain." It is a very adroitly constructed Socratic dialogue, the only one of length we have from Fielding, in which the Gentleman representing the Government wins over an Alderman who, though professing to be a Republican (that is, a follower of Harrington, the author of "Oceana," who would substitute a republic or commonwealth for the monarchy), is at heart a Jacobite masquerading under abstract political theories. The candidates whom the Alderman promises to vote for are Sir Thomas Leadenhead and Mr. Toastum, of whom the former is a Jacobite belonging to that cowardly class of men who "prudently refrained from drawing their swords; but . . . gloriously and openly . . . drew their corks in the Pretender's favour"; and the latter is a discontented Whig, "who hath joined with this Jacobite, and would join with the Devil himself, to work himself into employment, which he despairs of being let into under the present Administration." Against these candidates who know nothing of public affairs are set "two worthy gentlemen, Sir John Protestant, and Mr. English," whose names promise well for their character. Making the Gentleman of London his mouthpiece, Fielding defends almost every phase of the Government's policy, foreign and domestic— not only what the Government has done but what it intends to do. Occasionally he lets slip a humorous sentence, as

* "The Gentleman's Magazine," June, 1747, p. 300.

when in arguing ably in favour of septennial against triennial Parliaments, he remarks that so short a time as three years would hardly give the Opposition "time to enflame the people, to invent grievances, and sufficiently to circulate falshoods against the King and his Administration." It is rather disconcerting to find the author of "Pasquin" relaxing in his attitude towards placemen, pensioners, and bribery. Though he does not fully approve of the corruption which was as openly practised by the Pelhams as by Walpole, he minimizes its extent and influence. He even thinks that there is a sort of defensive corruption which is justifiable. This is what he says:

"Indeed, to speak a bold political Truth, some Degree of Corruption always hath attended, and always will attend a rich and flourishing Nation. . . . Nothing, I apprehend therefore, can appear more unjust than this Charge of Corruption on the present Government; which neither introduced nor can possibly cure it. And can we expect, that when the Enemies of the present Establishment, are so manifestly busy in employing every Art, fair and foul, open and secret, to corrupt the Nation; to mislead, inflame and bribe them against their own true Interest, and against the King and his Administration; that the Government should sit still and use no Attempts for its own Security. To defend yourself with the same sort of Weapons by which you are attacked, hath always been held lawful. . . . In this defensive Way only the present Government can be fairly said to apply to any Arts of Corruption; and in this sense, I sincerely think, every honest impartial Man will own, that some Degree of it may be necessary to preserve not only the King on his Throne, but the Religion and Liberties of this Nation; all which are by the blackest Corruption attempted to be undermined."

Extracts from this pamphlet, of which there was a second edition, were widely quoted in the newspapers and magazines. It was at once a defence and a programme. Fielding, supplied with the necessary information, stated the issues on which the election was fought; and the Government which he supported won.

In the midst of renewed hack-work, Fielding married his housekeeper Mary Daniel, who had been his wife's maid. The marriage took place on November 27, 1747, at St. Bene't's, Paul's Wharf, an obscure London Church most suitable for quiet or semi-private marriages. In the parish register, Mary Daniel is very properly described as a spinster of St. Clement Danes in the Strand, wherein lay, as we have seen, Old Boswell Court. She was a citizen's daughter who had to earn a living, perhaps in consequence of the death of her father, for there is no reference to him then or subsequently, though her mother is mentioned by Fielding himself a few years later. At the time of her marriage she was twenty-six years old.* Her portrait painted by Francis Cotes after Fielding's death still exists somewhere—"a very fine drawing," it is said, "of a very ugly woman."† It is noticeable that Fielding, though he speaks in his "Voyage to Lisbon" of her tenderness, amiability, and fortitude in the face of trouble, is silent on the question of good looks. It was Charlotte Cradock, not Mary Daniel, whom he thought excelled all other women in beauty. Fielding took his bride to Twickenham, where they lived for a year in a house in Back Lane, now called "Holly Road," a narrow winding lane behind King Street.‡ It was "a quaint, old-fashioned wooden structure" not far from the river down to which ran from King Street other grassy lanes. The old house gave way fifty years ago to a row of three ugly brick cottages, over the entrance to one

---

* She was buried at St. Stephen's, Canterbury, May 18, 1802. The parish register gives her age as eighty-one.

† Dobson's edition of "A Voyage to Lisbon," 1892, p. 247.

‡ R. S. Cobbett, "Memorials of Twickenham," 1872, pp. 52 and 358-359.

of which has been inscribed Fielding's name. There in Back Lane was born the first child of the marriage—a son William, who, according to the parish register, was baptized on February 25, 1748. Twickenham seems to have been chosen as a place of retirement for Mrs. Fielding, while her husband must have remained much of the time in London.

The marriage exposed Fielding to considerable banter and abuse. Smollett, for example, introduced Fielding and Lyttelton, under fictitious names, into his first edition of "Peregrine Pickle"—the former as "Mr. Spondy" who married "his own cook-wench," and the latter as Gosling Scrag, a gracious patron who condescended to give the bride away. Worse than this, a long article in "Old England," for April 23, 1748, represented Fielding as applying with his wife for his tickets to a box in the theatre and being refused on the ground that the woman with him was not his wife but only a maid or a woman of the town who could not be admitted into the company of ladies. It was a marriage, too, that his friends had to apologize for if they remarked about it at all. At best Fielding had taken a wife socially beneath him; he had done exactly what Mr. B. had done in "Pamela,"—for which Fielding had ridiculed him in "Joseph Andrews." Fielding's first biographer, Arthur Murphy, passed over the marriage as if there had been none, though he knew of it and was acquainted with the second Mrs. Fielding. What the prim Sarah Fielding, the friend of Richardson, thought of her brother's marriage, is not recorded; but his cousin Lady Mary Wortley Montagu observed, as an example of his happy temper, that "his natural spirits gave him rapture with his cook-maid." Lady Mary, however, did not wholly disapprove of her cousin's conduct. The views of that branch of the family were given by her grand-daughter, Lady Louisa Stuart, who remembered what she had heard in her youth. The passage is the last word on Fielding's second marriage. Remarking on the beauty of the first wife and Murphy's silence with reference to the second, Lady Stuart goes on to say:

"His biographers seem to have been shy of disclosing that after the death of this charming woman he married her maid. And yet the act was not so discreditable to his character as it may sound. The maid had few personal charms, but was an excellent creature, devotedly attached to her mistress, and almost broken-hearted for her loss. In the first agonies of his own grief, which approached to frenzy, he found no relief but from weeping with her; nor solace, when a degree calmer, but in talking to her of the angel they mutually regretted. This made her his habitual confidential associate, and in process of time he began to think he could not give his children [there was, however, only one child] a tenderer mother, or secure for himself a more faithful housekeeper and nurse. At least this was what he told his friends; and it is certain that her conduct as his wife confirmed it, and fully justified his good opinion."[*]

Perhaps Smollett's assertion, not quite direct, that Lyttelton was present at the marriage to give the bride away, should be ascribed to mere rumour or ill-natured fiction; but it is certain that Lyttelton and Fielding were drawing together in a closer friendship than ever before since their days at Eton. To the outward view Lyttelton's political career had not been distinguished for its consistency. Long in the forefront of the opposition to Walpole, he had failed to support, after Sir Robert's downfall, the Wilmington Ministry though it contained many of his political friends, had indeed intrigued with Pelham for its overthrow, and had now become, as has been said earlier, a Lord of the Treasury in the new Administration known

[*] "The Letters and Works of Lady Mary Wortley Montagu," 1861, I, 106.

as the Coalition or the Broad Bottom Ministry. More than this, he had apparently sought at one time an alliance with Walpole. By his political enemies, he was regarded as a renegade who had deserted his former colleagues and the Prince of Wales, the figurehead of the old Opposition. In fact, his Royal Highness, piqued by his conduct, had dismissed him from a post that he held as a favourite in the Prince's household. Much the same shifting character was also charged against Pelham, Pitt, and other Whig leaders who had come into power after the death of Wilmington.

Criticism of their measures to cure the wounds of the rebellion, was accompanied by a torrent of abuse from the newspapers, the most scurrilous of which, said Fielding, was "The London Evening Post." Hardly second to this tri-weekly was "Old England," written chiefly by "Argus Centoculi," who sometimes, as a variation on his "Argus of the Hundred Eyes," signed himself "Porcupine Pelagius," the pseudonym employed by the author of "The Causidicade." Among other anti-ministerial newspapers were "The Westminster Journal," managed by Richard Rolt; and Walpole's old organ, "The Daily Gazetteer," in which the leading writer, said to have been "W. Horsly," commented on current events under the assumed name of "The Fool," meaning thereby not a dunce but a wise man of the Shakespearean breed. In short, there had not been since the demise of "The True Patriot" a London newspaper of any importance that gave full and ungrudging support to the Coalition. Wherefore, according to current gossip which hit near the truth, it was decided to call in once more Fielding to champion the Government's policies and ridicule its critics. Lyttelton, whose career especially stood in need of defence, was the active agent in thus stripping the Bar again of "a notable ornament."

II

The new periodical, the first number of which appeared on December 5, 1747, was called "The Jacobite's Journal" and purported to come from the pen of "John Trott-Plaid, Esq," a variant of "John Trot," the pseudonym of a former contributor to "The Craftsman." It was issued every Saturday at twopence a copy. As in the case of "The True Patriot," the booksellers interested in the project were Cooper and Woodfall, with the addition of "C. Corbett, in Fleet-street." Among these names was included for a time "Mrs. Nutt, at the Royal-Exchange"; and the first number gave as the printer "W[illiam] Strahan, in Wine-Office-Court, Fleetstreet." At all these places advertisements and letters were received for the author. Besides having the same two booksellers for its main support, "The Jacobite's Journal" much resembled in form and style its predecessor. It had the usual four pages, beginning with a political essay, followed by foreign and domestic news, with which Fielding played delightfully in the character of Punch, and advertisements, which consisted mostly of books, though there were admitted a few notices of remedies of the better sort. Here was announced the publication of "Clarissa Harlowe," "Roderick Random," "The Castle of Indolence," and the fourth edition of "Joseph Andrews." A moderate amount of advertising was also supplied by the Admiralty Office; and the Government purchased, according to rumour, two thousand copies or more of each issue for free distribution by post among the inns and alehouses throughout the kingdom.

No one could doubt, after reading a few numbers, that John Trottplaid was Henry Fielding. Never was Fielding happier in his humorous comment on the news of the day; never more generous in the praise of his friends living or dead, whatever their rank—whether among the nobility and gentry or among the actors and tradespeople of London. When it was lamented that the Earl of Cromarty, a Scottish lord who had joined Charles Edward, should be stripped of his title and banished for life to a place near Exeter, Fielding in his love for the West remarked on the mildness of the punishment: "If Ovid had been obliged to have exchanged Scotland for Devonshire, he had never written his *Tristia.*" When the roof of Westminster Hall became ruinous and had to be repaired with new spars, he observed: "Some will have it that the *floor* of Westminster-Hall hath been long more ruinous than the roof." News, afterwards found to be incorrect, reached him that his kinsman Henry Gould (subsequently Sir Henry) had died while on the Western Circuit; and Fielding wrote:

"This young gentleman (who was of the Middle-Temple) had great Parts, and had with great Diligence applied them to the study of his Profession; in which he was arrived at a very extensive Knowledge, and had very early in Life acquired much Reputation."

On the death of the poet Thomson, he said:

"This Morning at Four o'Clock died of a violent Fever, at his House in Kew-Lane, the celebrated Mr James Thompson, Author of the Seasons, &c. an honest Man, who has not left one Enemy behind him. His Abilities as a Writer, his Works sufficiently witness to all the World; but the Goodness of his Heart, which overflowed with Benevolence, Humanity, universal Charity, and every amiable Virtue, was best known to those who had the Happiness of his Acquaintance; by every one of whom he was most tenderly beloved, and now most sincerely and most deservedly lamented."

All this good feeling, finely expressed, had also pervaded "The True Patriot"; it was the unmistakable mark of Fielding's hand.

The novelty of "The Jacobite's Journal" lay in its humorous conception. The English Jacobites, whom fear had kept quiet during the invasion of the Pretender, crept from cover as soon as all danger to their lives and estates was over. Many of them were, of course, perfectly honest in their political views. They looked upon the Georges as intruders, and the living descendant of James the Second as the rightful King of England. Here and there, by the ostentatious display of their principles, they came into conflict with the established Government. Jacobite disturbances at Oxford, for example, led to the arrest of several students of Magdalen College, who were brought up to London, fined, and barely escaped imprisonment for their insults "to his Majesty's Crown and Government." Among people who had no real interest either in the Stuarts or in the Hanoverians, Jacobitism became a fashion. At taverns and country houses they openly drank bumpers to "the King over the water" in noisy scenes often ending in tumult and riot. Though the Highlanders were forced to discard their peculiar dress, it was partially appropriated by the English Jacobites, of whom the women wore plaid petticoats, and the men laced waistcoats of the same kind. Plaids were especially conspicuous at hunting matches and horse races. A party of sportsmen near Lichfield, said Smollett, not only adorned themselves with plaids, but hunted with hounds clothed in variegated colours, and—to complete the absurdity—dressed the fox in a red uniform.

Just what had caused this outbreak of Jacobite madness Fielding was uncertain. Some, he claimed, attributed it to the heats of the summer of 1747; others to the mildness of the Government rather than to the mildness of the season; while many thought it had something to do with "the great plenty of good liquor, neither malt or cyder having been ever cheaper than lately." At any rate, the Jacobites were a large and flourishing party who deserved to have an organ of their own; hence the establishment of "The Jacobite's Journal." True, most of the London newspapers, Fielding admitted by way of apology for his own undertaking, are secretly Jacobite, but their authors are afraid to speak out directly in favour of the principles of their party, lest they be laughed at by the sane and judicious. Moreover, these newspapers are wretched productions written by a set of Grub Street hacks beneath contempt. The articles of "The London Evening Post," as everybody knows, are "low, quibbling, unintelligible"; the author of "The Westminster Journal" dwells in "Cimmerian darkness"; and the Argus of "Old England" has long since appeared "with all his eyes out." On the other hand, "The Jacobite's Journal" will be managed by "one who hath more wit and humour in his little finger (according to a common expression) than these writers have in their whole bodies"; himself a Jacobite, he will explain all the esoteric doctrines of the sect, and faithfully defend them; he will patiently endure all the ridicule which will be heaped upon him for thus setting forth and advocating policies conducive to the good of his country. Such is the ironical point of view that Fielding assumed in his "Jacobite's Journal." It is the irony of "Jonathan Wild" applied to the newspaper—not only to the leading articles, but even to many of the news-items. Just as in that novel Fielding told the story of a scoundrel as if he were himself the scoundrel; so here he proclaims himself a Jacobite in order the better to laugh his countrymen out of their political follies.

Emblematic of his design, Fielding placed at the head of "The Jacobite's Journal" a woodcut, supposed to have been drawn by Hogarth from hints supplied by the author himself.* It was, said Fielding, "a contrivance of mine

* S. Ireland, "Graphic Illustrations of Hogarth," 1794, I, 148.

(the expence of much laborious thinking) to do honour to
the Jacobite Party.'' In this curious frontispiece are seen
two Jacobites—a man and a woman—dressed in the fashionable plaids and riding on an ass. The man, who sits
astride in front, a Highland cap raised aloft in one hand,
a cup in the other, is shouting a huzza; while the woman
directly facing the reader, one hand grasping a French
sword, the other resting on the rump of the beast, is
bawling in unison. A sly Jesuit in the garb of a bare-
footed friar is leading the ass by a rope over which is flung
a copy of ''The London Evening Post,'' upon which the
hungry animal is munching. To the tail of the ass is
fastened a copy of Harrington's ''Oceana'' emblazoned
with the fleurs-de-lis of France. In the background lies
the city of London.

To this picture were given, said Fielding, various inter-
pretations. Some readers thought the ass symbolized the
author himself, arguing that, if an ass in Scripture once
spoke, it might be inferred that his descendants had learned
to write. Again, he had heard it suggested that the Jesuit
stood for the old Chevalier, while the two other figures
represented the young Chevalier and his mistress Jenny
Cameron. Still others recognized in the plaids the features
of certain squires and gentlewomen whom they had seen
riding to the fox-chase. But all these resemblances to particular persons were, Fielding avowed, fanciful. The
plaided man and woman (presumably his wife) were merely
types having no definite originals; and the ass on which
they rode was designed to figure neither the author nor
other gentlemen of the press, but the whole body of Jacobite doctrine. He hoped that no offence would be taken at
the emblem, for none was intended. To be sure, the ass
had come to be regarded in modern times with some dis-
respect, but he was not so held by the ancients—neither
by the Jews, who worshipped his golden image, nor by the

Greeks and Romans, who related of him most instructive stories. To them he was a noble animal so remarkable for his patience and firmness that, however much he might be beaten, whipped, or kicked, he would still trudge on without altering his pace. Rightly considered, the ass thus admirably symbolized the Jacobites, whom no force of argument has ever been able to swerve from their principles. If it be objected that the firmness of the ass and the Jacobite inclines to obstinacy, it should be remembered that every virtue in excess borders upon its corresponding vice; for such is the teaching of all the philosophers, ancient and modern.

Several minor details of the print Fielding left to his readers to work out for themselves. They would see in the French sword and the fleurs-de-lis the Jacobite intrigues with France, and in the "Oceana" hanging at the ass's tail a hit at those Republicans who, though they wished to rid England of her kings, preferred the Stuarts to the House of Hanover. They were the tag end of the Jacobite party. Equally clear to everybody would be the meaning of the Jesuit, for from the Protestant standpoint the Church of Rome was the instigator of all disaffection with the House of Hanover. Similar views Fielding had already expressed in his "Dialogue between a Gentleman of London . . . and an Honest Alderman." In his print he depicted, as he had described in his pamphlet, "that notable and mysterious union of French interest, Popery, Jacobitism, and Republicanism; by a coalition of all which parties this nation is to be redeemed from the deplorable state of slavery, under which it at present labours." The art of man, he remarked by the way, could not carry higher than this, "the glory of Jacobitism."

Like the explanation of his frontispiece, the irony of the leading articles had to be patent in order to be effective. In mock praise of the Jacobites, Fielding divided them into classes, pointed out the external marks by which they might be detected, and reduced all their political opinions to nonsense. A parallel was drawn between Jews and Jacobites, in which both were shown to possess the same characteristics—superstition, stubbornness, and a headlong temper. Both had lost their anointed kings, and both were still looking for a Messiah who had already come. A parody on Ovid's "Art of Love," which a fictitious correspondent, who had read Fielding's paraphrase of that poem, professed to have translated from a Latin original called "De Arte Jacobitica," instructed the Jacobites in the rules necessary for winning over their country by deceit and misrepresentation, by feigning a love where there is none. A learned treatise on fables being advertised, Fielding made use of the book for an analogous account of the origin of Jacobitism out of ignorance and oral tradition founded upon it. As the Jacobites were all heavy drinkers, Fielding thought that the word designating them was in some way derived from *Bacchus,* otherwise *Iacchus,* from which one may easily pass to Iacchites, or, in English pronunciation, *Jackites.* But Parson Adams questioned this etymology, and challenged him to go a step further and show how *Jackites* became *Jacobites,* how the "middle syllable," as it was called, ever got into the place where it now stands. According to the Hebrew scholar, the word *Jacobite* could come only from *Jacob,* meaning "a supplanter," which exactly described not only the man in Scripture who bore that name but also a party always intriguing for power under the pretence that the existing Government is damnable.

A fictitious correspondent such as Parson Adams was an editorial device for removing the ironic masque whenever Fielding wished to deal a direct home thrust. As John Trottplaid, he was bound to write in the character of a Jacobite; but as a country parson, a Quaker, or any other

fanciful contributor, he might become an avowed Hanoverian, assailing the Jacobites and repelling their attacks
on the Government. More than once Mr. Trottplaid was
censured in his own newspaper for stirring up political
quarrels at a time when the people should present a united
front against their common enemy across the Channel. Let
these dissensions continue, declared Fielding through an
alarmed correspondent, and there will soon be no British
nation for the Jacobites to disrupt; it will become a dependency of France. Despite sober communications in this
style, the ironic tone of the newspaper was maintained by
the editorial comment which accompanied them. Though
he had dedicated his talents, Mr. Trottplaid said, to the
Jacobites, a man of his fair temper could not justly refuse
to let a poor devil on the other side occasionally address
the public through his columns. He had no fear that harm
would result from this impartial policy, for no argument
had ever yet prevailed against Jacobitism. Of course, it
would be better if he could count upon more correspondents
within his own party; but for some unknown reason there
was a dearth of them. Doubtless many Jacobites had failed
to contribute to his journal because they were unable to
write; but that could not be true of the whole party, for he
had already published several Jacobite effusions and there
were more in his desk. To prove his point, Mr. Trottplaid
inserted an illiterate letter from a Somerset squire in denunciation of the window-tax. "I put out," wrote the
squire, "one haf of my windows last year, and if there
comes another [tax], Ile put out t'other haf.—D–n me
a man may drink in the dark, and mayhap he may then be
the buolder in toasting honest healths." This letter of an
old Jacobite who sat in the dark and drank to the King
over the water, breathed, Mr. Trottplaid remarked, that
honest, hearty, patriotic spirit which distinguishes the
country gentlemen of England from all other people in the

world. If Parliament had a majority of them, there would be no doubt about the future of Great Britain.

In the heat of political warfare, Fielding did not hesitate to hurl the word Jacobite against anyone who criticised the Pelham Ministry. Applied generally, the charge meant that all the disaffected Whigs and the remnant of the old Tory party were but Jacobites in disguise. Fielding's newspaper had run through only a few numbers before the tables were turned against him by an unknown pamphleteer of considerable ability. The lively controversy centred round the character of Thomas Winnington, the politician, who had suddenly died, the year before, of a cold. It was a notorious case of improper treatment by Dr. Thomas Thompson, who subsequently attended Fielding in a serious illness. A Tory by birth and education, Winnington became, on entering Parliament, a zealous supporter of Walpole, and, after Sir Robert's downfall, so ingratiated himself with the two succeeding Ministries that he held under them the lucrative post of Paymaster-General of the Forces. To the King he was "the honestest man" in the public service; to others he appeared to have sacrificed his political principles, if he ever had any, to a desire to stand well with the Court.

About the first of December, 1747, while Winnington's career and death were still subjects for gossip, a mischievous enemy published a pamphlet on him, called "An Apology for the Conduct of a late celebrated Second-rate Minister." Title-page and preface asserted that the manuscript had been found after Winnington's death among his papers; that its genuineness was attested by the author's well-known hand and style. In this spurious autobiography, Winnington was made to flaunt his Jacobitism and to claim that most of the Whig leaders since the Revolution of 1688—Harley, Godolphin, Marlborough, Walpole, and the present Ministers even—were really Jacobites;

that, though appearances might be to the contrary, they were always waiting for a turn in the affairs of state which would enable them to restore the Old Constitution, as it was called, that is, the relation between King, Lords, and Commons which existed under the Stuarts. A plausible case was made out, for party leaders had indeed carried on flirtations with the Jacobites. Walpole, it is well known, intrigued more than once for their votes. But the contention that a deliberate scheme for betraying the people into the hands of the Pope and the Stuarts had been worked out in secret by successive Whig Administrations was preposterous despite its cleverness.

The pamphlet created a sensation. Throughout the winter it was the talk of everybody. Winnington's executors offered a reward of fifty pounds for the discovery of the author, but he was not found. What did he mean by it? Was it written in seriousness or in irony? Was it, as the executors claimed, a forgery, or a genuine document which they wished to suppress? Assuming it to be a forgery, what facts lay behind it? Was Walpole a Jacobite? Were the present Ministers secretly Jacobites also? Would they have put the young Chevalier on the throne, had they dared? These questions, so far as prudence would permit, were discussed in several pamphlets—perhaps there were a half-score of them. In one having as title "The Patriot Analized," a gentleman of London collected the various opinions of the town in a letter to a friend at Worcester, the constituency that Winnington represented in Parliament. Coffee-house politicians, physicians, merchants, aldermen, Quakers, nonjurors, stock-jobbers, apothecaries, parsons, members of Parliament, lawyers and law students, ladies, some married and some unmarried, the company at Drury Lane—Mrs. Clive, Mr. Garrick, Mr. Cibber,—all gave their views in imaginary conversations.

After reading the attack on Winnington, Fielding ironically congratulated "Father Paul Maskwell of the Society of Jesus" on his "excellent treatise"; and a week later entered the fray in earnest with "A Proper Answer to a late Scurrilous Libel, entitled, *An Apology for the Conduct of a late celebrated Second-rate Minister.*" This counterblast, too long for his newspaper, was issued as a shilling pamphlet on December 24, 1747,* under the pseudonym of "the Author of the *Jacobite's Journal.*" Fielding had no special concern for the memory of Winnington, except to say that a man of his position could never have written himself down to posterity as a hypocrite and impostor; that the author of the "Apology" was a jester or a madman— certainly a liar "capable of asserting falsehoods blacker than hell itself." Fielding's pamphlet was rather an answer to the arraignment of the Whig party and the Church of England since the Revolution of 1688; and what particularly aroused him was the apologist's insinuation that certain members of the Government—Pelham and Chesterfield, for example—who had just suppressed the rebellion, were nevertheless Jacobites like their predecessors. It was, said Fielding, "the honestest Ministry with which any nation hath been blessed"; and of Henry Pelham, he declared, "he hath indeed a mind which no difficulties can conquer, nor any power corrupt."

Fielding's "Answer" lent gaiety to the absurd controversy. The wits who pounced upon him declared his performance dull; and though he had written his pamphlet at white heat, they asked him why he was so cool in the defence of his party if he really believed in its principles. It was thus intimated that he might be a Jacobite at heart as much as were his political friends, who would together display their real colours when the opportune moment arrived. Indeed, so perfunctory was the reply to the attack on Winnington from this pensioner of the Government, that he

* Announced for that day in "The Jacobite's Journal," Dec. 19, 1747.

would seem to be the author of the attack also. To go no
further, these insinuations were made in the pamphlet to
which reference has already been made—"The Patriot
Analized." Here is a bit of dialogue re-arranged from the
interviews in that work:

"*A Bookseller.* Ah, Sir, you know not what F———g
could do if he were willing. The Fault lay in the Heart and
not in the Head. Had he not approved of the *Apology* in his
Heart, you would have seen him mince and hash it so as
to make half the Town weep and the other laugh. Don't
you think the Pen that writ *Pasquin, Joseph Andrews,* and
the *Champion,* could have answered the *Apology,* if he had
had the Will?

"*A Bencher of the Middle Temple.* But I can't see why
the Author of the *Jacobite Journal* should want that Will.

"*A Bookseller.* Alas, Sir! You forget the Power of
Necessity. If a Man, that wants Bread, can establish a
Paper by the P[os]t Off[ic]e taking off *Two Thousand*
every Week, is he not more excusable than a Man of Fortune, who Votes against his Conscience and the Interest of
his Country, for a Place or Pension?

"*A Bencher of the Middle Temple.* I detest the latter,
and can't excuse the former; it being possible that his
wavering Principles had brought him to the Necessity of
writing for Bread.—But as to the *Apology,* the Answerer
shews his want of Power much more than Deficiency of
Will, which he plenteously lays out in the foulest, lowest,
poorest Language that ever paper was stufft with.

"*A Student of the Law.* What would you say, if the
Apology had been wrote by the Answerer himself? 'Tis
a common Device among such Writers as find themselves
obliged to vary their Productions according to the Whim,
Caprice, or Persuasion of the employing Bookseller. But
whether or no the Author of the *Jacobite Journal* was that
of the *Apology,* 'tis evident, by the Shallowness of the

Answer, that the *Apology* was unanswerable, or that the Answerer, being of the same Principles with the *Apologist,* was unwilling to efface any Impressions such a Work as the *Apology* might have made on the Mind of the Subjects.''

This and other attempts to draw Fielding out further were unavailing; he let his ''Answer,'' which went into a second edition, speak for itself. One of the pamphlets against him brings us back to ''The Jacobite's Journal.'' It bore the title, ''A Free Comment on the Late Mr. W—g—n's Apology for his Conduct,'' and purported to be a letter from a lady disguised as ''C'' to her friend ''Harriott'' in the Country. Lady C receives a visit from Lady Fanny which is duly reported to Harriott. Lady Fanny becomes ruffled at the rumour that she is the original of the brawling Highland woman riding the ass in the frontispiece of ''The Jacobite's Journal'':

''*Lady Fanny.* Good-Morrow, my Dear; have you heard the News?

''*Lady C.* Yes; that Lady Fanny —— was she, whom F——g represents in a *Plaid Jacket,* in the Front of his *Jacobite* Journal.

''*Lady Fanny.* The Whirling Coxcomb! What had he to do with ridiculing any Party, who had travell'd round the whole Circle of Parties and Ministers, ever since he could brandish a Pen? But I suppose he has got a *Pension* for answering People with his Nonsense, to draw off their Attention from What's *doing amiss,* as one of his fellow *Journalists,* some time ago, had, for holding his Tongue— Well may —— be raised in a *Day,* when Publick Money is thus lavish'd on Weather-Cocks and Jackalls.''.

It is not known that Hogarth—if the frontispiece of ''The Jacobite's Journal'' be his—had in mind a particular person when he designed the Highland woman; but this assumption would be in accord with his practice. What is certain is that Fielding withdrew the woodcut—the block was somewhat worn—after the twelfth number, assigning, among several humorous reasons, "the many gross and absurd misconceptions" which had been vented against it by the public. The disappearance of the frontispiece was followed by the announcement in the seventeenth number (March 26, 1748), that the author of "The Jacobite's Journal" had decided to pull off the masque which he had been wearing through the winter. Then and there John Trottplaid renounced forever "all the principles of a Jacobite, as being founded on certain absurd, exploded, tenets, beneath the lowest degree of a human understanding." "In plain fact," said Fielding, "I am weary of personating a character for which I have so solemn a contempt." Besides his own dislike—"abhorrence" is his word—of the part he was playing, the jest had become stale. "I have observed," Fielding remarked justly, "that tho' irony is capable of furnishing the most exquisite ridicule; yet as there is no kind of humour so liable to be mistaken, it is, of all others, the most dangerous to the writer. An infinite number of readers have not the least taste or relish for it, I believe I may say do not understand it; and all are apt to be tired, when it is carried to any degree of length." Beyond these considerations lay the fact that a Jacobite disguise had become impracticable. From all sides, in newspapers and pamphlets, the assaults on the Ministry grew more and more determined every week. These assaults could not be withstood by irony alone; nor was it always convenient to send forth various imaginary correspondents to repel them. Everybody knew that John Trottplaid was an alias for Henry Fielding. And why keep up the fiction longer? In Fielding's phrase, Jacobitism had ceased to be "a joke"; "The Remembrancer," an anti-ministerial newspaper established the previous December, was advising the people "to rise and do themselves justice"; the time had arrived for an open fight. Irony still remained a powerful weapon for Fielding, but he was now free to use any other weapon known to political warfare.

The Ministry was assailed for what it did, for what it failed to do, and for what it had no intention of doing— for a war which it inherited from the Walpole Administration and to which it was opposed, for not prosecuting the war with vigour whenever there was a rumour of defeat, for not making peace on any terms that France would accept, and then for making peace as soon as there was a decent opportunity, for novel schemes of taxation which were proposed not by its own members but by others, and for suppressing the freedom of the press though it never went beyond an occasional prosecution for libel. This method of attack Fielding called "the art of contrariety," or "of abusing on both sides of the question," in order to bring into the Opposition men "of different and repugnant opinions"—Jacobites and Republicans, Tories and Whigs, Churchmen and Dissenters; it resembled, he said, the forestroke and backstroke in cudgel-playing whereby an ingenious champion may put his adversary aside his guard and easily break his head; or the lawyer's dragnet, that summary charge of many crimes against a miserable defendant "which no innocence can possibly escape"; or the potion which an unskilled physician, uncertain of his diagnosis, compounds of many ingredients, in the hope that some at least of his "contrariant medicines" may hit the disease in the spot his ignorance has unhappily missed.

Against adversaries who fought in this underhanded manner, Fielding pretended that no headway could be made by a champion conversant with only the honourable rules of the game. So it would be better, he thought, to acknowledge defeat at once and give one's attention to some scheme for silencing the enemy. Since the temper of the public would not permit any restriction on the liberty of the press, three or four members of the Ministry might resign in favour of its most scurrilous defamers, such as the editors of "Old England," "The London Daily Post," and "The Daily Gazetteer." The most serious objection to this transfer of power would be perhaps the doubt whether these gentlemen of the press were perfectly qualified for the highest offices of state. As a compromise, they might be erected into a "Board of Supervision" with Argus of the Hundred Eyes as chairman, to whom the Ministry should be required to submit all its measures for approval before bringing them forward in Parliament. Though this method would subject the councils of the Ministry to some delay and to the danger of discovery, the inconvenience would be counterbalanced by the great sanction thereby given at home and abroad to all political transactions. If neither of these schemes seemed feasible, no one could object to the establishment of a "Hospital for Scoundrels," after the plan of the Foundling Hospital, where the entire host of Grub Street scribblers could be fed and clothed at less expense than the public was then paying for their scandalous nonsense.

More formidable than these literary hacks, were the hostile pamphleteers, among whom often lurked a political leader or someone of equal ability whom he employed to write for him. No anti-ministerial pamphlet of consequence ever escaped a hot retort in "The Jacobite's Journal." More than once the editor, with all the force of his eloquence, defended Pelham against the charge of bribery and Lyttelton against apostasy. One passage at arms has a personal interest because of an antagonist whose identity was not then suspected. It occurred over "A Letter to the Tories," a ministerial pamphlet of ambiguous authorship, flaying the old Walpole Administration and threatening stern measures against that combined Opposition of the disaffected such as Fielding had several times described. This vigorous pamphlet, it was generally supposed, came from

Lyttelton, though he probably never saw it before he read it in print. Sure in his own mind that the letter was Lyttelton's, Horace Walpole fell upon it in "A Letter to the Whigs," which was succeeded by a second and a third letter—all in defence of his father's policies and in denunciation of Lyttelton, the time-server, the turncoat, the courtier, who had boxed the political compass. It was not safe to attack Lyttelton while Fielding was alive. Denying, "upon certain knowledge," that Lyttelton wrote "A Letter to the Tories," Fielding riddled young Walpole's replies with fact, sarcasm, and contempt.* It was a superb vindication of Lyttelton's career and character. In the next number of "The Jacobite's Journal" the author of "A Letter to the Whigs" half apologized for the appearance of a second edition which his publisher had just brought out. The humour of this clash with Walpole lies in the fact that Fielding did not know with whom he was contending; he surmised a Jacobite, probably a weak-minded woman of the party, so feeble and ill-informed was the author. No wonder that Horace Walpole never placed a very high estimate upon Fielding's wit and humour.

Ridicule of the newspapers went on in "The Jacobite's Journal" without interruption. In their name, Fielding advertised for "new Aspersions to be cast upon the Ministry" since those current had become stale, and the editors were at their wit's end to coin without assistance fresh ones. He extracted from "The London Evening Post" and the rest examples of "Jacobite wit," puerile and ineffectual, for the edification of his readers; rearranged their news-items as a supplement to the wonders in Baker's "Chronicle"; reprinted with remarks or parody their satirical verses on trade, war, and peace; and once put into rhyme the contents of a typical number. These anonymous scribblers he denounced as "the scandal of the press" and

* "The Jacobite's Journal," April 2, 1748.

"the disgrace of the age," whose productions every man of common sense should be ashamed of reading. They ought to be extirpated from society or sent back to the clerkships and manual trades from which they originally sprang.

By way of jest, it was gravely announced in a summer issue of "The Jacobite's Journal" that all the Grub Street writers had gone into the country to do harvest work for the farmers. On their return to town, they found that their places had been taken by a recent convert to Jacobitism, one Anna Maria Supple, who for half their pay was writing the leading articles in "Old England" and "The London Evening Post," besides furnishing a few papers upon naval affairs in "The Fool," and composing an occasional pamphlet like "The Letters to the Whigs." Her son, a boy just eight years old, was the author, her husband said, of most of the satirical "varses," as the lad called them, in "The London Evening Post." The writers who had turned harvesters for the season were consequently thrown into great distress; and were forced to appeal through their friends to the editor of "The Jacobite's Journal" to give them employment, else they would starve. Though reluctant to take over gentlemen who had no talent except to throw dirt, Mr. Trottplaid was eventually persuaded to try "Morgan Scrub, Grubstreet-Solicitor, whileom Author of Old-England," in the mean capacity of collector and arranger of his news. The fictitious Scrub, bitter towards a party that had refused him the bread necessary to sustain life, poured forth his Billingsgate against "The London Evening Post" conducted by "an infernal blockhead" and "jack-ass." In thus pitting one anti-ministerial newspaper against another in an imaginary squabble, Fielding created a very humorous situation which enabled him to burlesque admirably the vituperation of the current defamatory style.

However low Fielding might descend for his humour, he rarely reached direct personal abuse. His quarrel was with Grub Street as represented by the writers on the newspapers of the Opposition. He must have known who the men were that called themselves "Argus Centoculi" and "The Fool"; and, following the example of Pope, he might have pried into their lives for scandalous incidents. That he would not do. Nor did he print their names with the vowels out, leaving the initial, middle, and final consonants—a common practice in his time as a means of escaping an indictment for libel. Only when burlesquing the style of others was he accustomed, in his own phrase, to "embowel or rather emvowel" words; and he expressed contempt for the intelligence of the judge who in a case of libel decided for the defendant on the ground that it was not certain who was meant by a row of consonants about which nobody else had any doubt. Always Fielding respected anonymity if a writer chose it, and avoided the scurrilous anecdote though he might have it at hand. With Fielding the point of attack was not so much the individual behind the masque as the class to which he belonged. What he sometimes said about the personality of an anonymous writer was so obviously fictitious that no one could regard it as having any basis in fact.

It was not so with the gentlemen of the press whom he infuriated by his irony and ridicule. "A heavier load of scandal," said Fielding while writing "The Jacobite's Journal," "hath been cast upon me, than I believe ever fell to the share of a single man." The assertion is true for the literary men of the eighteenth century if we except Pope. With no disguise beyond casting out the vowels of his name, he was pelted in verse and prose, often in company with Pelham and Lyttelton. Pelham became "Palaam," a wretched pun upon "Balaam," who held conversations with the ass that wrote "The Jacobite's Journal.'' Lyttelton was known as ''Little-Tony'' to rhyme with ''money,'' or as ''Selim Slim,'' so named in derision from the character of Selim in ''The Persian Letters'' and from the extreme thinness of his person. According to ''The London Evening Post,'' Trottplaid or F———g was the hireling of these politicians; the ''magpie'' whom ''Patron Slim'' taught to scream obscene phrases, the meaning of which he did not know; ''a dolt,'' ''an obsequious fool,'' ''an incorrigible blockhead,'' ''a reptile scribbler,'' or ''a madman'' found straying in St. James's Park, whom his friends ought to commit to the care of the learned Dr. James Monro, physician to Bethlehem Hospital for the insane. In ''Old England'' ''Aretine'' had an open letter addressed to Selim Slim, censuring Lyttelton for taking into his service ''the outcast of the playhouse! the refuse of the booksellers! the jest of authors, and the contempt of every ingenious reader.'' But all this was very mild compared with a character-sketch of Fielding which Argus Centoculi subsequently printed from the pen of ''Porcupine Pelagius.'' Fielding was there made to say of himself down to the time that he reached a haven of rest as ''the pensioned scribbler'' of the Pelham Ministry:

''Hunted after Fortune, and lived on Kept-Mistresses for a while; scored deep at the Taverns, borrow'd Money of my Landlords and their Drawers; burrough'd in privileg'd Places among the Flatcaps of the Town, . . . abused my Benefactors in the Administration of public Affairs, of religious Dispensations, of Justice, and of the Stage; hackney'd for Booksellers and News-Papers; lampoon'd the Virtuous, wrote the Adventures of *Footmen,* and the Lives of *Thief-Catchers;* crampt the Stage, debased the Press, and *brought it into Jeopardy;* bilk'd every Lodging for Ten Years together, and every Alehouse and Chandler's Shop in every Neighbourhood; Defrauded and revil'd all my Acquaintance, and being quite out of Cash, Credit and

Character, as well as out of Charity with all Mankind, haunted by Duns and Bumbailiffs, hollow'd, hooted at and chased from every Side and by every Voice, I escap'd with whole Bones indeed, but d—bly mangled into these Purlieus of Safety, where no venemous Creatures dare enter.''*

Summarizing the attacks upon him, Fielding declared that the writers on the anti-ministerial press, as soon as they got hold of his name, "attempted to blacken it with every kind of reproach; pursued me into private life, *even to my boyish years;* where they have given me almost every vice in human nature." "Again," to quote further, "they have followed me, with uncommon inveteracy, into a profession, in which they have very roundly asserted, that I have neither business nor knowledge: and lastly, as an author, they have affected to treat me with more contempt, than Mr. Pope, who had great merit and no less pride in the character of a writer, hath thought proper to bestow on the lowest scribbler of his time. All this, moreover, they have poured forth in a vein of scurrility, which hath disgraced the press with every abusive term in our language." It was impossible, he said, for any man to defend himself against slander so determined and malicious. He could nevertheless console himself with the reflection that those who knew him would not take their opinion from those who knew him not. And then for the amusement of his readers, he illustrated by the death of Socrates how the scandalmonger, having a few facts, may pervert them to his purposes. Fielding called it "the Art of mixing up Truth and Falsehood." Socrates, it is well known, might have escaped from prison had he so desired; but he chose to die in the midst of his disciples after those wonderful conversa-

* "Old England," March 5, 1748. For other attacks, see "Old England," April 23, 30, June 25, and Nov. 12, 1748; and "The London Evening Post," March 12-15, 15-17, 29-31, April 7-9, July 28-30, Sept. 13-15, 17-20, Oct. 8-11, Nov. 5-8, 1748, and many other issues of these newspapers.

tions on the immortality of the soul. When his wife Xan-
thippe visited him on the morning of the last day, he was
disturbed by her loud lamentations and requested a friend
to remove "the troublesome woman." These are the facts
according to Plato; but had there been an "Athenian
Evening Post," the editor would have inserted the following paragraph on the occasion:

"WE HEAR the famous Atheist *Socrates,* who was lately
condemned for Impiety to the Gods, refused to go out of
Prison, tho' the Doors were set open, and defied the Government to execute him; a fresh Instance of his Obstinacy.
He persisted likewise in uttering the most horrid and
shocking Blasphemies to the last; and when his Wife, who,
WE HEAR, is a Woman of remarkable Sweetness of Temper,
and whom he hath very cruelly used on many Occasions,
went to take her Leave of him, he abused her in the grossest
Language, called her by several opprobrious Names, and
at length prevailed on one of his Gang, who were there to
visit him, to kick the poor Woman down Stairs; so that
she now lies ill of the Bruises she received."*

Inasmuch as "men of the best and most solemn characters" had no certain redress at law for libels against
them, Fielding decided to erect a "Court of Criticism,"
with himself as judge and lawmaker, for "the well-ordering
and inspecting all matters any wise concerning the Republic
of Literature, and for the correction and punishment of all
abuses committed therein" by the horde of "loose, idle,
and disorderly persons, calling themselves authors." It
would not be, he promised, merely "a Court of Damna-
tion," for he intended to recommend every book or writing
in which he could discover the least merit. The public was
strictly charged not to purchase any new book or to attend
any new play at the theatres until it had received the approbation of the court. Bills of complaint might be presented

* "The Jacobite's Journal," June 11, 1748.

in person or by letter; and in answer to them authors might appear with witnesses and counsel if they wished. Whichever way it happened, a fearless judge would render an impartial decision. All proceedings of the court, which would sit weekly, were to be reported by the clerk in "The Jacobite's Journal" and nowhere else. The account of these transactions, begun in the seventh number, was continued down through the thirty-third, with four omissions in weeks when there came from the press no book worth the slightest consideration.

Before his court Fielding summoned the worst literary offenders to meet their fate. "The Fool" and the editor of "The London Evening Post" were easily convicted of scurrility. The author of "The Letters to the Whigs" was adjudged guilty of calumny; and a sentence of infamy was accordingly pronounced against him. "Porcupine Pelagius," none other in the court's opinion than "Argus Centoculi" under another name, was denounced in a scathing address to the culprit for libelling the law, the church, and the editor of "The Jacobite's Journal" in "Old England" and various satirical poems such as "The Causidicade" and "The 'Piscopade"; but in view of the scribbler's wretched condition, the court thought it sufficient to commit "Porcupine Pillage" to "the Bridewell of Billingsgate" for a month and to stand for a full day in the pillory of "The Jacobite's Journal" with two opprobrious Latin verses pasted over his head. Ever since 1743, a literary hack connected with the newspapers had been collecting stray poems and publishing them under the title of "The Foundling Hospital for Wit"; hence Fielding's "Hospital for Scoundrels." This writer, known as "Samuel Silence," pleaded so pathetically his poverty in excuse for the crime of attempting to impose bastard wit upon the public for true and legitimate humour, that the judge not only dismissed him but gave him a half-crown to purchase bread.

Much fun was derived from Thomas Carte's "General History of England," the first volume of which made its appearance in December, 1747. This work, based upon considerable research, would have met with a favourable reception but for an unfortunate note asserting that one Christopher Lovel of Bristol, while at Avignon in 1716, was cured of "a scrofulous humour" on his neck by the touch of the Old Pretender, though the head of the House of Stuart at that time had been neither crowned nor anointed. By the Jacobites the miracle was regarded as absolute proof of the Chevalier's pure blood, of his descent from a race of kings that for a long succession of ages had touched for the king's evil. Immediately the wits fell upon Carte and the newspapers professing to believe the idle tale which he told; and the Common Council of London, who had been aiding Carte in his work, withdrew their subvention of fifty pounds a year. Carte was duly seized and brought before the Court of Criticism, on an indictment for stealing his silly story from an old woman with the intention of deceiving weak and credulous people. Though the prisoner pleaded not guilty, the charge was clearly proved against him, and he was judged to be and to remain perpetually under the contempt of the court. The next week Mr. Carte's counsel explained to the court that the note on Lovel got into the history through the carelessness of a scribe while the author was asleep; whereupon the judge, taking into consideration the infirmities of the historian, ordered his clerk to erase the word "contempt" and to write in its place the word "compassion," so that the sentence of condemnation would read that the said Carte was merely an object of compassion.* Continuing a jest that pleased the town, Fielding published an ironic protest, signed "True Blue," from the Jacobites of Manchester against his endeavours to discredit the miraculous cure of

* "The Jacobite's Journal," Feb. 20 and 27, 1748.

Lovel, accompanied by a blank-verse poem in mock praise of the "Immortal Carte"; and when the ass and his retinue were removed from the front of "The Jacobite's Journal," the emblem was given to Mr. Carte that it might be prefixed to the next volume of his great work.

In this foolery occurred an interesting episode. Of the many pamphlets in circulation for and against Carte one was sent forth by Cooper in January, 1748, entitled "A Letter to John Trot-Plaid, Esq; Author of the Jacobite Journal. Concerning Mr. Carte's General History of England." The anonymous author, claiming to belong to the Scots branch of the historian's family, styled himself "Duncan MacCarte, a Highlander," and dedicated his six-pence worth of wit to the patrons of his distinguished kinsman. Though slight in texture, the pamphlet is a well-sustained piece of irony, in appearance lauding Carte's history for its clear and vigorous style, full and accurate facts, jocose and smart thrusts at the new kings, their ministries, and their measures, but in fact utterly condemning the book as the work of a blunderer whose head is but a confused jumble of ideas. On reading the effusion, Mr. Trottplaid found that it contained wit and humour, and so recommended it to his brother Jacobites throughout the kingdom.* The man who perpetrated on the public a joke in which Mr. Trottplaid and Mr. MacCarte regaled each other with mutual flatteries was Samuel Squire, afterwards Bishop of St. David's. At the time he addressed Fielding as "Dear Trott," he was Archdeacon of Bath and Chaplain to the Duke of Newcastle.

Once Judge Trottplaid gave way to justifiable anger. For a year or more Samuel Foote, the actor and manager of Covent Garden Theatre, had been diverting the town with satirical performances mixed with mimicry. Few of them were ever published, but their general character is

* "The Jacobite's Journal," Jan. 30, 1748.

known from the accounts of people who saw them. At first
Foote confined his talent mostly to the rival players at
Drury Lane, whom he introduced, says Tate Wilkinson,
in a long procession, mimicking the voice, features, and
gestures of each as he went along. He was particularly
severe on Garrick, who sometimes hesitated in "dy-dy-
dying" speeches; and on Quin, whose sonorous voice and
heavy manner suggested a watchman crying: "Past twelve
o'clock and a cloudy morning." Macklin was hit off in
"Othello's occupation 's gone"; and Peg Woffington, who,
though most beautiful, had a squeaking voice, was shown
as an orange woman at the theatre, screaming to ladies
and gentlemen to purchase her oranges, nonpareils, and the
book of the play. During the last season, Foote had extended his mimicry to politicians, members of the bench
and bar, and various odd characters in the theatrical district such as Mr. Cock the auctioneer. The Government
attempted to enforce the Licensing Act against him, but
the adroit actor evaded the law by converting his performance into a loose entertainment that could not be considered as a play. He called it "a dish of chocolate" or "a
dish of tea" to which the public were invited if they wished
to come. When in danger of an indictment for libel, he
displayed his defiance of the persons he had ridiculed by
impersonating Sir Thomas de Veil, the late Bow Street
justice.

Coming to the rescue, Mr. Trottplaid scored hard this
mimicry of his helpless friends as "indecent, immoral, and
even illegal." Foote thereupon retaliated by exhibiting
Fielding himself in his bill of April 18, 1748, and perhaps
at other times. As appears from "Old England" of June
25, Foote's Fielding came on the stage shabbily dressed in
complete black, except for "two or three chasms in his
galigaskins, and the flap of his shirt hanging out." He
seems to have had in his mouth a quid of tobacco which he

ostentatiously removed before beginning a facetious address to the audience on his life and character. What the law had failed to do was now accomplished by the Court of Criticism. "Samuel Fut, of the Parish of St. Giles's, Labourer," who got his bread by his "hatchet-face" instead of his hands, was indicted for hacking and hewing gentlemen "in a certain part called the character." Though the culprit at first took his arraignment lightly, even mimicking the judge, his conviction was swift. Then the Court, venting wrath, scorn, and contempt, pronounced an ignominious sentence upon the defacer of God's images; and that the buffoon might not escape punishment, proceeded to inflict it himself before the prisoner was removed from the bar with a countenance as disfigured as was Parson Adams's in that contest with the hostess of a village inn.*

The Court of Criticism is memorable for Fielding's extension of the olive branch to Richardson, his enemy and traducer. The first part of "Clarissa Harlowe" then appearing, the Court set its approval upon two letters of imaginary correspondents who had vigorously defended the novel against the sneers of hostile critics.† Thanks were also given to Mr. Thomson for his "Castle of Indolence," excellent throughout and containing "an extremely delicate" and "just" compliment to Lyttelton. Praise was likewise bestowed upon his friend Edward Moore's "Trial of Selim the Persian," a creditable allegorical poem, inspired by a gentleman of "unblemish'd and unstain'd character"; and upon the same author's comedy entitled "The Foundling," from which Fielding later took the sub-title of "Tom Jones." The play was interrupted the first night because the audience saw in Faddle the

* "The Jacobite's Journal," April 30, 1748.

† "The Jacobite's Journal," Jan. 2, 1748. See also the number for March 5, 1748.

rascal an allusion to some well-known person. The court, after a rigid examination of its plot and characters, decided that it was on the whole a good comedy, and ordered the management of Drury Lane to proceed with its performance. In this pleasant and facetious way Fielding commended books, plays, authors, and actors, whenever he saw merit in them. There was, however, one glaring exception. No word of approval greeted the publication of "Roderick Random," which Fielding read; which, then in a second edition, was advertised almost continuously in Fielding's newspaper. Unfortunately Smollett was a Scotsman, and that meant a probable Jacobite.

On the approach of the harvest season, Fielding gave notice that the Court of Criticism would suspend its sittings until the Grub Street writers had finished their work in the fields. In the same issue (July 23, 1748), the news of the day was given for the first time with slight editorial comment. The inference is that Fielding then entrusted the management of his journal to another and went down to the summer Assizes in the West. If this be so, it was the last time that he prepared briefs for his Somerset clients. On his return to London four or five weeks later, his interest in "The Jacobite's Journal" had greatly waned: the Court of Criticism never sat again; the news was left unadorned with wit. His most notable leaders thereafter were on the Peace of Aix-la-Chapelle, which put an end to a long and fruitless war. As the Jacobite hope of aid from France was now forever lost, Fielding could see no reason for the existence of his newspaper. In his opinion, he had done his best to stay the progress of Jacobitism during a crisis in the nation's history, though he had never been deluded by a hope of eradicating political principles founded upon heredity and folly. There is, he said, no receipt to cure fools. He would, however, admonish the Jacobites to become good and faithful subjects of *"the Powers that be,"* since "*these Powers* will most certainly *continue to be,* in defiance of all which the Courts of *Rome* or Hell can devise against them." With these parting words, on November 5, 1748, "The Jacobite's Journal" made its exit—an event that Fielding celebrated by advertising the fourth edition of "Joseph Andrews."

Of its forty-nine leaders, nearly if not quite all were from the editor's pen, whether they were cast in the form of an essay or a series of letters. About the essays there can be no doubt whatever. If any of the letters came from genuine correspondents, they were so made over that they became Fielding's in their humorous phrasing. To this assertion only one exception is probable. The letter of Honoria Hunter—number 30,—whose Jacobite father would prevent her from marrying Philander because his great-grandfather was a Whig, may have been written by Sarah Fielding. Several leaders consisted mainly of quotations from some current pamphlet; and while the editor was away in the summer, an article from Addison's "Freeholder" was slipped in to fill up the number. But in all these cases, the introductory or closing remarks were Fielding's. In short, "The Jacobite's Journal," like "The True Patriot," appears to have been a single-handed performance, except for the assistance which the editor received from an occasional correspondent and from a hack employed to collect and arrange the news. The hack was probably Parson Young, who had just revised for Millar "The History of the Wars of Alexander the Great"—a translation formerly made by John Digby from the Latin of Quintus Curtius.* As soon as it began to show signs of decline, Fielding had to endure much coarse wit from the other newspapers. "Selim Slim," said "The London Evening Post," remonstrated with him for his dulness and threatened to take away his pension; but all in vain. Mr.

* "The Jacobite's Journal," Dec. 26, 1747.

Trottplaid, mortally affected in the head, grew weaker and weaker in every number until death released him from suffering. The epitaph was supplied by "Old England" on November 26. It began—

> Beneath this stone,
>   Lies Trotplaid John,
> His length of chin and nose;
>   His crazy brain,
>   Unhum'rous vein
> In verse and eke in prose.

It is not certain, however, that Fielding the political writer was yet quite dead; possibly he extended the merry warfare over into the winter. At this time John Perceval, the second Earl of Egmont in the Irish peerage, came to the front as the leader of the Opposition in the House of Commons. He is "the Right Honourable Lord Percival," who subscribed for Fielding's "Miscellanies." Perceval, representing Westminster, had entered Parliament in 1742 as a Patriot, but in course of time he turned against his party and lost his seat at the next election. He was helped to another seat by Pelham, and in like manner he turned against the Pelham Ministry also, and began to intrigue with the English Jacobites. By his friends he was admired as an independent; by those whom he had betrayed he was denounced as twice a deserter. No one, however, could soberly deny his conspicuous ability. In vindication of his career, Perceval published, late in December, 1748, a severe attack upon the Ministry, under the title of "An Examination of the Principles, and an Enquiry into the Conduct, of the Two B*****rs." The two brothers were Henry Pelham and the Duke of Newcastle, who, Perceval declared, had "improved every weakness, and all the wickedness of this age, to the establishment of their own absolute and unconstitutional power." To these false and treacherous men he refused to surrender his understanding and the welfare of his country.

Perceval's assault upon the Government drew the fire of its friends, among whom was the author of "A Genuine Copy of the Tryal of J - - - - - P - - - - - - l, Esq; &c. Commonly call'd E - - - - - of E - - - - - - - - - . . . . Try'd on Wednesday the 22d of February, at the Old-Bailey. For several High Crimes and Misdemeanours. . . . Taken in Short-hand by a Barrister at Law, and Revis'd and Publish'd by Order of the Judges." The pamphleteer arraigned "J—— P——l of the parish of St. Martin's in the fields, in the county of Middlesex, Esq.," on an indictment charging him with deserting, at the instigation of the devil, "the cause and colours" under which he had enlisted, with betraying "the secrets of private and friendly conversation," and with lying about his former friends in a scandalous and malicious pamphlet calculated to "promote sedition, confusion, and contempt of all government" and to serve "the base, low, and interested views, of a cheat and imposture." The case was argued before the Lord Chief Justice Truth by Serjeants Clear-Doubt, Puzzle, and Clenchit; and despite the fog which the counsel for the defence created and threw over it, an impartial jury decided that the prisoner was "a deserter, not only from his late masters, but from all the masters he ever served." Thereupon the court sentenced him to make a journey on an ass through the principal streets of Westminster, preceded by marrow-bones and cleavers to herald his approach.

"The Tryal" was a vigorous piece of rough and gross ridicule from a writer who was more than a match for Perceval. Who was he? Suspicion at once fell upon Fielding. "A despicable ministerial pamphlet," said Argus of the hundred Eyes, "has lately made its appearance in town, . . . in which, or I have lost my cunning, I discover the cloven foot of my old friend Justice Trotplaid, under the

direction of the excellent Selim Slim.''* Against the as-
cription of this pamphlet to Fielding are certain minor
technicalities of style; and it is hard to account for the name
of "R. Freeman" on the title-page as publisher. Other
considerations of equal weight, however, point to Fielding.
The burlesque of the contending serjeants is in line with
what we have in "Joseph Andrews"; and the method of
dealing with Perceval is a continuation of the mock trials
conducted by Mr. Trottplaid in "The Jacobite's Journal,"
down to the use of similar phrases. These resemblances
cannot be accidental. Either Fielding or a clever imitator
shot this bolt at a spurious Patriot and disguised Jacobite.

III

The time had now come for a recognition of Fielding's
services to his Majesty's Government, which—men and
measures—he had ably championed for three years against
bitter and unscrupulous enemies. Besides the Pelhams and
Lyttelton, he possessed another staunch friend in the Administration—the rich and powerful Duke of Bedford, the
First Lord of the Admiralty and Privy Councillor since
1745. Upon the Duke, as chief of the Admiralty Office, fell
the brunt of criticism for the conduct of the war on the
sea. Again and again Fielding came to the rescue of "a
noble Duke of the highest rank, the most extensive property, and the most unblemished honour, and whose labours
have . . . been indefatigable for the service of his country,
and crowned with most eminent success.''† It was a just
tribute to the man during whose administration a success-
less war on land had been partially redeemed by victories
at sea. In February, 1748, the Duke of Bedford resigned
from the Admiralty, and entered the Cabinet as Secretary
for the Southern Department, "to the great joy," remarked
Fielding, "of all who wish well to the true interest of

* "Old England," March 25, 1749.
† "The Jacobite's Journal," Jan. 30, 1748.

their country."* Fielding, it is apparent, once had the ambition to end his career on the King's Bench like his kinsmen among the Goulds; but his hopes must have dwindled in the face of broken health and the difficult enterprise of making a living. He had no good reason to expect more than he now received. On the recommendation of Lyttelton, the Duke of Bedford obtained for him a place in the Commission of Peace for Westminster, to fill one of the two vacancies which occurred that year. The fiat authorizing the appointment bears the date of July 30, and his commission that of October 25, 1748. The next day he took the usual oaths, and six weeks later he was presiding over the justice court in Bow Street, Covent Garden. The town, passing by his immediate predecessor, regarded him as heir to the mantle of Sir Thomas de Veil, long the terror of the theatrical district. Colonel de Veil, as he was called, had died two years before. That a playwright whose farces were running at the theatres should be installed in Veil's place as a Justice of the Peace, had for the wits a humorous aspect. Men and women of the kind represented in some of his plays, Fielding the magistrate was now sending to jail.

It was quite common for a Bow Street justice to have his jurisdiction extended over the entire county of Middlesex; otherwise many criminals, by passing into the city of London, could escape him. Fielding at once saw the necessity of this extension; but he was unable to qualify, on the score of property, for a county magistrate, who must possess real estate to the value of £100 a year. In this difficulty he wrote the following letter to the Duke of Bedford, who owned most of Bloomsbury and Covent Garden:

"Bow Street. Decr. 13. 1748.

"My Lord,
    Such is my Dependence on the Goodness of your Grace, that before my Gout will permit me to pay my Duty to you

---

* "The Jacobite's Journal," Feb. 20, 1748.

personally, and to acknowledge your last kind Favour to me, I have the Presumption to solicit your Grace again. The Business of a Justice of Peace for Westminster is very inconsiderable without the Addition of that for the County of Middlesex. And without this Addition I cannot completely serve the Government in that office. But this unfortunately requires a Qualification which I want. Now there is a House belonging to your Grace, which stands in Bedford St., of 70l. a year value. This hath been long untenanted, and will I am informed, require about 300l. to put in Repair. If your Grace would have the Goodness to let me have a Lease of this House, with some other Tenement worth 30l. a year, for 21 years, it would be a complete Qualification. I will give the full Worth for this lease, according to the valuation which any Person your Grace shall be pleased to appoint sets upon it. The only favour I beg of your Grace is, that I be permitted to pay the Money in two years, at four equal half-yearly Payments. As I shall repair the House as soon as possible, it will be in Reality an Improvement of that small Part of your Grace's estate, and will be certain to make my Fortune.

"Mr. Butcher* will acquaint your Grace more fully than perhaps I have been able to do; and if Your Grace thinks proper to refer it to him, I and mine will be eternally bound to pray for your Grace tho I sincerely hope you will not lose a Farthing by doing so vast a service to,

My Lord your Grace's

Most obliged most obed^t humble servant

H. FFIELDING."†

The Duke of Bedford was more generous than Fielding anticipated. Instead of troubling him with a house that

---

* Mr. Butcher was the Duke's agent.

† First published in "Correspondence of John Fourth Duke of Bedford," 1842, I, 589-590. Printed from the autograph at Woburn Abbey by Miss Godden in "Henry Fielding," p. 196.

would have required an expenditure of £300 for repairs, he gave him a lease for twenty-one years of various small properties having a clear rental value of £100 per annum, and described as "several leasehold messuages or tenements lying or being in the several parishes of St Paul Covent Garden, St Martin in the Ffields, St Giles in the Ffields, and St George Bloomsbury, co: Middlesex, now in the occupation of his tenants." Pursuant to this ingenious arrangement, Fielding qualified, on January 11, 1749, as a Justice of the Peace for the County of Middlesex, and immediately took the oaths of the office "at the General Quarter Sessions of the Peace at Hicks Hall, St. John Street."* Subsequently he met the current religious tests necessary to a servant in his Majesty's Government. On Sunday, March 26, he received the Sacrament of the Lord's Supper at St. Paul's, Covent Garden, according to the usages of the Church of England; and on April 5, after again receiving the Holy Communion, he put his signature to declarations against the doctrine of transubstantiation, and the power of the Holy See, abjured King James and his descendants, and promised allegiance and faithful service to King George. These oaths and declarations were properly attested by Charles Tough, the minister of his parish and by other credible witnesses. Thereupon Fielding, supported by the Duke of Bedford, entered upon the vast labour of ridding Middlesex of thieves, highwaymen, and robbers in order that life and property might be safe. That is a remarkable story never yet half told; but it must be held in abeyance, for "Tom Jones" had just appeared.

* Record Office. Middlesex Guildhall. "Oaths taken by Justices of the Peace, 1746-50," p. 187. Owing to some inaccuracy in the first declaration or to some alteration in the leases, Fielding took a similar oath, leaving out the Bloomsbury leases, on July 13, 1749 (*ibid.*, p. 191). The details connected with Fielding's appointment were first discovered and assembled by Miss Godden in her "Henry Fielding," pp. 173, 175, 194-198.

CHAPTER XVII

THE PUBLICATION OF TOM JONES

It has been often lamented that Fielding, when he discovered his talent in "Joseph Andrews," did not proceed
forthwith to write a novel free from all dependency upon
Richardson, in fulfilment of the vision he then had of a
great comic epic in prose, which should be for modern
England what the comic counterpart of the Iliad had been
for ancient Greece. Such, it is clear from the dedication of "Tom Jones" to Lyttelton, was the desire of his
friend and patron, who believed him possessed of the extraordinary endowments requisite for the undertaking.
Though Fielding regarded Lyttelton's desire as hardly less
than a command, neither time nor circumstance then seemed
favourable. The fact is, Fielding's mind soon became
engrossed with the law; and so fierce and scurrilous were
the attacks upon him by Grub Street for what he had
written and for what he had not written, that he resolved
to publish nothing more for the amusement of the public.
His "Miscellanies," as I have related, was to be his last
book in general literature. The next year, in the summer
of 1744, he did indeed write a preface to "David Simple"
to please and aid his sister; but it was made the occasion
for a solemn declaration that he had given up the struggle
for literary fame, upon which he had come to look with
contempt.

Unexpectedly, however, the insurrection of 1745 drew
him into patriotic journalism, where his ability to deal
with exactly contemporary life and affairs shone with very

99

great brilliancy. The time had arrived for "Tom Jones"
if that "newspaper of many volumes," as he called it, were
ever to be written. Fielding's circumstances were then
made easier by the steady income week by week from the
sale of his journals, of one of which the Government apparently took, as was then said, two thousand copies; and he
may have received gifts of money from Lyttelton towards
the support of himself and family. Without Lyttelton's
assistance, he declared in the preface to "Tom Jones," the
novel "had never been completed." It was to this friend,
he added in explanation, that he really owed his existence
"during great part of the time" he was engaged upon
its composition, covering "some years" of his life. Along
with Lyttelton Fielding alluded to Ralph Allen, who
together were in Fielding's estimation "two of the best and
worthiest men in the world," who were "strongly and
zealously my friends." Their generosity, he means to
say, gave him the time—it can hardly be called leisure—to
write "Tom Jones," the labour, in his own phrase, of
"some thousands of hours."

The thousands of hours that Fielding, already becoming
infirm with the gout, was able to devote to "Tom Jones"
were clearly distributed over the three years, 1746-1748.
Of these years, the period when he was least interrupted by
hack-work fell between the discontinuance of "The True
Patriot" in June, 1746, and the establishment of "The
Jacobite's Journal" in December, 1747. The novel, I take
it, was begun as early as the summer of 1746, and continued at a steady though not uniform rate through 1747
and 1748, despite the extra labours of "The Jacobite's
Journal," down to a few months before its publication in
February, 1749. Though not an historical novel, "Tom
Jones" has, in harmony with the ancient epics, a slight
historical background in the insurrection just preceding
its composition. To be precise, its main action—the jour-

George, Lord Lyttelton

From a mezzotint by G.H. Every after a painting by Sir Joshua Reynolds at Hagley

ney of Jones up to London and his experiences in town—
covers five weeks in November and December, 1745, while
companies of foot are on the way north to reinforce the
Duke of Cumberland, and the young Chevalier is threatening to march on the capital. Squire Western is one of those
English Jacobites whom Fielding scored in his newspapers;
his sister is a Hanoverian—"a Hanoverian rat," her
brother calls her—whose political principles are derived
from the numerous Whig pamphlets in circulation; and
Sophia, because of her great beauty, is suspected, when on
her travels, of being Jenny Cameron, one of the Chevalier's
"ladies" trying to escape capture. Again, like Fielding
himself, Tom Jones is "a hearty well-wisher to the glorious
cause of liberty, and of the Protestant religion"; while
Partridge, his companion on the road, is a secret and deluded Jacobite who has been assured by a Roman priest
that "Prince Charles is as good a Protestant as any in
England." Though Partridge is ready, out of friendship
to Jones, to risk his life with him on the battlefield in defence of the House of Hanover, he cannot be persuaded to
join in a health to King George; the barber will fight against
his own cause but not drink against it. Thus, while Fielding was writing "Tom Jones," all the events of 1745 as
related in "The True Patriot" were fresh in his memory.

Many, too, are the correspondences in thought and sentiment between "Tom Jones" and "The Jacobite's Journal," which indicate nearly if not quite simultaneous composition. Into the novel Fielding carries over his gibes
at the newspapers and the reptile critics, his denunciation
of the slander and scurrility aimed at him; and alludes to
the political questions which divided parties in 1747-1748.
The character of Blifil, for instance, illustrates all that he
was saying in "The Jacobite's Journal" on the art of
prevarication whereby truth is twisted into falsehood by
clever suppressions and the adroit turn of phrases. It is

the art, said Fielding, of conveying "a lie in the words of truth." In several issues of his newspaper, the editor advocated a plan for providing for the widows and children of the clergy, based upon an essay by Humphrey Prideaux, the Dean of Norwich. It was a subject that greatly interested Fielding at that time; and in the characters of Mrs. Miller, Mrs. Honour, and Mrs. Partridge, he would represent, going so far as to add a footnote, the distress or disaster that overtakes the wives and orphans of the poor clergy who are unable to make a decent provision for their families. Of these three women, one is reduced to letting rooms to lodgers and would have starved but for the assistance of Allworthy; another becomes a waiting-maid in a squire's household; and the third marries a poor schoolmaster and dies in poverty. Finally, there is Squire Western, who surely has a cousin in the Humphry Gubbins that sent Jacobite letters to Mr. Trottplaid cast in the Somerset dialect. The portraits of Western and Partridge were resented by the Jacobites, who regarded "Tom Jones" as a political document in line with "The Jacobite's Journal." To them the novel was a challenge to renew the warfare. Having "humourized" disaffection out of the land, said "Old England" ironically, the "ingenious brain" of Mr. Fielding now proposes "to amuse and laugh us into virtue."

These considerations only fix within the limits of two or three years the composition of "Tom Jones" as a whole. It is hazardous to go a step further and attempt by the use of parallels and allusions, unsupported by external evidence, to define the month or the season when Fielding wrote each of the eighteen books into which the novel is divided. For example, in the fifth chapter of the thirteenth book he quotes in a footnote an advertisement of a pugilist dated February 1, 1747—a full year, as we shall see, before the chapter could have been written. To illustrate his text, the advertisement was taken from an old newspaper which Fielding had by him or from that commonplace book which, he informs the reader, it was his custom to keep. Hence, this note with specific date has no value for the purpose in hand. Similarly, in the first chapter of the seventh book Fielding quotes a passage from Boyse's "Deity," with the remark that it was published "about nine years ago." As the poem appeared towards the end of 1739, the inference may be drawn that Fielding composed the chapter late in 1748. Such may have been the case; but if so, then Fielding left this initial chapter until the narrative part of "Tom Jones" was nearly completed; it cannot be that he was writing the seventh book in the autumn of 1748 or in any part of that year.

The reference to Boyse raises the question whether the introductory chapters throughout the novel were not an afterthought. Though that is hardly probable, I surmise that several of them had to wait for the conclusion of the novel. Only a few of them have any organic connection with the story; for the most part they are mechanically adjusted to it by a sentence or two, or are completely independent essays on the art of fiction such as might go in one place as well as another. The initial chapters to books fifteen and sixteen, it will be observed further, are not only short but perfunctory as if the author, writing one essay after another in a series, had grown tired of a plan which he felt bound to carry out to the letter in order that no book might be without an introduction. To sum up without more illustrations, the endeavour to follow Fielding closely in the composition of "Tom Jones" leads into a perilous road for two reasons. He probably did not write more than half of his initial chapters as he went along with his story; and it was clearly his custom in revision, perhaps as the book was going through the press, to insert such references or allusions to persons and events as would give point to his narrative and comment. There is the well-known anecdote* that Fielding promised Mrs. Hussey, a charming and vivacious mantua-maker in the Strand, that he would introduce her into "Tom Jones"; but having forgotten the promise until the last moment, he then hastened to the printer and found a suitable place for her in the third chapter of the tenth book, where, to give the reader an idea of Sophia's affability, he compares her happy disposition with that of "the celebrated Mrs. Hussy," whom everybody in London knew.

Still, despite all difficulties, it is possible to point out two or three stages in the composition of "Tom Jones." Certain of the initial chapters contain references or quotations so interwoven with the text that they could not possibly have been late adornments; nor is it at all probable that these specific chapters were written after the novel was otherwise complete. To be well on the side of safety, I will consider only two of them. Nobody certainly can doubt that Fielding began the novel with the first chapter, wherein he promises to treat his readers in accordance with "the highest principles of the best cook which the present age, or perhaps that of Heliogabalus, hath produced." Just as this skilled master of the feast first sets plain things before his hungry guests and afterwards regales them, as their appetites gradually decrease, with highly seasoned dishes, hashed and ragoo'd in the French and Italian styles, until he reaches "the very quintessence of sauce and spices," so Fielding would represent human nature in all its phases from plain and substantial country people up to the life of the town, seasoned with all the follies and vices of France and Italy as well as of England. Now, this entire chapter is but an elaboration of a letter signed "Heliogabalus," which we have already quoted from "The

* J. T. Smith, "Nollekens and his Times," edited by W. Whitten, 1917, I, 104-106.

True Patriot'' under the date of December 3, 1745. There was nothing, it will be remembered, except what he could eat, that Heliogabalus liked better than Mr. Trottplaid, for the editor so dealt with the questions and news of the day as to please an epicure of the most exquisite palate. He began, said his admirer, with a sober essay, and ended as he ought, with humorous comment on current events, thereby giving ''a delicious flavour'' to what would otherwise be ''flat and insipid.'' In both the newspaper and the novel, Fielding was perhaps paying a compliment to ''a famous cook'' named Lebeck, whose house, a few doors from Mrs. Hussey's, was made conspicuous by a large portrait of himself hung out for a sign.* The letter of Heliogabalus, which of course Fielding himself wrote, is as conclusive evidence as one can get, in the absence of a diary, that ''Tom Jones'' was not in the making on December 3, 1745; it is also indicative that the day when Fielding sat down to his novel was not far off—no farther at most than the six months ahead when ''The True Patriot'' came to an end.

This conclusion receives support from references to Dr. John Freke in the fourth chapter of the second book and again in the ninth chapter of the fourth book. During the autumn of 1746, this London surgeon and dabbler in natural science was involved in a controversy with William Watson over the nature of electricity. In June Watson had published an account of some very interesting experiments much like Franklin's; and in October Freke set up a wild theory against him in ''An Essay to shew the Cause of Electricity; and why some Things are non-electricable.'' Fielding's references are to Freke's pamphlet. The first of them, taken by itself, might be regarded as an interpolation made during revision; but when considered with the second, the inference is inevitable that Fielding was writ-

* ''Nollekens and his Times,'' 1917, I, 105.

ing "Tom Jones" at the very time the discussion was at its height. In the second reference Fielding asks Mr. Freke, before publishing "the next edition of his book," to inquire into certain analogies between frictional electricity and the effects of the switch when applied to a shrew, first to inflame and then to quiet her. The next or second edition of Freke's essay appeared in November. Hence, unless we are to suppose Fielding unaware of this fact, he was midway in his fourth book by November, 1746. To be exact, he had then composed 279 pages.

Another stage in the progress of "Tom Jones," no less definite than this, is marked by the chapter placed at the head of the twelfth book. It is an essay concerning plagiarism, based upon a passage in the preface to the Abbé Banier's "Mythology and Fables of the Ancients," which Fielding half seriously interprets to imply that a writer may take whatever he pleases from Latin and Greek authors without appending place or name, provided he preserve strict honesty towards his poor brethren still living. The translation of the French savant's compendium from which Fielding quotes, though it had first appeared several years before, was advertised by Andrew Millar as "this day published" in "The Jacobite's Journal" for January 9, 1748.* This was a new edition. Three weeks later, on January 30, the Court of Criticism recommended the work to the public "as the most useful, instructive, and entertaining book extant"; and on February 20, Mr. Trottplaid ran up a parallel between Banier's disquisition on the origin of fables and the origin of Jacobite

---

*Fielding appears to have written the advertisement. I surmise that William Young made the translation under Fielding's supervision. The book in question is "La Mythologie et les Fables expliquées par L'Histoire," 3 tom., Paris, 1738-1740. The English translation, brought out by Millar, appeared in instalments, 1739-1741. It is advertised as complete in four octavo volumes in "The London Magazine," Feb., 1741, X, 104. This work Millar reissued in 1748.

doctrines. Inasmuch as Fielding never again quoted from Banier, it is a safe assumption that his praise of the work here in "Tom Jones" for its "great erudition" and "equal judgment" was nearly contemporary with the similar encomiums passed upon it in "The Jacobite's Journal" of January 30, 1748. This means that by February Fielding had written eleven of the eighteen books of "Tom Jones," or 1,097 of the 1,818 pages (not counting the dedication and title-pages) comprised in the novel. There yet remained for the year 1748 about seven hundred pages.

The speed with which Fielding composed these later books might be deduced by a Sherlock Holmes from an incident in the plot. As related in the eleventh chapter of the thirteenth book, Sophia went with a companion to the theatre to see a new play; but they both fled before the end of the first Act, terrified by a violent conflict between those who came to applaud and those who came to damn the performance. A struggle of this noisy character between two parties—the one for and the other against an author—was no very uncommon occurrence. Several of Fielding's own plays had gone down to a like disaster in the uproar of the audience. It so happens, however, that exactly what Sophia saw on that memorable night appears to have occurred at Drury Lane several times in February and March of 1748 during the performance of "The Foundling," that comedy by Fielding's friend Edward Moore. Whether to withdraw the play or to go on with it was the question at intervals for a month. While the town divided on its merits, Fielding (as has been related in the previous chapter) came forward with a just appreciation of its art in his Court of Criticism for March 19, 1748; and when his own novel was ready for the press he honoured Moore by appropriating the title of the play. The novel was to be called "The History of a Foundling." Its longer title was an afterthought. So great was Fielding's interest in the threatened failure of his friend's comedy that he may indeed have had it in mind when he sent Sophia to the theatre and then home again in fright. Between the quotation from Banier and the first mention of the disturbance at the theatre, there intervene 210 pages. Supposing the play to have been Moore's, the time between the composition of the two passages was roughly six weeks. That is, Fielding was then writing at the rate of nearly 150 pages a month, in addition to his work on "The Jacobite's Journal." If he continued at this rapid pace, he should have had the end in sight by the summer of 1748.

This is precisely what happened, as may be seen from the following document:

"June 11 1748

Rec^d of Mr. Andrew Millar Six hundred Pounds being in full for the sole Copy Right of a Book called the History of a Foundling in Eighteen Books. And in Consideration of the said Six Hundred Pounds I promise to asign over the said Book to the said Andrew Millar his Executors and assigns for ever when I shall be thereto demanded.

£   s   d.
£600,   00,   00.   HEN: FFIELDING

The said Work to contain Six Volumes in Duodecimo."*

When Fielding signed this receipt, "Tom Jones" could not have been completed. At least Fielding was engaged, we must suppose, through the summer and early autumn in readjustments, revisions, and the composition of several of those introductory chapters, which he said cost him more labour than all other parts of the novel. The dedication was written in October or early in November.

As in the case of Homer, many places have claimed the honour of giving birth to "Tom Jones." The only clue that the author cared to put into the hand of the reader

* Taken from the autograph in the library of J. P. Morgan, Esq. It is a scrap of foolscap, 3¼ inches in length by 7¾ inches in width.

may be found in the first chapter of the thirteenth book. When Fielding there had a vision of his future fame, of the time when "I shall be read, with honour, by those who never knew nor saw me, and whom I shall neither know nor see," he was writing in a "little parlour" as meanly furnished as the narrow box that would soon contain him. About the room were "his prattling babes," whose innocent play and laughter had been often hushed that he might be quiet in his labours. It was Harriot playing with William. In that parlour, wherever it may have been, were written long stretches of "Tom Jones." It was not in the house at East Stour, for the Fielding farm had long been in possession of another. There is an old story that Fielding composed parts of the novel on the tennis court at Sharpham during the intervals of the game. Just as the younger Pliny found hunting and Addison found wine conducive to composition, so Fielding, it used to be said, received the greatest assistance from tennis.* The tale is too absurd for comment. Nor is it probable that Fielding was then spending his summers in the house at the foot of Milford Hill near Salisbury, now that his wife Charlotte had long since been dead. Nor had he yet taken Fordhook House at Ealing on the Uxbridge Road beyond Hammersmith, nor the house at Barnes across the Thames in Surrey, where it is said he dwelt later. All these places must be eliminated from serious consideration; for during more than half the time Fielding was at work on "Tom Jones," parochial taxes were assessed against him as tenant of a house in Old Boswell Court, covering the entire year 1746 and three quarters of the year 1747.† In November, 1747, he gave up the house in Old Boswell Court and took one, as I have already related, for Mrs. Fielding out at Twickenham. In the face of these records, the old romantic

* Burke, "History of the Commoners," 1838, III, 570.
† Mr. J. Paul de Castro, "Notes and Queries," 12 S. I, 264 (April 1, 1916).

stories must collapse. While Fielding was engaged on "Tom Jones," he had just two places of residence—Old Boswell Court and Twickenham. Accordingly, houses which long ago disappeared were the real scene of his "vast labours."

To these cold facts may be adjusted, however, one or two stories. Tradition has been persistent that "Tom Jones" was partly written in a house at Twerton-on-Avon, a village a mile and a half below Bath and close enough to Prior Park for a visit there every day. To this effect we have a detailed account from a contemporary writer—the Rev. Richard Graves, still remembered as the author of an amusing romance against the Methodists called "The Spiritual Quixote." A native of Gloucestershire, Graves graduated at Pembroke College, Oxford, and for some years held a fellowship in All Souls. In 1748, he was appointed to the rectory of Claverton, a parish two or three miles to the west of Twerton. As he was not inducted into the living until the next year, and did not come into permanent residence until 1750, the chances of a personal acquaintance with Fielding are about even. But he was on intimate terms with Allen, who purchased in 1758 the manor of Claverton; and he mentioned among his friends several persons of distinction who came incidentally into the life of Fielding—Lord Camden, Warburton, Shenstone, and Lady Luxborough, for example. After acquiring Claverton, Allen used to dine every week at the manor-house. "I dined there," says Graves, "more than once with Mrs. Fielding, the author of 'David Simple.' . . . Mr. Allen very generously allowed her one hundred pounds a year." Gossipy and garrulous, Graves knew all about the local celebrities. For a half-century he walked the Bath hills—a welcome guest everywhere. In the anecdotes which he left about Allen, in a little posthumous volume entitled "The Triflers," he says that Fielding "dined

Drawn from M. Allens Plan.   Taste in Miller Sculp.

PRIOR PARK. the Seat of Ralph Allen Esq.r near Bath.

PRIOR PARK. la Résidence de Raoul Allen Escuyer près de Bath.

almost daily" at Prior Park, and lived, "while he was writing his novel of Tom Jones," at Twerton in "the first house on the right hand, with a spread eagle over the door."

It is difficult to find any reason for doubting the clergyman's word. The old stone house, easily identified, has been named, as I have said earlier, "Fielding's Lodge." As one enters through the quaint doorway, there is, curiously enough, a "little parlour" to the left with an ancient fireplace, unchanged since Fielding sat and wrote there. There may have been "a little parlour" also in the houses which Fielding occupied in Old Boswell Court and at Twickenham; so it must be left undetermined where he composed the most eloquent passage that ever came from his pen. On the supposition that he wrote the famous invocation with which the thirteenth book opens in immediate sequence to the twelfth book, he must have been then in town conducting "The Jacobite's Journal." But that initial chapter, standing by itself, might have been written earlier or later than the narrative surrounding it. All that can be said with certainty is that the "little parlour" at Twerton fits exactly into the situation as Fielding describes it. To sum up without pressing this detail beyond warrant, the positive assertion of Graves, combined with the chronology of Fielding's other literary activities, clearly indicates that the first books of "Tom Jones" and some of the later chapters were composed at Twerton. Nothing stands in the way of the assumption that Fielding, after he had given up "The True Patriot," spent the summer and autumn of 1746 at Twerton and that he returned for briefer periods the two following years. So London, Twickenham, and Bath must divide the honour of being the birthplace of "Tom Jones." Before the novel had passed through the press, Fielding had permanently settled in Bow Street as a justice of the peace. His house, of which the Duke of

Bedford gave him a lease, stood on the west side of the street, near the present public house known as "The Grapes."* In the dedication of "Tom Jones," he thanked the Duke for his "princely benefactions."

Another story takes us into the midlands for a scene some weeks before Fielding gave his manuscript to the publisher. Lyttelton's country seat was at Hagley in Worcestershire. The seat of the Earl of Denbigh was at Newnham Paddox near the eastern border of Warwickshire. To the south in the same shire lay the fine estate of Sanderson Miller on the Edge Hills overlooking the village of Radway. This country gentleman, now almost forgotten, was a conspicuous figure in the mid-eighteenth century, skilled in agriculture, Gothic architecture, and hospitality. A graduate of Oxford, he had acquired a love of old books, which he gathered about him in a large library. At this time he was only thirty-one years old, and had recently married "a sweet little woman," to repeat the phrase of one who knew her. His house, called Radway Grange, had been built from the stones of an old monastery which once stood on its site. On the summit, two miles from the house, he was then erecting a tower to mark the spot where King Charles fixed the royal standard before descending the hill to give battle to Lord Essex. The scenery, beautiful in itself, had been made more beautiful by hanging woods and ornamental trees of his own planting. The squire, described as good-humoured, convivial, and facetious, liked to have about him his friends among the Whig politicians and men of letters, whom he lavishly entertained. A short time before the publication of "Tom Jones," he had as his guests the elder Pitt, Lyttelton, Henry Fielding, and a kinsman of the novelist, whose name is given in the story as George Fielding. It is uncertain who this fourth mem-

* Mr. J. Paul de Castro, "The Modern Language Review," April, 1917, p. 233.

ber of the company was. Both the Earl of Denbigh and Edmund Fielding had had brothers named George, but they had been long since dead after honourable careers in the army. The only living George Fielding closely connected with the family was a half-brother of Henry, born of Edmund Fielding's second marriage. This young man may have been the person intended by the narrative; but it is more likely that some confusion has arisen in the account—that George Fielding has been brought into the story in place of William Fielding, the Earl of Denbigh. While on this visit to Radway Grange, "the great novelist," it is said, read the manuscript of "Tom Jones" to the "distinguished audience" seated about him in the dining-room, that he might have their comment before his final revision. It is a scene of surpassing interest, if it be true.

And no suspicion rests upon the tradition except in the matter of a few ornaments which are here mostly suppressed. The story was told long ago by George Harris in his Life of Lord Chancellor Hardwicke,* who was a frequent visitor at Radway and whose house at Wimpole was made over on designs furnished by Miller. It has recently been retold with more definite details in "Rambles round the Edge Hills and in the Vale of the Red Horse," by the Rev. George Miller, a descendant of the hospitable squire. Writing to Miss Godden in 1907, Mr. Miller repeated the story as given here and added: "My father told me this often and he had the account from his grandmother, who survived her husband several years and who was the hostess on the occasion."† Pitt, a most intimate friend of Sanderson Miller, was doubtless making one of his long visits at Radway. Fielding perhaps had been staying with Lyttelton at Hagley, and thus went over to Miller's with him, while the Earl of Denbigh was invited in to com-

* "Life of Lord Chancellor Hardwicke," 1847, II, 456-457.
† Miss Godden, "Henry Fielding," p. 179.

plete the company for a fortnight's entertainment. To commemorate the visit, Pitt, according to the story, planted three trees, and Miller placed near them a stone urn.

No record of the conversation on this memorable occasion has survived. But the Earl of Denbigh, according to tradition, was very fond of his cousin Henry, and liked to engage him in wit-combats. Perhaps it was at Radway Grange that he quizzed "Harry" on the proper spelling of the family name and provoked the retort quoted in the first pages of this biography. Sanderson Miller should have been pleased with the portrait of Mr. Allworthy, a country magistrate like himself, of large estate, having the same love for planting and architecture. Lyttelton, we have Fielding's word for it in the dedication of "Tom Jones," saw the novel in manuscript and passed a favourable judgment upon it, while suggesting alterations which the author adopted. From a most unexpected source the information now comes that the admiration of both Lyttelton and Pitt was so great that they everywhere recommended the forthcoming novel to their friends. Three months after the appearance of "Tom Jones," "Old England" published a most scurrilous attack on Lyttelton for permitting the novel to be dedicated to him. It is in the form of a long letter from "Aretine" to "Selim Slim," dated May 27, 1749. The passage from the disreputable newspaper which concerns us here, begins:

"Not only the Dedication, but common Fame is full of the warm Commendations you have given of the aforementioned *Romance*. You have run up and down the Town, and made Visits, and wrote Letters merely for that Purpose. You puffed it up so successfully about Court, and among Placemen and Pensioners, that, having catched it from you, they thought it incumbent upon them to echo it about the Coffee houses; insomuch, that all the Women laboured under the Burthen of Expectation, 'till it was midwived into the World by your all-auspicious Hand, and proclaimed by them to be the goodest Book that was ever read.

"While it was yet in Embrio, or rather, after it was licked up into *Wit* and *Humour,* and dished finely up in Lavender, your Zanies puffed and blew it up so into Fame, among his old Masters the Booksellers, that they begun to lament their Want of Discernment touching the Value of the *precious Jewel,* which, like the Cock in the Fable, they had despised and cast away on the very Dunghill they found it in. But, by the Care of yourself and Brother Deserter, *Two of the best and worthiest who are strongly and zealously his Friends,* (yclept the Poet and the Orator!) he has been so improved and polished, as to exhibit finer Lustres than ever blazed from the great Diamond, which founded the Family of one of his said Two *best and worthiest* Friends. Lo! the Effects of the Public Treasury and Pay-Office!"

Through the ill-nature and malice of these paragraphs is visible what happened. Only the concluding sentences need comment. By the "two best and worthiest friends," a phrase inaccurately quoted from the dedication to "Tom Jones," Fielding meant Lyttelton and Allen. But Aretine did not understand it quite that way. The second friend he derisively called "the Orator" in contrast with Lyttelton "the Poet," and identified him with the head of "the Pay-Office" in antithesis with the head of "the Public Treasury." "The Orator" was William Pitt, the Paymaster-General of the Forces. It was his grandfather Thomas Pitt, Governor of Madras, who once possessed "the great Diamond" to which Aretine refers. He purchased it in India for a small sum, and sold it to an agent of Louis the Fifteenth for £135,000, thereby laying the foundations of the family estate, and contributing to the crown jewels of France. By common report, then, Pitt as well as Lyttelton knew the merits of "Tom Jones" while the novel was yet in manuscript, bore a hand in its revision, and helped spread abroad its fame. All this tends to confirm the tradition that Pitt, Lyttelton, Fielding, and Tom Jones passed a merry time together at Sanderson Miller's seat on the Edge Hills.

A little gossip may be traced to the author's household. While Fielding was still at work on "Tom Jones," his sister Sarah began a book called "The Governess," on the education and behaviour of girls. Jane Collier, who was intimate with the Fieldings, if indeed she did not live with them, wrote to Richardson on October 4, 1748, that brother and sister were both strongly opposed to corporal punishment, to "all the party of the Thwackums' (as Mr. Fielding calls them)."* And among others who saw and approved "Tom Jones" before it reached the general public, was Lady Hertford, soon to become the Duchess of Somerset. This aspirant to literary patronage, who in bygone days had received the homage of Thomson and had rescued Savage from the gallows, lived some miles from London out on the Bath road—at Percy Lodge, which as the former residence of Lord Bathurst had many literary associations with Addison, Pope, Congreve, and Gay. There Lady Hertford amused herself with gardening, books, rural verses, and correspondence with literary friends. On November 20, 1748, she wrote to Lady Luxborough, the sister of Lord Bolingbroke, then living in retirement at Barrells in Warwickshire:

"I have been very well entertained lately with the two first Volumes of the *Foundling,* written by Mr Fielding, but not to be published till the 22^d of *January;* if the same Spirit runs through the whole Work, I think it will be much preferable to Joseph Andrews."†

* Barbauld, "Correspondence of Samuel Richardson," II, 63.

† Thomas Hull, "Select Letters between the late Duchess of Somerset, Lady Luxborough . . . and Others," 1778, I, 85.

THE PUBLICATION OF TOM JONES

It is not probable that Fielding read from his manuscript to Lady Hertford or lent it to her for quiet perusal. Apparently not only her ladyship but several other friends of the author were honoured by advance copies of the first volumes as soon as they came from the press in the late autumn of 1748. Certain it is that Lady Hertford was not the only person to inform Lady Luxborough of the unpublished novel which people of fashion were writing and talking about. "I remember," Lady Luxborough wrote to the poet Shenstone in retrospect, "I heard so much in Tom Jones's praise, that when I read him, I hated him."* This praise, however, had the desired effect on the sale of the novel; for Lady Luxborough procured and began reading the complete "Tom Jones" immediately after its publication, and in turn recommended it in letters to her own friends.

Lady Luxborough had to wait for her copy, however, a month or two longer than she expected. January passed and the novel was still in press. But in "The St. James's Evening Post" of January 24, 1749, Millar set February 10 for its appearance. It is not quite certain that the novel was ready even then; for not till February 28 did Millar advertise it as actually published. The notice as it appears in "The General Advertiser" for that and subsequent dates has been often quoted:

"This Day is published, in Six Vol. 12 mo.

THE HISTORY OF TOM JONES,

A FOUNDLING.

—Mores hominum multorum vidit.—

By HENRY FIELDING, Esq;

It being impossible to get Sets bound fast enough to answer the Demand for them, such Gentlemen and Ladies

* "Lady Luxborough's Letters to William Shenstone," 1775, p. 369.

as please, may have them sew'd in Blue Paper and Boards, at the Price of 16s. a Set, of

A. Millar over against *Catharine-street* in the *Strand.*"

Most interesting is the address to the public with which the advertisement concludes. So eager were gentlemen and ladies to obtain the novel at once that they were willing to take copies in paper and boards at sixteen shillings a set, a reduction of two shillings from the regular price. This offer Millar repeated in newspapers for a week, by which time the first impression of "Tom Jones" had probably been sold before the copies could be bound. The curiosity of the public, it may be said, had been skilfully awakened by Pitt, Lyttelton, Lady Hertford, and many others whose names are not known; but this curiosity was really based upon the admiration which Fielding's friends expressed for him and his book.

In accordance with the promise Fielding made when he gave Millar a receipt for six hundred pounds, he assigned the copyright in "Tom Jones" to his publisher on March 25, 1749. The verbose document runs:

"Know all Men by these Presents that I Henry Fielding of St. Paul's Covent Garden in the County of Middlesex Esqr for & in consideration of the Sum of Six hundred Pounds of lawful Money of Great Britain to me in hand paid by Andrew Millar of St. Mary le Strand in the County afores^d Bookseller, the Receipt whereof is hereby acknowledged and of which I do Acquit the s^d Andrew Millar his Executors & Assigns, have bargained sold delivered assigned & set over all that my Title Right and Property in & to a certain Book printed in Six Volumes, known & called by the Name & Title of The History of Tom Jones, a Foundling, invt': written by me the s^d Henry Fielding, with all Improvements, Additions or Alterations whatsoever which now are or hereafter shall at any time be made

THE
HISTORY
OF
TOM JONES,
A
FOUNDLING.

In SIX VOLUMES.

By HENRY FIELDING, Esq;

——*Mores hominum multorum vidit.*——

LONDON:

Printed for A. MILLAR, over-againſt
Catharine-ſtreet in the *Strand.*
MDCCXLIX.

by me the s^d Henry Fielding, or any one else by my authority to the s^d Book To Have and to Hold the s^d bargained Premises unto the s^d Andrew Millar, his Exors Admors or Assigns for ever And I do hereby covenant to & with the s^d Andrew Millar his Exors Admors & Assigns that I the s^d Henry Fielding the Author of the s^d bargained Premises have not at any time heretofore done committed or suffered any Act or thing whatsoever by means whereof the s^d bargained Premises or any part thereof is or shall be impeached or encumbered in any wise And I the s^d Henry Fielding for myself my Exors Admors & Assigns shall warrant & defend the s^d bargained Premises for ever against all Persons whatsoever claiming under me my Exors Admors or Assigns.

In Witness whereof I have hereunto set my hand & Seal this twenty fifth day of March One thousand seven hundred & forty nine

H FFIELDING   [Seal]

Signed sealed & delivered
by the within named Henry
Fielding the day and year within
mentioned, in the presence of

JOS. BROGDEN''*

The sum which Millar gave for the book was considered very handsome, though in proportion to the size of the novel, it was little more than Fielding received for "Joseph Andrews." That is, Millar paid him one hundred and eighty-three pounds and eleven shillings for "Joseph Andrews" in two volumes, and six hundred pounds for "Tom Jones" in six volumes. "Old England" insinuated that this ready money enabled the bankrupt author to settle with his creditors, who expected nothing, at a shilling in

---

* From the autograph in the library of J. P. Morgan, Esq. Folio. 12⅝ inches by 8⅛ inches. In the manuscript there is a line over *xo* and likewise over *mo* in *Exors* and *Admors* to indicate that the words are abbreviated.

the pound;* and there was a rumour, repeated by Horace Walpole, that Millar, finding the novel "sell so greatly," added another hundred to the original amount.†

The man who witnessed the agreement was Joshua Brogden, Fielding's clerk in the Bow Street court. By its terms, strictly interpreted, Fielding assigned his title, right, and property only in a "certain book printed in six volumes," called "The History of Tom Jones, a Foundling." In case the novel should be issued in another form—say, in a less number of volumes—the question might arise whether the copyright would cover that also. On the other hand, the copyright included "all improvements, additions or alterations whatsoever which now are or hereafter shall at any time be made" by Fielding or anyone else on his authority. This clause, though it is but a common stipulation, half reveals a curious detail concerning the publication of "Tom Jones." Within a month after its first appearance, Fielding was far advanced in a revision of the novel.

Immediate revision was rendered imperative on account of the numerous errors that crept into the text owing to the haste with which the novel had been at last put through the press. Most of them were due to the compositors, who occasionally misread the manuscript, but more often merely dropped out or repeated small words like *is, can, in, at,* and *not. Square* was once turned into *Squire;* and *Mr. Anderson* became *Mr. Enderson.* Other errors, such as the use of a wrong pronoun or the misplacing of a phrase, may be more definitely ascribed to the author. Twice Fielding fell into uncertainty over the age of his hero in the story of Tom's growth through boyhood, making him nineteen years old when he should have been seventeen, and nineteen when he should have been twenty. Once Mrs. Miller was called Mrs. Cannister—because, I daresay, the author had

---

* "Old England," May 27, 1749.

† "Letters of Walpole," edited by Toynbee, II, 384.

in mind the real name of the clergyman's widow whom he was depicting in the character. The slips of compositor and author, taken together, were quite enough to blemish the pages. In ordinary circumstances neither Fielding nor Millar would have let a book like this go to the public. As a makeshift, space was provided after the table of contents in the first volume for a page of errata, having at the head a request that the reader make for himself some sixty-odd corrections. Of the list of errata, two things are to be observed. First, it is confined mostly to the author's mistakes, mixed here and there with a few of the compositors' many blunders. Hence it was prepared by Fielding himself. Secondly, it covers only five volumes, though the sixth volume has some of the most glaring lapses in the entire novel. Not only, then, was Millar unable to bind copies fast enough to meet the demand, but he felt constrained to print them before the proofs could be properly corrected by his hacks and before the author had time to read the last volume for alterations.

It was a shrewd guess of Mr. Frederick S. Dickson, the only bibliographer who has ever examined with care the first edition of "Tom Jones," that preparation was begun for a new edition "about the time the sixth volume went to press";* that is, in February, 1749. In fact, there were two new editions—one in six volumes at the old price, and another in four volumes, which sold in blue paper covers at half a guinea and bound at twelve shillings. According to "The St. James's Evening Post," the four-volume edition was published April 13, 1749. At the same time Millar announced the six-volume edition "on a large Letter, pr. bound 18s." As he said nothing about being able to supply it in paper covers, the inference is that this was the new edition in six volumes. On the same day,

* "Life and Writings of Fielding," by Keightley, edited by Dickson, 1900, p. 132.

it would therefore seem, "Tom Jones" reappeared in two quite different styles of dress.

At first sight the second edition in six volumes differs from the first only in the absence of the errata. The phrase, "the second edition," nowhere appears; type and paper are the same; and the paging is kept uniform with the edition having the errata. Close inspection, however, reveals the story of what happened. The table of contents is re-spaced so as to extend into the page formerly given to the errata; the first volume has a new tailpiece; the title-page of the fifth volume ends in a misprint; and most, though not all, of the slips made by author and compositor have been corrected, including, with two exceptions, those contained in the errata. Moreover, though each volume has the same number of pages as the corresponding volume of the first edition, scores of individual pages differ either in the number of lines or in the last words and phrases. It looks as if Millar, not anticipating the immense demand, distributed the type, and so had to reset the entire novel. There is really no other conclusion. Labour was cheap and the compositors were asked to do their work over again. "Tom Jones," as the novel appeared in February, is a most rare book. It is this second edition or impression here described—call it what you will—that has long passed for the first.

Simultaneously another set of compositors was put to work on the four-volume edition. They made all the changes indicated in the errata, and corrected many verbal inaccuracies besides, though not in exact conformity with the new six-volume edition. On the whole, they were more careful than their brethren. Near the same time a "Tom Jones" in three volumes was also brought out in Dublin. Since this edition failed to incorporate all the corrections called for by the errata,—indeed, none of those covering the first three books,—the certain inference is that it was

The Reader is defired to correct the following
E R R A T A.

V O L. I. Page 11, line 25. for *was* read *had.* p. 52, l. 18.
dele *that.* p. 57, l. 12. for *Military* read *Militant.* p. 60, l.
6. for *this* read *it.* p. 68, l. 14. read *what it.* p. 99, l. 12. for
bore read *borne.* p. 151, l. 19. for *feventeen* read *nineteen.* p.
209, l. 15. for *he could* read *could.*

V O L. II. Page 29, l. 14. read *twenty.* p. 86, l. 13. read
whipped at. p. 195, l. 24. dele *on.* p. 230, l. 21. for *thefe* read
they. p. 273, l. 16. for *bore* read *borne.* p. 289, l. 4. for *Wrath*
read *wroth.* p. 306, l. 22. for *fuffered* read *induced.*

V O L. III. Page 19, l. 10. dele *that.* p. 27, l. 28. read *as he
never concealed this Hatred.* p. 40, l. 10. for *fatisfied* read *convinced.* p. 57, l. 26. read *preferves and requires.* p. 134, l. 2.
dele *that.* l. 9. dele *fo.* p. 238. l. laft, for *proflitute* read *profligate.* p. 274, l. 21. for *thofe* read *they.* p. 277, l. 21. read
Affronts. p. 294, l. 16. read *Louage.* p. 307, l. 8. dele *Doomf-
day Book,* or. p. 330, l. 14. read *came.* p. 348. l. 12. put a come,
Comma only after *charming.*

V O L. IV. Page 35, l. 1. read *pricked up.* p. 90, l. 20. read
they are effected, l. 25. dele *fuch.* p. 91, l. 3. for *Cafh* read
Gold. p. 110, l. 12. for *our* read *old.* p. 111, l. 22. for *which*
read *and.* p. 120, l. 1. dele Comma after not. p. 122, l. 8. dele
by. p. 169, l. 27. read *think it material.* l. 28. dele *fo.* p.
179, l. 3. for *its* read *her.* p. 185, l. 14. read *the Truth, of
this Degree of Sufpicion I believe.* l. 23. for *who* read *which.*
p. 193, l. 11. for *Crime* read *Shame,* p. 212, l. 16. for *nor*
read *and.* p. 231, l. 13. for *by* read *for.* p. 235, l. 20. for
rifen read *raifed.* p. 270, l. 9. read *Lalagen.* p. 294, l. 13. for
Alternative read *Alteration.*

V O L. V. Page 66. l. 20. for *Cannifter* read *Miller.* p. 113, l.
1. read *Characters.* p. 172, l. 6. read *exifting.* p. 181, l. 6. for
in read *on,* p. 182, l. 11. read *bringing her into.* p. 223, l. 12.
dele *not.* p. 249, l. 25. read *fat.* p. 251, l. 27. read *two or
three.* p. 263, l. 20. read *Lady.* p. 272, l. 12. dele *that.* p. 274,
l. 10. dele *as.* p. 282, l. 11. for *for* read *on.* l. 25. read *ever.*
p. 283. l. 9. read *in his Way.*

set from the first London edition in six volumes. Hence, towards the close of March, not two but three groups of compositors were engaged on new editions of "Tom Jones" —enough to satisfy for the present an eager public throughout the kingdoms of Great Britain and Ireland.

There was yet to be one more London edition of "Tom Jones" in four volumes before the year closed. Millar announced it in "The St. James's Evening Post" for December 9-12, 1749, as "this day published," though it is dated 1750. The advertisement assured the reader that the novel had been "carefully revised and corrected," but whether by the author or by someone else was left ambiguous. No such phrase, however, appeared on the title-page. Except for the date 1750, and a new tailpiece to the first volume, this edition looked like another issue of the first one in four volumes. Nevertheless, the novel was largely if not entirely reset, and "cured" here and there of slight errors, real or imaginary. Word-catchers had taken Fielding to task for the Dutch word *Trachtchugt*,* which, they said, should be spelled *Trachtchuyt*. In the new edition, the word was first changed to *Treckschuyte*. Again, in all the earlier editions, Thwackum, while speaking of Black George in contempt, had called him "Black Jack."† Thwackum was now made to give the gamekeeper his usual nickname. In the first case, the compositor had merely misread the manuscript; in the second case, Fielding evidently intended that Thwackum should refer to the gamekeeper as a "Black Jack." As of these two corrections, so of the rest. None of them was probably made by Fielding himself; none rose beyond the intelligence of a bookseller's hack.

Startling as it may appear, there is not a trace of evidence that Fielding ever read "Tom Jones" after March,

---

* Bk. XIII, Ch. I. The modern spelling is *Trekschuit* for the Dutch canal-boat.

† Bk. III, Ch. IV.

1749, when he looked through most of the novel for the new edition in six volumes to be published the next month. As it was, he must have read mainly for verbal errors, else he would not have let stand several inaccuracies in the narrative which have been observed by readers ever since his day. Nearly as obvious, for example, as that oversight with reference to the age of his hero, which he corrected, was a sudden transition in the course of three or four weeks from mid-summer to mid-winter, which he left uncorrected. Nor, when he reached the sixth volume in revision, did he look sharply, if at all, at the text for slips of the compositors. Attention, I think, has never been called to the most corrupt passage to be found anywhere in the novel. It occurs during a conversation in the eighth chapter of the sixteenth book, where Lady Bellaston addresses Sophia's maiden aunt, Mrs. Western, first as "Bel" and then as "Bell." Nowhere else in the novel is it certain that a Christian name was given to Mrs. Western. Once Lady Bellaston had earlier referred to her as "Di," short for "Diana," because of her imperious bearing and air of virginity, and men had called her "the cruel Parthenissa" in verses scratched upon windows, which she immediately broke into a thousand pieces. But Parthenissa and probably Diana were sobriquets not names, quite different from "Bel" or "Bell," which I surmise got into the text through a blunder. I say "surmise," for not a sentence of "Tom Jones" exists in manuscript for verification. It was, however, the custom of authors in the eighteenth century, so far as we know it, to abbreviate words wherever they were disposed to do so. No one, for instance, would have thought it necessary to write out on all occasions the names of the characters in a play or a novel. Much was left to the printer. So I take it that in this passage Fielding in his haste wrote merely "Bel" or "Bell" when he meant Lady Bellaston; and that the compositor at this point misunderstood him. Probably the manuscript was not clear. Except that "Bel" was altered to "Bell" in the four-volume edition dated 1750, the text remained unchanged during Fielding's lifetime. The conversation was first set straight by Murphy in 1762, in his second edition of the author's works. This confusion of names, be it noted, occurred on page 67 of the sixth volume of "Tom Jones" as originally published. The list of errata for this edition, it will be remembered, did not cover that volume. It accordingly seems certain that Fielding left all corrections therein to Millar and his men, never going through the proofs for himself.

By April, 1749, "Tom Jones" was for Fielding a thing of the past. Critics might snarl, but he gave no heed to them. No copy of the novel appears in the catalogue of his library advertised by the auctioneer a few months after Fielding's death. Like many other novelists, Fielding did not ponder his works for his own edification; they were written for the delight of a public willing to pay for them. Not that Fielding wrote "Tom Jones" just for money, though we may be sure that if Millar offered him another hundred in April, he took it. As he sat in his little parlour with the manuscript spread out before him, he could hear the clink of the shining heap that was to be his and could already feel the warmth of the comfortable house that it would bring to himself and family; but he declared that gold was not his inspiration; it was his reward for a book upon which he had expended thousands of hours and into which he had put all the wit and humour of which he was master.

CHAPTER XVIII

THE RECEPTION OF TOM JONES

The story of the hundred pounds, coupled with the patronage of Lyttelton and the Duke of Bedford, led Sir Walter Scott to say that "Tom Jones" was greeted "with unanimous acclamation." The assertion is quite untrue. The novel evidently had a wide sale for those days; probably ten thousand or more copies were printed the first year; everywhere it supplied among the upper and middle classes a topic for conversation; but the public divided into hostile camps on its merits. It was still almost as true as in Pope's day that

> Parties in Wit attend on those of State,
> And public faction doubles private hate.

Fielding's praise of Lyttelton and the Duke of Bedford at once drew the fire of the whole mob of writers employed against the Ministry. Moreover, Richardson three months before had published the last volumes of "Clarissa Harlowe," with which "Tom Jones" came into rivalry. From the first Richardson and his coterie were very bitter against Fielding, as if he had no business to enter the lists for public favour at this time. As a result, we have few unbiassed estimates of "Tom Jones" by Fielding's contemporaries; we have unmeasured praise from some of Fielding's friends, though fewer instances of it than one would expect; we have unmeasured abuse from his enemies. But outsiders, with here and there an exception, did not quite understand Fielding's drift; they expected to find in

126

"Tom Jones" as in "Clarissa" one or more models of perfection; whereas they found men and women such as they had seen and known in real life; and they were nonplussed by Fielding's frank realism. The great fame of "Tom Jones" belongs to later times, when neither private friendship nor malice nor envy could warp the reader's judgment. With this explanation and caution, I will proceed to the real story of how the novel was received when first published. Fact may seem stranger than fiction.

Of Fielding's friends, where were Pitt and Lyttelton, both of whom had commended the book while it was in manuscript? In their published works neither "Tom Jones" nor Fielding is even mentioned. A passage, to be sure, in one of Lyttelton's "Dialogues of the Dead" compliments Fielding for "a true spirit of comedy, and an exact representation of nature, with fine moral touches"; that dialogue, however, was written not by Lyttelton, but by his friend Elizabeth Montagu, the Blue Stocking, who in general put Richardson above Fielding. Where was Garrick, whose Hamlet Fielding had praised for its perfect naturalness? Where was Allen, whose character had been drawn in Squire Allworthy? Where was Warburton, in whose hands, said Fielding, had been placed the key to the treasures of ancient learning? The guest of Allen at Prior Park in the summer of 1749, Warburton was sending to Richard Hurd at Cambridge news of the literary world, but he condescended to no phrase in favour of a writer who had bestowed upon him many an undeserved compliment. Two years elapsed before the world knew that he rated Marivaux and Fielding foremost among those novelists who have given "a faithful and chaste copy of real life and manners." Both Shenstone and Lady Luxborough preferred "Joseph Andrews" to "Tom Jones." Writing to the poet from Barrells, March 23, 1749, Lady Luxborough says in the midst of her letter:

"I might live at least five hundred years in this place before one quarter of the incidents happened which are related in any one of the six volumes of Tom Jones. I have not yet read the two last; but I think as you do, that no one character yet is near so striking as Adams's in the author's other composition, and the plan seems far-fetched; but in the adventures that happen, I think he produces personages but too like those one meets with in the world; and even among those people to whom he gives good characters, he shews them as in a concave glass which discovers blemishes that would not have appeared to the common eye."*

A similar opinion was expressed by Lady Mary Wortley Montagu. Since 1739, Lady Mary had been living abroad, and so did not see "Joseph Andrews" when it first appeared. But in September, 1749, her daughter, the Countess of Bute, sent her a box of books containing this novel, presumably the recent edition of it, and "Tom Jones." On the first of October, she wrote back, from Lovere, Italy, to her daughter:

"My Dear Child,—I have at length received the box, with the books enclosed, for which I give you many thanks, as they amused me very much. I gave a very ridiculous proof of it, fitter indeed for my granddaughter than myself. I returned from a party on horseback; and after having rode twenty miles, part of it by moonshine, it was ten at night when I found the box arrived. I could not deny myself the pleasure of opening it; and, falling upon Fielding's works, was fool enough to sit up all night reading. I think Joseph Andrews better than his Foundling."

In course of time, Lady Mary, however, reversed her judgment. She admired, says her grand-daughter Lady Stuart, "Tom Jones" above all her cousin's books, and wrote in her own copy *Ne plus ultra,* though she was sorry

* "Letters of Shenstone," 1775, p. 88.

that Fielding "did not himself perceive that he had made Tom Jones a scoundrel; alluding to the adventure with Lady Bellaston."*

Unqualified admiration, so far as we have a record of it, came from humbler sources. "The London Magazine," owned and managed by Thomas Astley, led the way late in February, 1749, with a "Plan of a late celebrated Novel," highly laudatory throughout of a book "which has given great amusement, and, we hope, instruction to the polite part of the town." To his summary of what the reader would find in it, the writer added:

"Thus ends this pretty novel, with a most just distribution of rewards and punishments, according to the merits of all the persons that had any considerable share in it; but this short abstract can only serve as an incitement to those, that have not yet had the pleasure of reading it; for we had not room for many of the surprizing incidents, or for giving any of them in their beautiful dress."

This is the first account of "Tom Jones" to appear in print. The name of the man who wrote it is not known; but two or three things about its publication are certain. Astley, who had been giving his support to the Government, was so well disposed towards Fielding that he made the novel the subject of his leading article for the month. The reviewer was likewise a close friend, who could see no fault whatever in the book; indeed, as this number of "The London Magazine" was issued near the first of March, within a week after the publication of "Tom Jones," he must have been among the favourites who had advance copies—one of the men called Lyttelton's "zanies" by irate "Old England," because they had praised the novel up and down through the coffee-houses. The first review of "Tom Jones," spreading its fame through Britain, was thus an echo of what Lyttelton and Pitt had said of the

* "Letters," 1861, I, 107; II, 185-186.

novel. Perhaps it was directly "inspired" by the one or the other of them. If this be so, it atones in a measure for the silence of their own books.

It is noteworthy that this appreciation of "Tom Jones," which sounds very like one of those extended press notices prepared nowadays in the publisher's office, did not appear in "The Gentleman's Magazine," owned and edited by Edward Cave—a periodical mildly opposed to the Government and coloured by the literary views and prejudices of Dr. Samuel Johnson. The Great Cham of literature was thoroughly committed to the interests of Samuel Richardson. The author of "Clarissa," he said, "had picked the kernel of life, while Fielding was contented with the husk"; and in another figure (which Richardson had himself used), "that there was as great a difference between them as between a man who knew how a watch was made, and a man who could tell the hour by looking on the dial-plate."* It was, I suppose, Fielding who could explain the mechanism of a watch to a reader who had patience enough to listen; it was Richardson who constructed the clock on whose bright dial one might see at a glance where the hands stood. The one lost himself in unimportant details; the other gave broad and clear pictures of human nature. To Johnson "the virtues of Fielding's characters were the vices of a truly good man." Quite naturally, then, it was not "The Gentleman's Magazine" but its rival that described "Tom Jones" as a prose epic "calculated to recommend religion and virtue, to shew the bad consequences of indiscretion, and to set several kinds of vice in their most deformed and shocking light." The one magazine was the champion of Fielding, the other of Richardson and his friends; the one took "Tom Jones" for its literary article in February; the other took Dr. Johnson's "Irene," which Garrick's company was performing at Drury Lane.

* Boswell, "Life of Johnson," 1835, III, 38-39.

THE RECEPTION OF TOM JONES

Nevertheless, "The Gentleman's Magazine" could not ignore a "Tom Jones"; it might refrain from reviewing the novel and lament that the world, which ought to be reading Newton's "Milton" and Warburton's "Shakespeare," "is run a madding after that fool parson Adams, and that rake Tom Jones"; but it had to reckon with contributors who thought differently. The artist who drew the emblematic frontispiece to the volume for the year gave an obscure place to "Tom Jones" at the bottom of a pile of miscellaneous books representing the annual output. Upon "Tom Jones" rests "Clarissa"; and near them stands a bottle of Nantes with a sprig of laurel stuck into its mouth. While reprinting from the newspapers several attacks on Fielding, the editor also admitted from a correspondent a conversation supposed to have taken place between Allworthy and Western over the reform of the Prayer Book, besides a new country dance called "Tom Jones," with the music and a full description of the movements. Another correspondent, who signed himself "Tho. Cawthorn," ventured to send in a poem addressed "To Henry Fielding Esq; On reading his inimitable history of Tom Jones." Hitherto, the poet said, fiction had dealt with characters either "vilely bad" or "greatly good," the one class "exciting horrour," the other "promoting sleep"; but when genius spoke,

> Life dropt her mask, and all mankind were men.

Then something happened, though we do not know what. Perhaps Richardson's friends remonstrated with Cave for lending the authority of his magazine to the dethronement of "Clarissa," and warned him to read hereafter with more care poems from unknown contributors. The editor evidently took it for granted that the poem came from James Cawthorn, the master of the Tunbridge Grammar School, whose occasional poems were very well known. At the schoolmaster's request, he inserted in a later number of "The Gentleman's Magazine" a notice to the effect that "the verses to Henry Fielding, Esq;" were not written by this poet, but by another man of the same surname.* The explanation pleased Fielding's enemies. Still, the spurious Cawthorn by a clever ruse had succeeded in his aim; he had misled a hostile editor into publishing a poem in praise of "Tom Jones."

Of spontaneous tributes like this, there were many instances. In May, 1749, was established "The Monthly Review," the first of the magazines devoted wholly to a description and estimate of current books. It was conducted by Ralph Griffiths and his wife, who kept a bookshop in St. Paul's Churchyard. Dr. Johnson thought the new magazine a dull performance and charged Griffiths with forcing the hacks who wrote for him to read the books they reviewed. "The Monthly Review" appeared two months too late for an account of "Tom Jones," but Griffiths and his men were always quick to meet attacks upon a work so "generally esteemed" as "Tom Jones" and upon "so considerable a writer as Mr. Fielding." Dr. John Hill, who afterwards worked up a quarrel with Fielding, advised a gentleman compelled to retire to the country on account of ill health, to take with him only the Bible, a chapter in which he would find "as much a novelty as one in 'Tom Jones' . . . when new fallen from the almost creative pen of its author."† "The Ladies Magazine" had verses "On the incomparable History of Tom Jones," beginning—

> Hail! happy Fielding, who with glorious ease,
> Can'st Nature paint, and paint her still to please.

* "The Gentleman's Magazine," Aug. and Oct., 1749, XIX, 371 and 464. See also pp. 547-550; and XX, 179, 229, and 252; and "An Examen . . . of Tom Jones," 1750, p. 118.

† "The Inspector," as reprinted, Vol. II, 1753, No. 94, p. 74.

Each humorous incident is finely hit,
With justness, symmetry of parts, and wit.
Nature throughout the drama plays her part,
Behind the curtain lurks assisting art.*

The same idea was better expressed without the aid of verse by Allan Ramsay, the portrait painter, in a casual remark on "Tom Jones" as the highest type of "an artful story, . . . where the incidents are so various, and yet so consistent with themselves, and with nature, that the more the reader is acquainted with nature, the more he is deceived into a belief of its being true; and is with difficulty recall'd from that belief by the author's confession from time to time of its being all a fiction."† With wider sweep, Christopher Smart the poet, who knew Fielding personally, said of him and his novels: "Through all Mr. Fielding's inimitable comic romances, we perceive no such thing as personal malice, no private character dragged into light; but every stroke is copied from the volume which nature has unfolded to him; every scene of life is by him represented in its natural colours, and every species of folly or humour is ridiculed with the most exquisite touches. A genius like this is perhaps more useful to mankind, than any class of writers; he serves to dispel all gloom from our minds, to work off our ill-humours by the gay sensations excited by a well directed pleasantry, and in a vein of mirth he leads his readers into the knowledge of human nature; the most useful and pleasing science we can apply to."‡ Nothing much better than these words of Smart and Ramsay, long since forgotten like the pamphlets in which they occurred, has ever been spoken of Fielding's art. It was an art almost concealed by nature.

Before the year was over, anonymous scribblers began

---

* "The Ladies Magazine," April 20-May 4, 1751, II, 202.
† "A Letter . . . Concerning Elizabeth Canning," 1753, pp. 16-17.
‡ From "A Letter" prefixed to "The Hilliad," 1753.

to trade on Fielding's fame. In November, 1749, appeared, for example, "The History of Tom Jones the Foundling, in his Married State," a novel in three books, based on the old characters, who were brought back to Somersetshire. Lady Bellaston, out of envy, tries in vain to break up the happy marriage, and Tom Jones develops into a prudent country squire. This continuation of the famous novel has been often ascribed to Fielding despite a preface which says that "Henry Fielding, Esq; is not the author of this book, nor in any manner concerned in its composition or publication." The warning should have been unnecessary, for the novel bears, said "The Monthly Review," no marks of Fielding's "spirit, style, or invention." The best thing about it is the banter of Fielding in the preface, where the writer laments that his novel was not warmly recommended by an Honourable Lord of the Treasury before it appeared in public, but hopes that it may now engage that gentleman's attention. In his want of a patron at Court, the author dedicated his book to "the Right Honourable Elizabeth, Countess of Marchmont." Two years before, the Earl of Marchmont, who figures in the "History of the late Rebellion," which Fielding may have written, had married the daughter of a linen-draper. Therein lay the jest of the dedication.

Then followed, in February, 1750, a more pretentious imitation entitled "The History of Charlotte Summers, the Fortunate Parish Girl," which extended to four books in two volumes. The heroine, taking her name from Fielding's Charlotte, is another Pamela with variations: in the end she proves to be of rank, refuses to marry the man who would deceive her, and gets a gentleman for a husband. The author, whose name has never been discovered, claimed to be, in a literary sense, a natural son of Fielding, about whom he discourses in the most intimate terms. His sketch of his father, with whom he may have had no personal acquaintance, is interesting in that it reflects the contemporary view of a young man not wholly devoid of talent. In a long passage on "Tom Jones" and "Clarissa," he says:

"I happened the other Day to be in Company with a very judicious ancient Gentlewoman of my Acquaintance, and our Conversation turned on these two wonderful Performances, of which she gave the following Character: I have read both these Authors, and have been highly entertained with each in his Way. The one tickled me till I had like to die of laughing, and the other moved me so I had like to have died crying. . . . The Truth is, my worshipful Father is naturally a Man of good Humour himself, and resolved to be pleased as easily as he can; he has so little Bile in his Constitution, and so large a Quantity of Mercury, he is seldom or never sad himself, and in writing his *Tom Jones,* he wrote nothing but what tickled his own Fancy, and never put Pen to Paper but when he was perfectly pleased with himself and all about him; by this Means nothing flowed from him but what was facetious and witty. On the other Hand, the Historian of *Clarissa* . . . never wrote till he had wrought up his Imagination into a real Belief of the Reality of the Misfortune of his Heroine. His Sighs, his Tears, and Groans guided his Pen, and every Accent appears but the Picture of his own sad Heart, that beats with tender Simpathy for the imaginary Distress of his favourite Fair. Thus both these great Men while they were writing for the Entertainment of the Public, were pleasing themselves in their different Tastes; *Tom Jones* was pleased when he laughed, and *Clarissa* when she cried."

By way of parenthesis, the author of "Charlotte Summers" observed what no one else has ever pointed out—that Fielding, in his description of the feast which awaits the reader of "Tom Jones," provides nothing to drink. How so essential an article could have been omitted puzzled him, for his father was "no enemy to a chearful glass." In the new novel drinkables are added to the viands.

The next year "Tom Jones" and its imitators and critics supplied another young man* with material for "An Essay on the New Species of Writing founded by Mr. Fielding"— a shilling pamphlet of forty-six pages, which "The Gentleman's Magazine" mentioned with contempt. It is, indeed, an immature production of a young gentleman, but it has some significance as a reply to malicious criticism of Fielding and as an honest appreciation of his art. Mild strictures are passed upon parts of "Joseph Andrews" and upon the story of the Old Man of the Hill, "though," says the author, "I have heard that there is such a character." Notwithstanding these slight blemishes, Fielding is boldly proclaimed "the English Cervantes," and his works are declared to be "in every body's hands." On the whole, "Joseph Andrews" is good and true to life, and "Tom Jones" is perhaps "the most lively book ever published."

Apart from these things are two quite different pieces whose origin is involved in mystery. In April, 1748, there appeared in London, bearing Cooper's imprint, a shilling pamphlet called "The Important Triflers. A Satire";† but no copy of the London edition of the satire, evidently an anonymous publication, is now discoverable. "The Important Triflers," however, has survived in a Dublin reprint, of sixteen pages, dated just a year later, on the title-page of which the work is ascribed to "Henry Fielding, Esqr; Author of Tom Jones." It is a journal in verse of the fashionable town lady from the time she rings for breakfast until she says her midnight prayers and goes to bed to dream of the opera with which she has closed a day crowded with frivolous diversions. There are brief character-sketches of fashionable people known to the

---

* Probably Francis Coventry, author of "Pompey the Little," 1751.

† "The Gentleman's Magazine," April, 1748, XVIII, 192.

author, who appear with the vowels taken out of their names; while the shopkeepers fare better, as when Kitty and her friends say:

> Now and then, for a Frolick, we rove up and down,
> And strole, like wild Creatures, half over the Town:
> Call at *Highmore's,* at *Hudson's,* and step up to *Cock's;*
> See the Lyrichord, Wax-work, Bear, Horse, or an Ox,
> Stop at *Chenevix, Deard's,* and, in passing by, pop
> In the Laceman's, the Mercer's, and Millener's Shop.

The young ladies—Kitty, Mariana, Philadella, and two more—sign an affidavit, in the presence of "H. Z.," to the effect that the poet tells their true story; and an advertisement gives the information that the author once wrote out the journal "for the amusement of a learned and ingenious lady" who was staying at Bath, and subsequently interspersed the narrative with Latin quotations, adding translations for the English reader. At the request of the same "learned and ingenious young lady," who asked him for something extempore, he subjoins, in the character of "Captain Cockade," a neat rendering of four lines from Tibullus; and then concludes with "The Poet Bewitch'd: or, the Muse set at Liberty," consisting of wild paraphrases out of the Latin poets in praise of Bella, who outshines all the Graces.

The other piece has a similar but not identical history. In the register of books for April and May, 1749, given in "The London Magazine" for May, was listed "Three Letters to the Fool, on Subjects the most interesting." There was no further description, and no copy of the London edition has ever been found. But what purports to be a second edition, reprinted in Dublin the same year, has escaped oblivion. The full title of the reprint is *"Stultus* versus *Sapientem:* In Three Letters to the Fool, on Subjects the most Interesting." The author is declared to be "Henry Fielding, Esq." This is a small political

THE HISTORY OF HENRY FIELDING

pamphlet, of only twenty-three pages, dealing ironically with Irish affairs, in letters which Thomas Stupidius addresses to "The Fool," the name assumed by the editor of "The Daily Gazetteer," the violent anti-ministerial newspaper. Thomas Stupidius is bitterly opposed to the great improvements in the economic condition of the Irish people under the Pelham Ministry. He particularly denounces the encouragement given to the linen industry by means of bounties, and those "cursed Protestant schools," supported by private charity, wherein children "are taught to read the Bible . . . and still more infamously employed in tilling the land, spinning, weaving, or some other manual operations, unknown to their forefathers." He longs for the restoration of the good old times when the children were kept in "indolence and rags," and the priests frightened "these little reptiles" with purgatory and hell. The pamphlet seems to have been written to praise the work done in Ireland by Lord Chesterfield as Lord Lieutenant and by his successor and kinsman, the first Earl of Harrington.

Doctors will disagree on the authorship of this and the other pamphlet. The Dublin editor altered the date of the affidavit to which the young ladies of "The Important Triflers" set their names, making it "16° Aprilis, 1749," instead of 1748, and also adjusted a line in the poem itself to the new date. These minor details, however, do not touch the question at issue. It is merely my own opinion that Fielding originally composed the verses at Bath in the circumstances described in the advertisement. They are in the light and playful mood so common in his occasional poems; and the translations from the Latin are like the free and facetious paraphrases seen all through his work and culminating in "The Covent-Garden Journal." Similarly "*Stultus* versus *Sapientem*," slight as it appears, is in line with the irony of "The Jacobite's Journal," which he had edited; it is the laudation of men whom he had there lauded; and the economic position taken in the pamphlet is the same that Fielding afterwards elaborated elsewhere. In the second letter of Tom Stupidius to the Fool, we read: "The riches and prosperity of a nation are in proportion to their inhabitants properly employed." In "A Provision for the Poor," which we know Fielding wrote later, we read: "It is not barely . . . in the numbers of people, but in numbers of people well and properly disposed, that we can truly place the strength and riches of a society." Taking everything into consideration, we may, I think, restore the two lost strays to the Fielding fold. If they add nothing to his literary reputation, they have a bibliographical interest, and show that his name was worth something to Dublin publishers in 1749.

In the meantime, "Tom Jones" was making its way abroad in a French dress. In June, 1749, Pierre-Antoine de la Place, who had just published his "Théâtre Anglais," read the novel and could not resist, he says, the temptation to translate it into his own language. Fearing that he might be anticipated by others, he set to work at once and completed his task before the year was out. The result was not so much a translation as an adaptation and abridgment according to principles explained in a letter which La Place addressed to Fielding in English and afterwards turned into French by way of preface or introduction to his volumes. "I have never seen you, Sir," said the translator, to paraphrase his French, for his own English has been lost, "but I love you; I do not know you, but I admire you. . . . And yet if Mr. Fielding had written his novel for the French, he would probably have suppressed a large number of passages, which, though excellent in themselves, would appear out of place to French readers, who, when once interested in an intrigue, become impatient of digressions and dissertations, or a treatise on morals, and regard all these ornaments, however fine, as obstacles to the pleasure which they are in haste to enjoy.'' For this reason La Place proceeded to make over "Tom Jones" in accordance with French views of what a novel should be. "I have done," he said, "no more than the author himself would have done," had he been a Frenchman. On this assumption, he cut down the novel a full third—from six to four duodecimo volumes; compressed the narrative wherever he wished by giving the gist of it; abridged the dedication; and sent the initial chapters with two exceptions to the scrap heap. His opinion was that these ''preliminary discourses,'' as he called them, might make a little volume, if printed separately, as instructive as amusing, but that they could not be tolerated as a part of the novel. In this mutilated version "Tom Jones" crossed the Channel and was read by Prince Charles Edward Stuart. The volumes were rendered unusually attractive by sixteen plates designed by Gravelot, who from a long residence in London knew English life much better than the translator.

Like many other French translations of English books, the ''Histoire de Tom Jones, ou L'Enfant Trouvé'' was first printed in London, *chez Jean Nourse,* and then in Amsterdam, "aux Depens de la Compagnie"; that is, at the expense of a group of French booksellers residing there. Thence it spread to their agents in France and Germany. Copies for Dresden bore the imprint of ''George Conrad Walther Libraire du Roi, Avec Privilège de Sa Maj. le Roi de Pol. Elect. de Saxe.'' Those for Paris, it was said by ''The Gentleman's Magazine,'' were the ones ''artfully'' described on the title-page, to translate the French phrase, as ''printed for Mr. Nourse in London.'' Other copies had on the title-page Paris, Reims, Geneva, or merely ''En France.'' In France poor "Tom Jones" met with a rebuff. According to "Old England" for April 7, 1750, ''A-la-Main,'' a Paris newspaper much quoted in London, had the following announcement in its issue for the sixteenth of March:

"An Arrêt of the Council of State is issued for suppressing a certain immoral Work, entitled The History of Tom Jones, translated from the *English*."

The prominence that Argus Centoculi gave to the word immoral in his translation of the decree shows with what delight he received the news. It was intimated in "The Gentleman's Magazine"* that French ladies were shocked by Tom's breaches of faith to Sophia and that parents exclaimed against her running from home in search of him. This was doubtless the immorality which the French saw in "Tom Jones." It was a question of differences in race and custom. As Fielding well knew, the irregularities of youth were easily pardoned in England; a girl who fled after her lover from a suitor whom she hated, was in fact a heroine in that land of liberty. The stay to the sale of "Tom Jones" in France appears to have been brief, for within a year the novel was having "a vast run" there. It was also immediately translated into Dutch and German.

Thus far, discordant notes have entered now and then into the story I have told of the praise lavished upon "Tom Jones." It will be equally entertaining to reverse the process, to throw the emphasis of the narrative upon the discords. Strike a balance and we shall have the truth. By Fielding's enemies, "Tom Jones" was as completely damned as the worst of his comedies. First of all, there was Samuel Richardson. What he thought of "the bastard" may be seen in the Barbauld correspondence and in those unpublished letters which passed between him and his friends, now preserved at the South Kensington Museum. Twice in "The Jacobite's Journal," Fielding had expressed the highest admiration for "Clarissa Harlowe" when the first two volumes of that novel made their

* March, 1750, XX, 117-118.

appearance. "Sure this Mr. Richardson," he wrote there, "is master of all that art which Horace compares to witch-craft,

> . . . pectus inaniter angit,
> Irritat, mulcet, falsis terroribus implet,
> Ut magus . . ."

This apt quotation from Horace, Richardson conveyed to a postscript appended to his last volume for the purpose of explaining how "Clarissa Harlowe" differed from all other novels; and an admirer paraphrased the passage for the opening lines of a "sonnet" subsequently placed before the preface:

> O master of the heart! whose magic skill
> The close recesses of the soul can find,
> Can rouse, becalm, and terrify the mind,
> Now melt with pity, now with anguish thrill.

The complete "Clarissa" thus bore, though impressed by other hands, the finger-print of Henry Fielding. The anonymous poet could do no better than expand his words for adulation; Richardson could do no better than employ them for a disquisition on the novelist's art. Before the last instalment of "Clarissa" was published, Fielding, probably in a conversation with Richardson, advised him to give the novel "a happy ending." Beyond this private advice, which the author heard also from Lyttelton, the poet Thomson, and others, Fielding never went in his strictures on "Clarissa Harlowe." Who was right, it matters not; for Richardson could brook no criticism. Whoever questioned his infallibility lost at once his favour, which could be won back only by the most abject flattery. Such was the temper of this irritable little man who wrote a very great novel. He never forgot, too, as his letters show, Fielding's "rude engraftment" on "Pamela"; and when "Tom Jones" now appeared on the heels of "Clarissa

Harlowe," it seemed to him as if there were a premeditated design on Fielding's part to injure him with the public. A word in praise of "Tom Jones" set his shrunken heart boiling with rage and envy; a word in disparagement of the novel set it beating at a happy pace. Some of his friends shared his moods; others mildly remonstrated with him.

The first instalment of "Clarissa Harlowe" fell into the hands of Lady Dorothy Bradshaigh, the wife of a Lancashire baronet. Carried away by the pathos of the story, she opened a correspondence with the author under the assumed name of "Mrs. Belfour." Beyond all others, she pleaded with him to save "the divine Clarissa" from the fate she saw impending; but in the end she became partially reconciled to "the murder" of the heroine, and was ready to place her heart in the keeping of the great and good Mr. Richardson. Having been informed by Richardson as late as the autumn of 1749 that he had not yet read "Tom Jones," she knew how she ought to receive the book if she were to please her friend. So she wrote to him:

"As to Tom Jones, I am fatigued with the name, having lately fallen into the company of several young ladies, who had each a Tom Jones in some part of the world, for so they call their favourites; and ladies, you know, are for ever talking of their favourites. Last post I received a letter from a lady, who laments the loss of her Tom Jones; and from another, who was happy in the company of her Tom Jones. In like manner, the gentlemen have their Sophias. A few days ago, in a circle of gentlemen and ladies, who had their Tom Jones's and their Sophias, a friend of mine told me he must shew me his Sophia, the sweetest creature in the world, and immediately produced a Dutch mastiff puppy."

Lady Bradshaigh, however, was perplexed by Richardson's utter condemnation of a book that he had never read. Under date of December 16, 1749, she again wrote to him:

"I shall not say a word more toward persuading you to read Tom Jones, and beg pardon for having done it; but I meant not to compell; how could you insinuate such a thing. You really seem not only grave, but angry with me. Had you gone thro' it, your censure or praises would have had agreeable weight with me, as some things I approve, but disapprove many more. I should have been glad to have known how far my opinion corresponded with yours. . . . As to my pointing out the moralities which I think may be found in this work, I must beg to be excused; for as you think the piece not worth your perusal, I must think that a research is not worth my trouble, tho' I persist in thinking there are many good things in it."

It is not recorded what emotions were awakened in Richardson by this letter. Two months later Lady Bradshaigh came up to London, threw off the disguise of "Mrs. Belfour," and met the author of "Clarissa" under very romantic conditions. One day he remarked to her that an extraordinary compliment had just been paid to him by the author of "Charlotte Summers." Richardson referred, of course, to that comparison between himself and Fielding, but was careful not to mention his rival's name. From Reading on the way home, Lady Bradshaigh sent Richardson a letter containing a reference to the conversation: "When I saw you last, I forgot to tell you I had read Charlotte Summers; but I did not find any thing relating to you, like what you told me. I doubt I do not well remember what he says; but I think it is, that we are taught the art of *laughing* and *crying*, from your *melancholy* disposition, and Mr. Fielding's *gay* one; and I think passes a compliment upon each, though perhaps he might design to sneer. There are very different kinds of laughter; you make me laugh with pleasure; but I often laugh, and am angry at the same time with the facetious Mr. Fielding.''* So it was that a compliment intended rather for Fielding than for Richardson was turned by flattery into a sneer.

Always fearing to contaminate his own mind with "Tom Jones," Richardson likewise asked the daughters of Aaron Hill—Minerva and Astraea—to read the novel and give him their candid opinion of it. He expected that their comment would be most scathing, for they had wept, when little girls, over "Pamela," and had been taken by their father to see the great author. Richardson's request reached the young ladies in a little Essex village where the Hills resided. The father, though suffering from a violent colic, acknowledged the receipt of the letter, and said that had not good nature turned the girls into nurses, "they wou'd have obey'd you instantly, about *Tom Jones;* and they will certainly have sauciness enough to do it—being, of late, grown borrowing customers to an Itinerary Bookseller's Shop, that rumbles, once a week, through Plaistow in a wheelbarrow: with chaff enough, of conscience, and sometimes a weightier *grain* that now and then turns up among the heap, and looks like a temptation." From that strolling vendor Astraea and Minerva—and there was a Urania also—purchased their "Tom Jones." On July 27, 1749, the girls laid "their two wise heads together" and framed a reply to Mr. Richardson. Both Astraea and Minerva signed it, but it was written, Mr. Dobson says, by the fair hand of Astraea. As their father had predicted, it was a saucy letter. Although they felt at first, they said, some reluctance in opening a novel that had so coarse a title as "The Foundling," they quickly discovered "much (masqu'd) merit" in the six volumes, "both of head, and *heart,*" mingled, however, with "a bantering levity" in the treatment of serious matters. Mr. Richardson, they

---

* For the letters between Richardson and Lady Bradshaigh, see Barbauld, "Correspondence of Richardson," IV, 280, 309, and VI, 7.

thought, might find the novel not unworthy of perusal, if he had sufficient leisure for it. As the letter progressed, it became more and more difficult for them to maintain a just balance between praise and censure and to restrain their genuine delight. Near the close they declared in summary:

"It is an honest pleasure which we take in adding, that (exclusive of one wild, detach'd, and independent Story of a *Man of the Hill,* that neither brings on Anything, nor rose from Anything that went before it) All the changeful windings of the Author's Fancy carry on a course of regular Design; and end in an extremely moving Close, where Lives that seem'd to wander and run different ways, meet, All, in an instructive Center.

"The whole piece consists of an inventive Race of Disappointments and Recoveries. It excites Curiosity, and holds it watchful. It has just and pointed Satire; but it is a partial Satire, and confin'd too narrowly: It sacrifices to Authority, and Interest. Its *Events* reward Sincerity, and punish and expose Hypocrisy; shew Pity and Benevolence in amiable Lights, and Avarice and Brutality in very despicable ones. In every Part it has Humanity for its Intention: In too many, it *seems* wantoner than It was meant to be: It has bold shocking Pictures; and (I fear) not unresembling ones, in high Life, and in low. And (to conclude this too adventurous Guess-work, from a Pair of forward Baggages) would, every where, (we think,) *deserve* to please,—if stript of what the Author thought himself most sure to *please by.*"

The favourable impression which "Tom Jones" made upon Minerva and Astraea amazed Richardson. In his reply a week later, on the fourth of August, he half promised to give the novel a perusal since they recommend it, but in the meantime he would show them what kind of book they had admired and let them into the character of the author. The most piquant paragraph runs:

"I must confess, that I have been prejudiced by the Opinion of Several judicious Friends against the truly coarse-titled Tom Jones; and so have been discouraged from reading it.—I was told, that it was a rambling Collection of Waking Dreams, in which Probability was not observed: And that it had a very bad Tendency. And I had Reason to think that the Author intended for his Second View (His *first*, to fill his Pocket, by accommodating it to the reigning Taste) in writing it, to whiten a vicious character, and to make Morality bend to his Practices. What Reason had he to make his Tom illegitimate, in an Age where Keeping is become a Fashion? Why did he make him a common—What shall I call it? And a Kept Fellow, the Lowest of all Fellows, yet in Love with a Young Creature who was traping after him, a Fugitive from her Father's House?—Why did he draw his Heroine so fond, so foolish, and so insipid?—Indeed he has one Excuse—He knows not how to draw a delicate Woman—He has not been accustomed to such Company,—And is too prescribing, too impetuous, too immoral, I will venture to say, to take any other Byass than that a perverse and crooked Nature has given him; or Evil Habits, at least, have confirm'd in him. Do Men expect Grapes of Thorns, or Figs of Thistles? But, perhaps, I think the worse of the Piece because I know the Writer, and dislike his Principles both Public and Private, tho' I wish well to the *Man*, and Love Four worthy Sisters of his, with whom I am well acquainted. And indeed should admire him, did he make the Use of his Talents which I wish him to make, For the Vein of Humour, and Ridicule, which he is Master of, might, if properly turned, do great Service to the Cause of Virtue."

The poor girls, though crushed by the vehemence of Mr. Richardson, refused to be convinced against their will.

Unable to reply for themselves, they entrusted their pen to Aaron, who wrote to Richardson on August 11:

"Unfortunate *Tom Jones!* how sadly has he mortify'd Two sawcy Correspondents of your making! They are with me now: and bid me tell you, You have spoil'd 'em Both, for Criticks.—Shall I add, a Secret which they did not bid me tell you?—They, Both fairly *cry'd,* that You shou'd think it possible they cou'd approve of Any thing, in Any work, that had an *Evil Tendency,* in any Part or Purpose of it. They maintain their Point so far, however, as to be convinc'd they say, that *you* will disapprove this over-rigid Judgment of those Friends, who cou'd not find a Thread of Moral Meaning in Tom Jones, quite independent of the Levities they justly censure.—And, as soon as you have Time to read him, for yourself, 'tis there, pert Sluts, they will be bold enough to rest the Matter.—Meanwhile, they love and honour you and your opinions."*

There is more of the correspondence, but these extracts are enough. It was a comic situation. Richardson hesitated "to bestow a reading" on "Tom Jones" because it was a most immoral book written by "a very indelicate, a very impetuous" gentleman; and so, after failing with Lady Bradshaigh, asked two innocent girls to read it for him and tell him what they thought of it. They reported that it was a much better book than rumour had led them to anticipate; that it was in fact well planned, well executed, and just in its rewards and punishments. Whereupon Richardson, without having ever read the novel, informed these amateur critics that they were mistaken; that author and book were thoroughly corrupt. It would be a pertinent question to ask how Richardson, if he had never read "Tom Jones," knew its contents so well, how he knew, for

* For the Richardson-Hill correspondence, see the Forster Collection of MSS., Vol. XIII, in the South Kensington Museum, published in part in Dobson's "Henry Fielding," 1900, pp. 189-195.

example, that Sophia was "so fond, so foolish, and so insipid." Perhaps the question ought not to be pressed. Whatever the answer, we have here that kind of harmless hypocrisy which Fielding delighted to expose in all his novels.

Richardson's denunciation of "Tom Jones" was by no means confined to his correspondence with the Hills and Lady Bradshaigh. Over in Paris he had an admirer in J. B. Defreval, who supplied him with the first of the commendatory letters prefixed to the third edition of "Pamela." A year after the rumour that "Tom Jones" had met with disaster in Paris, Richardson casually inquired in the postscript of a letter to his friend whether it was true "that France had virtue enough to refuse a licence for such a profligate performance" and added: "Tom Jones is a dissolute book. Its run is over even with us." The reply, from which I have already quoted a phrase, could have brought little comfort to Richardson. So brief was the prohibition that M. Defreval had never heard of it. "I am sorry to say it," he wrote, "but you do my countrymen more honour than they truly deserve, in surmising that they had virtue enough to refuse a licence to *Tom Jones:* I think it a profligate performance upon your pronouncing it such, for I have never read the piece, though much extolled; but it has had a vast run here this good while, and considering how things go on, I don't believe there is now a book dissolute enough to be refused admittance among us."*

Of his correspondents, who had read the book, Richardson could find only one to agree in the utter condemnation of "Tom Jones." That was a certain Solomon Lowe known as the author of a "Critical Spelling Book" on new principles. Lowe, whose family had been captivated by "Clarissa Harlowe," wrote Mr. Richardson a brief letter

* Dobson, "Samuel Richardson," 1902, p. 129.

on July 10, 1749, inviting the author to favour him and his daughters with his company or to let them know when he would have a vacant hour to receive them at his own home. "The more critically your performance," he said of "Clarissa," "is considered, the more unexceptionable it appears, nay the brighter it shines. The fame of it (I find by Cave's magazine) is got into Holland; and I do not doubt but all Europe will ring of it: when a Cracker, that was some thousand hours a-composing, will no longer be heard or talkt-of."* With this opinion Richardson could find no fault. He carefully folded the letter, wrote on the back "Cracker, T. Jones," and laid it aside for posterity.

It is a long descent from Samuel Richardson, from Solomon Lowe even, to Bampfylde Moore Carew, who diverted the public at the expense of "Tom Jones." Moore, the son of a clergyman down in Devonshire, ran away, when a mere boy, from his school at Tiverton, and joined the gypsies, of whom many years later he was elected king, thereby becoming the head of all the mendicants and vagabonds in England. In 1745, he published an auto-biography—"The Life and Adventures of Bampfield Moore Carew"—believed to be in the main truthful, which was reissued with additions in the autumn of 1749, under the title of "An Apology for the Life of Mr. Bampfylde-Moore Carew, Commonly call'd The King of the Beggars." Carew, according to the narrative, was twice transported to the American colonies and traversed the Atlantic sea-board from Maryland to Massachusetts Bay. His book is a most interesting story of a clever swindler, valuable, too, for its comment on men and manners of all degrees at home and abroad. It is almost certain that Fielding had met this man who plied his trade vigorously at Bath and through the West. On one occasion, it is said, Carew got a half-crown from Ralph Allen by assuming the part of a

* Forster Collection, Vol. XV.

poor lunatic. As a former king of gypsies, the notorious vagabond resented the chapter in "Tom Jones" on his ancient and honourable order, and so rewrote a good part of his autobiography in order to draw a parallel, "after the manner of Plutarch, between Mr. Bampfylde-Moore Carew and Mr. Thomas Jones." Not that Carew himself actually held the pen; he had an "historiographer," to whom he told his story—one who could dress it out in the true Defoe style, thought to have been the wife of his publisher, Mr. Robert Goadby; but more likely the scribe was someone in the bookseller's employ. This so-called second edition of the "Apology," having no date on the title-page, appeared in the spring of 1750, as may be seen from an address to the reader dated February 10, and from many reviews of it during the summer. A dedication "To the Worshipful Henry Fielding, Esq." ridiculed the style of "Tom Jones" and Mr. Fielding's moral and literary opinions; a few pages at the end of the volume gave an epitome of the novel, purporting to be "The full and true History of Tom Jones, a Foundling; without Pattering," but more remarkable as a tissue of adroit misrepresentations. It is very amusing to see the greatest rascal in all England picking flaws in the conduct of Tom Jones.

And yet Carew was able to work out a plausible parallel between himself and Fielding's hero, for there are in the career of Tom Jones some traces of the rogue, which came over from the older picaresque novel. Nor was Carew without a degree of success in his many parodies on Fielding's style. No one needs to be told what passage he had in mind when he began his account of the death of Clause Patch, "the good old King of the Mendicants," with the apostrophe: "Reader, if thou hast ever seen that famous picture of Seneca, bleeding to death in the bath, with his friends and disciples standing round him; then mayst thou form some idea of this assembly." A good story was told, too, with reference to the gypsies described in "Tom Jones." While on the way to London, Tom and Partridge were overtaken at night by a storm and took refuge in a barn where a band of gypsies with their king were carousing. Carew declared that he was that king and well remembered the visit. As Mr. Fielding had said, he entertained his guests hospitably, had a pleasant conversation with them, and sent one of his men to guide them on the road to Coventry; but Mr. Fielding's report of that conversation and of a shameful incident which occurred during the evening were utterly false, and calculated to cast scandalous aspersions both upon himself and his subjects. Did Carew fabricate that scene as a jest? or did he and his mendicants on some occasion really give Fielding shelter from a storm while travelling in the West?

All the time "Old England" kept up a flow of Billingsgate against a "motely History of Bastardism, Fornication and Adultery." "Aretine" was uncertain whether the book deserved greater censure for its immorality than for its irreligion—for the scenes with Molly Seagrim, Mrs. Waters, and Lady Bellaston than for depicting Parson Supple as a fool and the Rev. Mr. Thwackum as a rascal. From the literary point of view, "Tom Jones" was declared to be beneath contempt. Readers whose hunger had been whetted by the first chapter, expected a feast, but instead of that they had been fed upon "whip-sillabub"— mere froth and air. Accordingly, if "Old England" at any time condescended to point out Mr. Fielding's many slips and blunders, the public should understand that it did so, not because the novel was worthy of "regular criticism," but because the world should know what a sorry performance it was. To this newspaper must be given the honour of calling attention to what has often been regarded—by Coleridge, for example,—as "a chorographic mistake" in the description of Allworthy's seat. The squire's mansion was situated on the southeast slope of a Somersetshire hill, from which one could see a river meandering for miles through woods and meadows until it emptied itself into the sea, "with a large arm of which, and an island beyond it, the prospect was closed." On this passage "Aretine" remarked triumphantly:

"To reconcile this Description with Probability will be the Difficulty; for, unlucky for our Author, the Counties of *Devon* and *Dorset* stretch out between *Somersetshire* and the sea; and if we place this Seat in the *North-West Part* of that Shire, the Hills of *Devon* will intercept the View to the Sea: And if we should imagine the Scite to be in the *South-East* Part of that County, then *Dorsetshire* interferes, with an Extent of Ground of no less than 30 Miles across to *Portland,* which, if the Author means any thing, must be the Island that terminates the Prospect. A most extensive Ken indeed! and shews the accurate Author endued with more than a *second-sighted* Mind."*

This ill-natured criticism, breaking the bounds of newspaper leaders, overflowed into a pamphlet entitled "An Examen of the History of Tom Jones, a Foundling. . . . In Two Letters to a Friend. Proper to be bound with the Foundling." Some of the advertisements in "Old England," beginning on December 9, 1749, added: "In which the bad morals, unnatural descriptions, inconsistencies, improbabilities, impertinent shew of learning, and false pretensions of wit, of that droll performance, are exploded. Designed to rescue true taste from the sophistry of the farcical author." The pamphleteer, who adopted the pseudonym of "Orbilius," the Roman grammarian, was probably a writer on the staff of "Old England." He repeated, sometimes quoting them, the blunders that "Aretine" had discovered in "Tom Jones," advertised his "Examen" in "Old England" along with the satires of

* "Old England," May 27, 1749.

"Porcupinus Pelagius," and surely had the hundred eyes of "Argus Centoculi." The man who thus multiplied himself was also, I daresay, the word-catcher that assisted Carew with the revision of his "Apology." We cannot certainly call him by name. Was he that Macnamara Morgan, to whom has been attributed "The Causidicade"? Or had another Porcupine stolen the pen of the old one?

Through more than a hundred pages, Orbilius took up "Tom Jones" chapter by chapter, finding or fabricating mistakes in every one of them and damning every character. If readers should observe, he remarked, a certain strangeness in his style, that was because he had decided to adopt Mr. Fielding's "elegant termination of *th* instead of *s*" in the third person singular of the auxiliary verbs *do* and *have;* though he would refrain from imitating, except in quotations, that author's pleonasms such as "the final end," for "the end" by itself seemed able to do the business. Whenever he hit upon a genuine slip, he was, of course, in glee. For example, Fielding apparently ascribed the proverb, "Evil communications corrupt good manners," to Solomon instead of St. Paul or Menander; whereupon Orbilius remarked, "Read your Bible, Mr. F. before you cite from it again." When Fielding despaired of making "shine" a scene which he would like to write and so omitted it, Orbilius told him that he could make this and all the dull passages in his book "shine" by casting them into the flames. At the end, however, the critic relented far enough to say: "Yet have I no personal pique against this gentleman; but admire some irregular touches of wit and morality, which, like the few fertile spots to be seen among the most barren parts of the Alps, may be found in travelling thro' his volumes."

A few months later, the humorous climax of censure was reached in "Old England." During the spring of 1750, London was visited by two earthquakes, which occurred just a month apart, on February 8 and March 8. Houses rocked, chairs shook, pewter rattled, chimneys tumbled, people ran into the streets, "the councillors in the Court of the King's Bench and Chancery in Westminster Hall were so alarmed that they expected the building to fall." While the inhabitants were in consternation, an astrologer predicted a third and worse earthquake for the fifth of April. Though the prophecy was not fulfilled, quivers continued at intervals far into the summer. The earthquakes were preceded and followed by terrific storms of wind and rain and hail; while at night the heavens throughout England were all illumined with the Aurora Borealis, and meteors exploded with dreadful detonations. At Fielding's old home in Salisbury was seen "an extraordinary phenomenon, being a very luminous collection of vapours, that formed an irregular arch, like rock work, and extended across the horizon, waving like flames issuing from fire. After a short continuance, it disappeared at once, the sky being very clear, and more enlightened than by the stars only." Some people tried to find humour in this turmoil of earth and heaven. Fashionable ladies in Westminster, we are told, "were so ludicrously profane as to send cards thus inscribed: 'I invite your ladyship to the earthquake on —— next.'" But when the night approached for the third earthquake, great numbers left their houses, walked in the fields, lay in boats, sat in their coaches, and thronged the roads as far as Windsor until daybreak came and the danger was over.

The strange occurrences were the theme of numerous pamphlets written in jest or in earnest. One of them was a letter from the devil, who congratulated the people of London on their conduct before and after the earthquakes; others explained the commotions in earth and air from natural causes; but most discerned in them the hand of the Almighty. In March, Thomas Sherlock, the Bishop of

London, came out with a "Pastoral Letter," calling the people to repentance, of which ten thousand copies were sold in two days and forty thousand were distributed to the poor. Inasmuch as the earthquakes were hardly felt outside London and Westminster, it was clear to the Bishop that the tremendous shocks had been directed by the immediate hand of God against "these two great cities" because of their infidelity, lewdness, and debauchery. And then, near the time the town was to be shaken by the third earthquake, "Old England" admonished the people to heed the voices of heaven ringing in their ears, to mend their ways, to cease from gaming and masquerades, and from all manner of loose and profane pleasures. What above all else had reduced London to a sink of abominations, declared Argus of the Hundred Eyes, was the reading of lewd books, especially one called "Tom Jones" which, to the shame of England, had been greedily devoured by everybody. On the other hand, it was intimated, Paris had preserved her morals by suppressing the novel, and so had escaped the earthquake and meteors. But in England, earthquakes still threatened; and night after night "streams of a dark-ruddy fire" continued to shoot from the heavens "in a menacing manner," with now and then "a mild gleam of light" higher up in the sky as a sign, perhaps, "of mercy after judgment." The conclusion was that the surest way to appease the wrath of the Almighty would be for Parliament to pass an Act prohibiting the sale of "Tom Jones" and all other books so clearly designed in cool and diabolical malice to corrupt the religion and morals of the nation.

And there was an equally humorous sequel. One of the wise men who forecast the third earthquake was a "crazy life-guardsman" named John Misavan. He belonged to Lord Delawar's troop of horse then stationed in London. Claiming that "the intelligence was communicated to him by an angel," Misavan warned the public that the most dreadful of all earthquakes would soon be upon them; that the Thames would wash away London Bridge, that Westminster Abbey would be laid level with the ground, that the earth would open in a great many places and swallow up numberless buildings and people. Alarmed by the impending disaster, men and women of all classes visited and questioned the prophet and came away still more frightened. "Certain persons of a great family having been to hear him, they were so terrified, that they sent to Mr. Whiston the astronomer, to know if it was possible for any man to foretell an earthquake; his answer was, that no man could without divine inspiration; but that in foreign countries, where earthquakes were more common, they seldom had two, but they had a third to succeed." Thereupon Fielding as the principal justice of the peace for London and Westminster intervened. On the night before the earthquake was to occur, he summoned John Misavan into court and committed him to Newgate "with strict orders to chain him down in one of the cells." Rarely in literary history has an author been able to get so complete control over a hostile critic, and thereby forestall an earthquake threatening his readers with destruction.*

* The story of the earthquake may be followed in "The Gentleman's Magazine" and "The London Magazine," March, April, May, June, 1750; and with greater detail in the newspapers of the year. Prof. J. E. Wells called my attention to two pamphlets dealing with the case of Misavan, of which one has the following title: "The False Prophet Detected: Being a particular Account of the Apprehending John Misavan. . . . With his whole Examination before the Worshipful Justice Fielding, and his Commitment on Wednesday Night to Newgate, with strict Orders to chain him down in one of the Cells, as a Warning to all Persons how they are guilty of such wicked and blasphemous Crimes."

157

CHAPTER XIX

THE ART OF TOM JONES

I

Regard "Tom Jones" as you will—from the standpoint of mere artifice, characters, or ethics—and it will turn out to be an innovation in the history of fiction, no less unexpected than the meteors and earthquakes that were let loose after its publication. Hitherto those novelists who had aimed at a portrait of contemporary manners had taken as the basis of their plots a story from real life, and embroidered it with fictitious details. Such, so far as one can divine it, had been the method of Defoe in "Moll Flanders" and even in "Robinson Crusoe." Such, too, was the method of Richardson in "Pamela." Twenty-five years before "Pamela" was written there had actually lived in England a Mrs. B., who had reformed and married a rake and was then living happily with him after all his villainous attempts to undo her. Exactly as in the novel, the girl had tried to drown herself in a pond as the only escape from the wiles of the young gentleman. Richardson let his imagination play upon this story and spun it into a novel of four volumes. As he possessed the dramatic sense lacking in Defoe, he was able to give to his narrative the form of bourgeois comedy. He took the drowning incident for his climax of distress, introduced, in the character of Mr. Williams, a foil to Mr. B., and eventually wrought the conversion of his hero by placing in his hands the journal of Pamela which laid bare all her suffering for virtue's sake. From the structural point of view, this dramatic manner was the novelty that Richardson at a stroke brought into fiction.

In his next novel, "Clarissa Harlowe," he did not go to fact directly for his story, but made such changes in the plot and characters of a "Pamela" as were necessary to turn it from a bourgeois comedy into a bourgeois tragedy. In the process of transformation, he left real life further and further behind him; never strong in the motivation of his characters, his art in this respect weakened with age until he had nothing to offer but portraits of ideal goodness and villainy—Clarissa, Lovelace, and that monstrous compound of all the Christian virtues, Sir Charles Grandison, who was the logical outcome of his method.

Fielding set about quite differently. In "Joseph Andrews" he adopted, as I have remarked in discussing that novel, a conventional type of dramatic structure as old as the Greek drama—what Aristotle called the procedure by "revolution and discovery"; but within that framework he put incidents and characters drawn from his own observation and sometimes from his most intimate experience; he kept close to men and women as he knew them, none of whom were without their weaknesses, and several of them were rogues. Rarely was there any idealizing. For this reason the characters depicted in "Joseph Andrews" were denounced by Richardson and others as "low." In reply to his critics, Fielding more than once admitted the truth of their strictures, but contended that, with here and there an exception, life *is* really "low," in the sense that few men are always governed by disinterested motives; that no writer can pursue a series of human actions and keep entirely clear of human frailties and vices. This cannot be gainsaid. It must, however, be admitted that the realistic aim in "Joseph Andrews"— Fielding knew it as well as his critics—was obscured by his parody of "Pamela" and his direct imitation of "Don Quixote." These secondary aims, which had led Fielding into exaggeration, burlesque, farce, and some horse-play, were mostly to disappear in "Tom Jones," a novel that was to present on a large scale the pure comedy of English life. In these essential aspects "Tom Jones" was to differ from "Joseph Andrews"; it was to be the fulfilment of that earlier design of a comic epic such as Homer might have written. The plot was to be artificial; but the characters were to be real men and women. Some account of Fielding's art at its maturity is the subject of this chapter.

Being a dramatist, Fielding could not conceive of a novel without an elaborate plot. Of itself the plot of "Tom Jones" was to him a source of amusement and just pride. In his assignment of the novel to Millar, he declared that the story had been "invented" as well as written by himself. Upon his plot, too, he depended for keeping his readers alert through six volumes. From the first they became interested in the mystery of Tom's parentage, and as they progressed, other mysteries rose one by one out of the narrative; and at last they were all cleared up by a succession of discoveries accomplished in perfect ease and with fine strokes of humour and social satire. It was almost as if one were present at the representation of a score of comedies, some pathetic, some burlesque, others possessing the gay wit of Vanbrugh or Congreve, and all united in a brilliant conclusion, where every character was rewarded in accordance with his deserts as Fielding understood them, except that the author was inclined to mercy rather than to strict justice in the case of hypocrites and villains. When the curtain was rung down, there was nothing left, in the language of the time, "for God Almighty and another world." The drama was all played out to the very end, where it exploded in a burst of mirth. Fielding's contemporaries had never seen anything so clever

off the stage. Lady Luxborough, to be sure, before she had
read the novel entire, thought the plan "far-fetched"; and
Richardson, who professed to have never read it at all,
pronounced it "a rambling collection of waking dreams";
but to Allan Ramsay the painter "Tom Jones" was above
all other novels "an artful story" and average readers,
like the daughters of Aaron Hill, were impressed by Mr.
Fielding's "regular design" whereby the lives of all the
characters, which had seemed to run in different ways,
were eventually brought together in an extremely moving
close." So Coleridge, who exclaimed: "What a master of
composition Fielding was! Upon my word, I think the
Oedipus Tyrannus, the Alchemist, and Tom Jones the three
most perfect plots ever planned."

If Coleridge's exclamation cannot be accepted at full
value, it is still true that "Tom Jones" has an excellent
plot. The wonder is, not that the practised hand of a
dramatist succeeded so well in the mere mechanism of his
novel, but that the mechanism, except occasionally in the
last volume, does not obtrude, that characters and incidents
are inseparable, the one appearing to determine the other.
This is all the more remarkable when we consider that
"Tom Jones" is, to a large extent, a novel of reminiscences
having as its motto, *Mores Hominum Multorum;* Fielding
called it "a history," meaning thereby that many of its
characters were drawn from real men and women, that
many of its incidents had come within his observation. Not,
of course, that each character had an exact original, nor
that every real incident occurred just as it is given in the
story, nor indeed that there was an absence of pure fiction.
To take thus the most interesting experiences of a lifetime
and adjust them, without the perversion of their essential
truth, to the requirements of a rather intricate plot, was an
artistic triumph of the first order. No one had ever done
that before in a novel.

THE HISTORY OF HENRY FIELDING

Obviously the course of a man's life is known in its entirety by no one except the man himself. He alone can tell of the people whom he meets, what they said and what occurred. The outsider must be content to pick up scraps of information here and there, and piece them together as best he can. It is therefore impossible to say just how far Fielding mixed fact with fiction in a novel that reads as if it were all true. Generalizations such as I have made in the preceding paragraphs on his procedure rest upon a partial, indeed a very fragmentary knowledge of his life. Still, enough of it is known to warrant them, if a biographer may infer the direction of the wind from the way in which a few straws blow.

Fielding himself, in the dedication to "Tom Jones" and elsewhere, encouraged the reader to identify Mr. Allworthy with Ralph Allen of Prior Park, and in another place emphasized the resemblance by drawing a sketch of his friend as an example of "the truly benevolent mind" which he designed to depict in the character. Allworthy's mind, he said in substance without mentioning the name, was but a copy of Allen's. True, he added that it was a copy of Lyttelton's and the Duke of Bedford's also; but the afterthought was by way of compliment; it was Allen's virtues that he wished to immortalize. Fielding, it should be observed, never quite asserted that Allworthy was a portrait of Allen; but when the novel was completed, the character displayed so many of his traits that it was everywhere regarded as such by persons who knew him. In Allworthy's kindliness, generous spirit, hospitality, and charities, they saw at once their friend at Prior Park.

It was a very close parallel when Fielding said of Allworthy: "Above all others, men of genius and learning shared the principal place in his favour; and in these he had much discernment: for though he had missed the advantage of a learned education, yet being blest with vast

natural abilities, he had so well profited by a vigorous,
though late application to letters, and by much conversation with men of eminence in this way, that he was himself
a very competent judge in most kinds of literature.'' Both
men possessed large wealth, both were agreeable in person,
of good constitution and solid understanding; both, for all
their intercourse with the world, were slow in detecting a
rogue, so ingenuous were their own characters; both were
benevolent to the point where benevolence becomes a weakness, having a comic aspect when imposed upon by ad-
venturers. Like many self-educated men of humble birth,
Allen acquired from books a stately and pompous manner
of speech, as if that were the style among the learned,
which Fielding consistently imitated, often with a touch
of quiet humour as in that long oration which Allworthy,
sitting up in bed, delivered to his family when he thought
he was going to die of a severe cold. And when Mr. Allworthy, on a morning in May, walked out on the terrace of
his mansion to view the rising sun and to thank God that
he had another day to devote to the welfare of the distressed, that was certainly Ralph Allen walking on the
terrace of Prior Park to enjoy the fresh air, ''the blue
firmament,'' and the distant view of Bath—the home of his
many benefactions.

And yet only a few details of Allen's life were made use
of in the plot of ''Tom Jones.'' Allen had no sister living
with him, took no pair of nephews into his family to rear,
and, after losing his wife, did not remain long a widower.
Fielding here dealt in correspondences rather than in
actual incidents; he amused himself by imagining how an
Allen, who received into his household all sorts of people,
would behave if they should happen to be Blifil, Tom Jones,
Square, Thwackum, and the rest of that motley company.
It may seem that Fielding went very far in giving him an
illegitimate nephew; but Allen was not over-nice on the

question of birth, for he had himself married for his first wife the natural daughter of General Wade. Taking incidents and traits of character together, Allworthy, then, appears as a shadowy counterpart of Allen—a likeness rather than a portrait.

In the same way, Allworthy's seat is not a reproduction of Prior Park. Allen's house was of the Corinthian order, while Allworthy's is Gothic. Fielding liked better the latter style; at least he chose it for his magnificent Palace of Death in his "Journey from this World to the Next"; and he must have heard much praise of Gothic architecture from Sanderson Miller, who was then adding Gothic turrets and windows to the old Tudor house at Radway. So either as an expression of his own preference or as a compliment to Miller, Fielding gave Allworthy a Gothic instead of a Grecian house in which to entertain his friends. Nor could Allen, standing on the terrace of Prior Park, have had that panoramic view described in the fourth chapter of "Tom Jones." There was, indeed, just as Fielding says, a spring near the top of the hill from which a stream flowed over cascades down to a lake in front of the house. The cascades and the lake Allen would see and also the Avon threading its way through the valley below; but he could not have seen either the Avon or any other river meandering for several miles "through an amazing variety of meadows and woods, till it emptied itself into the sea, with a large arm of which, and an island beyond it, the prospect was closed." Extensive as is the view from Prior Park, there is no sight of the sea; nor, near at hand, of "an old ruined abbey, grown over with ivy."

These discrepancies have puzzled critics ever since "Tom Jones" was written. The author of "An Examen," as well as "Old England," ridiculed the whole scene as impossible anywhere in Somersetshire. Coleridge wondered from what point of vantage Fielding saw a "ridge of wild mountains, the tops of which were above the clouds,'' and re-marked that the clouds must have been ''uncommonly low,''* for the so-called mountains of Somersetshire are only hills. Of later date, Thomas Keightley, who once made a study of the topography of ''Tom Jones,'' came to the conclusion that ''the real site of Allworthy's mansion'' was not Prior Park at all, but Sharpham Park near Glastonbury, the home of Fielding's grandfather.† Had Keightley visited Sharpham, he would have discovered that the manor house and the prospect in no wise correspond with the description of Allworthy's residence; but a walk of a few miles would have brought him to the very place which was in Fielding's mind. Had Keightley climbed Tor Hill, to the northeast of Glastonbury, the magnificent panorama for which he was searching would have opened full upon his view. On this elevation, some five hundred feet above the sea, surmounted by the lofty tower of St. Michael, he would have beheld near at hand, just as Fielding had done many times when a boy, the ruins of Glastonbury Abbey; on all sides he would have seen a landscape diversified by villages, hills, lawns, and woods; to the northwest the Mendip Hills, extending to Weston-super-Mare; to the westward the river Brue winding through distant meadows until it joins the Parret, the Quantock Hills with clouds trailing over them, and, if the day were clear, a wide sweep of the Bristol Channel, islands, and shipping even. It was Stert Island in Bridgewater Bay that closed the prospect, a short distance beyond where the united waters of the Brue and the Parret find their home.‡ There on the slope of Tor Hill, Fielding placed the mansion of Squire Allworthy, giving it the Gothic

* MSS. notes to his copy of ''Tom Jones'' in the British Museum, I, iv.

† Keightley, ''Life and Writings of Fielding,'' edited by Dickson, Cleveland, 1907, p. 88.

‡ For the scene, see W. Phelps, ''Somersetshire,'' I, 493.

style of Radway Grange and introducing into the foreground the artificial cascades and lake of Prior Park. No detail of the composite scene appears to have been fictitious.

In marked contrast with this scene, Fielding did not describe the habitation of Squire Western at all. He merely says that his manor was contiguous to Mr. Allworthy's estate, and that the two seats were upwards of three miles apart, a distance which Tom could run in less than half an hour. The two families pass to and fro—walk or ride—but never a word escapes from Fielding in the way of definite description. It would, therefore, seem as if Fielding wished to conceal the identity of his Jacobite squire, a character that he knew would be resented by his political opponents; and he succeeded so well that no one has ever quite found out the original of this gentleman who went to bed drunk every night. A tradition says that he was Sir Paulet St. John—"a downright country squire," who was created a baronet in 1772, and died in 1780 at the age of seventy-six. The story got into print, a century ago, in an obituary notice of a grandson, Sir Henry P. St. John, who took the name of Mildmay on acquiring by marriage the estates of that family.* Assuming that there was a Squire Western in the St. John or the Mildmay family, it is likely that Fielding also had in mind Carew Hervey Mildmay, who died without male issue in 1784 at the age of ninety-four. Like Squire Western, he was a Tory; he sat in Parliament for Harwich back in Queen Anne's reign, was secretary to Lord Bolingbroke for a time, and a friend of Pope's. Loud-mouthed and blatant, Horace Walpole called him "Old Mildmay, whose lungs and memory and tongue will never wear out." It is said that he did not forget his gun when he came up to

* "Notes and Queries," 11 S. VI, 470 (Dec. 14, 1912). See also W. Phelps, "Somersetshire," I, 435, and J. Collinson, "Somerset," II, 75, and III, 446.

London, and once shot a woodcock near Regent Street, then in the fields. Mildmay had two estates—one at Queen-Camel, some thirteen miles from East Stour where Fielding used to hunt, and the other at Low Ham, a scant eight miles from Glastonbury. Fielding could hardly have missed an acquaintance with him, though it is of course another question whether Squire Mildmay really sat by the side of Sir Paulet St. John for the portrait of Squire Western.

By a better tradition Salisbury can claim a whole group of characters. The inn at Salisbury where "the great Dowdy" frightened strangers by playing the part of a ghost or a madman, rattling his chains and humming a catch along the gallery, was quickly localized by readers in the town. It was "The Three Lions," afterwards called "The Three Golden Lions," on the corner of Winchester Street and the Market, long since displaced by a bank. The landlord was a William Hooper, while the performer is said to have been one of the three sergeants at mace; that is, a minor officer of the Corporation who had the honour of carrying a mace in the Mayor's procession. If this be so, Fielding gave him a fictitious name; for, though Doughty (which Fielding rendered "Dowdy") has long been a common name in the town, it was borne by no city official in Fielding's time. The three sergeants at mace from 1734 to 1762 were Samuel Smith, Daniel Pearce, and Thomas Biddlecombe, of whom the last figures most in the Corporation Records,* and enjoyed the longest service. But according to "The Salisbury Journal" for January 18, 1762, Pearce was the merry ghost. Again, Dowling, the

---

* Minutes of the Corporation, examined by Mr. Thomas H. Baker of Salisbury, July, 1911. The Salisbury traditions in general are given by H. Hatcher in "Old and New Sarum, or Salisbury," 1843, p. 602, quoted in "Notes and Queries," 3 S. V, 385-386 (May 7, 1864). Mr. J. Paul de Castro throws unnecessary doubt on the Salisbury traditions ("Notes and Queries," 12 S. III, 466-467, Nov., 1917).

dishonest lawyer, who received the last message of Mrs. Blifil as she lay dying of the gout at Salisbury, was identified with a lawyer named Stillingfleet. To go a step further, he was probably the Robert Stillingfleet to whom Fielding conveyed his property at East Stour on its way to Peter Walter, another scoundrel. The land-agent of Peter Walter thus became the legal adviser to young Blifil. Fielding knew where to go for his villains—back in the memories of his life at East Stour and Salisbury.

He also found at Salisbury, says the same tradition, the two scholars—the one a divine, the other a deist—whom Allworthy took into his household for the instruction of his nephews Tom and Blifil, on the liberal principle that the doctrine of the Christian church should be supplemented by the most recent contributions of philosophy. Thwackum who held par excellence the post of tutor was drawn, it has been asserted by local antiquaries, from Richard Hele, master of the school in the Cathedral Close. Hele, a graduate of Balliol College, Oxford, was a small pluralist holding at the time of his death the vicarage of Britford near Salisbury and a prebendary's stall in the Cathedral besides the mastership in the school which he presided over for a half-century. In 1727, he received the degree of Master of Arts from King's College, Cambridge. He died in 1756 at the age of seventy-seven. A mural tablet, erected to his memory in the Cathedral, describes him as upright and diligent (*integer* and *sedulus*) in his calling both as a priest and as a schoolmaster. Not much more is known of Richard Hele; but perhaps the virtues recorded in his monument suggest some of those humorous infirmities embodied in Thwackum: a zeal for learning that made necessary the habitual use of the birch, in accordance with the formula, "Castigo te non quod odio habeam, sed quod amem," a zeal for the established church that led him to declare in all religious disputes: "When I mention religion, I mean the Christian religion; and not only the Christian religion, but the Protestant religion; and not only the Protestant religion, but the Church of England."

With Thwackum's hot disputant, one can be more definite. Square's original was Thomas Chubb, a native like Hele of Salisbury, where he kept a tallow-chandler's shop, but employed his leisure in theological studies, from which he emerged as a deist, though not an unqualified one. His death occurred two years before the appearance of "Tom Jones." To his many tracts, which display an elevation of mind, Fielding was considerably indebted. Chubb's "Reflections on Virtue and Happiness," for example, anticipated, at least, the best things that Fielding ever said on "the benevolent temper" as illustrated in the remarks and character of Allworthy. Nevertheless his lack of scholarship and training in the schools exposed him to easy ridicule; one could but smile at titles like "A Vindication of God's Moral Character." He had, too, a "darling phrase," which popped up on all occasions. It appeared, for instance, in his definition of reason as "that *reflecting power* of the mind, by which we are enabled to discern and judge of the fitness or unfitness, of the agreement or disagreement, of the good or evil, and of the truth or falshood of things." So whether an act were good or bad, he repeated many times over, was dependent upon whether "it was *consistent* with, or *repugnant* to the *nature* or *truth* of things."* No one need be told that Fielding parodied the phrase in the formula by which Square measured "true honour and true virtue"; to wit, by "the unalterable Rule of Right and the eternal Fitness of Things." Though Chubb, in contrast with Square, was a man of blameless character, the two philosophers were equally disputatious. This is evident from Chubb's many controversies with

* See Chubb's "Treatises," 1730, p. 366, and elsewhere.

eminent divines and from the fact that he formed a club at Salisbury for the discussion of his favourite doctrines. Did Fielding while living in Salisbury sometimes attend the meetings of the club? Did he actually witness a passage at arms between Chubb and Hele? These are questions to be asked, though they cannot be definitely answered. It is most probable, however, that Fielding was present on more than one occasion.

Concerning Sophia Western, Fielding left no doubt. This charming girl he meant as a portrait of Charlotte Cradock as she was when he first saw her in the freshness of youth and beauty at Salisbury—where he danced with her, addressed verses to her, and in the end fell upon his knees. Twice in "Tom Jones" he made the identification complete. Sophia, he declared on her entrance into the novel, was "a copy from nature," as lovely as the Venus of Medici, lovelier by far—and here there is a touch of irony—than all the beauties whose portraits hang in the galleries of Hampton Court or all the toasts of the Kit-Cat; "most like," if there must be a comparison, "the picture of Lady Ranelagh; and I have heard more still to the famous Dutchess of Mazarine; but most of all, she resembled one whose image never can depart from my breast, and whom, if thou dost remember, thou hast then, my friend, an adequate idea of Sophia." And when the portrait was nearly finished, he told the reader that all the worth which he had ascribed to Sophia "once existed in my Charlotte." In both of them, Fielding would have us believe, were the same constancy and devotion, in both the same intense passion combined with good sense, the same sweet but firm insistence that they be free to heed the promptings of a heart that never betrayed them.

And there is Tom Jones himself, who likewise reflects Harry Fielding as he was in his impetuous youth, when he tried to run away with Sarah Andrew and perhaps did

Ortance Manzini Duchesse de Mazarin *etc.*

P. Lely pinx. N? Vischer excudit A. De Blois fecit.

The Duchess of Mazarine

actually elope with Charlotte Cradock. Like Fielding, Jones was blessed with a fine, frank, open face, though the author did not give him his own features, nor his own herculean frame. The "large calves" and "broad shoulders" which enter into Thackeray's description of Jones, are imaginary. Fielding rose above six feet, while Tom, it is to be inferred, was several inches shorter. When the lad enlisted as a volunteer, the sergeant, contrasting him with another recruit, who was "near six feet, well-proportioned, and strongly limbed," reported to the commanding officer that Jones "would do well enough for the rear rank." As represented in the art of the period, Tom was a comely boy, five feet eight or nine inches in height, quite overshadowed by Partridge or Black George towering above him. That was the correct conception of the boy's appearance. His temper, like Fielding's, was generous, humane, and brave; and he had a high sense of honour. As a boy, he might on occasion lie, but that, so far as we know of it, was always to shield another, never to conceal his own acts. He was gay and good-humoured, wild and reckless in conduct and conversation. His vices, such as they were, never flowed from villainy, but from the animal within him; they might all be resolved into a want of foresight or of due thought of consequences. He was a strong anti-Jacobite and zealous in the cause of Protestantism. His career, however, must not be regarded as the autobiography of young Harry Fielding, despite the fact that certain episodes in it have often been given a personal application. It is in their general character, not in the details of their conduct, that the two boys most resemble each other.

Finally there is Lady Bellaston, with whom gossip associated Lady Townshend (Etheldreda Harrison, wife of Charles Lord Viscount Townshend), a woman of great wit and beauty but of notorious character. Lady Townshend was the mistress of Thomas Winnington, the second-rate minister whose political career Fielding had defended in a pamphlet; and she afterwards figured as Lady Tempest in Francis Coventry's "Pompey the Little," a novel dedicated to Fielding and actually ascribed to him by Lady Luxborough. These facts bring Lady Townshend within Fielding's observation, but not within his personal acquaintance. It is improbable that he ever spoke a word with her. This not uncommon type of woman he needed if he was to "ragoo" the life of the town, and he took her. If he had Lady Townshend in mind, her intrigue with Winnington was no more to him than were other similar alliances which gave piquancy to the scandal spread abroad in letters and conversation everywhere.

Lady Townshend nearly ends the list of the partial portraits that were known or suspected in "Tom Jones" within a reasonable time after the publication of the novel. The only additions were the gypsies, probably as a jest, and the Man of the Hill, who, Fielding says, was born in 1657 at Mark, a village nine miles to the northwest of Glastonbury. Numerous as are the identified models, they are few in comparison with the total number of characters in the novel, which, counting those merely mentioned as well as those that actually appear, falls little short of two hundred. All that swarming host, I believe, came directly out of Fielding's memories. Under fictitious names, or no names at all if the author could not recall them, still exist in "Tom Jones," the circumstances of their lives altered at will, men and women whom Fielding knew or heard of in London and the West. This conclusion receives support from the remark which Fielding made to Mrs. Hussey, the mantua-maker in the Strand, to whom he is reported to have said that he intended to introduce into "Tom Jones" "the characters of all his friends." Had he aimed at a complete statement, he would have added that many persons whom he disliked might be found there also.

Of his friends and acquaintances, some bear their real names. The men and women thus honoured, however, do not enter largely into the story; and in most cases, they pass in review for a compliment merely. Pitt, it is said, had transfused the whole spirit of Demosthenes and Cicero into his speeches; Sophia Western, could she have had her own way, would never have played any pieces but Handel's; Warburton held the key to the treasures of ancient learning; and the "great reputation" of Bishop Hoadly was not forgotten. Fielding did not mention by name his sister Sarah; but the book that Sophia was reading in her chamber, when interrupted by her aunt, was evidently "David Simple"—"the production of a young lady of fashion, whose good understanding," Sophia thought, "doth honour to her sex, and whose good heart is an honour to human nature." Sophia's mistake in calling the author "a lady of fashion" was quickly corrected by Mrs. Western, who remarked that she was indeed "of a very good family" but not seen much "among people one knows." It was Lord Hardwicke, the friend of Sanderson Miller, that Fielding had in mind when he paid a tribute to "The Lord High Chancellor of this Kingdom in his Court"; where conscience "presides, governs, directs, judges, acquits, and condemns according to merit and justice; with a knowledge which nothing escapes, a penetration which nothing can deceive, and an integrity which nothing can corrupt."

Esher, where "the days are too short for the ravished imagination," was the seat of Henry Pelham in Surrey. The London surgeon whose name the Man of the Hill had forgotten, though he remembered that it began with an R, was John Ranby, principal Sergeant-Surgeon to the King and Fielding's own physician—a man having "the first character in his profession," besides being "a very generous, good-natured man, and ready to do any service to his fellow-creatures." And so the compliments were meted out down to actresses like Mrs. Cibber and Kitty Clive (who were accorded a footnote); Philip Francis, whose version of Horace was several times quoted; Nathaniel Hooke, the Duchess of Marlborough's scribe and author of the Roman history; and the ingenious Philip Miller, sometime foreman of the Botanical Gardens at Chelsea and author of "The Gardener's Dictionary," who, however accurately he might describe a plant, advised his readers, if they would know anything about it, to look at it while growing in the garden.

The philosopher Square, when he went to Bath to drink the waters, consulted Dr. Brewster and Dr. Harrington, who told him that he was past hope of recovery and must prepare in haste for another world. These two well-known physicians were subscribers to Fielding's "Miscellanies." While at Bath, too, Beau Nash took Harriet aside and warned her against the attentions of Fitzpatrick; and the coach that conveyed her and her maid to Upton belonged "to Mr. King of Bath, one of the worthiest and honestest men that ever dealt in horse-flesh, and whose coaches we heartily recommend to all our readers who travel that road." The "Justice Willoughby of Noyle, a very worthy good gentleman," who committed a horse thief taken at the Hindon fair, was one of the Willoughbys of West Knoyle in Wiltshire, presumably the Richard Willoughby, Esq., who put down his name for a copy of the "Miscellanies."* West Knoyle and Hindon were but a few miles to the north of Fielding's former estate at East Stour, in the neighbourhood of which he had known, I daresay, a Jemmy Tweedle who played his fiddle at wakes and fairs, the Misses Potter whose father ran the Red Lion, and the rest of those country

* R. C. Hoare, "The Modern History of Wiltshire," 1822, I, 41.

girls with their lovers, including a Molly Seagrim. On his travels Jones put up at the Bell Inn in Gloucester, kept by a brother of "the great preacher Whitefield," where indeed this leader of the early Methodists was born. Fielding, as will become apparent, had stayed many times at that hostelry, and liked both the master and his wife. On no other minor characters in "Tom Jones" did he dwell with so pleasant recollections. Mr. Whitefield, who was "absolutely untainted with the pernicious principles" of his brother, he regarded as "a very honest plain man . . . not likely to create any disturbance in church or state"; while his wife was in person "a very fine woman, . . . who might have made a shining figure in the politest assemblies." On the recommendation of her husband's brother, she had tried Methodism for three weeks; but having experienced during that time no "extraordinary emotions of the spirit," she wisely decided to abandon the sect, and to give her attention to the comfort of her guests, all of whom were "extremely well satisfied in her house."

The way Fielding brought in his two peers, the painter and the player of the age, was superb. Three of his characters, he said, had already sat for Hogarth, and he wished that he could borrow his friend's pencil to make them appear as lifelike in his own pages. Anyone, however, who was curious to know just how they looked, might view them in Mr. Hogarth's prints. Thwackum was the gentleman in the Harlot's Progress seen correcting the ladies in Bridewell; Mrs. Partridge "exactly resembled" that masculine woman of the preceding plate, pouring tea in a mean London lodging just as a magistrate enters; and Bridget Allworthy was the withered lady of a Winter's Morning "walking (for walk she doth in the print) to Covent-Garden church, with a starved foot-boy behind carrying her prayer-book." And when Fielding got Partridge to London, he took him, with Jones and Mrs. Miller, to the theatre to see Garrick in Hamlet, Prince of Denmark; and thereby left, in the comment of the country schoolmaster, the most graphic account that has come down to us of a performance by the actor whom the town thought "the best player who was ever on the stage." To this opinion, repeated by Mrs. Miller, Partridge retorted with a sneer of contempt: "He the best player! . . . Why I could act as well as he myself. I am sure if I had seen a ghost, I should have looked in the very same manner, and done just as he did. And then, to be sure, in that scene, as you called it, between him and his mother, where you told me he acted so fine, why, Lord help me, any man, that is, any good man, that had had such a mother, would have done exactly the same. I know you are only joking with me; but, indeed, madam, though I was never at a play in London, yet I have seen acting before in the country; and the King for my money; he speaks all his words distinctly, half as loud again as the other.—Any body may see he is an actor." This wonderful scene, which began as a gentle parody on Sir Roger de Coverley's visit to the theatre when "The Distrest Mother" first appeared, was thus turned to the most convincing praise of the ease and naturalness with which Garrick played his parts.

What Garrick was in acting, what Hogarth was in painting, Fielding aimed to be in the novel. Though there might be a heightening of characteristics, restrained burlesque even, all must rest upon human nature as it is; all characters, all incidents, whatever the recombinations, must be in harmony with the real world as one observes it. By necessity, this view of art resulted in a large number of characters not far removed from actual portraits; and the occasional use of real names known to everybody lent to the narrative the atmosphere of biography rather than fiction. It was a marvellous art.

THE ART OF TOM JONES

II

The ease with which the story flowed from Fielding's pen—"commencing strikingly, proceeding naturally, ending happily"—was likened by Sir Walter Scott to "the course of a famed river, which gushes from the mouth of some obscure and romantic grotto—then gliding on, never pausing, never precipitating its course; visiting, as it were, by natural instinct, whatever worthy subjects of interest are presented by the country through which it passes— widening and deepening in interest as it flows on; and at length arriving at the final catastrophe as at some mighty haven, where ships of all kinds strike sail and yard."* Beginning with Allworthy, the novelist introduced, never before he needed them, one member after another of the squire's household until it was complete. After Allworthy came his sister Bridget, a spinster "somewhat passed the age of thirty," her elderly housekeeper Deborah Wilkins, and the foundling, whom the squire discovered one night asleep in his bed as he was preparing to step in after he had said his prayers—supposed to have been placed there by Jenny Jones, a trollop (so his sister and Deborah called her) of the neighbourhood, who had visited the house the day before. Among the guests at the good man's table were two brothers named Blifil,—the one a doctor, the other a captain on half pay,—of whom the latter, a young man thirty-five years old and a great master of the art of love, succeeded in winning the reluctant Bridget for a wife. Eight months after the marriage was born their only child, the Master Blifil of the story. A mile away was the habitation of George Seagrim the gamekeeper, known as "Black George" because of his large black beard; and fifteen miles distant—at "Little Baddington," that is, Little Badminton, perhaps—lived Partridge the schoolmaster, whose wife had learned to cook in Allworthy's kitchen. In the opinion

* "Introductory Epistle" to "The Fortunes of Nigel."

of the district, this Partridge was the father of Tom Jones, for Jenny Jones had been a servant in the schoolmaster's family, and an apt pupil in the Latin language under his instruction. Mr. Allworthy, overlooking in his good nature the accident of birth, resolved to give Tom and Master Blifil the same education as if both were his legitimate nephews, and so installed for the purpose those strange gentlemen, Thwackum and Square.

The adjoining manor belonged, as we have related, to Squire Western, whose beautiful daughter was two years younger than Tom. Her mother dying when the girl was only eleven years old, Sophia had fallen to the care of her nurse Mrs. Honour and her maiden aunt Mrs. Western, a woman who prided herself on a complete knowledge of the world. The two families, antagonistic in their politics, were brought closely together by Tom's poaching with Black George on Squire Western's preserves, which led to the gamekeeper's dismissal, but interfered in no way with a growing intimacy between Tom and Western, for Tom was a sportsman after the squire's heart, never stopping for ditches and barred gates in pursuit of the hare. As Tom grew older, he spent much of his time at Western's house, where he fell desperately in love with Sophia; and she returned the passion in all its intensity. But for the boy's uncertain parentage, there would have been no question about a speedy marriage. The alternative was to force Sophia to marry Master Blifil, by which means the two estates—Allworthy having no children—could be as surely united. But of all young men whom she had ever seen, Sophia hated Blifil the most. It was a situation very common in English life—the struggle between parental authority and the love of those whose happiness is most concerned.

To lay these foundations required nearly a third of the novel. Infants had to grow up—Tom, Blifil, and Sophia—

to the ages of twenty-one, twenty, and nineteen respectively before the main action could begin. Their education had to be explained, and their traits of character unfolded. Thwackum and Square, though they were still to come in for the close, had to be unmasked; and Captain Blifil was destined to die early of apoplexy while taking a walk through the grounds of Squire Allworthy which he expected would soon be his. Likewise Tom's mother, if she were not really a trollop, had to be removed. Finally, Tom himself must have an intrigue with Molly Seagrim, the gamekeeper's daughter; he must thrash Thwackum, and for his escapades be banished forever from Allworthy's sight. All this part of the novel was cast in plain and direct narrative, varied by conversation, in the manner of the epic; but towards the end of the sixth book Fielding rather abruptly shifted to the dramatic manner, his mind bent upon working out a situation which he had explained in great detail. For this purpose he now turned his characters out into the open air, on roads which were eventually to bring them to London, where the action could be terminated with striking contrasts of incident and character.

This procedure was similar to that in ''Joseph Andrews,'' the scenes of which were laid on the highway between London and Salisbury, with an extension farther westward to East Stour. The background of roads in ''Tom Jones,'' until one reaches the main route from Coventry to London, is less obvious, and has perplexed all commentators except Keightley, who suggested, though he could not quite make it out, that Fielding had in mind for his earlier stages the road from Glastonbury or Sharpham Park northward to Hagley Park, Lyttelton's seat in Worcestershire. Keightley's surmise was in the main right. That road Fielding must have traversed many times when, after riding the Western Circuit, he paid a visit to his friend; indeed it may have been in part the road that he took when, during the composition of "Tom Jones," he went to Hagley and thence to Radway to read the manuscript to Lyttelton, Pitt, and Sanderson Miller. Here again we see in another aspect the realism of Fielding's art. Just as he developed his characters from people whom he knew, so when he sent them on a journey he put them into roads with which he was perfectly familiar. The names of their halting-places he sometimes gave and sometimes suppressed in order that the identification might not be complete. Such in his view was fiction as distinguished from fact.

When Tom Jones was dismissed by Squire Allworthy with five hundred pounds to shift for himself, he walked "above a mile," not knowing in his distraction whither he went, until he came to a brook, where he threw himself down in despair and lost the pocket-book containing the little fortune with which he was to make his start in the world. That purse was shortly found by Black George, who, after playing with his conscience, decided to keep it. Thence Jones proceeded to "a house not far-off" for materials to write a farewell letter to Sophia; and then, having met Black George at the brook whither he had returned to search for the purse, he went on half a mile further to an alehouse to await a reply. He duly received, not a reply, but a passionate note which Sophia had written earlier that morning. The same day he reached "a town about five miles distant," where Black George overtook him with a purse of sixteen guineas from Sophia, being all the ready money she had in her possession, and where the next morning a messenger delivered to him all his effects left behind, and a letter from Blifil saying that no reconciliation with Allworthy was possible and that he must immediately leave the country. That unnamed town was doubtless Wells, five or six miles from Glastonbury, near which Fielding placed the seat of Allworthy.

Certain that he could never regain the favour of All-worthy, Jones "determined to seek his fortune at sea"; and with this intent, he set out with horses for Bristol; but his careless guide got on the Gloucester road, which brought them towards dark to Hambrook, a village five miles to the northeast of Bristol and, as the landlord of the public house where they put up said, about "thirty miles" from Squire Allworthy's. At Hambrook, Jones encountered a company of soldiers on the way north to reinforce the army of the Duke of Cumberland against the Highlanders, and was easily persuaded by the sergeant to join them as a volunteer instead of going to sea. The next morning he accordingly marched off with his new companions a day's journey to their halting-place for the night at a nameless inn—probably at Cambridge, a village having an inn—on the Gloucester road. There Jones had a quarrel with Ensign Northerton, from whom he received a broken head, which was patched up by the barber-surgeon of the place—none other, it turned out, than Partridge, who had finally settled in the village after the disgrace of being the reputed father of Tom. Owing to his wound, Jones was left behind by the soldiers, on the understanding that he would endeavour to overtake them at Worcester. The old schoolmaster became quickly attached to Jones and insisted, though a Jacobite, on attending him to the wars, if he could not be persuaded to return home. Thenceforth the two travellers were inseparable like Joseph Andrews and Parson Adams in the earlier novel.

After a day's rest, Jones and his companion walked on to Gloucester, where they arrived in time for dinner with Mr. Whitefield at the sign of the Bell; and thence, just as the clock struck five, set forward at a rapid pace towards Worcester under the light of a full moon; but when some miles out of Gloucester, Jones insisted that they take a road to the left (when they should have kept to the right), for he saw directly ahead on the left hills which he had been told lay not far from Worcester. The road which they turned into by mistake was probably the Ledbury road, along which they would have seen in the moonlight the distant Malvern Hills. Late at night they came to the foot of "a very steep hill," and saw through the trees a glimmering light, which guided them to the habitation of the Man of the Hill. Jones won the favour of the old recluse by driving off a band of robbers, and sat up with him till daybreak to hear the story of a life of disillusion, which was ending in complete retirement from the world. In the morning they climbed the hill, "where one of the most noble prospects in the world presented itself to their view." Looking towards the south, Jones could trace his whole journey from Gloucester. On that morning the hero again showed his prowess by rescuing a Mrs. Waters from Ensign Northerton, who, travelling with her from Worcester to Bath, enticed her to the woody slopes of this lonely place that he might strip her of all valuables. This Mrs. Waters proved to be, by a later discovery, the former Jenny Jones, who, like Partridge, had long ago fled from home to escape the dishonour of bringing Tom into the world.

The scene of these encounters, which Fielding called "Mazard Hill," has never been determined. I do not think, however, that the hill is quite imaginary. "The nearest town," the Man of the Hill told Jones, "was Upton-on-Severn." It has been conjectured that Fielding was thinking of Bredon Hill, from which indeed Tom might have had that extensive prospect; but Bredon lies far to the east across the Avon; whereas "Mazard" should be a few miles to the southwest of Upton. To the westward the view from this beautiful town is closed by the long line of the famous Malvern Hills, appearing in some lights to be one continuous hill. So they looked to Partridge the next day when he cast a glance to "yon high hill," which his imagination peopled with ghosts and the devil. To suit the narrative, it must have been one of the southern and lower summits that Tom climbed, not far from Little Malvern. In perfect harmony with his custom, Fielding called the hill "Mazard" because its crest resembled a mazard or bowl, and then gave it a philosophic recluse in place of the legendary hermits with which Malvern story abounds.

Taking under his protection Mrs. Waters, whose identity as yet remained a secret, Jones escorted the lady to Upton and went directly to "that inn which, in their eyes, presented the fairest appearance to the street," where they had dinner and tea and remained overnight. The honour of entertaining these guests is claimed for the White Lion, then as now the chief hostelry in the town.* This inn was the scene of the ludicrous battle between Jones, Partridge, and Mrs. Waters on the one side, and the landlord, land-lady, and Susan the chambermaid on the other. But adventures more material to the plot also occurred there before morning. Mrs. Fitzpatrick, a niece of Squire Western, stopped at the inn for rest and horses in her flight from her husband; and though he came up at midnight, she managed to get away before he discovered her. That night, too, Jones fell a victim to the charms of Mrs. Waters. And to look backwards, within a week after Allworthy turned Jones away, and as the day was almost at hand for the marriage of Sophia and Blifil, the distracted girl stole at night from her father's house, with the intention of seeking refuge with Lady Bellaston, a relative living in London; but learning from her guide on the way to Bristol, the same one that her lover had employed, that Tom had gone north by way of Hambrook, she set forward in hot haste on his

---

* For this and other local traditions, see "A New Pictorial and Descriptive Guide to Malvern," London, n. d.

track, and reached Upton very late on the night he stayed there with Mrs. Waters. Being informed by her maid Mrs. Honour how matters stood, she bribed Susan to place her muff, with her name on a piece of paper pinned to it, in Tom's empty bed, and before daybreak left for London, followed by Mrs. Fitzpatrick. Across the Severn, Mrs. Fitzpatrick overtook her, and the two ladies, recognizing each other, rode onward side by side. Two hours after they had gone, arrived Squire Western with his loud halloo, who joined in a neighbouring fox-hunt, and was soon prevailed upon to return home. On the discovery of the muff, Jones forgot Mrs. Waters, forgot the wars and the sea, and, unable to obtain horses, hastened forward on foot with Partridge "in quest of his lovely Sophia, whom he now resolved never more to abandon the pursuit of."

Besides the advantage of horses, Sophia had a start of nearly three hours ahead of Tom. She and Mrs. Fitzpatrick, riding at a good pace, arrived that morning at "a promising inn" on the London road, six miles from Coventry, and, utterly exhausted, slept through the rest of the day. Well they might have been tired out, for they had ridden above forty miles at a gallop in the course of a scant seven hours, and Sophia had had no sleep for two nights. Though Fielding gives few details of that hard ride, it is clear that some fifteen miles northeast of Upton the ladies struck into a cross-road running between the counties of Worcester and Warwick, over which, eastward and northward, was their main course until they reached the post-road from Chester to London; and then, turning to the right, they had a short stretch along this "wide and well-beaten road" to their inn. In the evening, they met there an unnamed Irish peer, a friend of Mrs. Fitzpatrick, who like themselves was on the way to London, and offered to take them up in his coach and six. Without doubt this meeting-place was Meriden,* a pleasant village, with a green and a church on the hill, exactly six miles to the northwest of Coventry, and a mile from the point where Sophia turned into the London road. It was on the direct route of the Irish peer from Holyhead and Chester; it was also on the route that Fielding would likely have taken from Hagley Hall to Radway Grange on to London. The inn where the author, as well as his characters, may have spent a night more than once, was called the Bull's Head, "a celebrated sleeping-house for families travelling to and from London, and much famed for its cellars and fine ale."† According to Fielding, the master of the inn was curious to know all about his guests; while his pipe, his nods, his grave manner in short, gave him the reputation of possessing great wisdom and insight into character, which he displayed on this occasion by divining for himself and his good-natured wife that Sophia must be Jenny Cameron, the Pretender's mistress, on her way to join her lover in town. These suspicions produced a hurricane when they reached the ears of the chaste Mrs. Honour; but the hurricane was silenced by the discreet Sophia; and a journey of two days in the Irish nobleman's coach brought the ladies to London.

All this time Jones was in eager pursuit. Perplexities arose when he came to cross-roads, and to a wide common where the footsteps of Sophia's horses, owing to the frozen ground, were hard to trace. But at one difficult point, he met a beggar who had found a pocket-book containing a hundred-pound bank-bill, which Sophia had dropped; at another he fell in with the Merry Andrew of a puppet-show, who had seen Sophia and could tell him the direction in which she was going; and at an alehouse where he took refuge from a violent storm, Partridge saw sitting by the fire with a plaster on his face the very lad who had attended

* First identified by Mr. Frederick S. Dickson in unpublished MSS.
† Thomas Sharp, "An Epitome of the County of Warwick," 1835, p. 115.

185

Sophia from Gloucester to the inn on the London road, and who was now on the way home. The boy was easily persuaded by the usual "golden arguments" to lend himself and his horses to conduct Jones to Meriden, where they arrived at three o'clock on the second day from Upton. Going on to Coventry that night, Jones lost his way, encountered a band of gypsies in a barn, and so did not reach the town until twelve o'clock. Two hours later he set out by post for London on the most direct road via Daventry, Stoney Stratford, Dunstable, and St. Albans, just missing Sophia at the last two places, and disarming, near Barnet, a highwayman who attempted to wrest from him Sophia's pocket-book. Late that evening Jones entered London by way of Highgate through Gray's Inn Lane, and put up at the Bull and Gate in Holborn.

To this journey—a long loop from the neighbourhood of Glastonbury to the north through the midlands to London— Fielding gave the entire second third of his novel; that is, volumes three and four. His delight in consorting with people on the road perhaps militated against his sense of proportion; memories of his own travels over much of that route came to mind, and the impulse to describe them could not be withstood. Still, though events occurred that had little or no bearing on the fortunes of Tom or Sophia, it can hardly be said that the background is too elaborate. Some embroidery was necessary if there was to be an interesting tour of the inns down in the West. Many of the incidents, of course, looked directly forward to the last stages in the plot. Sophia's muff and pocket-book, which Tom picked up by the way, he clung to until they could be placed in the hands of the owner. Again, the lost Partridge and Jenny Jones—Tom's reputed father and mother —reappeared in readiness for the dénouement; and Dowling, a most material gentleman, was seen flitting about the country, sure to be in London when the time for it should come. A footman of the Irish peer conducted Jones to the lodgings of Mrs. Fitzpatrick, who later informed Tom where he could find Sophia; and even the highwayman had a rôle left for him in the closing scenes.

It is against two long episodes that most persistent objection has been made. The inclusion of those episodes may be explained if not justified. Both Tom and Sophia had been bred in the country; Tom, so far as we know, had never been in London; nor Sophia since she had grown up. Their journey was designed as a preparation for scenes and associations quite different from any that they had been a part of. They were to learn something of a highly seasoned life by contact with it at inns; they were to have that knowledge supplemented by accounts from persons who had passed through it all. What the career of a gentleman in town was likely to be Jones heard from the Man of the Hill on a memorable night; what dangers environ matrimony Sophia heard from her cousin Harriet at the inn by the London road. Episodes like these had the sanction of Cervantes and the best story-tellers from the Greek romancers down through the literature of the Renaissance to the eighteenth century; they were a survival of the Homeric epic. It was held that they lent variety to the narrative, besides filling in pauses when the main story stood still. Tom, for example, had the remnant of a night to pass with the Man of the Hill in a cottage where there was no place to sleep; and Sophia and Harriet had an evening for conversation at an inn where there was nothing else to do. It is Fielding's distinction that he did not introduce these episodes merely to fulfil the time-honoured aims of the novelist. Mrs. Fitzpatrick's story brought out facts pertinent to the main narrative; and though the Man of the Hill was but a passing incident, his story, detachable as it is, remained in Tom's mind for warning and enlightenment. At best, episodes may be bad art; but such art as they have, Fielding closely studied for new effects.

Keeping a just balance between the parts, Fielding reserved the last third—volumes five and six—of his novel for the town and his conclusion. Here the background was mainly Westminster, where Fielding lived and had done his work. Tom's lodgings, whence he set out with Mrs. Miller and Partridge to see Garrick's Hamlet, were in Old Bond Street. The site of Lady Bellaston's house, where Sophia lay concealed, could not be given for obvious reasons, but it was somewhere in that fashionable quarter. The masquerade was at Heidegger's in the Haymarket, and the private rooms where Lady Bellaston unmasked for Jones that night were in a street near Hanover Square. Squire Western, whom Fielding brought to town over the great western road by way of Basingstoke, with Black George in his company, put up his horses at the Hercules Pillars at Hyde Park corner, and afterwards migrated to an inn in Piccadilly; while his sister took more genteel lodgings not far away. Squire Allworthy, following them with Master Blifil, went directly to rooms always kept ready for him at Mrs. Miller's. Dowling, in London ostensibly on business for Western, was uncovered at a hedge tavern near Aldersgate. Jenny Jones, alias Mrs. Waters, who had been drinking the waters for a few days with Mr. Fitzpatrick at Bath, accompanied the Irish gentleman to London in the search for his wife. The gatehouse in which Tom was confined after his duel with Fitzpatrick must have been the one to which Justice Fielding was committing young gentlemen at the very time his novel appeared. The marriage of Tom and Sophia, which was private like both of Fielding's own marriages, took place in the chapel at Doctors' Commons.

In his disguise as historian, Fielding thought it necessary to state not only *where* but also *when* the events of his novel occurred. The time that Tom or Sophia leaves one place and arrives at another, it has been casually observed, is sometimes given to the very hour. This procedure points to a most careful time-scheme, which has been worked out in minute and interesting detail by Mr. Frederick S. Dickson.* The first six books of the novel, in which Fielding selected and summarized incidents, cover more than twenty years; the last twelve books, comprising the dramatic action, cover, according to Fielding's various headings, about forty-two days; but there are overlappings which reduce the forty-two days to thirty-seven or thirty-eight. This short period which settled the fortunes of Tom Jones fell, as one may see from the novel, in the last two months of 1745. To quote a conspicuous passage, Fielding remarked, when Tom encountered the soldiers at Hambrook, that "this was the very time when the late Rebellion was at the highest; and indeed the banditti were now marched into England, intending, as it was thought, to fight the King's forces, and to attempt pushing forward to the metropolis." The Highlanders crossed the English border on November 8, took Carlisle on November 14, and entered Derby on December 4, expecting to reach London by Christmas. Hence the dramatic action of "Tom Jones" began after the middle of November.

Having obtained this date, Mr. Dickson ingeniously fixed the exact day by Fielding's references to the moon. When Jones, three days after leaving Hambrook, sallied out of the Gloucester inn with Partridge just as the clock was striking five one evening, the moon, "with a face as broad and as red as those of some jolly mortals, who, like her, turn night into day, began to rise from her bed, where she had slumbered away the day, in order to sit up all night."

* "The Chronology of 'Tom Jones,'" in "The Library," July, 1917, pp. 218-224; and an unpublished "Index to 'Tom Jones,'" in the library of Yale University.

Fielding meant to say that there was a full moon; in fact, he actually used the phrase in the account of Mrs. Waters, whom Jones rescued the next morning at the foot of Mazard Hill. This unfortunate woman had set out, it is related, with Northerton from Worcester on that morning at five o'clock, above two hours before daybreak, under the light of the moon which was then "at the full." Two days after the adventure at Mazard Hill, while Jones and Partridge were at dinner in an alehouse, "night came on, and as the moon was now past the full, it was extremely dark." According to the London almanacs for 1745, the moon was at the full at one a.m. on November 28; and rose, about an hour after sunset,* at 4.48 p.m. at Greenwich on November 29, or, if the necessary correction be made, at 4.58 at Gloucester. It was, then, on the evening of November 29 (which would be regarded as a night of the full moon) that Jones took leave of the Whitefields at Gloucester, whose clock was two minutes fast! The conclusion is inevitable that Fielding, in his aim to give an air of perfect reality to "Tom Jones," actually consulted an almanac for his sun and moon; that he constructed the dramatic action throughout on a time-scheme as carefully prepared as if he were writing a play.

For the benefit of anyone disposed to doubt that Fielding would adjust his narrative to the moon, it may be added that when Elizabeth Canning, a few years later, swore before him as justice of the peace that she had been conveyed by two ruffians from London on a January night, he tested the probability of her story by recourse to an almanac to see whether there was then a moon. He found that "it was within two days of the new moon,"† when the suburbs of London were veiled in complete darkness. Hence the time was most opportune for an abduction. In

---

* Nov. 29, the sun rose at 8.10 and set at 3.50, Greenwich time.
† "The Case of Elizabeth Canning," 1753.

those days, before gas and electricity, the moon was for all honest travellers a most welcome lady of the night.

On the assumption that Jones left Gloucester on the evening of November 29, most of the events from Allworthy's dismissal of Tom may be followed day by day to the end. The details of the journey are so clear that no difficulty arises until the scene shifts to London. For example, to omit much of the journey, we have:

Nov. 24. After a midday dinner, Allworthy turns Tom out of doors.

Nov. 27. Tom falls in with Partridge, disguised as a surgeon-barber.

Nov. 29-30. Tom's adventures at Mazard Hill.

Nov. 30. Midnight, Sophia steals from her father's house.

Nov. 30-Dec. 1. The night at Upton.

Dec. 1. Sophia, followed by her father, reaches Upton early in the morning. Squire Western forgets his daughter in pursuit of the hounds. Parson Supple, who was in his company, keeps in the rear to meditate "a portion of doctrine for the ensuing Sunday." At 10 a.m. Sophia arrives at Meriden. Jones passes the night at the puppet-show inn.

Dec. 3. Tom and Sophia arrive in London.

Dec. 7. Tom meets Lady Bellaston at the masquerade, and attends the lady to her private apartments.

Dec. 8. Partridge gets a £50 bank-bill broken for Tom. The second interview with Lady Bellaston.

Dec. 15. Sophia goes to the theatre; returning early, she meets Jones at Lady Bellaston's.

Dec. 17. Squire Western rescues Sophia from Lord Fellamar at Lady Bellaston's house and takes her to his lodgings in Piccadilly.

Dec. 21. Jones and Partridge see Garrick in "Hamlet." Allworthy and Blifil arrive in London.

Dec. 22. Tom fights a duel with Fitzpatrick and is committed to the gatehouse.

Dec. 25. The climax of Tom's distress, when told in the gatehouse that Fitzpatrick's wound will likely prove mortal, and that the lady whose charms overcame him at Upton is his mother.

Dec. 28. Tom is released from the gatehouse.

Dec. 29. The marriage of Tom and Sophia, who set out for home two days later.

This is but a mere sketch of the time-scheme from the last chapters of the sixth book to the fall of the curtain. Each day is crowded with events, which are frequently assigned to definite hours. Within this period, Fielding made, so far as I can detect, not a single positive error. True, in the last book where he hurried on feverishly with his mind intent on the close, he did not keep, as Mr. Dickson has remarked, the incidents of one day quite distinct from those of another; but that was a partial reversion from the dramatic to the epic manner with which he began "Tom Jones." He simply said "about six days" for the final book, thinking that information a sufficient guide at a point in the plot where the exact distribution of events was no longer essential. The reader, too, would understand that the six days did not include the look into the future, when Sophia became the mother of two children destined to have Abraham Adams as their tutor in place of Roger Thwackum. There are, however, some inadvertences, none of which amounts to an error. For example, on that night when Partridge was held spellbound by Garrick's Hamlet, the great actor was in Dublin, where he had gone for the season. No one, I daresay, observed the slip, for Garrick returned to London in May, 1746, and then appeared several times in the rôle at Covent Garden.

Again, to follow Mr. Dickson's lead, no account was taken of the six Sundays which fell within the limits of his dramatic action. Each book was said to occupy a certain number of days or hours; and Sunday, like all the other days of the week, had to shift for itself. The Sundays were November 24, and December 1, 8, 15, 22, and 29. It was quite appropriate that Sophia should be married on Sunday; but it is rather strange that she should go to the theatre, as she did, on Sunday, and that Partridge should be ordered by Jones to go out and get a fifty-pound bank-bill changed on a day when the brokers were taking a rest. It is stranger still that the pious Allworthy should send Tom out into the world after a Sunday dinner, and that Squire Western and Parson Supple should go a fox-hunting on the next Sunday, while Jones—this is not so strange— attended a puppet-show on the same evening. Jones fought his duel on Sunday; and by a similar coincidence the day when Partridge informed him that Mrs. Waters was Jenny Jones, his own mother,—that day was Christmas. It would seem as if Tom might have been spared this news until the next morning. The truth is, of course, that Fielding, if he considered the Sunday and Christmas question at all, decided to disregard it in the interest of an uninterrupted narrative. It was impossible for him to let his characters rest or to send them to church for spiritual comfort in the midst of momentous occurrences.

The only real error anywhere in the time of "Tom Jones" was pointed out by a contributor to "The Gentleman's Magazine" for May, 1791, whose discovery has since been honoured by the comment of several learned men. In the eleventh chapter of the fifth book, Tom gave Thwackum and Master Blifil a terrible trashing. The battle occurred, says Fielding, on "a pleasant evening in the latter end of June, when our hero was walking in a most delicious grove," and encountered there his tutor and the young squire. Three weeks later, according to the time allotted by Fielding to the following book, Tom was dismissed by

Allworthy and within a few days was on his "midwinter" travels when the nights were "cold," and the Highlanders were well over the border. How, it has been asked, can these "winter transactions" be reconciled with the summer scene in the grove? They cannot be reconciled, for there is no way to stretch three weeks and some odd days into five months. Keightley sought to palliate the inconsistency by assuming that the author purposely introduced the anachronism in imitation of Cervantes in "Don Quixote"; that is, to mystify the reader.* Is not Sancho Panza seen riding on an ass that he had lost in a previous chapter of the celebrated novel? Keightley's hypothesis is interesting, but it fails to consider that Fielding's aim was more realistic than Cervantes's; that elsewhere his time-scheme approaches perfection.

Fielding's error, it must be conceded, is positive and glaring; it cannot be explained away, but it may be accounted for. Despite the fact that "Tom Jones" appears to be admirably organized, Fielding did not write with a definite plan laid out before him; he doubtless knew from the first how in general the novel was to end; but it developed day by day under the inspiration of his pen. There were to be those scenes on the estates of Allworthy and Western and adventures on a journey to London, where the curtain was to be rung down. His slip occurred just as he was making the transition from the estates to the road. A grove on an evening in June was a most appropriate place for Tom to meditate on Sophia, for him to meet Molly, and incidentally to be surprised in his amour by Thwackum and Master Blifil. A grove in midwinter could have offered no concealment to the intrigue. When Fielding described that scene, the journey to London existed only in prospect; perhaps he then had no design of placing it in the winter. That was a detail rendered necessary if Tom

* Keightley, edited by Dickson, pp. 90, 107-108.

were to come into contact with the soldiers marching against the Chevalier. This curious shift from summer to winter, Fielding probably never observed, for slight alterations, such as he elsewhere made for his second edition, would have removed the anachronism.*

A good historian or biographer should let his readers know how old his characters are in order that youth and age may be duly considered in passing judgment on their conduct. Well aware of this principle, Fielding tells us in many cases their exact age, or when they were born, or supplies a clue to the information. It was really a part of his time-scheme. His oldest character was the Man of the Hill, who had reached the age of eighty-eight and could still climb Mazard Hill. Next to him came Mrs. Wilkins, who was in her fifty-second year when Allworthy ordered her to take the infant Tom from his bed to her own room, and seventy-three when she fell into a rage because her master did not mention her by name in his will. Miss Bridget Allworthy, the boy's real mother, was somewhat past the age of thirty at the time of his birth; while Jenny Jones, to whom the child was laid, was probably no more than twenty. Tom himself was born about the first of May, 1724; Master Blifil in 1725, Sophia in 1726, and Molly Seagrim in 1727. Tom was fifteen years old when he gave the bird to Sophia, and twenty when he first imagined himself in love with Molly. Thwackum, already a fellow of a college, with a reputation for learning, must have been towards thirty when he undertook the tuition of the boys; and Square, "a profest master of all the works of Plato and Aristotle," seems to have been a year or two younger.

Partridge, when he was charged with being the father of Tom, was "a jolly, brisk, young man" not quite thirty years

* There is a minor anachronism in the allusion to Dr. John Ranby. Though he was not born until 1703, he was consulted by the Man of the Hill as early as 1681.

old; he was nearly fifty-one when Tom took him to the theatre. Lady Bellaston was passing from the summer into "the autumn of life," though "she wore all the gayety of youth both in her dress and manner." Allworthy—who, married in his youth and lost his wife in 1719, after she had given birth to three children, all of whom died in infancy—should be, at the beginning of the novel, not much above thirty, though he was rather grave for his years. It was a slight inconsistency for him to speak, as he did once, of his sister as being "many years younger" than himself. Western was then only a young squire probably just married; but when he entered the novel to play his rôle, he appears to be above forty, while Allworthy had advanced to fifty-odd by 1745. The fact that Fielding left the age of these two squires to be inferred from hints was due, I think, to a desire not to make quite obvious the parallel between them and two gentlemen well known at Bath. Allen was born in 1694; like Allworthy, he married probably in 1716, and like him buried his wife within a few years. Their ages, on which Fielding was not specific, nearly corresponded also. The same thing is equally true of Western and his supposed original, Sir Paulet St. John, who was born in 1704. This probable identification makes, as it ought, Squire Western twenty-two when Sophia was born, and nearly forty-two when she ran away.

It is perhaps also incumbent upon a professed historian to give the full names of his characters as well as their ages. In this respect Fielding was at variance with Lord Clarendon and the usual practice. Sophia Western and Tom Jones, to be sure, were honoured with complete names; so were Bridget Allworthy, Deborah Wilkins, and many others; but no Christian name adorned Tom's real father, the handsome young Mr. Summer, nor Sophia's father, Squire Western, nor her mother, nor, to add to the list, Dr. Blifil, Dowling, Mrs. Miller, Parson Supple, the Irish

peer, Lord Fellamar, and Lady Bellaston. Squire Allworthy conferred his own name on Tom Jones, and so was
entitled to Thomas, though he never appears as Thomas
Allworthy in the narrative. Except for his epitaph we
should never know that Captain Blifil's name was John;
and except for the signature to a letter, that his son Master
Blifil could claim a name beginning with "W." Likewise
the boys' tutors when they signed a letter became for once
Roger Thwackum and Thomas Square. Partridge, when
living in obscurity, was called "Little Benjamin," from
which we infer, though we do not know, that his name was
Benjamin. Sophia's aunt Mrs. Western, as we have
remarked, was once addressed as "Di" and once as "Bell";
her cousin Harriet was just "Harriet," until she became
Mrs. Fitzpatrick; and her maid Mrs. Honour would also
have remained without a surname had she not once added
Blackmore in a signature. Betty and Susan answered for
several chambermaids and maids in waiting. Innkeepers
Fielding usually let go without any names at all, though
he singled out the Whitefields and "Robin" of Hambrook.
Similarly there were nameless lawyers, surgeons, and
physicians, old women, guides, and footmen—and one
Quaker shorn of his name. The effect thus produced was
that of casual history or memoirs in which the writer
forgets as many details as he remembers.

So unconcerned a manner, charming in itself, led to occasional slips in the narrative which, like that sudden passage from June to midwinter, might have been corrected
by an alteration in word or phrase or by the addition or
suppression of a sentence. Many of these lapses—real and
imaginary—have received the attention of critics ever since
the author of "An Examen" discovered that Fielding
quoted the classics from memory without consulting his
books. Keightley observed several inconsistencies and Mr.
Dickson has apparently found them all. To disregard the

most trivial ones or those where the trouble is clearly with the critic rather than with the author, there remains the following incomplete list of curiosities:

At the outset of his travels, Tom received a letter from Sophia at an alehouse; and then, taking leave of Black George, who had placed it in his hands, he "set forward to a town about five miles distant" (vi, 12). In the meantime, the gamekeeper returned to Squire Western's house, where Sophia's maid gave him a purse of sixteen guineas to be delivered to Tom. "Black George," it is said, "having received the purse, set forward towards the alehouse" (vi, 13). With some perplexity to the reader, Fielding failed to add that the gamekeeper, not finding Tom at the alehouse, went on and overtook him on the road to the town some five miles ahead. In fact, the delivery of the purse is inferred rather than directly stated anywhere.

This purse contained all of Sophia's ready money; and she lost after leaving Upton the hundred-pound bank-note which her father had given her, "and which, within a very inconsiderable trifle, was all the treasure she was at present worth" (xi, 9). How, then, did she pay for horses, guides, and entertainment at the inns? Well, six days elapsed between Sophia's gift to Jones and her own departure— ample time for a wealthy squire's daughter to scrape together enough guineas to take her to the inn on the London road, where she first discovered the loss of the bank-bill after she had settled her reckoning and made the landlord a present. The rest of the journey cost her only the "trifle" at the bottom of her purse, for she rode in the Irish nobleman's coach. Still, Fielding here left too much to the intelligence of some readers. All would have been plain had he included money among the other details of the preparation which Sophia and Honour made for the journey.

At the same inn by the London road, Dowling told Jones

that he had never had the happiness to see Mr. Allworthy and had seen Master Blifil but once (XII, 10). This is in accordance with the preceding narrative; and yet three weeks later Dowling was in London, a favourite with Blifil and a steward to Allworthy, who had recommended him to Western (XVII, 7). How this happened Fielding did not stop to explain.

Mrs. Miller, it is said, learned of Tom's connection with Allworthy, "either by means of Partridge, *or by some other means natural or super-natural*" (XIV, 5); but only two chapters before this, Fielding explained in detail how she acquired that knowledge, partly from Partridge, and partly from Allworthy himself in a previous visit to London. The phrase which I have put in italics should have been deleted. Again, Mrs. Miller had two daughters, seven years apart in age (XIII, 5); but later on, when the virtuous widow related her history, she said she had enjoyed the happy marriage state for only five years (XIV, 5). Her husband was a clergyman.

If this unintended slur on the character of Mrs. Miller was the most amusing of Fielding's lapses, a worse one was still to occur. In the tenth chapter of the last book, Allworthy "returned to his lodgings" at Mrs. Miller's from a visit to Sophia, sent for Jones, and "explained to him all the treachery of Blifil." In the next chapter while Jones, in continuation of the scene, was telling Allworthy and Mrs. Miller how he had gained his liberty, the story was broken off by a paragraph beginning "When Allworthy returned to his lodgings, he immediately carried Jones into his room and then acquainted him with the whole matter" about Blifil; and then Mrs. Miller, in her desire to be present at the reconciliation, entered the room with "a gentle rap." In other words, Allworthy returned to lodgings he had not left, and twice told Jones of Blifil's treachery; Mrs. Miller entered a room where she had been all the time, and, we may add, twice congratulated Jones on the happy turn in his fortunes. This is the sort of thing certain to happen sometimes when a novelist writes a chapter without reading over the previous one written a day or two before.

It would be hypercritical to ask, as Mr. Dickson has pleasantly done: Why did not Jones remember his promise to reward the beggar who found Sophia's purse? Why did not Sophia likewise fulfil her solemn engagement to reward Mrs. Honour to the utmost for her fidelity? Instead of that, she did not, so far as the reader knows, even pay Mrs. Honour her wages when she dismissed her. And finally, when Mr. Abraham Adams was taken into All-worthy's house, what became of the parson's wife and six children? These questions have a sort of answer. The beggar, we may suppose, received a liberal reward when Jones returned home, though Fielding neglected to say so. Mrs. Honour found a mistress more to her liking in Lady Bellaston. And as to Parson Adams, he was now a widower and his children had doubtless grown up and long since left Mr. Booby's parish to make their fortunes in the world.

When the slips, omissions, or inadvertences—whatever they may be called—in "Tom Jones" are thus brought together, it is remarkable, says Mr. Dickson, how few they are in comparison with "the harmonies." Fielding had an extraordinary memory, which enabled him to carry through hundreds of pages the varied details on which he built the last books. All along he played with the secret of Tom's birth, giving hints as to who he was but never betraying the secret. A reader may feel certain that Partridge and Jenny Jones were not his parents; but that does not give him any positive clue to the mystery; he hardly picks up the clue when Mrs. Blifil is disposed of by death. But if he looks back after finishing the novel, it is another story: he then sees that Tom's real mother conducted herself just as a woman of her character would in the circumstances. By the time Tom had his quarrel with Northerton at a nameless inn on the Gloucester road, perhaps Fielding had already planned to have his hero arrested and sent to the gatehouse for murder after his arrival in London. He there provided Tom with a sword which he wore by his side against the day when he should be called upon to run Fitzpatrick through the body. It is really amusing to see how Tom clung to that sword, as he should, through the long journey to town; how he used his fists or a cudgel in the contests with ordinary people by the way, drawing but once—it was when he stood guard over a prostrate highwayman—the sword which Fielding had reserved for a duel with a gentleman. To cite one more instance, the night at Upton was a forecast of that scene of deep humiliation when Partridge visited Jones in prison and told him who Mrs. Waters really was. Throughout "Tom Jones" there is this looking forwards and backwards. Such lapses as occur now and then may be mostly laid to the interruptions of journalism and the illness to which Fielding referred in setting pen to the last book. They are unimportant; they may be paralleled in Scott, Dickens, and Thackeray; they merely show the fallibility of genius. The wonder is that any man having no definite plan on paper and depending solely upon memory and prevision, could ever have composed so large and so harmonious a novel as "Tom Jones."

Those who have most praised the art of "Tom Jones" have had in mind the final complication of the plot and the dénouement which quickly follows. Here Fielding was confronted by several problems. He had to punish Tom for his follies (to use no harsher word), to display, as an offset to them, the best elements in his character, to lay bare the intrigues against him, unmasking one by one the villains, and to remove, by disclosing the mystery of Tom's birth, a conventional bar to the marriage with Sophia. For these purposes he cleverly assembled, as I have earlier remarked, his characters in Westminster, summoning several of them even from Ireland, and then set them into various relations with men and women of the town. His procedure, though on a larger scale, was much like that in many comedies of the time, his own "Miss Lucy in Town," for example.

It was Lady Bellaston who suggested to Lord Fellamar that Jones be impressed as a vagabond and sent to sea, for she had no further use of him, and his lordship would thereby be rid of a rival for the hand of Sophia. Four days later, while the press gang was lying in wait for him near the lodgings of Mrs. Fitzpatrick, Jones encountered, as he was leaving the house, her husband, who in a fit of jealousy hit him over the head and received in return the hero's sword half through his body. The officer in command of the gang rushed up with his men, seized the victor, and delivered him over to a constable. Tom thus found himself committed to the gatehouse awaiting an indictment for murder. Fitzpatrick was dying, and witnesses were eager to swear that Jones struck the first blow. For six days Fielding kept Tom locked up, with Tyburn all the time staring him in the face; and then, thinking that he had undergone sufficient punishment, set him free by the simple device of letting Fitzpatrick live. Three persons were at hand who knew the secret of Tom's birth. Jenny Jones alias Mrs. Waters related to Mr. Allworthy all the circumstances in which his sister Bridget fell in love with Mr. Summer; how Bridget intended to marry him, but was prevented by the young man's sudden death from smallpox, and so brought a fatherless child into the world; how Jenny and her mother nursed the infant till the day it was placed in Mr. Allworthy's bed; and the girl was amply paid for shielding the spinster from all suspicions of maternity. Dowling had heard the same story from Bridget, then the

widow Blifil, as she lay on her deathbed at Salisbury. Her
statement, carefully written out, the attorney had brought
to the house of Mr. Allworthy at the time of the squire's
illness, but the letter had been intercepted by Master Blifil,
who, being now confronted by the evidence, confessed all
his villainy. After this revelation, there was little to
choose between Tom and Blifil on the score of birth; both
had the same mother who had conducted herself in the
same way with her two lovers. That one boy had a father
while the other had none, was a mere accident; had Captain
Blifil like Mr. Summer contracted the smallpox or some
other mortal disease, Master Blifil would have been illegitimate as well as Tom Jones; as it was, his birth was
rather premature. With this happy turn of affairs Mr.
Allworthy was content, and Squire Western, who loved
Tom in his heart, was in glee.

Only Sophia had to be reckoned with. By this time Jones
was, from the point of view of the eighteenth-century
gentleman, reinstated in his former character. The dying
confession of Square relieved him of the charge on which
Allworthy had turned him off, and disclosed the machina-
tions of Master Blifil against him. It became known to
friends, too, that Black George had stolen the five hundred
pounds which Jones lost by the brook-side. More than all
else, Tom's restoration of peace and happiness in the
household of Mrs. Miller brought into light his finest qualities, whereby those who intrigued against him were shown
to be the real villains. Nothing was left to explain except
his follies and vices—his dealings with women, in a word.
Mr. Allworthy lamented them, but was willing to accept a
sincere repentance, being certain that faults due to the
wildness of youth would soon pass; whereas Squire Western
really gloried in all of Tom's escapades because they proved
him to be a man. Sophia, of course, could not agree with

her father; nor could she regard as complacently as Mr. Allworthy her lover's shortcomings.

Her attitude is most interesting. In the first place she loved Tom to desperation; and the story of the deceits practised against him awakened her pity. She wished that his conduct had been otherwise, but she hardly expected to find a woman's delicacy in the male sex; she must admit a certain grossness foreign to herself. She insisted, however, upon being assured of one thing: that Tom had been faithful to her from the day he had had any hope of winning her hand. This was easily done. The intrigue with Mrs. Waters at Upton, Jones had refused to continue after their arrival in London. He had also declined a marriage with the rich Mrs. Hunt and a liaison with Mrs. Fitzpatrick. Not only was he no profligate himself, but he had prevailed upon Nightingale to marry the girl whom this young man had betrayed. What still troubled Sophia was Tom's proposal of marriage to Lady Bellaston at the very moment he was professing undying love to herself. As soon as Tom explained to her that the proposal was a device, suggested by Nightingale, for ridding himself of her ladyship, Sophia's resistance broke down. It was all over when Tom, seizing Sophia's hand, led her to the glass, and asked her to look upon her charming self as the surest pledge of his constancy. There was some sparring for time on Sophia's part in order that Tom might be put to a further test, but the impetuous temper of Squire Western would brook no delay of the marriage beyond the next morning.

III

Historians, Fielding used to say, generally agree on the time and place of an action, but disagree on what the action was and how it should be interpreted; and therefore on whether the actor was an honest man or a rogue: while he himself, it should be understood, was not so much interested in when and where an act took place as in its quality and in who committed it; that is, as in the characters of history. All his characters, he claimed, are in harmony with human nature; all do what real men and women of their temper would do in the same circumstances. To keep them true to life, he let his memory, as I have shown, play about persons whom he had known; they were his models, so to speak. As experience taught him not to expect, except in rare instances, unalloyed goodness or unalloyed villainy in the world, so in his novel there should be mainly "mixed characters," few if any either wholly good or wholly bad. This does not mean that Fielding was free from traditional and rather artificial methods in moulding his observations. As in "Joseph Andrews," his mind sometimes, though not so often, recurred to Cervantes. Don Quixote sallies forth on adventures, is dubbed a knight, and picks up Sancho Panza when he discovers that he needs a squire. Tom Jones sets out on a journey, purchases a sword on the first opportunity, and falls in with Partridge, who is as much a Cervantic creation as was Parson Adams. This odd, garrulous, superstitious schoolmaster never fathoms, despite hard experiences, the motives of men, and reads life in the light of his whimsical dreams, much as Parson Adams read it in the light of ancient literature, and Don Quixote in the light of romances of chivalry. Likewise Squire Allworthy, with a difference, is in line with the knight and the parson; he is blinded by the glare of an unblemished character into taking hypocrites and pretenders for what they seem; only the most conclusive evidence can induce him to change his favourable opinion of men by whom he has been grossly deceived.

Other characters, not having the Cervantic cast, display an unmistakable kinship with several in "Joseph Andrews." The Man of the Hill is a Mr. Wilson of darker fibre; each has had his experiences in the world; and each, becoming disenchanted, has retired from it into seclusion. Lady Bellaston and Lady Booby, though there are personal differences, represent the same imperious and sensual type of woman in full middle age. Joseph Andrews is kept from a liaison with Lady Booby by his love for Fanny; Tom Jones, more a man of the world, submits, under not quite the same conditions, to the proposal of Lady Bellaston. Mrs. Honour is another Mrs. Slipslop, ignorant and Malapropian in speech, though a less farcical creation. Finally, the same theory of humour underlies both novels. The characters are mainly built upon some affectation, flowing from vanity or hypocrisy, and they are all unmasked in the end. What keeps them from becoming artificial is the fact that Fielding's theory of comic art was restrained and enriched as he went along by his personal observations in a world of men and women. Theory was but a guiding principle with him. Art and nature played into each other's hand without conscious effort.

This is a general statement requiring modification. Art and nature were not always completely fused. A clear instance is Master Blifil. Fielding began well by making him a sober, discreet young man as a foil to Tom, who lacked these qualities, but eventually transformed him into a villain, pure and simple, with hypocrisy so ingrained that he ceased to be a comic character, despite the humorous touch at the end where he turns Methodist in the hope of marrying a rich widow of that sect. It is noteworthy that no original for Master Blifil has ever been suggested. Of course not; for he was drawn not from life, but from the stage. Thwackum and Square, though rather artificial creations, are always entertaining, for they have enough of reality in them to support the humour. Neither of them really has a bad heart; but their natural feelings have been overpowered and atrophied by moral speculations. Of the two, Square is the more human. When he bites his tongue, his unalterable rule of right and the eternal fitness of things does not prevent him from uttering an oath or two; and he shows that he is composed of flesh and blood when Jones discovers him in Molly Seagrim's garret. At last, too, he renounces his atheism and repents of all the injuries that he had done Tom by conniving at the villainy of Blifil. That the character of Thwackum might not be misread, Fielding added a paragraph on him, saying that, though he was proud and ill-natured, he was an excellent scholar, strictly severe in his life, honest, and most devout in his attachment to religion. Still, it is unfortunate that such an explanation was made necessary lest the reader should interpret him otherwise.

Neither is Allworthy quite successful. His head is sacrificed to his heart; he is saved from being a fool by a certain quiet humour and a determination, when once undeceived, to punish the rascals that have fed upon him. It is rather curious that Fielding is silent on the politics of Allworthy, who was evidently, like Tom, an adherent of the House of Hanover. At times there are approaches to a contrast between him and the Jacobite Squire Western, but for some reason the opportunities are allowed to slip away. Again, Mrs. Fitzpatrick and Lady Bellaston are not so much individuals as representatives of a class. On the other hand, the antithetical elements are finely "mixed" in Diana Western, Mrs. Honour, Bridget Allworthy, and the housekeeper Deborah Wilkins. Certain resemblances have been pointed out between Mrs. Honour and the nurse in "Romeo and Juliet."* They result, I daresay, from the fact that both Shakespeare and Fielding depicted the characters from real life. Bridget Allworthy is an amusing prude and hypocrite, who cannot withstand those instincts which she affects to abhor. Her weakness was gently treated by Fielding; he let her die before the main action of the novel

* "Notes and Queries," 10 S. VII, 444-445 (June 8, 1907).

began in order that she might escape the humiliation of exposure.

Theory was overlooked in the portrayal of Sophia Western. She is the refined product of memory and of a grief that could never pass. To create her, Fielding had merely to imagine how a Charlotte Cradock would have comported herself, had she been a squire's daughter without a mother to guide her when the time came to choose a husband. From the twentieth-century point of view, Sophia can claim few accomplishments. Her nurse and her aunt, a woman of the world, were her only instructors. There was no governess, no boarding-school. She learned to play old English tunes on the harpsichord to please her father, and Handel to please herself; in Fielding's phrase, she became "a perfect mistress of music." She read moral tales and essays of the kind Sarah Fielding wrote, and had a just appreciation of them—but she was put through no programme of hard studies, no foreign language, no mathematics. She was "perfectly well-bred," though lacking somewhat in that ease which can be acquired only in polite society. From her father and Parson Supple she heard the grossest anecdotes and scandal, when they were in their cups; and yet she preserved the purity of her own imagination. She was amiable and of gay temper, becoming grave only on the most serious occasions. She loved her father rather more than she ought and ministered at all times to his whims. If he asked her for his favourite song or that she join him in the hunt, she consented without the slightest show of reluctance, though the request might not be to her taste. In return, her father prized her above all other creatures except his kennel, and placed her, when only eighteen years old, in command of his house and at the upper end of his table.

By her ready obedience she seemed to anticipate all his wishes except one. She could go so far as to promise never to marry against his inclinations; but her heart rebelled against a husband whom she could never love and who could never love her; she preferred death to a life of misery. While Blifil was deceiving her father and Mr. Allworthy, she felt rather than knew him to be base and treacherous; she just hated him and let it go at that without explanation. Sophia, however, was not a girl who blindly followed the impulse of her emotions; she possessed patience, excellent practical sense, and a determination from which she could not be swerved; indeed, Lord Byron thought her too "emphatic." She had the prudence of a Pamela, but its mission served a higher purpose. Pamela would have jumped at a marriage with Blifil and trusted to herself to make him over. Sophia by her strategy escaped a loveless match and married the man who, everybody at last said, should be her husband. Long before the enfranchisement of her sex, Sophia Western fought out the first great battle. In her case there could be no forced marriage; all the time-honoured torments—threats, upbraidings, insults to her modesty, imprisonment in her room, bread and water—availed not to break the spirit of this independent girl. Throughout the struggle she was quiet and self-poised; and when the victory was won she became more charming than ever.

Without question, the squire her father is the character into which Fielding put the most colour; but it did not show all at once. In this respect contrast him with his neighbour. Allworthy is a character of one consistent piece from the moment he is introduced into the novel to his last appearance. Always the same, he is a stationary figure, whose kindness, simplicity, and generous nature shine in the varied lights turned upon him. He may be read in any scene where he converses at length. This was inevitable; for Fielding began the portraiture with Ralph Allen definitely in mind. Not so with Squire Western. When this man first appears, he is without any distinctive characteristics whatever. He is merely a fox-hunting squire who will permit no poaching on his game. The fact is, Fielding had here, at the outset, no individual as his model. That came later and perhaps one can determine just where. By degrees, we are told that Western was fonder of his daughter than of any other person, that he got drunk, that Sophia played the old jigs for him; we may hear him utter an ordinary oath or two, and learn that his thoughts, to the neglect of Sophia, were in the field, the stables, or the kennel. Whenever he was occasionally brought on the stage, he spoke as others spoke, in commonplace phrases. On the whole, it was a tame beginning, in which we see the author casting about for characteristics capable of humorous development. This "preserver of the game" was first mentioned in the second chapter of the third book; but it was not until the tenth chapter of the fourth book—a full hundred and twenty-five pages ahead—that he became the Squire Western whom we know. Then, over the table with his curate, he first fell into his native Somerset dialect and soon into his odd oaths referential. At that point the character took definite shape; at that point Fielding's imagination began its wild play about a distinct individual whom he developed, under the excitement of Sophia's refusal to marry Blifil, into a veritable whirlwind of contending passions. The height of the storm was reached in the scenes with his sister Diana, which, brutal as they are, have never been equalled for humour in this language of ours; in them is all the raciness of our speech in conjunction with action that suits the word.

Only one criticism, I think, has ever been preferred against this marvellous creation. When in London, the squire gave the lie to Captain Egglane, who brought from Lord Fellamar the challenge to a duel; whereupon the gentleman struck him with his stick over the head and sent him howling and capering about the room. That incident, said Scott, was a mistake; "as an English squire, Western ought not to have taken a beating so unresistingly from the friend of Lord Fellamar; we half suspect that the passage is an interpolation."* The scene is not an interpolation; it is in the first edition. Who then was right—Fielding or Scott? Did Fielding, as it is implied, slip into the inconsistency of making a coward of the man who had earlier in the novel pommelled Thwackum and Blifil? I think not. Rightly interpreted, Western, though no coward, was never very brave. He could threaten, browbeat, and even use his fists or his whip on Somerset boys and schoolmasters; but the situation was not quite the same in London. He did not know the ways of the town, having been there only twice before in his life; he thought that he could give the lie as safely to a gentleman as to his sister or to a booby squire. Unarmed at the time, he was taken off his guard when Captain Egglane boxed his ears with a cane; and in perfect harmony with his temper, the squire, who always gave free vent to pleasure or pain, howled under the smart of the blow. Had he been armed, he would have retaliated; in fact, he immediately challenged the Captain to fight him on equal terms, either with bare fists or single sticks. The invitation was declined. The scene just borders upon farce; but it is really in accord with Western's character.

Fielding knew the English Jacobite better than Scott; he knew that beneath his noise and bluster there was no uncommon bravery. The character is full of surprises, because he was created piecemeal, because his conduct depends upon circumstance and the violent emotions awakened by contradiction or by acquiescence in his whims; he could weep as well as curse. Before Fielding finished with this man, he exhibited him in all his phases—in his igno-

---

* "Henry Fielding" in "Lives of the Novelists."

rance, prejudices, brutality, profanity, and grossness. At length the sky cleared, and Squire Western was left with the one abiding passion out of which the storm had risen—an unmeasured affection for his daughter. As a last look at him before the curtain is rung down, Fielding lets us see Western in the nursery of Sophia's children, declaring that "the tattling of his little grand-daughter, who is above a year and half old, is sweeter music than the finest cry of dogs in England." There have been other country squires in our literature; if none of them have been so gross, none have been so real and human.

As in "Hamlet," the problem of "Tom Jones" is the hero himself. Not because Fielding is obscure, but because the character raises certain moral questions, humorously casuistical, on which men are bound to differ. The author plays delightfully, if one is interested in old books, with the Earl of Shaftesbury's formal "Inquiry concerning Virtue"—with his lordship's "mere goodness," "natural affections," "moral sense," and sharp distinctions between good and evil. This essay, like others in the "Characteristicks," had profoundly influenced Fielding; in a sober mood he would have accepted as completely as did Square the moral doctrines of "the Great Lord Shaftesbury." He never burlesques or parodies Shaftesbury, never quite uses his phrases; he rather puts to a sort of humorous test his lordship's ethical system by bringing it into conjunction with real life. From the moment we first see Tom, he has all of Shaftesbury's "social virtues"; he is kind, considerate, and generous. He climbs a tree overhanging a canal, to recover Sophia's pet bird which Blifil had set free, and falls, the branch breaking, into the water; when Sophia's horse rears and throws her, Jones catches her before she can strike the ground, at the expense of breaking his left arm. In heeding the impulses of his heart, he falls into indiscretions that run from these instances of personal harm to acts which appear as vices and which are indeed near allied to them; he is lacking in all the practical virtues, such as Master Blifil's prudence and caution, and so becomes in the general view "his own worst enemy."

The stigma upon his birth never soured his happy disposition; but it led to insults which he bravely answered with his fists, to neglect on the part of his tutors, to the use of the birch as the main instrument of instruction. Tom never got very far, I daresay, in his Latin, never went to Eton or the university. He was a better boxer than Latinist. This handsome, full-blooded boy became an idler. At first he was puzzled and then amused by the moral and religious formulas of Square and Thwackum, once venturing to inquire of them whether they knew of any rules by which one could make an Allworthy. His foster-father was an ideal by which the better side of his character, to use a Wordsworthian phrase, was moulded in "silent sympathy." But there were other influences at work upon him. Thrown upon himself, he became intimate with Black George and his family, where his affections received their first stain. In company with the gamekeeper, he robs an orchard, steals a duck, and poaches on Squire Western's manor. The duck and most of the apples were appropriated by Black George and he shot the partridge; but Tom, not being an expert in hiding, was the one caught and made to smart for not recognizing the usual distinction between *meum* and *tuum*. To relieve the distress that later fell upon the gamekeeper's family, Tom sells for half their value a pony and a very fine Bible that Allworthy had given him; and easily yielding to the animal within him, is corrupted by the gamekeeper's daughter Molly, with whom he imagines himself in love. Moderate in the use of wine, the boy once overdrank in his joy at the unexpected recovery of Allworthy whose death sentence the doctor had pronounced; under the influence of the wine, he sought to renew the intrigue with Molly, and quarrelled with Blifil and Thwackum. Such was the lad Tom Jones, whose character is easy enough to read as one stands off from it; sound at heart, his affections had been swerved into dubious conduct by evil companions. Fielding put nothing heroic into his composition, and made his power of resistance but moderate. The word "duty" formed no part of Tom's vocabulary.

The author amuses himself as well as the rest of us by letting a philosopher and a theologian debate the questionable points in Tom's behaviour. Both Thwackum and Square judge an act by abstract rules; they never take into account the circumstances in which it is committed; they never regard motives; they always leave out of consideration the "natural goodness of heart." Though they may hotly disagree on the grounds of their decision, their verdict is in general the same: that Master Blifil is an exemplary young man, and that Tom was born to be hanged. Both, for example, praised Blifil for his dastardly act of freeing Sophia's little bird, and equally condemned Tom for his attempt to regain it. According to Thwackum, Blifil merely did his duty when he tossed the bird into the air; according to Square, he was merely restoring to the creature that liberty which belonged to it by the laws of nature. Neither of them considered that Blifil really stole the bird and that Tom tried to restore the property to its owner. It was doubtless wrong for Tom to conceal his escapades with Black George, but his unwillingness to betray his associate to ruin brought out a sense of honour which was neglected by his tutors in their utter condemnation.

Likewise, to sell valuable presents from Allworthy was in itself an act not to be commended; but it should be remembered that Tom disposed of them, not because he had no regard for them, but as the only means at hand for aiding a family threatened with starvation. On the sale of the Bible there was not perfect harmony in the views of the theologian and the deist. Thwackum looked upon the transaction as sacrilege, and so whipped Tom forthwith; while Square thought that, if a book were to be sold, it might as well be the Bible as any other, and pointed his argument with "the story of a very devout woman, who out of pure regard to religion, stole Tillotson's Sermons from a lady of her acquaintance." Wine was a solace to both of them; both were heavy drinkers; but they frowned upon the animal spirits awakened in Jones by a few bumpers; had he drunk enough to induce the stupor that overtook them, all would have been well. Finally, on the affair with Molly Seagrim, they made no allowance for Tom's youth, for the fact that he never did her or any other woman the slightest harm; the intrigue was in the abstract an open defiance of the Scriptures and "the eternal fitness of things"; it was not a mere blemish upon the boy's character to be removed by advice; it showed a thoroughly corrupt nature which no castigation could cure. All the time the man habitually loose in his relations with women was Square himself.

Philosopher and theologian were not present to pass upon the later phases of Tom's conduct; the journey to London left them behind. In their place, Fielding's fellow novelists and critics have pronounced judgment. The night at Upton, which most troubled Jones, has usually been condoned; the crux of the character has always been the affair with Lady Bellaston. Richardson put the case bluntly against Fielding when he said that Tom was "a kept fellow, the lowest of all fellows," at the time he pretended to be in love with Sophia. In agreement with Richardson, Scott thought that Tom was "unnecessarily degraded" by the incident, and surmised, in accounting for it, that "Fielding's ideas of what was gentleman-like and honourable had sustained some depreciation, in consequence of the unhappy circumstances of his life, and of the society to which they condemned him.'' These, then, are the charges, better known perhaps by Thackeray's repetition of them: Tom sold himself to Lady Bellaston; the fact debased the character to a point from which there could be no recovery; and the author himself, owing to his low associations, was unaware that he had made of his hero, to repeat Lady Mary's phrase, ''a sorry scoundrel.'' In reply, Coleridge absolved Fielding of the insinuation that he was lacking in a sense of honour, and suggested that it was a mistake to test Tom by the manners of a society which did not exist in 1745. Fielding's failure, if there be any, he attributed to the fact that Tom was not made to feel the full force of his degradation as soon as he understood what his relations had been with Lady Bellaston. The addition of a paragraph or two, Coleridge held, would have restored the moral and artistic equilibrium of the character; and thereby removed from ''Tom Jones'' ''any just objection'' to the novel on the score of immorality.*

This is all admirably said; it is not, however, the last word on Tom Jones. As Coleridge hints, there was nothing unusual in the kind of intrigue which Tom carried on with Lady Bellaston; it was indeed a common occurrence, not in the low life to which Scott consigned the author but in the fashionable life of the town such as Fielding knew equally well if not much better. Neither Pitt nor Lyttelton, who were familiar with the manuscript, made any objection, so far as we know, to an intrigue which was allowed to stand after that consultation over the novel at Radway Grange. The conclusion is that they as well as the author saw nothing in Tom's connection with Lady Bellaston out of harmony with contemporary manners, or inconsistent with the young man's character as previously depicted. Per-

* ''The Complete Works of Coleridge,'' edited by Shedd, New York, 1884, IV, 381.

haps they observed certain extraordinary circumstances passed over by the critics, by Coleridge even. Tom Jones was an ingenuous lad bred in the country; he had never been in London before; he may have had a mistaken sense of honour, but he had only one weakness approaching a vice, and for that weakness Fielding resolved to degrade him and make him suffer to the utmost. Tom did not pursue Lady Bellaston; he was in no mood for an amour; he fell in with her while searching for Sophia; and she trapped him at the masquerade which he attended in the hope of discovering Sophia. When he walked behind Lady Bellaston's chair to her rooms, he supposed that she was Mrs. Fitzpatrick who could inform him where Sophia might be found. Lady Bellaston withdrew her masque, and Tom accepted a challenge to love in the spirit of a challenge to fight.

Withal, he wished to keep on good terms with Lady Bellaston, for she evidently knew the hiding-place of Sophia. His last shilling gone, he accepted a fifty-pound note from her ladyship and another gift a day or two later, of which ten pounds went immediately to the relief of a family in sickness and dire distress. Altogether he had several interviews with Lady Bellaston, but only two of them, which occurred on succeeding nights, were in private. As soon as he was able, he cut himself free from a relationship with which he was disgusted. It took him about a week to do that. Could Fielding have anticipated the objections of the Victorian age to the episode, he might have deleted certain phrases and substituted others for them; but he was portraying a young man of his own time. In his meditations, Tom thought not so much of his own "misery" as of Lady Bellaston's honour and of his ingratitude towards her from a gentleman's point of view. Fielding rightly reserved for the scene of Tom's humiliation that day in the gatehouse when Partridge misinformed him that

Mrs. Waters was his own mother. Those were rightly the most terrible hours in the young man's career. Still, it remains true that "Tom Jones" has suffered most in popularity because of Lady Bellaston. Take her out of the novel, and it would become a book for the fireside. Fielding has here paid the penalty for strict fidelity to the society of which he was a part. It is a penalty which must be paid by all writers who depict characters which, however true to human nature, fall under the ban of later and perhaps better times. A Lady Bellaston, disappearing from decent society, then becomes repugnant to that large majority of readers who have no historical sense, who look upon manners, not as ever changing, but as fixed and everlasting.

Incidentally, the question has been often asked: "Why did Fielding further degrade Tom Jones by making him illegitimate?" Richardson, who was repelled by the "coarse" sub-title of the novel, first put the question, and once answered it by insinuating that the first Mrs. Fielding was perhaps a "bastard." Though the circumstances of her birth are unknown, there is no reason for casting this aspersion upon the beautiful Miss Cradock. If one must find a specific instance of illegitimacy within Fielding's observation, there is the first wife of Ralph Allen. But uncertainty of birth is a literary *motif* hoary with age. It is in Shakespeare and in Euripides, to go no further backward. Just before Fielding began "Tom Jones," Mrs. Haywood published a novel called "The Fortunate Foundlings"; and when he was at work upon it, Edward Moore brought out the comedy of "The Foundling." The point tacitly urged against Fielding is his treatment of the theme. With the romancers, the foundling always turns out to have had honest parents; the solution of the mystery thus satisfies the most delicate and chaste imagination. Fielding, I take it, should have had a secret marriage between Mr.

Summer and Miss Bridget Allworthy. It would have been as easy to do that as to kill off the young man with the smallpox. By a mere flourish of the pen, he might have removed a stain from Tom and his mother, and kept his morality on a high plane. To say all this is but to restate the old quarrel of romance against realism. Fielding took over from fiction and the drama a hackneyed type of mystery and gave it fresh interest by correlating it with English life in the country. As a realist, this was the only course open to him. "Tom Jones" might be rewritten as a romance, but it would then cease to be "Tom Jones"; there could then be no Bridget Allworthy of flesh and blood; and with her would be washed out several other characters and all that social satire centering about her frailty and that of the Captain Blifil who became her husband.

Nowhere does Fielding's irony cut deeper than in those passages where he relates the attempts of the amiable hypocrites to visit upon Tom the sins of his parents, unless it be in the final chapter where Parson Supple is married to Mrs. Waters, and Partridge to Miss Molly Seagrim. The entire portrayal of Tom Jones is of course irony. It is the art of "Jonathan Wild" and numberless comedies refined to a greater degree of subtlety. A boy, whose moral code is of necessity defective, is sent out into the world and receives a temporary smirch from the contact. But he quickly learns his lesson and becomes in the end a most respectable country squire. Never does Fielding set the seal of his approval upon the boy's conduct as a whole. On the contrary, he condemns much of it.

Throughout the novel, the author himself is always present in the full maturity of his powers. There is no dramatic aloofness such as we associate with French literary art. "No man," said Fielding in agreement with Horace, "can paint a distress well, which he doth not feel while he is painting it," and "I never make my reader laugh heartily but where I have laughed before him.'' That is, the characters were to Fielding real men and women in whose joys and sorrows he shared as if they were his own friends or acquaintances. His presence is felt quite as much as Tom's, for example, when the young man, confronted by a duel, has to reconcile the code of honour with the teachings of Scripture. Fielding doubtless smiled there with his reader when Tom's scruples were quieted by the assurance, coming from a parson over a bowl of punch, that a certain latitude might be granted to a gentleman, or that there must be a mistake, somewhere or other, in the translation or in the understanding of the command that we should love our enemies and do no murder.

Likewise, though the plot has its logic, Fielding is never a detached spectator merely interested in the solution of his problem; he thrusts himself in with remarks, anecdotes, and disquisitions, becoming a sort of ubiquitous character whose appearance anywhere on the scene is conditioned by neither time nor place. Consequently the action is often suspended in order that the author may speak *in propria persona,* and pass sentence, as a Bow Street justice ought, on the conduct of his characters. This procedure Fielding likened to the parabasis of ancient comedy, where the chorus, between the Acts as it were, turned to the audience and addressed it directly. In fulfilment of his design, he comments on the follies of Tom Jones, foreshadows the punishment that will be meted out to them, and warns his young readers against imitation. If we look for a moral, here it is: ''Prudence and circumspection are necessary even to the best of men. They are indeed as it were a guard to virtue, without which she can never be safe.'' According to his temper, one will like or dislike this kind of novel which ''Tom Jones'' established in English fiction. If we wish to do our own moralizing, we must shun Harry Fielding, the grandson of an archdeacon. And

yet it may be worth while to listen to a preacher who turns
the light of his experience and humour on the devious ways
of mankind.

It is right to consider apart from these casual parabasis-
openings those long initial chapters to the successive books
which were eliminated in the first French translation of
"Tom Jones" and which some readers still pass by. They
have little or no direct connection with the story, and so
their presence may be explained rather than justified. In
them Fielding, saturated with Cicero, Shaftesbury, and the
New Testament, elaborated piecemeal a theory of morals
based upon "goodness of heart," and out of his wide reading and practice in the drama set forth a complete art of
fiction. They are essays, which have less finished analogues
in many leading articles that Fielding had written for his
newspapers. In Fielding's view, the essays lent dignity
to the novel, which in his day was despised as a literary
form. Those dealing with conduct supplied the reader with
an extensive background of morality with which to judge
the behaviour of the characters; those dealing with the
novelist's craft described the "new province of writing"
which he had discovered. The novel of real life was then
in its infancy. No one before Fielding had ever written a
novel comparable with his in its reliance upon contemporary manners and the facts of human nature. He accordingly felt it necessary to state in clear words his
general design, his moral code, and his method of procedure
with plot and characters. It would not have served his
purpose to have published these essays by themselves; in
order to gain the attention which he wished for them, they
must be bound with his novel. Had Fielding lived in
the nineteenth century, there might have been no introductory chapters. He could have reserved for the great quar-
terlies what he had to say on the art of fiction. What he did
say in the only place at his command, we now read not be-

cause the essays are an organic part of the story but because they embody profound observations on art and life united with matchless irony and humour.

If either the story or the introductory chapters—one and not the other—were to be lost, many would be unable to decide which could go with the less pain. On this point George Eliot was uncertain, but she lamented the departure of those Georgian days "when summer afternoons were spacious, and the clock ticked slowly in the winter evenings"; when there was leisure to listen to the digressions of Fielding, "when he seems to bring his armchair to the proscenium and chat with us in all the lusty ease of his fine English."* Scott had no doubt about his choice: he would have sacrificed the novel, despite his high regard for it, to the essays. "Those critical introductions," he declared, "which rather interrupt the course of the story, and the flow of the interest at the first perusal, are found, on a second or third, the most entertaining chapters of the whole work." It would be difficult to imagine "Tom Jones" without its initial chapters; and were they removed, I suspect that one would find it quite another book.

* "Middlemarch," Bk. II, Ch. XV.

CHAPTER XX

THE MIDDLESEX MAGISTRATE

I

THE RIOTS OF 1749

The man who wrote "Tom Jones" was already presiding as principal justice over the Bow Street police court, before which came business from all parts of the metropolis. By Fielding's friends, the position was regarded as lucrative as well as honourable, being worth, if the justice insisted on his full fees, a thousand pounds a year. Relying too much upon this assurance, Fielding entered upon his duties in the winter of 1748-1749, and began sending thieves and footpads to the Westminster jail where Tom Jones had spent an unhappy week. Among his first cases recorded in the newspapers, is the following from "The St. James's Evening Post" for December 8-10, 1748:

"Yesterday John Salter was committed to the Gatehouse by Henry Fielding, Esq; of Bow Street, Covent Garden, formerly Sir Thomas De Veil's, for feloniously taking out of a Bureau in the House of the Rev. Mr. Dalton, a Quantity of Money found upon him."

The man whose bureau was robbed may have been the Rev. John Dalton, known for his sermons and verses and for a sentimental friendship with Lady Luxborough and the Duchess of Somerset. He was a canon of Worcester, and the rector of St. Mary-at-Hill in London.

In a more serious case, given in the same newspaper a week later, the culprit bore the surname of Fielding's hero;

and the justice or his clerk took the occasion to enlighten the public on the law relative to the crime:

"Yesterday one Jones was brought before Henry Fielding, Esq; at his House in Bow Street, for barbarously and wantonly wounding a young Woman on the Head with a Cutlass the Night before, without any Provocation; the young Woman had the good Nature to forgive the Assault, but the Justice nevertheless committed the Offender to the Gatehouse, for being found arm'd with so dangerous a Weapon in the Streets, contrary to Law; and it's hoped that all Persons who have lately been robb'd or attack'd in the Streets by Men in Sailors Jackets, in which Dress the said Jones appeared, will give themselves the Trouble of resorting to the Prison in order to view him. It may perhaps be of some Advantage to the Publick to inform them (especially at this Time) that for such Persons to go about armed with any Weapon whatever, is a very high Offence, and expressly forbidden by several old Statutes still in force, on Pain of Imprisonment and Forfeiture of their Arms.''*

A few weeks after this, the jurisdiction of the Bow Street court was extended, as I have related earlier, over the entire county of Middlesex, enabling the justice to make commitments for similar or graver offences to places of confinement more dreaded than a gatehouse or a bridewell. To the New Prison in Clerkenwell went, for example, James Wood (brother of Peter and William Wood living at the Star in the Strand) for stealing a large quantity of human hair from Mr. Burket the merchant, "who hath been sollicited and offered a bond of 100 l., not to appear against him at the next Sessions at the Old Bailey''; and

---

* Fielding's cases were very fully reported by his clerk, first in ''The St. James's Evening Post,'' and later in ''The Covent-Garden Journal'' and ''The Public Advertiser.'' Some of them may be found in ''The Gentleman's Magazine'' and ''The London Magazine.''

to the same place was conveyed, "under a strong guard," a man who kept an alehouse in the Beaufort Buildings, charged with commanding, aiding, and abetting men at a neighbouring wharf to steal great quantities of coals, knowing them to be stolen. To Newgate went Mary Anthony and Mary Batty for assaulting Elizabeth Coxen on the highway, and taking her straw hat and a lace handkerchief; Catherine Butler for assaulting and wounding one of her own sex in head and throat with a case-knife; John Cropley for falsifying accounts; Thomas Pady on suspicion of breaking into a dwelling-house and taking coin; Joseph Mottley alias Dowdle for rescuing from custody a man who had just picked a gentleman's pocket of a handkerchief; and James Jewell, a sailor, for stealing from a jeweller in New Street, Covent Garden, a gold ring, though he left behind a brass one in its place.

Amid these sordid surroundings, Fielding had settled with his family by the first week of December, 1748. The court room was on the ground floor, where his clerk, Fielding says, sat "almost sixteen hours in the twenty-four, in the most unwholesome as well as nauseous air in the universe." Nor was there long escape from that fetid atmosphere for the justice himself. He might retire to his private apartments, but even when there he was subject to call at any time for counsel or to order a commitment. Since the birth of his son William, his family had been increased by a daughter Mary Amelia, baptized on January 6, 1749;* and there was living with him his unmarried half-brother John, born in 1721† of General Fielding's second marriage, whom he greatly loved for his character and the misfortune of having been totally blind since the age of nineteen. The two brothers were inseparable. A week before the publica-

---

* Registers of St. Paul's, Covent Garden, Jan. 6, 1748, O. S.

† Burke's "Peerage," 1916. John Fielding alludes to the accident which caused his blindness, in the preface to "The Universal Mentor," 1763.

tion of "Tom Jones," they opened, in conjunction with other partners, a "Universal Register Office, opposite Cecil-Street, in the Strand." The design of the office, according to a plan drawn up by Henry, was "to bring the world, as it were, together into one place, . . . the buyer and the seller, borrower and lender, landlord and tenant, the tutor and the pupil, the master, the scholar and usher, the rector and curate. . . ."* John became the manager. The ambitious undertaking, which had been suggested to "Messires Fielding and Company" by a passage in Montaigne, throve especially as an agency for houses and servants. More commodious quarters becoming necessary, the office was moved to the corner of Castle Street, opposite the New Exchange in the Strand, and a branch was established in Bishopsgate Street. On Henry's recommendation, John was soon to be appointed an assisting justice in the Bow Street court. By 1751, the blind brother who, it has been said, came to know all the notable criminals of London by their voices, had received his commission;† and from the beginning, it is evident, John's knowledge of the underworld, derived from his business, was of great assistance. Fielding was also very fortunate in having a most faithful and efficient clerk in that man who never complained of the long days at his desk—one Joshua Brogden, who had served in the same capacity under Sir Thomas de Veil. He is the man who witnessed the assignment of "Tom Jones" to Andrew Millar. Of his constables, Fielding could always rely upon Saunders Welch of Holborn, "one of the best officers," he said, "who was ever concerned in the execution of justice." Thus equipped with assistants, and fortified by a small income from an employment bureau in

---

* See "A Plan of the Universal-Register-Office," 1752, and subsequent editions. The body of the pamphlet, running on *hath*, is clearly the work of Henry, while a preliminary address "To the Reader," running on *has*, bears the signature "John Fielding."

† Miss Godden, "Henry Fielding," p. 232.

which he owned twenty shares,* the author of "Tom Jones" undertook the task of rendering life and property safe within the county of Middlesex.

Now and then we may get a glimpse of his household and court; even see how he was living and how he conducted business. First of all, there is that oft-quoted passage in one of Horace Walpole's letters, wherein the wit relates what he has heard of Fielding's ménage, to illustrate the text that life when deprived of its masque is quite different from what it appears when dressed for the ball. Writing from his house in Arlington Street, on May 18, 1749, Walpole sends to his friend George Montagu all the news and scandal that can be crowded into a most amusing letter. The famous passage on Fielding runs:

"Take sentiments out of their pantoufles, and reduce them to the infirmities of mortality, what a falling off there is! I could not help laughing in myself t'other day, as I went through Holborn in a very hot day, at the dignity of human nature; all those foul old-clothes women panting without handkerchiefs, and mopping themselves all the way down within their loose jumps. Rigby gave me as strong a picture of nature: he and Peter Bathurst t'other night carried a servant of the latter's, who had attempted to shoot him, before Fielding; who, to all his other vocations, has, by the grace of Mr. Lyttelton, added that of Middlesex justice. He sent them word he was at supper, that they must come next morning. They did not understand that freedom, and ran up, where they found him banqueting with a blind man, three Irishmen, and a whore, on some cold mutton and a bone of ham, both in one dish, and the cursedest dirtiest cloth! He never stirred nor asked them to sit. Rigby, who had seen him so often come to beg a guinea of Sir C. Williams, and Bathurst, at whose father's he had lived for victuals, understood that

* The number given in his will.

dignity as little, and pulled themselves chairs, on which he civilized.''*

This racy anecdote, which Scott thought most "humiliating," should not be taken literally; large allowance must be made for a twofold distortion, first by Rigby the political parasite, who resented Fielding's coolness, and then by Walpole, whose malicious phrasing and aristocratic sense of superiority to the vulgar herd supplied the seasoning. Walpole is the only authority for the tradition that Fielding sponged upon Sir Charles Hanbury Williams, or that he dined too often with Earl Bathurst, at whose table had sat Pope and Swift, Congreve and Prior. Withdraw the wit and the animus from Rigby's story, and there still remains a vivid scene of Fielding with his family and guests after the day's work was supposed to be over. The "blind man" was, of course, John Fielding; and the "whore" none other than Mrs. Henry Fielding, a woman from the common walks of life, and, I daresay, not very careful about the appearance of herself or her table. Who the Irishmen were, we do not know; but Fielding mentions in various places Irish acquaintances, whose fresh wit he evidently relished. It was a plain man's board around which Fielding, his wife and brother, and three casual guests drew for conversation over cold mutton and a bone of ham. Whatever resentment the justice felt at the intrusion of Rigby and Peter Bathurst, he strove to conceal it as soon as he knew who they were; and if he followed his rule of action, he immediately committed the culprit to Newgate on the oaths of the two gentlemen.

Whenever the public service demanded it, Fielding kept his court open all night, though by law and custom all persons arrested at night were to be held by the constable until morning. Having received, for instance, information one evening that a large number of people were at a

* "Letters of Horace Walpole," edited by Toynbee, II, 383-384.

gambling-house in the Strand, too many for the constables to handle, he sent for a party of soldiers from the Tilt-Yard to aid them in the arrests. It took the justice till two o'clock in the morning to dispatch the forty-five gamblers that were brought in; of whom six were admitted to bail and the rest were sent to the gatehouse. In lighter vein, we read: "The high constable of Westminster went about 12 o'clock to a private masquerade near Exeter Change, where several idle persons of both sexes were assembled, most of whom were apprehended and carried before Justice Fielding, who sat up all night to examine them; and several of them being found to be persons of distinction under 20, the justice not thinking proper to expose them, after a severe reprimand dismissed them all." Again, complaint being made on an evening that a set of apprentices had taken a large room at the Black Horse in the Strand, where they were performing, contrary to law, Otway's "Orphan," he issued a warrant to Mr. Welch the high constable, "who apprehended the actors, and conducted them thro' the streets in their tragedy dresses, before the justice, who out of compassion to their youth only bound them over to their good behaviour."

However severe Fielding might be with hardened criminals, he was invariably considerate in dealing with juvenile offenders like the masqueraders and amateur players, and with the aged and infirm who found their way into his court not so much because of wilful crime as indigence and distress. When three poor men, said the newspapers, were brought before him on a morning charged with begging, "they appeared to be in so dreadful a condition with sickness as well as poverty, that the Justice, having first relieved, dismissed them." Sometimes his good nature became, like Squire Allworthy's, pleasantly humorous. When, for example, Rich revived at Covent-Garden Theobald's pantomime called "Harlequin Sorcerer," with newly painted scenes and elaborate machinery, everybody ran to the theatre for a fortnight to see the spectacle. So great was the crowd one evening that "a lady lost one of her shoes going into the house and sat with a gentleman's glove on her foot; and the gentleman lost his hat and wig, and sat with a handkerchief over his head." A girl who had come all the way from Wapping, had her pocket cut off while before the door; and though she could not identify the thief, she immediately ran over, her face wet with tears, to the Bow Street court to enter a general complaint. Fielding listened to her patiently, tried to soothe her, and succeeded when he discovered that the tears flowed not from the loss of some fourteen shillings but from the loss of an entertainment on which her heart was set. As a dramatist whose plays were being performed every year, Fielding enjoyed for himself and his friends the freedom of the theatres. So he simply gave the heart-broken girl a pass to the gallery; her tears, running in brooks, dried up immediately, and she went back to the playhouse, content to lose half of all she possessed in this world's goods provided she could see the tricks of Harlequin and the many new and wonderful contrivances.

All the while Fielding was rising into eminence. No justice of the peace in his time was more competent; none ever had a higher conception of the office. To be certain of this, one has but to examine his legal tracts and his more important cases. In May, 1749, his brethren recognized his superior talents by choosing him chairman of the Quarter Sessions of the Peace for the city and liberty of Westminster;* and they continued to repeat the honour, six times in all, until his health completely broke down. So notable was his first charge, delivered on the twenty-ninth of the following June, that it was published three weeks

* "MS. Sessions Books for Westminster," Vol. for 1749, as quoted by Miss Godden, "Henry Fielding," p. 204.

later "by Order of the Court and the unanimous request of the Grand Jury."* There are a few other interesting details. The address was given in the Town Court-House near Westminster Hall. In the resolution which his Majesty's Justices of the Peace immediately passed, they thanked Henry Fielding, Esq., for his "very loyal, learned, ingenious, excellent and useful Charge, highly tending to the service of his Majesty and Administration and Government."† In scope and method it is certainly a model charge, on the lines of Lambarde, through the history of the institution of grand juries and observations on the high qualities demanded of them if they are to do their duty, down to the distinction between a presentment and an indictment and to specific instruction when to return a true bill. Everywhere are displayed learning, zeal, and acumen, with passages of grave and measured eloquence. "This ingenious author and worthy magistrate," said "The Monthly Review," "has, in this little piece, with that judgment, knowledge of the world, and of our excellent laws (which the publick, indeed, could not but expect from him) pointed out the reigning vices and corruptions of the times, the legal and proper methods of curbing and punishing them, and the great necessity of all magistrates . . . vigorously exerting themselves in the duties of their respective offices."‡

Fielding's charge was an address to the citizens of Middlesex as much as to the officers of the law; it was a manifesto setting forth the statutes relative to the minor crimes which then went unpunished, and a solemn warning that these statutes would now be enforced. This was really the reason for the publication of the charge. Fielding admonished the grand jurors that they were "the only

* "The St. James's Evening Post," July 18-20, 1749.
† The resolution was published with the "Charge."
‡ "The Monthly Review," I, 239-240 (July, 1749).

censors of this nation''; that as such it was their duty to inquire into all reports of misdemeanours which especially infested the public at that time, and to present the offenders for punishment to the justices of the peace in their neighbourhood. First of all, must be suppressed the brothels, which have spread throughout the metropolis into the suburbs, not merely because they are public nuisances but because they have become "seminaries of education," corrupting the minds and bodies of the next generation with vice and disease. With these houses must go, too, the dancing-halls, "where idle persons of both sexes meet in a very disorderly manner, often at improper hours, and sometimes in disguised habits''; for, though they pretend to be only "scenes of innocent diversion and amusement," they are, "in reality, the temples of iniquity." So also are the gaming-houses, which offered a difficult problem for the justice to solve. Here the aim should be, Fielding remarks, mainly to prevent gambling among the lower sort of people, those useful members of society who lose at the table all the benefits of their labour; whereas "for the rich and great, the consequence is generally no other than the exchange of property from the hands of a fool into those of a sharper, who is, perhaps, the more worthy of the two to enjoy it."

There is even a hint at the curtailment of theatrical performances of the kind that Foote was giving at Covent-Garden, where "the stage is reduced back again to that degree of licentiousness [or unrestraint] which was too enormous for the corrupt state of Athens to tolerate." Nor is the press forgotten. "Our newspapers," it is declared, "from the top of the page to the bottom, the corners of our streets up to the very eves of our houses, present us with nothing but a view of masquerades, balls, and assemblies of various kinds, fairs, wells, gardens, etc., tending to promote idleness, extravagance and immorality, among all sorts of people.'' Lastly, there is the offence of libelling, ''which is punished by the Common Law, as it tends immediately to quarrels and breaches of the peace, and very often to bloodshed and murder itself.'' To paraphrase Fielding, a man wins praise and honour and reputation, seeking no other rewards for noble actions; and then comes a miscreant to strip him of his good name and to expose him to public contempt. Long ago Demosthenes justly stigmatized the libeller as a ''viper, which men ought to crush where-ever they find him, without staying 'till he bite them.''

It is not easy, as Fielding found, to put into practice the excellent advice of the Greek orator. That sly viper Aretine, who still lay hiding in ''Old England,'' again poured forth his venom without being harmed by any heel. In a parody on the ''Charge,'' he accused the justice himself of all the misdemeanours enumerated in the pamphlet, and instructed the grand jury to present him to one of his brethren on the bench as ''a nuisance to civil society, the bane of peace, and the scandal of human kind.''* Had not, Aretine inquired, this same Fielding (now turned informer against the liberty of the press) once libelled whomsoever he pleased in his theatrical pieces and in a contemptible newspaper called ''The Champion''? To say the truth, there was some incongruity between Fielding the man of letters and Fielding the justice. Moreover, the large programme which he laid out for the officers of the law exposed him to ridicule, for it was impossible of fulfilment. And yet, the endeavour to transform the town into an earthly paradise was a noble ideal. What Fielding mainly hoped to do was to check the current vices by driving them from the streets and public places of amusement, so that they might not contaminate the young. By infusing new

* August 5, as quoted in ''The Gentleman's Magazine,'' XIX, 366-367 (Aug., 1749).

life into the grand juries and by warning the citizens against crime, he did all that one man could do in a depraved state of society. The vigour with which he administered the Bow Street court simply astonished the gentlemen of the press, who recorded day by day his many commitments.

His charge was delivered on a Thursday, just before he went into the country for the week-end. The place where Fielding sought deliverance from scenes of crime is not quite certain. There is a tradition, found in Lysons's "Environs of London,"* that he took, at this time or earlier, a house at Barnes across the Thames in Surrey, and on the way by boat to Twickenham, where he had passed some time after his second marriage. His "four worthy sisters," all unmarried, then lived at Ealing, Hammersmith. Wherever he went—whether to Barnes or Ealing or elsewhere,—dreadful riots, while he was away, broke out in the Strand. On Saturday evening, the first of July, three sailors belonging to the Grafton man-of-war visited a house at the sign of the Crown, where, it was claimed, they were robbed of more than thirty guineas by women who frequented or lived at the place. Being driven out, the men returned with a large number of other sailors; and when thus reinforced they broke all the windows of the house, demolished all the furniture, ripped the clothing from the backs of the inmates, piled up the spoils of war in the street, and set the heap ablaze. An immense crowd gathered to encourage the rioters or to share in the plunder; the parish engines were summoned, though they never arrived, to stay the flames which threatened adjoining buildings whose beams were already hot; beadles and constables bustled about, only to be jeered at; and no magistrate could be found who cared to meddle with the angry mob. Towards midnight

* 1792, II, 544. In 1792 the house was the property of "Mr. Partington."

guards were brought from Somerset House and the Tilt-Yard; and after desperate encounters the streets were cleared. Somehow, only a few of the rioters were arrested; of whom two were placed in a temporary night-prison under the house of a beadle named Nathanael Munns. The next night the mob again assembled, wrecked two other houses and burned the goods; wrenched the bars out of the windows of Beadle Munns's cellar and rescued his two prisoners with a yell.

It so happened, however, that just as this second riot was reaching its height, Saunders Welch of Holborn, who had been visiting a friend in the city, met the mob about midnight on his way homeward, and with the aid of a military force was able to drive the rioters from the streets before morning. Several of the ringleaders were apprehended and conducted under a strong guard to the New Prison. Still again, lawless crowds assembled on Monday morning and pressed into Bow Street to rescue anyone that might be brought there for examination. Such was the posture of affairs on Fielding's return from the country towards noon on Monday. The fearless magistrate immediately sent for a party of the guards to bring the ringleaders from the New Prison to his house, where they arrived amid uproar and shouts of "To the rescue!" In vain Constable Welch went among the mob and entreated them to disperse; in vain Fielding himself "from his window informed them of their danger and exhorted them to depart to their own habitations." Thereupon the justice dispatched a messenger to the Secretary of War for a reinforcement of soldiers to protect the court. That afternoon the rioters who had been arrested on the previous night were duly examined and nine of them were committed to Newgate, where they were conveyed in closed vehicles attended by the guards. All Monday night people dwelling along the Strand were in consternation, mobs were threatening to gather at points as far east as the Tower, all the streets in the danger zone were patrolled by soldiers as well as by peace officers, and Fielding himself sat up with Saunders Welch and a military officer until daybreak, ready to issue orders on a moment's notice. This vigorous action, which any justice of the peace might have taken on either of the preceding days, put an end to the riot and restored peace once more.

Among the prisoners whom Fielding committed to Newgate was a young man named Bosavern Penlez, who had been overtaken by the watch in Carey Street. At the time of his arrest he had in his possession a bundle of woman's apparel, which, it was alleged, belonged to the wife of Peter Wood a victualler, whose house was pillaged by the mob on Sunday night. Penlez tried to account for having laced caps and laced aprons on his person, but his story was rambling and inconsistent. The evidence was quite clear that he had taken part in wrecking Wood's house and had made off with all the goods he could carry. It was then very difficult to obtain a conviction under the Riot Act; indeed, since its passage in the first year of George the First, Fielding said that he could remember only two or three instances of its enforcement. Accordingly the public was surprised when, during the August session at the Old Bailey, a jury brought in a verdict against Penlez and a young associate named John Wilson, both of whom were identified by Wood, his wife, and a servant as among the men who tried to pull their house down. Long before the day of execution arrived, feeling ran high in favour of the condemned men who, it was claimed, were not the instigators of the riot, but only outsiders drawn into a crime by a laudable ambition to destroy a notorious brothel. The jury who had convicted them were induced to address the King in their behalf; and a similar petition to the Duke of Newcastle, the head of the Ministry, was signed by nine hundred inhabitants of the parish of St. Clement Danes, within which the riot had occurred. Wilson was reprieved and eventually pardoned; but Penlez was hanged at Tyburn on the eighteenth of October. His body was buried in the church of St. Clement Danes at the expense of his admirers, one of whom proposed "a monumental inscription" to the memory of a young man who sacrificed his life to "an honest detestation of public stews."*

The burial of Penlez by no means stayed the agitation over his fate. That inscription extolling his virtues was spread broadcast through the magazines and newspapers; and there followed, apparently by the same hand, a pamphlet called "The Case of the Unfortunate Bosavern Penlez," written by "a Gentleman not concerned" and having as its motto *summum jus, summa injuria*. Penlez, we are there told, was the son of "a reverend clergyman of the Church of England" and had just completed his term as apprentice to a peruke-maker, who could vouch for his "fair and honest" character. A trifle overheated with drink on the night of the riot as he was returning from a birthday party, he had fallen into the humour of a crowd bent upon the annihilation of a house whose existence was a scandal to all decent citizens. It was but a youthful freak; nothing more. Aside from this special pleading, the point was well made that Penlez had been illegally convicted at the Old Bailey because the Riot Act had not been read, as required by the law, at the time of the disturbance.

The case, thereupon getting into the Westminster election for members of Parliament, threatened to defeat Lord Trentham, the government candidate for re-election, because he had refused to sign the petition to the Duke of Newcastle for clemency to Wilson and Penlez. During the

* "The St. James's Evening Post," Nov. 2-4, 1749.

heated canvass in November the public was entertained with many broadsides and advertisements, including an ironical address to the electors by "Capt. Hercules Vinegar," as if it were from the pen of Fielding, though that of course was a jest.* So far as is known, Fielding had not used this pseudonym since he left "The Champion," and in any case he would not have written the broadside in question, for it was really aimed against Lord Trentham, his own kinsman and the brother-in-law of the Duke of Bedford. Fielding's name, however, did appear in an advertisement, which consisted of an affidavit sworn before him by one John Haines, a waiter at the King's Arms Tavern in Pall Mall, to the effect that Lord Trentham, so far as the deponent knew, was never so lacking in patriotism as to protect—such was the grievous charge—the French strollers who were playing at the Little Theatre in the Haymarket. At this juncture, on November 18, Fielding also published under his own name a politico-legal pamphlet (not wholly disconnected with the election), called "A True State of the Case of Bosavern Penlez,"† in defence of the Government, the conviction of Penlez, and his own part in the first stages of the case. Nothing, says Fielding, could have induced him to appear again as "a political writer" except a desire "to do an act of justice to my King, and his Administration, by disabusing the public, which hath been, in the grossest and wickedest manner, imposed upon" by pamphlets and newspapers which are making "a malefactor an object of sedition," transforming him into a hero, and arraigning "the most merciful Prince who ever sat on any throne . . . of blameable severity, if not of downright cruelty, for suffering justice to take place."

* "A True and Impartial Collection of Pieces in Prose and Verse . . . published . . . during the Westminster Election," 1749.

† "The St. James's Evening Post," Nov. 16-18, 1749.

Fielding explains the provisions of the Riot Act, gives reasons why it imposes the death penalty, prints all the depositions which were sworn before him, and concludes with an able summary. The clamour against the conviction has some excuse, it is admitted, in the desire of all good citizens to be rid of lewd and disorderly houses, but their zeal ought not to lead them to sanction open defiance of the law. Against these houses there is, they must know, a lawful remedy which every man has the power to apply. With the rioters themselves the laudable motive which they gave was, as the evidence showed, a bare pretence to shield them from punishment for theft and robbery. Rising to a climax, Fielding puts the rhetorical question: "When by our excellent Constitution the greatest subject, no not even the King himself, can, without a lawful trial and conviction divest the meanest man of his property, deprive him of his liberty, or attack him in his person; shall we suffer a licentious rabble to be accuser, judge, jury, and executioner; to inflict corporal punishment, break open men's doors, plunder their houses, and burn their goods? I am ashamed to proceed further in a case so plain, where the absurdity is so monstrous, and where the consequences are so obvious and terrible."

Nevertheless Fielding did not quite go to a full vindication of the judge who tried Wilson and Penlez at the Old Bailey. The public first learned in his pamphlet that the petitions to the King and the Duke of Newcastle in favour of Wilson were supplemented by the earnest efforts of Fielding himself, who, out of compassion for the young man ill in prison, secured bail for him before the trial. It is implied that he would have intervened for Penlez also, had not the grand jury found against him a capital indictment for burglary, as well as for riot, upon evidence such as "every impartial man must allow would have convicted him (had he been tried) of felony at least." That is, though

Penlez met a just fate, he was not tried on the indictment where the evidence against him was the strongest. There is, therefore, an intimation that the judge at the Old Bailey made a mistake, in not having Penlez arraigned—as the prosecutor, it is said, wished—on the indictment for burglary. What Fielding really did in his pamphlet was to lay before the public a case that was never tried and to invite them to act as the jury.

His frankness gave "Old England" a chance for another venomous attack upon him. Fielding shows, it is declared, an utter ignorance of the law he would expound, and is advised to read, before proceeding further in the business of his court, "the notes" of his grandfather, "old Judge Gould," though one may doubt whether he has enough intelligence to apply them. The magistrate's own words made it clear to Argus of the Hundred Eyes that responsibility for the death of the "unspotted" Penlez rested not with the King, not exactly with the Government, not with the judge and jury, but with a certain justice of the peace who first ordered his commitment—"a profligate . . . at the head of a gang of illiterate staffmen and information makers,"* and in secret partnership, some suspect, with the keepers of the wrecked bawdy-houses. This time Argus Centoculi seems to have rather overshot the mark; for he was asked by his brethren on the metropolitan press whether it might not, with as much reason, be inferred from his tenderness for Penlez that he was a sharer in the plunder of the thief. There was no reply to the retort. Fielding's pamphlet, abstracts of which were published in all the magazines and in many newspapers, had a sobering effect. It was a warning from the Government that rioters could no longer be certain of escaping with a fine and bail for good behaviour.

The long agitation over Penlez doubtless wore upon

* "Old England," Nov. 25, 1749.

Fielding; but there were more acute anxieties, of which the first was a shrunken purse. Although he had double the business of his predecessor, the income from his office, owing to his custom of composing quarrels, and his refusal to exact the usual fees from the very poor, dwindled from a possible £1,000 a year to a little more than £300 "of the dirtiest money upon earth," most of which he let remain with his clerk, and thought him "but ill paid" for those long days spent in a foul court room. In other words, his absolute integrity would not permit him to become "a trading justice" of the kind depicted in his Squeezum of "The Coffee-House Politician." How the "trading-justices" of the period filled their pockets, is described by Melville Lee in his "History of Police in England," where he says: "Those who did not actually accept bribes were usually ready to make a little extra money by the improper and wholesale bailing, not only of offenders who ought to have been kept in confinement, but of innocent persons also, who ought to have been immediately and unconditionally set at liberty. The system was to issue warrants against helpless people for imaginary crimes, and then to let them out on bail, the magistrate netting the sum of two shillings and fourpence every time he repeated the trick." In contrast with this practice, all that Fielding annually took for himself out of the legitimate fees cannot be estimated at more than £100 a year; and his interest in the Universal Register Office was a very uncertain source of supply. Strangely enough, from the modern point of view, he still continued to be consulted as a professional lawyer; in fact, of the fees that he received for his advice during his long practice at the bar, none are recorded by himself or his clients until after he became a justice of the peace. These occasional fees, however, from his friends must have been insignificant. Beginning to feel the pressure after six months in Bow Street, he applied for one of two positions formerly held by William Selwin, "counseller at law, solicitor to the excise and commissioner of bankruptcy." On the night after sending Penlez to Newgate, he dispatched the following letter to the Duke of Bedford:

"Bow Street. July 3. 1749.

"My Lord,

The Protection which I have been honoured with receiving at the Hands of your Grace, and the goodness which you were pleased to express some time since toward me, embolden me to mention to your Grace that the Place of Solicitor to the Excise is now vacant by the Death of Mr. Selwyn. I hope no Person is better qualified for it, and I assure you, my Lord, none shall execute it with more Fidelity. I am at this Moment busied in endeavouring to suppress a dangerous Riot, or I w^d have personally waited on your Grace to solicite a Favour which will make me and my Family completely happy.

I am, &c.,

H. FFIELDING."*

Fielding, it should be observed, did not ask for the position in the court of bankruptcy, which had been immediately filled after Mr. Selwin's death in June, but for the more agreeable one in the excise. The Duke hesitated for several weeks, and then appointed Dudley Baxter instead of Fielding, perhaps because he thought the Bow Street justice already had enough to do. Though Fielding may have been disappointed, he had no reason to complain greatly of his treatment, for the Duke of Bedford gave him "a yearly pension out of the public service money." The amount of the pension is not stated by Fielding, who relates the incident in his "Voyage to Lisbon." He only says that it "would have been larger," had the Duke known how small

---

* "Correspondence of John, Fourth Duke of Bedford," 1843, II, 35-36; and Miss Godden, "Henry Fielding," p. 209. From autograph at Woburn Abbey.

were the fees paid into the Bow Street court. Naturally, too, search has failed to discover any record of Fielding's pension among treasury warrants or elsewhere, for it was private business between him and the Duke of Bedford, and the payments were made from a general fund granted by the King for various purposes. It is known, however, that John Fielding, when he succeeded his brother at Bow Street, received from the Duke of Newcastle £200 a year in semi-annual instalments. The same amount was also paid to his associate Saunders Welch. Regularly as Lady Day and Michaelmas came round John dispatched a letter to the Duke of Newcastle, dunning him for payments long overdue.* Henry Fielding's pension was probably no larger than his brother's; it was just sufficient to render his circumstances tolerable for the present.

Moreover, Fielding was overwhelmed with business. As he was always ready to take prompt action, cases were every day brought before him which should have been heard by other justices. Fifty commitments a week were not unusual with him. So we are not surprised when we find him asking for aid. He wished, though he did not obtain it, that his clerk might be appointed an assisting justice whenever there should be a vacancy. On sending Lord Hardwicke a copy of his "Charge" and the draft of a bill relative to the suppression of footpads, he wrote:

"Bow Street, July 21. 1749.

"My Lord

I beg your Lordship's Acceptance of a Charge given by me to the Grand Jury of Westm.ʳ tho I am but too sensible how unworthy it is of your Notice.

"I have likewise presumed to send my Draught of a Bill for the better preventing Street Robberies &c. which yᵉ Lordship was so very kind to say you would peruse; and I

---

* Manuscript letters of John Fielding in the British Museum. For example, "Additional MSS.," 32868, f. 296.

hope the general Plan at least may be happy in your Approbation.

"Your Lordship will have the Goodness to Pardon my repeating a Desire that the Name of Joshua Brogden may be inserted in the next Commissions of the Peace for Middlesex and Westmin^r for whose Integrity and Ability in the Execution of his office I will engage my Credit with your Lordship, an engagement which appears to me of the most sacred Nature.

> I am, My Lord, with the utmost Respect
> and Devotion,
> > Y^r Lordship^s most obed^t most
> > > humble Servant

> > > > H. Ffielding.

To the Right Honble The Lord High Chancellor of G. Britain."*

This letter was followed by one to Lyttelton, which showed the same mixed motives of improving the public service and of helping a friend. Its occasion was the marriage of his patron to Elizabeth, daughter of Sir Robert Rich, whose fortune bore out her name; but its purpose was to recommend the appointment of Edward Moore as deputy licenser of the stage. For a year or two, since his panegyric in "The Trial of Selim the Persian," Moore had been seeking the patronage of Lyttelton, who had half promised him the withered laurel of Colley Cibber as soon as that poet should die. Human life, however, is so uncertain that Cibber gave signs of outlasting Moore; and in the meantime the young linen-draper who had turned poet and dramatist was finding it difficult to maintain himself with his pen; but for Fielding's hospitality and influence with the players and booksellers, he would have failed in literature as he had failed in trade. Just as Fielding had long ago

* British Museum, "Additional Manuscripts," 35590, f. 334.

befriended Lillo the jeweller's son, so he was now aiding
this vivacious young man of fresh and original talents,
rather strict in his moral and religious principles, for he
had been bred among the Dissenters and knew the follies of
polite society only by report. Moore's affairs assumed a
very serious aspect by his falling in love with Jenny
Hamilton, daughter of Charles Hamilton, table-decker to
the princesses. She was a sprightly girl if she be the author
of a poem on her lover which purports to have been addressed by her to the daughter of Stephen Duck, the peasant
poet who had once been Cibber's rival for the laurel. A
play upon her lover's name ends each stanza, of which the
last runs in one of the many versions:

> You will wonder, my girl, who this dear one can be,
> Whose merit can boast such a conquest as me;
> But you shan't know his name, tho' I told you before,
> It begins with an M, but I dare not say *More*.

While the poem, attributed by some to Thomas Francklin
the translator, was amusing the town, Fielding wished to
see the romance brought to a happy conclusion and to
obtain at the same time an officer for the Government who
would exert a salutary influence upon the stage. In these
circumstances, he laid the case before Lyttelton:

"Sir

Bow St. Augt 29, 1749

Permit me to bring up the Rear of your Friends in paying
my Compliments of Congratulation on your late happy
Nuptials. There may perhaps be seasons when the Rear
may be as honourable a Post in Friendship as in War, and
if so, such certainly must be every time of Joy and Felicity.
Your present situation must be full of these; and so will
be, I am confident, your future Life from the same Fountain. Nothing can equal the excellent character your Lady
bears among those of her own Sex, and I never yet

knew them speak well of a Woman who did not deserve their good words. How admirable is y^r Fortune in the Matrimonial Lottery! I will venture to say there is no man alive who exults more in this, or in any other Happiness that can attend you than my self; and you ought to believe me from the same Reason that fully persuades me of the satisfaction you receive from any Happiness of mine; this Reason is that you must be sensible how much of it I owe to your Goodness; and there is a great Pleasure in Gratitude tho it is second I believe to that of Benevolence: for of all the Delights upon Earth none can equal the Raptures which a good Mind feels on conferring Happiness on those whom we think worthy of it. This is the sweetest ingredient in Power, and I solemnly protest I never wished for Power more than a few Days ago for the sake of a Man whom I love, and that more perhaps from the Esteem I know he bears towards you than from any other Reason. This Man is in Love with a young Creature of the most apparent worth, who returns his Affections. Nothing is wanting to make two very miserable People extremely blessed but a moderate Portion of the greatest of human Evils. So Philosophers call it, and so it is called by Divines, whose word is the rather to be taken as they are, many of them, more conversant with this Evil than ever the Philosophers were. The Name of this man is Moore to whom you kindly destined that Laurel, which, though it hath long been withered, may not probably soon drop from the Brow of it^s present Possessor; but there is another Place of much the same Value now vacant; it is that of Deputy Licensor to the Stage. Be not offended at this Hint: for tho I will own it impudent enough in one who hath so many Obligations of his own to you, to venture to recommend another Man to your Favour, yet Impudence itself may possibly be a Virtue when exerted on the behalf of a Friend; at least I am the less ashamed of it, as I have

Bow H. Aug.st 29 1749

Permit me to bring up the Rear of your Friends
in paying my Compliments of Congratulation on your
late happy Nuptials. There may perhaps be Seasons
when the Rear may be as honourable a Post in Friendship
as in War, and if So, such certainly must be every
time of Joy and Felicity. Your present Situation must
be full of these; and so will be, I am confident, your
future Life from the Same Fountain. Nothing can equal
the excellent Character your Lady bears among her own
Sex, and I never yet knew them speak well of a Woman
who did not deserve it. How admirable is y.e Fortune
in the Matrimonial Lottery! I will venture to say there
is no Man alive who equals mon in this, or in any other
Happiness that can attend you than my Self: and you
ought to believe me from the Same Reason that fully persuades

Reduced Facsimile of a Letter to George Lyttelton, Esq.

...me of the satisfaction you receive from any Happiness of mine; this Reason is that you must be sensible how much of it I owe to your Goodness; and there is a great Pleasure in Gratitude tho' it is found I believe to that of Benevolence: for of all the Delights upon Earth none can equal the Raptures which a good mind feels in conferring Happiness on those whom we think worthy of it. This is the Sweetest Ingredient in Power, and I solemnly protest I never wished for Power more than a few Days ago for the Sake of a Man whom I love, and that more perhaps from the Esteem I know he bears towards you than from any other Reason. This Man is in Love with a young Creature of the most apparent Worth, who returns his Affections. Nothing is wanting to make two very miserable People extremely blessed but a moderate Portion of the greatest of human Evils. So Philosophers call it, and so it is called by Divines, whose Word is the rather to be taken as they are, many of them, more conversant with this Evil than ever the Philosophers were. The Name of this Man is Moore to whom you kindly destined that Laurel, which, tho' it hath long been withered, may not probably soon drop from the Brow of it's present Possessor; but there is

another Place of much the same Value now vacant; it is
that of Deputy Licenser to the Stage. Be not offended at
this Hint: for tho' I will own it impudent enough in
one who hath so many Obligations of his own to you, to
venture to recommend another Man to your Favour, yet
Impudence itself may possibly be a virtue when exerted
on the Behalf of a Friend; at least I am the less ashamed
of it, as I have known Men remarkable for the opposite
Modesty possess it with the Mixture of any other good
Quality. In this Fault then you must indulge me; for
should I ever see you as high in Power, as I wish, and as it is
perhaps more my Interest than your own that you should be,
I shall be guilty of the like as often as I find a Man in whom
I can, after much Intimacy discover no Want, but that
of the Evil abovementioned. I beg you will do me the Honour
of making my Compliments to your unknown Lady, and
believe me to be with the highest Esteem, Respect, Love and Gratitude

                                Sir,
                                  Y.r most Oblig'd
                                    most obed.t
                                      humble servant
                                        Henry Fielding

To the Hon.ble
George Lyttelton Esq.r

known Men remarkable for the opposite Modesty possess it with᷒ the Mixture of any other good Quality. In this Fault then you must indulge me: for should I ever see you as high in Power, as I wish, and as it is perhaps more my Interest than your own that you should be, I shall be guilty of the like as often as I find a Man in whom I can, after much Intimacy discover no Want, but that of the Evil abovementioned. I beg you will do me the Honour of making my Compliments to your unknown Lady, and believe mè to be with the highest Esteem, Respect, Love, and Gratitude

Sir,

Y᷒ most obliged

Most obed᷒

humble Servant

HENRY FFIELDING

To the Hon᷆᷆ᵇˡᵉ

George Lyttelton, Esq᷒''*

The request was not granted, though Lyttelton soon came to Moore's aid in other ways. There may have been some immediate assurances, for on August 10, 1749, Edward Moore led Jenny Hamilton to the altar.

The year of labour and new friendships closed for Fielding in gloom. Succeeding the controversies over Penlez, he was visited by the severest attack of gout that he had ever had. In "The General Advertiser" for December 28, we read: "Justice Fielding has no mortification in his foot as has been reported: that gentleman has indeed been very dangerously ill with a fever, and a fit of the gout, in which he was attended by Dr. Thompson, an eminent physician, and is now so well recovered as to be able to execute his office as usual." The physician who attended him was Dr. Thomas Thompson, the quack whose improper treat-

* From the autograph in the library of the Historical Society of Pennsylvania, Philadelphia.

ment of Winnington, the wits said, had put an end to that eminent statesman's career. Fielding knew the story, and yet employed him. The doctor had another patient in the house whom his physic could not cure. On December 17, 1749, Mary Amelia, who had breathed the Bow Street air a scant year, was buried at St. Paul's, Covent Garden. Her place was taken a month later, on January 21, 1750, by Sophia, christened after the daughter of Squire Western. But before the new year, beginning so auspiciously, was over, Fielding lost two of his sisters—Catherine and Ursula—who were laid at rest in Hammersmith; the former on July 9, the latter on November 12, 1750. A third sister, Beatrice, was buried by their side on the twenty-fourth of the following February. Of the spinsters only Sarah remained to survive him. His brother John soon married, took over as assisting justice a share of the routine business of the court, and thus enabled Henry to give more attention to literature and the larger questions arising out of his office.

During these months no cases comparable to the riots of 1749 came before the court, though organized disturbances threatened and demanded prompt action. With reference to one of them, Henry wrote to the Duke of Bedford:
"My Lord,

In obedience to the Commands I have the Honour to receive from your Grace, I shall attend to-morrow morning and do the utmost in my Power to preserve the Peace on that occasion.

I am, with gratitude and Respect,
My Lord,
Your Grace's most obliged
most obedient humble servant.
Bow Street,
May 14, 1750.''*

* Miss Godden, ''Henry Fielding,'' p. 221. From autograph at Woburn Abbey.

Fielding also nipped in the bud a conspiracy against the life of the Lord Chancellor entered into by the keepers of three notorious gambling-houses which had been closed by his lordship's order. In a letter to a lawyer named Hutton Perkins we see the two men preparing to confer over the case:

"Sir

I have made full enquiry after the three Persons and have a perfect account of them all. Their characters are such that perhaps three more likely Men could not be found in the Kingdom for the Hellish Purpose mentioned in the Letter. As the Particulars are many and the Affair of such Importance I beg to see you punctually at six this evening when I will be alone to receive you—and am,

Sir,
Y? most obedient humble servant
H. Ffielding.

Bow Street.
Nov? 25. 1750.''*

As time went on, only cases like these required Fielding's personal attention. Eventually, minor misdemeanors were left to his brother. Thus relieved from constant attendance in the court room, the principal justice was able to bring his intelligence to bear on the most difficult criminal problem of the time—the suppression of house-breaking and highway robbery within the metropolis and on the roads leading to it.

* British Museum, ''Additional MSS.,'' 35591, f. 147.

CHAPTER XXI

THE MIDDLESEX MAGISTRATE

II

WAR AGAINST ROBBERY AND MURDER

No description can easily exaggerate the lawless state of London when Fielding took office. The following item from the newspapers of December, 1748, is but typical of the violent crimes occurring every week and almost every day:

"This evening, as a gentleman and lady were going out of Drury-lane playhouse, a pickpocket snatch'd at the lady's watch, upon which the gentleman collar'd the fellow; but immediately another came to attack the gentleman, who behaved very gallantly, by immediately running the fellow thro' the body, and he died in half an hour afterwards. Not only pickpockets, but street-robbers and highwaymen are grown to a great pitch of insolence at this time, robbing in gangs, defying authority, and often rescuing their companions, and carrying them off in triumph."[*]

Horace Walpole, returning from Holland House on another evening, was robbed in Hyde Park, after the skin of one cheek had been grazed by the highwayman's bullet. Near the same place his uncle Horatio was stopped and had his face scorched with powder. These were common incidents within the heart of Westminster—in the Haymarket and Piccadilly, right under the Duke of Devonshire's wall. Within the memory of man, streets and roads had never been so infested with footpads, while highway-

[*] "The London Magazine," XVII, 570 (Dec., 1748).

men rode through the town to visit gambling-houses or to attend the masquerades. Sometimes these robbers waylaid people in daylight, but more often at night when they could escape under its cover. Nowadays there is no darkness for a city, but in Fielding's London the case was quite different. The lamps were never lighted until six o'clock in the evening, and those that did not flicker out before were extinguished at midnight; and when the moon was full they were not lighted at all. From midnight till sunrise might be seen the torch of the linkboy conducting some gentleman home, or the lantern of a watchman as he made his rounds. Save for these streaks of light, the town was as dark as Erebus; it was "the darkness visible" of Milton's Hell.

The watchmen in general were timid and feeble old men, engaged for a few pence a night. The constables to whom they handed over suspected persons were a grade better; but they were few in number and hard to find when they were wanted. Constable and watchman were as likely to be at an alehouse as on the streets. To tumble them into the gutter when they were in the way, and to run off with their staff or lantern or rattle, was more a jest than an offence. The whole story of the police system is summed up in the Penlez riots. The watch amounted to nothing; no constable except Saunders Welch did his duty; no justice except Fielding cared to interfere, for there was danger in the business. Not even this sort of protection was given to the outskirts of the metropolis, where the gentlemen of the road, in gold-laced caps with crape over their faces, waited on horseback for easy victims. Aware of this, the inhabitants of the suburbs organized themselves into a police to patrol the turnpikes until eleven o'clock at night, and then they went to bed. No one, if he could help it, ever entered London alone by night. Tom Jones, having only Partridge with him, tried it and succeeded, but he had to pass over the body of a highwayman. Fresh from the country, he did not know that it was customary for travellers who were forced to take the risk, to band together in companies well armed.

This influx of robbers was often attributed by newspapers to the large number of disbanded soldiers and sailors after the Peace of Aix-la-Chapelle, who, finding no other occupation, augmented the old gangs and formed new ones. Some of them were desperate characters; others, like the highwayman in "Tom Jones," were made criminals by necessity—they had to choose between starvation and robbery. If they reached Newgate or some other prison, their state became dreadful. "Graft" was rampant, there was no discipline, robbery and murder were frequent within the very walls, there was no sanitation, and the inmates died in shoals of jail fever. Before bringing prisoners into court, it was customary to wash them in vinegar that the infection might not take hold of judge and jury. If the highwaymen reached Tyburn, they were drawn there in carts, hanged in the presence of a vast crowd, wept over by sentimental women, and made heroes instead of objects of detestation. Such was criminal London as Fielding found it. In his contest with the corruption of the Walpole Government, he had assumed the rôle of Hercules slaying the hydra; he now undertook, in his own phrase, to cleanse the Augean Stables.

Had he been a soldier, his first endeavour would have been a reorganization of the police, the need of which was apparent. He had no more respect for the watch than had Shakespeare when the great dramatist drew Dogberry and his staff. Their ignorance, dishonesty, and general incompetency, are all depicted in "The Coffee-House Politician." The establishment of a new police system, however, required mature consideration; and Fielding decided for the present not to disturb a time-honoured institution, but rather to improve it so far as he could by recommending the retention of every constable who had proved efficient. In this indirect way, he gathered about him a group of officers who could be depended upon—so numerous in the course of a year or two that he was willing occasionally to spare one for the Commission of Peace or for a prison which needed a strong man over it. Thus he wrote to the Duke of Newcastle:

"My Lord,

It being of the utmost consequence to the Public to have a proper Person Keeper of the new Prison at this Time, I beg leave to recommend Mr William Pentlow a Constable of St George Bloomsbury to your Graces Protection in the present Vacancy. He is a Man of whose Courage and Integrity I have seen the highest Proofs, and is indeed every way qualified for the charge. I am with the most perfect Respect,
        My Lord,
            Your Grace^s most obedient and most
                humble servant
                    HENRY FFIELDING.

Bow Street, Jan. 15, 1750 [N. S. 1751]"*

Mr. Pentlow had distinguished himself in the apprehension of a gang of robbers; and as a reward he received the prison appointment on Fielding's recommendation, despite the fact that the Duke of Newcastle wished to place over the new prison in Clerkenwell a certain John Bland who had never learned to read or write. In a deed dated May 23, 1751, Fielding bound himself for £100 unto Thomas Lane, Esq., then chairman of the Middlesex Sessions, and two other justices of the peace, Luke Robinson, Esq., and Henry Butler Pacey, Esq., as a surety that William Pent-

* British Museum, "Additional Manuscripts," 32685, f. 59.

low would observe the conditions of the appointment.* Pentlow conducted himself so well in his new office that the justices of Middlesex at one of their Sessions subsequently thanked him for his vigilance and efficiency.† At the same time, Fielding drew up regulations for the guidance of the eighty constables within his immediate jurisdiction and afterwards encouraged Saunders Welch to publish a little treatise on the same subject so that constables might know precisely what was expected of them.

As a lawyer and justice, he saw at once that the existing statutes against violent crimes were inadequate; they seemed to be framed, he declared, more for the escape of highwaymen and footpads than for their conviction. Accordingly, he prepared during his first year in office, as the reader has probably observed, the draft of a "Bill for the better preventing Street Robberies," which he sent to the Lord Chancellor with his "Charge to the Grand Jury." Though the draft is no longer extant, we may assume from Fielding's subsequent proposals that it was a very drastic measure which the Government was not then ready to advocate. He was doubtless advised to try out the old laws. At any rate he adopted this course of action and pursued it with vigour. Quoting from the newspapers under the date of August 29, 1750, "The Gentleman's Magazine" says: "So many highway men and street-robbers are in custody on the impeachment of their accomplices, that the little prisons are quite full; notice was given in the papers, that those who have been robbed might see the impeached persons in Clerkenwell Bridewell, or at Justice Fielding's on their examination." Many of these robbers, however, were acquitted when brought to trial, owing to defects in the law.

And so Fielding resolved, as another point of attack, to

* Mr. J. Paul de Castro, "Notes and Queries," 11 S. II, 55 (Jan. 16, 1915).
† John Fielding, "A Plan for Preventing Robberies," 1755, p. 2.

address the public in the capacity of justice and moralist. The suggestion of a moral as well as a legal appeal perhaps came from his friend Isaac Maddox, the Bishop of Worcester, who delivered, on Easter Monday, 1750, an eloquent sermon before the Lord Mayor and the Magistrates of London, on "The Expediency of Preventive Wisdom," in which all the prevailing crimes were laid to inordinate gin-drinking. Others discovered the main source of crime in the many houses of ill fame. The time was ripe for a larger discussion of criminal London. On October 9, 1750, "The General Advertiser" came out with the interesting announcement: "We hear that an eminent magistrate is now employed in preparing a pamphlet for the press in which the several causes that have conspired to render robberies so frequent of late will be laid open; the defects of our laws enquired into, and methods proposed which may discourage and in a great measure prevent this growing evil for the future." And midway in the following January came the pamphlet itself, entitled "An Enquiry into the Causes of the Late Increase of Robbers," with a dedication to Lord Hardwicke.* The "Enquiry" appeared—by mutual arrangement, no doubt,—at the very time when the Government was ready to bring forward new criminal legislation. His Majesty's speech, in opening Parliament on January 17, 1751, recommended to Lords and Commons that they should make use of the present state of tranquillity "for suppressing those outrages and violences, which are inconsistent with all good Government, and endanger the lives and properties of my subjects." In its political aspect, the "Enquiry" was designed to mould the public mind in favour of the Ministry's proposals.

Fielding the moralist uncovered no esoteric or hidden causes for the violent crimes which rendered life hazardous in the metropolis. All his reflections were based upon a

* "The Gentleman's Magazine," XXI, 48 (Jan., 1751).

knowledge of the town which he had gained from long observation, and upon his experience as a Bow Street justice. Out of the mouths of men and women brought before him for examination, he had learned how they entered on their careers of crime, and by what means they had since succeeded. All the ins and outs of the underworld were a plain tale to him. Once the common people, he declares, were frugal and industrious; but since the introduction of trade with the wealth consequent upon it, a "vast torrent of luxury . . . hath poured itself into this nation," whereby "the manners, customs, and habits" of the lower orders, equally with the higher, have been "almost totally changed." Each rank in society is now emulating in expensive pleasures the next rank above. He was not much disturbed, he says, by the nobleman who apes a prince or by the gentleman who apes the nobleman; but there is reason for concern when "the tradesman steps from behind his counter into the vacant place of the gentleman," and reason for alarm when the confusion reaches "the very dregs of the people, who aspiring still to a degree beyond that which belongs to them, and not being able by the fruits of honest labour to support the state which they affect, they disdain the wages to which their industry would intitle them." The result is that "abandoning themselves to idleness, the more simple and poor-spirited betake themselves to a state of starving and beggary, while those of more art and courage become thieves, sharpers and robbers." "I remember," he says, "very lately a highwayman who confessed several robberies before me, his motive to which, he assured me, (and so it appeared) was to pay a bill that was shortly to become due." And again: "I once knew an honest gentleman who carried his wife and two daughters to a masquerade, being told that he could have four tickets for four guineas; but found afterwards, that in dresses, masques, chairs, &c. the night's entertainment cost him almost twelve. I am convinced that many thousands of honest tradesmen have found their expences exceed their computation in a much greater proportion. And the sum of seven or eight shillings (which is a very moderate allowance for the entertainment of the smallest family) repeated once or twice a week through a summer, will make too large a deduction from the reasonable profits of any low mechanic." These men who spend their earnings in pleasure neglect their business; and in the end "fill the streets with beggars, and the gaols with debtors and thieves." Fielding therefore advocated, in the interest of the general welfare, the passage of a law to retrench the places of amusement where the common people squandered their time and money and were tempted to crime.

With the Bishop of Worcester, Fielding agreed that the worst vice which has attended luxury is a "new kind of drunkenness . . . which, if not put a stop to, will infallibly destroy a great part of the inferiour people." "The drunkenness I here intend," he explains, "is that acquired by the strongest intoxicating liquors, and particularly by that poison called *gin;* which, I have great reason to think, is the principal sustenance (if it may be so called) of more than an hundred thousand people in this metropolis. Many of these wretches there are, who swallow pints of this poison within the twenty-four hours; the dreadful effects of which I have the misfortune every day to see, and to smell too. . . . Wretches are often brought before me, charged with theft and robbery, whom I am forced to confine before they are in a condition to be examined; and when they have afterwards become sober, I have plainly perceived, from the state of the case, that the *gin* alone was the cause of the transgression, and have been sometimes sorry that I was obliged to commit them to prison." This monstrous evil he would extirpate by prohibiting the manufacture of the "diabolical liquor" or by laying so severe an impost upon it that it would be placed entirely beyond "the reach of the vulgar."

Quite apart from murder and other crimes, legislators should soberly reflect upon the pernicious consequence of gin-drinking "to the health, the strength, and the very being of numbers of his Majesty's most useful subjects. . . . What must become of the infant who is conceived in *gin?* with the poisonous distillations of which it is nourished both in the womb and at the breast. Are these wretched infants (if such can be supposed capable of arriving at the age of maturity) to become our future sailors, and our future grenadiers? Is it by the labour of such as these, that all the emoluments of peace are to be procured us, and all the dangers of war averted from us? What could an Edward or a Henry, a Marlborough or a Cumberland, effect with an army of such wretches? Doth not this polluted source, instead of producing servants for the husbandman, or artificer; instead of providing recruits for the sea or the field, promise only to fill alms-houses and hospitals, and to infect the streets with stench and diseases?" If these considerations make no appeal, he adds with grim humour, there is one unanswerable reason for the suppression of the vice; and that is "the loss of our gin-drinkers: Since, should the drinking this poison be continued in its present height during the next twenty years, there will, by that time, be very few of the common people left to drink it." Well might Fielding make this prophecy; for the hundred thousand who lived upon gin comprised nearly a seventh of the entire population of the metropolis.

The breeding-place of the most eminent highwaymen he finds in the gambling-houses. Easy of access, they are frequented by all classes. A young gentleman perhaps is there bubbled out of his money, and in attempts to retrieve himself is lured on until he loses his estate. In desperation he turns sharper; and thereafter the transition is swift "from fraud to force, from a gamester to a rogue"; he joins a gang and takes to the road; that completes the process. The trouble here is not so much with the law as with the magistrates who have authority, if they will exert it, to destroy all gaming among the common people, no instance of which exists without their neglect or connivance. To make conviction somewhat easier, he advised that the law be so amended that the information of one instead of two witnesses should be sufficient for ordering a commitment. Still, by enforcing the law as it was, he declared that he had checked and discouraged public gambling within the liberty of Westminster. This policy, even though there were no new legislation, should now be extended to the entire county of Middlesex, that an end may be put to schools which educate for the road.

Terrible is Fielding's arraignment of the officers who administer the poor laws. Despite the high poor rates, equal almost to the land-tax, despite private donations, hospitals, and almshouses, the poor, generally speaking, "are in a very nasty and scandalous condition." The laws, though they have several imperfections, are not chiefly to be blamed for reducing the poor to the state of swine; the responsibility lies mostly with incompetent and corrupt overseers and churchwardens who pervert them for their own emolument. The very poor, as he has observed them, fall into three classes. First, there are those who are unable to maintain themselves owing to some weakness of mind or body. Eliminate from this class, which appears large, the impostors—such as the lame who when provoked use their crutches for weapons instead of supports, and the blind who when they hear the beadle at their heels outrun the dogs which had guided them before,—and the number of the really impotent left is so small that provision for them might be safely entrusted to private charity. It is

259

the second and third classes that stand in need of strict regulation; that is, "such as are able and willing to work" and "such as are able to work, but not willing." Notwithstanding the fact that the chief design of the various statutes has been to provide labour for the industrious poor and to compel the lazy to work, the overseers and church-wardens have, except in individual cases, totally neglected to perform their duties, giving as their excuse that, though the laws confer upon them authority to set the poor to work, they are not precisely mandatory. So long as the administrators of the poor laws take this view of their office, it is a farce for any justice of the peace to commit offenders to Bridewell, "there to be kept at hard labour," for these houses of correction, far from supplying work, have become "seminaries of idleness, and common sewers of nastiness and disease."

"What good consequence," he inquires of his readers, "can arise from sending idle and disorderly persons to a place where they are neither to be corrected nor employed; and where with the conversation of many as bad, and sometimes worse than themselves, they are sure to be improved in the knowledge, and confirmed in the practice of iniquity? Can it be conceived that such persons will not come out of these houses much more idle and disorderly than they went in? The truth of this I have often experienced in the behaviour of the wretches brought before me; the most impudent and flagitious of whom, have always been such as have been before acquainted with the discipline of Bridewell: A commitment to which place, tho' it often causes great horror and lamentation in the novice, is usually treated with ridicule and contempt by those who have already been there." Until the loophole through which the overseers crawl be closed by fresh legislation, it must be expected that many worthy magistrates will discharge offenders with a reprimand in hope of their reformation rather than send them to certain destruction.

Were measures to be taken, Fielding says, for the proper care and regulation of the present poor, and were their increase prevented by "some effectual restraints on the extravagance of the lower sort of people," it would be unnecessary for him to say more; "since few persons, I believe, have made their exit at Tyburn, who have not owed their fate to some of the causes before mentioned." But preventive legislation such as he advocates, interfering with British notions of liberty, is so difficult, he says, that he can hardly hope to make his views prevail. Perhaps he must be content to suggest certain palliatives, which, though they cannot work a cure, will reduce the number of robberies. As the law now stands, he adds, it is almost impossible to convict the receiver of stolen goods, for he is but an accessory to the crime and cannot be punished, however clear his guilt, if the thief is acquitted on some technicality. And yet, as everybody knows, the principal offender is the receiver of the goods, who keeps in his employ many of the younger thieves and pickpockets. If these nests are to be broken up, the law must make the reception of stolen goods an original offence and accept as evidence in little felonies the thieves themselves. Again, whenever a thief or burglar gets away with a booty of any value, he is almost sure of seeing it advertised within a day or two in one of the newspapers with the direction to bring the goods to a certain place where he will receive a reward for their return, and no questions will be asked. This public countenance to robbery by people who prefer an old watch or a diamond ring to the welfare of society, should be made a crime.

Render it harder not only for the thief to dispose of his winnings, but for him to escape. The problem here is how to catch the thief in a town where hiding-places are afforded by an immense number of lanes, alleys, courts, and by-places. The law against vagabondage, which prohibits the wandering of suspicious characters as well as of the poor from parish to parish, has long been in abeyance. So far as London and Westminster are concerned, everybody is permitted to go where he pleases. The requirement that no person shall be without a place of abode is technically evaded by the gangs of thieves and robbers who herd in so-called private houses, where they pay a penny a quartern for gin and twopence a night for lodging, and less if they sleep two in a bed. They lie promiscuously, no distinction being made for sex, in all the rooms from cellar to garret. Having sent Saunders Welch several times on search warrants to these miserable places, he once accompanied his constable to two little houses in Shoreditch, which they emptied of nearly seventy men and women, among whom was "one of the prettiest girls I had ever seen." She was just married to an Irishman who had brought her there to celebrate their nuptials. On searching the seventy inmates, the officers found upon them all (excepting the bride who had robbed her mistress) less than a shilling. Whereupon Fielding remarks: "The . . . wonder is, that we have not a thousand more robbers than we have; indeed, that all these wretches are not thieves, must give us either a very high idea of their honesty, or a very mean one of their capacity and courage." The law needed, according to Fielding, only slight amendment in order to give the magistrate power to send vagabonds to the parishes whence they came, where, among people who know them, it would "be impossible for them to steal or rob, without being presently hanged or transported out of the way."

The apprehension of felons hardened in crime has become, says Fielding, a very hazardous undertaking. Highwaymen often commit robberies in open daylight, in the sight of many people, and afterwards ride triumphantly through the neighbouring towns without molestation. A constable, though he may have a warrant in his pocket, dares not attempt an arrest; for the moment he interferes, an alarm is sounded, and twenty or thirty armed villains come to the rescue of the highwayman and to the death of the constable. Under the law private persons are encouraged by rewards to assist the officer and are even given power in certain crimes to apprehend felons without a warrant; but they rarely or never offer their services lest they gain the opprobrious name of "thief-takers." If the felon is eventually caught and arraigned, there is, for a variety of reasons, great difficulty in proving the charge against him. A highwayman usually knocks his victim down in the dark or flaps his hat over his eyes, thus rendering identification in many instances impossible. Moreover, persons who have been robbed are loath to aid the prosecution because of fear or indolence, expense or tenderness. For the fearful and indolent Fielding had only contempt; and to the tender-hearted he read a lecture, admonishing them to reflect upon the character of the villain for whom they show pity—a man "who deprives his countrymen of the pleasure of travelling with safety, and of the liberty of carrying their money or their ordinary conveniences with them; by whom the innocent are put in terror, affronted and alarmed with threats and execrations, endangered with loaded pistols, beat with bludgeons and hacked with cutlasses, of which the loss of health, of limbs, and often of life, is the consequence; and all this without any respect to age, or dignity, or sex." If the good-natured man places this picture before his eyes, he will see what figure in it deserves his compassion.

The case, however, is different with the poor man who hesitates to prosecute on account of the expense in time and money. In these cases, numerous in the aggregate, Fielding would transfer the cost of trial from the prosecutor to the public. He also argues for alterations in the rules of evidence so that the evidence of an accomplice may put a prisoner on his defence and "oblige him either to controvert the fact by proving an alibi, or by some other circumstance; or to produce some reputable person [to] his character." Under this rule, no honest man could ever be convicted, and we should see less often than we do now the villain triumphantly acquitted, laughing at the court, scorning the law, and vowing vengeance against his prosecutors, as he rides away to ply his trade with renewed confidence and greater cruelty than ever.

In conclusion, Fielding touched lightly upon pardons and the commutation of the death penalty to transportation, for he did not wish to offend the Government, which, throughout the reign of George the Second, constantly interposed its power to modify or stay the course of justice. He nevertheless utterly condemned in most respectful language the merciful temper of his Majesty as an encouragement to felons. "Pardons," it was his opinion, "have brought many more men to the gallows than they have saved from it." Punishment, if it is to deter crime, must be certain and swift. He proposed that public executions at Tyburn, long after the crime has been committed, be done away with, for they have completely failed to awaken in the spectators the detestation of the rogue which was once expected of them. Any man who sees a wretch hanged is so overpowered with compassion that he forgets the atrocious crime. Tyburn Jack becomes a hero if he conducts himself with spirit tempered with decorum; and the day appointed by law for his shame is regarded as a day of glory. Death to be most terrible must be, as Shakespeare knew, behind the scenes. When Garrick plays the rôle of Macbeth and comes running in with the daggers after murdering Duncan, "it is scarce a hyperbole," Fielding remarks, "to say, I have seen the hair of the audience stand an end. Terror

264

hath, I believe, been carried higher by this single instance, than by all the blood which hath been spilt on the stage." Taking his cue from this scene, Fielding brought forward a blood-curdling plan which he thought would meet all the ends that can be reasonably required of an execution. "Suppose," he says, "that the court at the Old Baily was, at the end of the trials, to be adjourned during four days; that, against the adjournment-day, a gallows was erected in the area before the court; that the criminals were all brought down on that day to receive sentence; and that this was executed the very moment after it was pronounced, in the sight and presence of the judges." It was quite needless for him to add: "I leave it to any man to resolve himself upon reflection, whether such a day at the Old Baily, or a holiday at Tyburn, would make the strongest impression on the minds of every one."

Fielding did not wish to leave with his readers so tragical a scene as this. His very last word, coming from a most humane mind, was a grave petition to the legislature to cast aside remedies of the palliative kind and to seek a cure through prevention for the ills under which the commonweal was suffering; that is, in accordance with his plan, "to put a stop to the luxury of the lower people, to force the poor to industry, and to provide for them when industrious," in order that there might be no excuse for crime on the score of necessity. "Not only care for the public safety, but common humanity," he says finely, "exacts our concern on this occasion; for that many cart-loads of our fellow-creatures are once in six weeks carried to slaughter, is a dreadful consideration; and this is greatly heightened by reflecting, that, with proper care and proper regulations, much the greater part of these wretches might have been made not only happy in themselves, but very useful members of the society, which they now so greatly dishonour in the sight of all Christendom."

If any other justice of the peace ever made so valuable a contribution to the literature of crime, I do not know his name. One is uncertain which to admire most—Fielding's exact knowledge of the law, his common sense, or that lofty idealism and faith in human nature which led him to believe that crime might some day have an end. It would be easy, in the light of Adam Smith, to riddle his political economy, for he had queer notions on the relation of wages to wealth, and to pick flaws in his scheme for banishing poverty from Great Britain. No one, however, in his time was able to point out any of his fallacies. Criticism of his views was in the main narrow and spiteful. A writer in "The London Magazine" asked him why he did not mention brothels among demoralizing places of amusement. Curiously, he appended to his treatise an advertisement of the Universal Register Office, where the public were told that they might obtain trustworthy servants quite different from those described in the "Enquiry." Though a reader would see at a glance that the puff was not written by Fielding, but by his brother John or someone else in authority, the magistrate's eye to business provoked a sneer at the "trading-justice."

So in February appeared "A Letter to Henry Fielding Esq; occasioned by his Enquiry"; and a few weeks afterwards: "Observations on Mr. Fielding's Enquiry . . . By Ben Sedgly, of Temple-Bar. To which are added Considerations on the Nature of Government . . . By Timothy Beck, the Happy Cobler of Portugal Street." Ben Sedgly was one of the writers on "The Westminster Journal," where he distinguished himself, said a newspaper brother, for dulness and an ability to empty a tankard of beer at a single draught. He was also a contributor to "The Student, or, the Oxford and Cambridge Miscellany," with which Christopher Smart, the poet, was connected. Timothy Beck, who wrote from "Portugal Street, Lincoln's Inn," claimed to be a cobbler who had turned author. How he happened to collaborate with Ben Sedgly, he told the public in the March number of "The Student." "As I begin to have the estimation of a wit," he wrote there, "and am looked upon as a man of importance, I have lately resorted to Ben. Sedgley's at the Ship and Anchor near Temple-Bar, where I am reputed to be so comical a fellow, that the landlord has persuaded me to assist him in publishing an answer to Mr. Fielding's Enquiry."* This is probably a fiction; Ben and Timothy appear to have been one and the same man, whose real name may have been Sedgly or Sedgley. Not so bitter as Argus Centoculi of "Old England," he more than once snarled at Fielding as in this low pamphlet. The justice is here taken to task, in a dull and laboured style, for failing to enumerate the vices of his own class, for false views on the English constitution, for wishing to bribe felons to turn state's evidence, and for the light manner in which he treated grave questions. But this time all abuse of Fielding fell flat. The "Enquiry" went into a second edition in April, and was reprinted by Faulkener, the Dublin publisher. "An admirable treatise,"† said Horace Walpole, who had sneered at the justice's household and cold mutton.

Likewise all the magazines, without exception, expressed admiration. "The Gentleman's Magazine," often chary of praise when Fielding was concerned, took the "excellent pamphlet" for its leading article; while "The Monthly Review," of more generous temper, said: "The public hath been hitherto not a little obliged to Mr. Fielding for the entertainment his gayer performances have afforded it; but now this gentleman hath a different claim to our thanks, for services of a more substantial nature. If he has been heretofore admired for his wit and humour, he now merits

* "The Student," II, No. 6, p. 215.
† "Memoirs of the Reign of George II," 1836, I, 44.

equal applause as a good magistrate, a useful and active member, and a true friend to his country." The Duchess of Somerset, scenting its literary aroma, rescued the "Enquiry" and Gray's "Elegy" from "an inundation of books," and prattled of them to Lady Luxborough.* Hogarth drew his "Gin Lane," depicting the physical ravages of "this new kind of drunkenness," the most horrible of all his plates. Following the address from the throne, Parliament appointed a committee, on which were placed Pitt and Lyttelton with Sir Richard Lloyd as chairman, "to revise and consider the laws in being, which relate to felonies and other offences against the peace"; and in the meantime, the Government, taking the alarm, offered a reward of £100, above all other rewards, for the apprehension of any robber in the streets of London or within five miles of the city, together with a free pardon for any accomplice (provided he were not guilty of actual murder) who should discover the offender. Fielding, we may be sure, did not countenance that absurd proclamation, expressive of utter helplessness. More than any other writer he had awakened the public conscience which was as yet uncertain of its course.

Robbery means murder. About "the scarlet sin," as it was called, Fielding said little in the "Enquiry," but took up the subject in "The Covent-Garden Journal," a periodical which he founded in January of the next year. Under date of February 1, 1752, we read: "More shocking murders have been committed within this last year, than for many years before. To what can this be so justly imputed, as to the manifest decline of religion among the lower people. A matter which, even in a civil sense, demands the attention of the Government." The week previous Fielding spent, at the request of the Lord Mayor, twenty-eight hours in taking depositions and examining suspects in a

* "Lady Luxborough's Letters to Shenstone," 1775, p. 237.

most barbarous murder, but was unable to fathom the mystery. While the justice was meditating over the cause and cure of the growing evil, he had a conversation with the Bishop of Worcester, under whose encouragement he published, on April 13,* "Examples of the Interposition of Providence in the Detection and Punishment of Murder."

This is a small pamphlet to be slipped into the pocket, appropriately dedicated to its sponsor and containing thirty-odd tragical stories to illustrate how "the most dreadful crime of murder" is very sure to be detected through some miraculous act of God, if the conscience of the murderer does not first betray him. Here we have Fielding, the perfectly orthodox preacher, attributing, as in "The Covent-Garden Journal," the increase of murders to a "general neglect (I wish I could not say contempt) of religion, which hath within these few years so fatally over-spread this whole nation"; and avowing his belief in por-tents and ghosts sent from heaven as a last resort to frighten the murderer into confession before the arrival of that awful day when, standing before "an offended Al-mighty," he shall be confronted by his victim, "in the pres-ence of all the Host of Heaven," and have justice demanded against his miserable soul. Fielding's instances to prove that murder will out, were taken from many sources, of which he cited a favourite book once mentioned in "Jona-than Wild"; it is "The Triumphs of God's Revenge against the Crying and Execrable Sin of Wilful and Pre-meditated Murther," a popular compilation made by John Reynolds, a merchant of Exeter back in the seventeenth century. In truth, Fielding's pamphlet is a sort of chap-book drawn from the old merchant's long treatise, supple-mented by modern instances such as the cases of Mary Blandy and Elizabeth Jeffries, who were hanged in the spring of this very year. On the title-page Fielding asserts

* Announced for that day in "The Covent-Garden Journal," April 11, 1752.

that he is the author of the introduction and conclusion, but is silent as to the rest. Presumably the old stories were compressed into short narratives by another hand—his sister Sarah's, or more likely William Young's, for there are indications that the parson was still collaborating with him. Fielding's presence, however, is manifest here and there, as in the comment on the second example, and in several anecdotes concerning divine intervention in cases of murder. One anecdote he heard in conversation with a Lancashire clergyman, who certainly told the truth; another from a gentleman who had attended celebrated trials; and still others from Irishmen who were eyewitnesses to what happened. Fielding, I fear, was rather credulous when it came to a supernatural story.

The chapbook, having nothing of a legal character, was a direct appeal to the masses whom he hoped to restrain from murder by bringing home to them the heinousness of the crime and the certainty of punishment either in this life or in the next. That the pamphlet might accomplish its mission, he gave away many copies among the poor; and requested the aid of others in its circulation. The price to patriotic gentlemen thus inclined was ten shillings a dozen. Under the date of April 13, it is announced in "The Covent-Garden Journal" of the next day:

"This Day Mr. Fielding began to distribute Gratis, his little Book, just published, which contains a great Number of Instances of the Interposition of Providence, in the Detection and Punishment of Murder. An Example, which, it is hoped, will be followed by all who wish well to their Country, or who have indeed any Sentiments of Humanity.—No Family ought to be without this Book, and it is most particularly calculated for the Use of those Schools, in which Children are taught to read: For there is nothing of which Children are more greedy, than Stories of the Tragical Kind; nor can their tender Minds receive more wholesome Food, than that which unites the Idea of Horror with the worst of Crimes, at an Age when all their Impressions become in great Measure, a Part of their Nature: *For those Ideas which they then join together,* as Mr. Locke judiciously observes, *they are never after capable of separating."*

Despite the reference to Locke, I trust that these tales of horrible murders were never introduced into the schools to disturb the innocent sleep of children. They were put to better use by "a certain colonel of the army," who, according to "The Covent-Garden Journal" of May 5, "bought a large number of the book . . . in order to distribute them amongst the private soldiers of his regiment." "An example," the author adds, "well worthy of imitation." On discharging a man, it was related, who threatened to kill his wife, Fielding placed in his hands a copy of "the little book against murder," with the injunction that he read it before he slept that night. Another time, after he had committed to Newgate a young man for cutting his wife's throat, the prisoner "begged the justice to give him the little book on the heinous sin of murder, lately published, which when he received, he shed a shower of tears, and wished he had read it before."

In the "Enquiry," Fielding had treated of poverty in relation to crime. Administer the poor laws honestly, and robbery will be reduced to a minimum—that was his main thesis. He there hinted, however, that he was engaged upon a plan to cure the body politic of extreme poverty altogether. The idea came to the front towards the close of the treatise, and he later brought it to the attention of Henry Pelham, Chancellor of the Exchequer.* The plan, long brewing in his mind, was finally set forth in "A Proposal for making an Effectual Provision for the Poor, for Amending their Morals, and for Rendering them useful

* "The Daily Advertiser," Nov. 25, 1751.

Members of the Society.'' A noble dedication to Pelham, dated January 19, 1753, assured the Prime Minister that the scheme, if carried into execution, would remove from society the evils of which all honest men complain and render famous with posterity a name loved and honoured by the humble author. Nowhere else did Fielding ever write with deeper emotion than in the pages that followed.

"There is," to quote briefly from the introduction, "not a parish in the liberty of Westminster which doth not raise thousands annually for the poor, and there is not a street in that liberty which doth not swarm all day with beggars, and all night with thieves. Stop your coach at what shop you will, however expeditious the tradesman is to attend you, a beggar is commonly beforehand with him; and if you should not directly face his door, the tradesman must often turn his head while you are talking to him, or the same beggar, or some other thief at hand, will pay a visit to his shop! I omit to speak of the more open and violent insults which are every day committed on his Majesty's subjects in the streets and highways. They are enough known, and enough spoken of.'' But, in contrast with these misdeeds of the poor, there is another picture which few have seen. He has seen it; Saunders Welch has seen it; and certain members of Parliament have been shocked by it. The poor who beg and steal and rob in the open, starve and freeze and rot when at home. "If we were to make a progress through the outskirts of this town," he says, recalling his own raids, "and look into the habitations of the poor, we should there behold such pictures of human misery as must move the compassion of every heart that deserves the name of human. What indeed must be his composition who could see whole families in want of every necessary of life, oppressed with hunger, cold, nakedness, and filth, and with diseases, the certain consequence of all these; what, I say,

272

must be his composition, who could look into such a scene as this, and be affected only in his nostrils?''

The question that Fielding first put to himself was how this appalling state of society had been produced. In the course of his studies he read and considered all the statutes relating to the poor and all that had been written about them from the original institution of Queen Elizabeth, and observed with close attention, year by year, the effects of the existing laws in so far as he was concerned in the execution of them. His conclusion, somewhat at variance with that of the ''Enquiry,'' was that the failure to deal rightly with poverty had arisen as much from defects in the laws as in the administration of them. He therefore recommended that they be all repealed and that a new comprehensive law be enacted to take their place. For the benefit of the legislature he outlined in a tentative way such a statute, and commented upon each of the fifty-nine articles that it might well contain. His most novel recommendation was that the county of Middlesex purchase three hundred acres of a common near Acton Wells, beyond Hammersmith, and there erect an immense workhouse, where all the very poor of the county, criminal and industrious, might be collected, controlled, and set to work. An elaborate plan of the buildings, estimated to cost £100,000, was drawn for Fielding by ''an eminent hand'' and published as a part of the pamphlet. The name of the ''eminent hand'' appears at the foot of the sketch as ''Tho�$ Gibson Archᵗ,'' hardly to be identified with Thomas Gibson the portrait painter, for he died in the spring of 1751, long before Fielding issued his ''Proposal.'' Still, Fielding had his scheme in mind as early as 1751, and he may have then called in the well-known painter to design his buildings.

The women were to be separated from the men, the worthy poor from the criminal; and all were to be supplied with instruments and material for profitable employment.

Those put to the hardest labour were to rise at four o'clock in the morning, attend prayers in the chapel precisely at five, begin work at six, and stick to it until seven in the evening, except on holidays, with an allowance of half an hour for breakfast and an hour for dinner. All who refused to work were to be transported. For his labour everyone was to receive a small wage dependent upon the value of the goods he produced, which he should be encouraged to spend in the furtherance of his trade. As Fielding reckoned it, the profit accruing to the county from this rigid employment of the poor would be £60,000 a year, a full equivalent of the amount which was then raised by the poor rates. The inference is clear that, if his ideas were adopted, the poor would no longer be a burden upon the public, and might perhaps be converted into a source of emolument. Certainly there would be no more taxes for their support. They would also forget the ways of crime, acquire the habit of work, and gradually, on being discharged, become valuable members of society. It was altogether a patriotic scheme, notwithstanding impracticable features, which Fielding broached that he might, to quote his own words, confer "a lasting benefit upon my country."

An advocate of large reforms never expects, if he be sane, that his entire programme will be put into effect; he accounts himself fortunate if half of it prevails. Fielding, who really had none of the reformer's confidence in schemes for the regeneration of society, often feared that the movement in which he took the lead outside of Parliament would come to nothing at all. In his pamphlets pale hope alternates with despair. He rather misjudged the temper of a public ready to listen to his appeals. Inebriates and beggars are a nuisance; people, even though long accustomed to be robbed on the streets and highways, do not relish being knocked on the head and surrendering their purses and watches; they are quite willing that the legislature take measures for their protection. The only question is, What shall be done? Hence arise differing opinions which may end in a struggle, always causing delay and sometimes wreck of the reforms.

The Government showed a good deal of tact by making the first assault upon gin, over the disastrous effects of which there was general alarm. As the law then stood, the tax on gin was only a penny a gallon; and the ordinary licence to sell it cost but twenty shillings a year, though distillers who retailed spirituous liquors on their premises had to pay five pounds. By 1751, there were 17,000 gin-shops "within the bills of mortality"; and the consumption of British spirits, mostly gin, amounted to 11,000,000 gallons, nearly double what it had been in 1743 when the tax was reduced from twenty shillings a gallon to the beggarly penny. So low was the tax that it seemed hardly worth while to enforce the law. At any rate, the number of unlicensed gin-sellers and gin-pedlars increased enormously in the metropolis. They carried on their trade with little disturbance until 1750, when, before the year was over, more than four thousand of them were convicted of selling spirits without a licence, and were accordingly fined ten pounds each, the penalty under the law. It was more difficult to suppress the hundreds of gin-shops run on a distiller's licence, with the aim of distilling just enough of the liquor to satisfy the requirements of the law. To the commissioners of excise was left the perplexing question to decide whether the gin sold over the bar was distilled on the premises. Needless to say, convictions were rare.

With these spurious distillers and licensed dealers mainly in view, Parliament passed the so-called "Gin Act,"* which received the royal assent on June 25, 1751. All licences held by distillers under the old law immediately ceased, and no more licences were to be granted to them.

* "Statutes at Large," 24 Geo. II, 40.

No spirituous liquor was to be sold or given away "in any gaol, prison, house of correction, workhouse, or house of entertainment for the parish poor." Hereafter all licences were to be confined to taverns, alehouses, inns, and coffee-houses, that is, to places where victuals were sold. The retail licence was raised from one to two pounds, and the tax on all low wines including gin from a penny to twopence halfpenny. At the same time, the powers of justices of the peace were so greatly enlarged that they became almost coequal with those of the commissioners of excise, penalties for offences against the law were made heavy, and rewards were offered to persons giving information that should lead to conviction. The new law did not go so far as Fielding advocated in the "Enquiry," but it met his milder recommendations: the number of gin-shops was diminished, the sale of spirits was prohibited in all penal and charitable institutions, and convictions were rendered less difficult. Had the Government attempted more, there would have been, to judge from past experience, tumults and riots.

Parliament, however, adjourned without enacting a law against robbery; and at the opening of the next session, on November 14, 1751, the King and the Government again declared that immediate action was necessary. "I cannot conclude," said his Majesty, "without recommending to you, in the most earnest manner, to consider seriously of some effectual provisions to suppress those audacious crimes of robbery and violence, which are now become so frequent, especially about this great capital; and which have proceeded, in a great measure, from that profligate spirit of irreligion, idleness, gaming, and extravagance, which has of late extended itself, in an uncommon degree, to the dishonour of the nation, and to the great offence and prejudice of the sober and industrious part of my people." On the twenty-sixth of the following March, the royal

assent was given to "An Act for the better preventing
Thefts and Robberies, and for regulating Places of publick
Entertainment, and punishing Persons keeping disorderly
Houses."* Nearly all the provisions of this statute were
in line with the preventive measures urged by Fielding in
the "Enquiry." Under the new law any person advertising a reward, with no questions asked, for the return of
lost or stolen goods, was made liable to a fine of fifty
pounds. The penalty extended also to the publisher and
the printer of the advertisement.

Likewise any person keeping a place of public entertainment in London or Westminster without a licence was
to forfeit one hundred pounds. As the power to issue the
licence was vested in the justices of the peace at their
Quarter Sessions, this clause gave them full control over
all music and dancing halls as well as gardens like Ranelagh and Vauxhall. To remove the danger of collusion,
the justices were to receive no fee for the licence. It was
further required that there be placed over the entrance
of every licensed resort an inscription in large letters
announcing that it was such, and that the doors be not
opened to the public until five o'clock in the evening. For
a breach of either condition, the law declared, the licence
shall be revoked. To encourage prosecutions of bawdy and
gambling-houses, it was provided that if two inhabitants
of any parish or place, paying scot and lot, give information
that results in the conviction of the keeper, they shall each
receive a reward of ten pounds. Constables were directed
to enter, on a proper warrant from a justice of the peace,
all suspected places and to seize any persons found therein;
and that the old disputes over the identity of the keeper
might cease, he was defined as the man who behaves as the
keeper. Moreover, justices of the peace were empowered
to examine on oath any suspected rogue or vagabond not

* "Statutes at Large," 25 Geo. II, 36.

only as to the parish where he was last legally settled but also as to his means of livelihood. If he could not give a satisfactory account of himself, he was to be committed to the house of correction, to await removal to the place where he belonged. Finally, in cases of felony, poor prosecutors might, at the discretion of the court, be relieved of all fees and be allowed a reasonable sum of money for their loss of time in attending the examination or trial. Such was the law, designed, said the preamble, to remove from the lower sort of people temptations to theft and robbery and to cure, so far as might be, the habit of idleness.

This statute was supplemented by "An Act for preventing the horrid Crime of Murder."* Parliament was not yet ready to end the holiday at Tyburn; that reform did not come until 1783; but in other respects the new law was conceived in the spirit of Fielding's recommendations. Sentence must be pronounced immediately after conviction; and unless the judge know reasonable cause for delay, the murderer must be executed on the next day but one after the sentence. During the interval the prisoner was to be kept in solitary confinement on bread and water, and no spirits were to be brought into his cell except on a physician's order. After the execution, his body must be immediately conveyed by the sheriff to Surgeons' Hall, there to be dissected and anatomized. The salutary effect of the statute was apparent at once. The glamour of Tyburn was departing. Jonathan Wild had steeled himself for the ordeal by draughts of punch and laudanum; the first murderer executed under the new law went to the gallows sober and, according to "The London Magazine," wept bitterly over his fate.

At the same session of Parliament were introduced other bills dealing with the subject of Fielding's pamphlets; but

* "Statutes at Large," 25 Geo. II, 37.

they all failed. It was proposed, for example, to put pawn-brokers, as well as the purveyors of amusement, under the close regulation of licences from the justices of peace, to fix their rate of interest, and to hold them to strict account for receiving goods suspected of being stolen. The bill passed the Commons but was rejected by the Lords. Two bills were also presented for the more effectual relief and the employment of the poor—the one framed in behalf of children and the other of the whole body of the poor. The design was to build county houses throughout England, where the helpless poor might be given profitable work. By general consent both measures were deferred to the next session for further consideration. To them Fielding alludes in his "Provision for the Poor," saying that they were in the hands of "two very honourable and learned persons"— Lord Hardwicke and Sir Richard Lloyd—for whom he has "a very high respect and esteem." Expecting that action would be taken on the opening of Parliament in January, 1753, he then brought forward his plan of a county house for Middlesex with suggestions for enlarging the scope of the intended legislation. Neither of the poor bills, against which a strong opposition developed, was pressed by the Government. The hostility of the public towards them and Fielding's proposal was expressed by the Rev. Thomas Alcock in an open letter addressed to "a Member of Parliament." Had they been put on the statute book, Fielding's workhouse would have been a natural consequence; the disastrous law of Elizabeth would have been repealed, and England would have obtained in 1753 what she had to wait nearly a century for.

Here arises the question whether any of the three measures which prevailed were drafted by Fielding for the Parliamentary committees appointed to prepare them. As the evidence is mostly internal, one first looks in them for the technical peculiarities of Fielding's style. The very obvious earmark, his use of *hath* for *has,* partially fails, however, when applied as a test to laws, inasmuch as the older inflection survived in legal documents long after it had ceased to be common in literature. The Act against murder, which runs on *has,* may be at once eliminated, although the lawyer who framed this statute had by him Fielding's "Examples of the Interposition of Providence," the first paragraph of which he condensed into his preamble. The Gin Act comes nearer to Fielding's door, for the author not only works into his preamble various phrases from the "Enquiry" but is also fond of *hath.* Still, I hardly think that Fielding wrote out a law which falls far short of what he urged, and hits the gin traffic through the distillers about whom he is silent in the "Enquiry." There remains the Act for preventing theft and robbery. No *has* or *hath* here helps solve the problem; the law contains neither form. The statute, however, follows exactly, though in different order, the most practicable recommendations of the "Enquiry," and employs Fielding's own language, little altered from the pamphlet, all the way through the caption, the preamble, and the many sections. The presumption is that the draft of the bill which Fielding sent to the Lord Chancellor in the summer of 1749 served as an outline for his address to the public in the "Enquiry," that he afterwards made such changes in the original draft as seemed desirable and submitted the revised bill to Sir Richard Lloyd, who introduced it into Parliament with minor alterations. Taken all in all, what Fielding accomplished in the way of reform legislation by aiding the Government is most impressive. It is a fresh chapter in history. He was the man behind the scenes.

Above all others, Fielding was, too, the magistrate to whom the Government looked for the enforcement of this legislation. He sent out his constables, sometimes going with them, to raid unlicensed places of amusement,—drums, routs, masquerades, and semi-public gardens. One morning Saunders Welch brought in thirty idle gentlemen and apprentices taken the night before from a gambling-house, the most notorious of whom were committed to prison; and the master, said the newspapers, was bound "with very great bail to the Sessions, where he will be prosecuted pursuant to the new Act of Parliament." This is the first of many direct blows that Fielding was now able to level against the keepers of gambling-houses. In conjunction with other justices of the peace, he also revoked licences for the sale of spirits; and tried to end all unlawful traffic in gin, though he found the statute inadequate for the purpose. Profane swearers on the street were haled into his court, and fined or sent to Bridewell, that he might check "the licentious insolence of the vulgar." Vagrants who appeared honest were discharged; the sick were recommended to the care of the overseers of the poor; and the rest were bound to good behaviour or sent to the house of correction until they could be removed to the parishes where they belonged. Within a fortnight after the law went into effect, fifty houses of ill fame in the Strand were closed, many keepers fled to escape prosecution, and for a time the streets were "cleared of ladies in an evening." So determined became the pursuit that complaint was made against the "very worthy and useful magistrate" on the ground that his over-zealous constables interfered with women of character who happened to be out after dark, and that he was crowding the prisons with multitudes of unhappy wretches, who when released would add to the swarm of beggars, unless they were permitted to return to their former courses for bread. There may have been point in the latter part of the criticism. Fielding's desire, of course, was to keep these women at work in houses of correction; but the law which he urged with this intent had failed. So he did the best that he could in the circumstances; and that was to strike terror into all who made a business of prostitution. Nothing more was ever said by the wits about his being in league with bawdy-houses.

Where Fielding partially failed at first was in the execution of the clauses in the new Act against violent crimes. The number of thefts and burglaries perhaps diminished, for no man who had lost his goods now dared advertise a reward for them; but footpads and highwaymen still flourished as much as ever. The fault clearly lay with the public, not with the justices. Though the statute gave Fielding powers, which he often exercised, to hold these men five days as suspected persons, it was necessary to order their release at the end of this period if no one appeared against them. To encourage prosecutors, he inserted week after week in "The Covent-Garden Journal" the following notice:

"All Persons who shall for the Future suffer by Robbers, Burglars, &c. are desired immediately to bring, or send, the best Description they can of such Robbers, &c. with the Time and Place, and Circumstances of the Fact, to Henry Fielding, Esq; at his House in Bow-Street."

This and similar appeals published elsewhere had little effect upon the prevailing apathy and fear. How great was Fielding's disappointment may be inferred from many items in his newspaper, of which this, under date of June 13, 1752, is an example:

"On Tuesday last the three Persons taken up on Suspicion of robbing on the Highway, were brought before the Justices to be re-examined; when, after all the Pains which the Justices had taken, and the Expence which they had been at in advertising, not one Prosecutor thought proper to appear. In a Nation where there is such Zeal for the Public in every Man's Bosom, it is wonderful there are no more Robbers."

Again, with a livelier touch of humour:

WAR AGAINST ROBBERY AND MURDER

"There are now several Dangerous mad People confined by the Justice, who must shortly be let loose; of which timely Notice will be given in this Paper, *that his Majesty's sober Subjects may shut themselves up in their Houses.*"

That members of Parliament might see how difficult it was to prevent, for lack of evidence, the escape of a prisoner whose guilt nobody could really doubt, they were invited to attend examinations at the Bow Street court. This was the way Fielding took to impress upon Parliamentary committees defects in the law or the narrow rules of procedure by which he was bound. The crisis came in the summer of 1753 when he was probing with indifferent success five murders, all of which had occurred within a week. The Duke of Newcastle, becoming alarmed, then sent a ministerial courier, Mr. Carrington, to summon Fielding for his advice on the best means of putting "an immediate end to those murders and robberies which were every day committed in the streets." As was the Duke's custom with inferiors, he did not condescend to discuss the problem with the justice, but employed a gentleman acting upon his instructions. The upshot of this conference, held at Newcastle House in Lincoln's Inn Fields, was that Fielding prepared and submitted to the Duke four or five days later—Mr. Carrington again being the messenger—a plan which he believed would be effective. Hitherto, the Government in moments of desperation had offered, as we have seen, a reward of £100 for the apprehension of a robber, and full pardon to the accomplice who betrayed him. This policy, says Fielding's brother John, begot a worse evil "by inducing a set of villains to decoy unwary and ignorant wretches to commit robberies, and then to make a sacrifice of them for the sake of the reward; while the real offenders not only escaped justice, but increased their barbarities even to murder." Fielding himself, who was careful not to criticise the powers that be, proposed that the Government, instead of issuing proclamations of large rewards, should deposit £600 in his hands to be used at his discretion. With this sum to draw upon, he guaranteed "to demolish the then reigning gangs, and to put the civil policy into such order, that no such gangs should ever be able, for the future, to form themselves into bodies, or at least to remain any time formidable to the public."* Fielding's plan, supported by all the arguments at his command, pleased the Duke of Newcastle and met with the approval of the Privy Council.

Fielding immediately collected a small company of thief-takers, "all men," he says, "of known and approved fidelity and intrepidity." Well armed but in citizen's dress, they were really a detective force supplementary to the constables and watch—the first, so far as I can discover, in English history. Their method was to haunt places in the metropolis where violent crimes were most often committed, to ride in stagecoaches approaching the town, and, whenever the opportunity came, to capture the robber or highwayman by some ruse or in open fight. Their first success was with a most desperate gang of cut-throats who, though only fourteen in number, were robbing, hacking and hewing their victims, says John Fielding, to such an extent that people were deterred "from passing and repassing on their lawful occasions after night." An informer, to whom Fielding paid a small sum, betrayed them into the hands of the thief-takers; a terrible struggle ensued in which one robber and one thief-taker were killed. Seven of the villains were captured and hanged, and the rest were driven either out of town or out of the kingdom. This vigorous action was continued until, says Fielding, all similar societies "were almost entirely extirpated." It took him only a few weeks to perform this great public service, at an expenditure of but a third of the money

* Introduction to "A Voyage to Lisbon."

placed at his disposal. During the weeks that followed, in the dark nights of November and December, 1753, not a murder or street-robbery occurred, he adds, either in London or in Westminster. This extraordinary statement is confirmed by comment in "The Public Advertiser" of January 1, 1754, on the complete success of "Mr F's Plan." Moreover, according to his brother John, the gangs were unable to form again on any sure footing so long as the mysterious plan, which was kept a secret, remained in operation. When the public eventually learned how Fielding had suppressed robbery, they were surprised at the simplicity of his method. The thief-takers did not belong, as was supposed, to the criminal class; they were reputable citizens and householders who had served as constables. The bravest of these men Fielding organized into his second force and placed them under the direction of that faithful public servant, Mr. Saunders Welch.* Now for the first time in many years, people went about their business or pleasure at night without the slightest fear of being waylaid by footpads. None but Fielding's bitterest enemies failed to give him credit for the new freedom. Occasionally he was attacked for relying upon informers; occasionally, out of malice, a murder or robbery was chronicled in the newspapers opposed to him; but in every case the report was proved to be false.

By the side of this victory over crime, the most sensational case that ever came before Fielding now appears insignificant. It is nevertheless a spectacle that must be presented for the light it throws upon Fielding's character. On the night of January 1, 1753, Elizabeth Canning, described as a servant girl barely eighteen years old, mysteriously disappeared from her master's house in Alder-

* On these paragraphs see John Fielding, "A Plan for Preventing Robberies," 1755, pp. 2-6; also "An Account of the Origin and Effects of a Police," 1758.

manbury, a street in old London; she remained away until the twenty-ninth of the same month, when she returned home in a miserable condition, ill clad and half starved. She had been robbed, she said, on New Year's night and spirited away by two ruffians to a house out on the Hertford Road, where she had been confined for four weeks in a dark room. The suspicion of her friends immediately fell upon a house of ill fame at Enfield Wash, some ten miles from London; and several substantial tradesmen in her neighbourhood united in a subscription to prosecute those suspected of the crime. They carried her out to Enfield, where she identified, in the presence of a constable, the mistress of the house, a certain Susannah Wells known as "Mother Wells," and charged one of the inmates, an ugly old gypsy named Mary Squires, with the maltreatment which had reduced her to the point of starvation. The gypsy, she declared, had cut off her stays on her arrival, thrust her into a hayloft behind the kitchen, with a jug of water and a few slices of bread, upon which she had managed to subsist until her escape through a window four weeks later. As she sat upon a dresser in the kitchen, other members of the household were also brought in for her perusal, some of whom she doubtfully recognized. They were a motley company, mostly of strange names. Among them were a son and two daughters of the gypsy, a young woman whose name, Virtue Hall, belied her occupation, and a married couple who gave their names as Fortune and Judith Natus. Mother Wells, whose husband had been hanged, was facetiously called "the hempen widow." They were all huddled into a cart and taken before the nearest justice of the peace, one Merry Tyshmaker of Ford's Grove. Each of them in turn denied ever having seen Elizabeth Canning before that day. The justice, however, committed Mary Squires and Mother Wells to different prisons—the former for robbing

the girl of her stays and the latter for keeping a disorderly
house. All the rest were reluctantly discharged.

The result was not satisfactory to Elizabeth Canning's
friends; for the two footpads who had robbed the girl of
her money and conveyed her out of London were not yet
discovered; and unless her evidence against Mary Squires
could be corroborated, the gypsy would certainly be acquitted when she came up for trial before a judge and
jury. In these circumstances, the prosecutors employed
a lawyer named Salt to seek expert advice. What occurred
subsequently is told by Fielding himself in a story which
may well be set against the Rigby anecdote related by
Horace Walpole. While the justice was drinking tea with
his wife and a lawyer on the sixth of February, his clerk,
he says, delivered him a case on which Mr. Salt the solicitor,
who was waiting in the court room below, wished to consult
him. As the request was accompanied by the usual fee,
Fielding accepted the document, but handed it to his wife
for safe-keeping, and directed his clerk to tell the solicitor
that he would take it with him into the country, whither
he was going the next morning, for careful consideration.
Very soon the clerk returned with Mr. Salt, who asked for
an immediate decision as the case involved a felony and
there was danger that the parties would escape. Thereupon Fielding invited Mr. Salt to sit down; and after they
had finished their tea, he read over the case and advised
his friend how to bring the offenders to justice. The
solicitor then expressed a strong desire that the Bow Street
justice receive the depositions in the case; but Fielding
at first declined the business, partly on the ground that the
crime had been committed in a distant part of the county,
in the neighbourhood of an excellent justice of the peace,
and partly because he had been "almost fatigued to death
with several tedious examinations" during the week, and
felt that he must refresh himself with a short rest in the

country, where he had not been, "unless on a Sunday, for a long time." Mr. Salt was so insistent, however, that Fielding consented to alter his plans and remain in town.

The next day Elizabeth Canning, so weak that she could hardly stand, was brought in to swear to the truth of an information prepared by Mr. Salt, setting forth all the details of her detention; upon which, the justice issued a warrant against all who should be found resident in the house of Mother Wells, as idle and disorderly persons. The constable found only Judith Natus and Virtue Hall, whom Fielding subjected to a most severe examination lasting until midnight. Judith, who could not be moved from her original declaration that she had never seen nor heard of Elizabeth Canning before this case came up, was discharged, with the caution that she should beware of perjury if she intended to give the same evidence at the approaching trial of Mary Squires at the Old Bailey. Virtue, so great was the power exerted upon her at this and a subsequent examination, eventually put her mark to an affidavit corroborating Elizabeth Canning's story; and declared that one of the footpads who waylaid the girl was John Squires, a son of the gypsy.

On the strength of this confession, Fielding ordered detainers for felony against Mary Squires and Susannah Wells to be sent to the prisons where they lay. No action was taken against the gypsy's son because Virtue's unsupported oath appeared insufficient for his arrest. Having delayed his vacation for a week, the justice now went into the country for the week-end. The case of Elizabeth Canning, so far as he was concerned, seemed to be closed; but on his return, three or four days later, he was persuaded by "several noble lords" and "gentlemen of fashion" to confront Mary Squires and Mother Wells with Elizabeth Canning and Virtue Hall, in the hope of obtaining a full confession. Among those who attended this final examination was Lord Montfort, the lover of cricket and horse-racing. Unawed by the noble presence, the prisoners could not be induced to confess the crime laid against them. On February 21, 1753, Mary Squires and Susannah Wells came up for trial at the Old Bailey and were convicted five days later—the former of robbing Elizabeth Canning of a pair of stays valued at ten shillings and the latter of being an accessory after the fact. Mary Squires was condemned to be hanged, and Susannah Wells to be burned in the hand and imprisoned in Newgate for six months. The sentence against Susannah Wells was immediately executed before a crowd of spectators who shouted with delight at the smell of the burning flesh; but the sentence against Mary Squires was stayed by the intervention of the Lord Mayor, Sir Crisp Gascoyne, who, by virtue of his office, presided at the trial, and was dissatisfied with the verdict. A fortnight later, Virtue Hall, on being examined by the Lord Mayor, declared that the testimony which she gave at the trial as well as her information before Justice Fielding was false; whereupon his Majesty, on the tenth of April, granted the gypsy a respite of six weeks and instructed the law-officers of the Crown to make a full examination of the case and submit their report to the next cabinet council.

The prosecutors of Mary Squires, it seems, had in their possession a number of certificates or affidavits tending to prove for her an alibi. Since these friends of Elizabeth Canning were loath to produce them, the Lord Chancellor and the Duke of Newcastle appealed to Fielding for his assistance, thinking perhaps that he had some of them, as was being insinuated by the partisans of the gypsy. Fielding replied in two letters which cleared him of the charge of suppressing evidence. It will be noticed that these letters were written at Ealing, which, though now a part of the metropolis, was then a quiet country village, with a church and manor house, six miles from Hyde Park Corner. In the summer of 1752 Fielding took a farm there called Fordhook, which became his country residence for the rest of his life. It was situated, according to local history, "on the Uxbridge road, at the distance of about a mile from the village of Acton, at the eastern extremity of Ealing."* Various assessments against the property while it was held by Fielding show that it was valued at seventy pounds a year.† The place was chosen, Fielding says in "A Voyage to Lisbon," because the soil was dry and the air the best in the kingdom, while a ridge of hills cut off the north wind, and distance protected him against "the smells and smoke of London." Besides these attractions, the house had a southern exposure. What a relief it must have been for Fielding and his family to exchange on a Friday or a Saturday that old Bow Street den for the pure elastic air of Fordhook! In his first letter from the country to the Duke of Newcastle, Fielding wrote:

"My Lord Duke

I received an order from my Lord Chancellor immediately after the breaking up of the Council to lay before your Grace all the Affidavits I had taken since the Gipsey's Trial which related to that Affair. I then told the Messenger that I had taken none, as indeed the fact is the Affidavits of which I gave my Lord Chancellor an Abstract having been all sworn before Justices of the Peace in the Neighbourhood of Endfield, and remain I believe in the Possession of an Attorney in the City.

"However in Consequence of the Commands with which your Grace was pleased to honour me yesterday, I sent my

---

* T. Faulkner, "History and Antiquities of Brentford, Ealing, and Chiswick," London, 1845, p. 266.

† Mr. J. Paul de Castro in "Notes and Queries," 12 S. I (July 1, 1916). The Ealing Rate Books show poor rates assessed against Fielding on Feb. 15, 1753, Sept. 5, 1753, and Sept. 18, 1754. Fielding's predecessor was Thomas Gurnell; his successor was John Ranby, the distinguished surgeon praised in "Tom Jones."

Clerk immediately to the Attorney to acquaint him with these Commands, which I doubt not he will instantly obey. This I did from my great Duty to your Grace for I have long had no Concern in this Affair, nor have I seen any of the Parties lately unless once when I was desired to send for the Girl (Canning) to my House that a great Number of Noblemen and Gentlemen might see her and ask her what Questions they pleased. I am, with the highest Duty,

My Lord,

Your Graces most obedient
and most humble servant
HENRY FFIELDING.

Ealing.   April 14, 1753
His Grace the
   Duke of Newcastle.''

In the second letter, Fielding added:

''My Lord Duke,

I am extremely concerned to see by a Letter which I have just received from Mr Jones by Command of your Grace that the Persons concerned for the Prosecution have not yet attended your Grace with the Affidavits in Canning's Affair. I do assure you upon my Honour that I sent to them the Moment I first received your Grace's Commands and having after three Messages prevailed with them to come to me I desired them to fetch the Affidavits that I might send them to your Grace being not able to wait upon you in Person. This they said they could not do, but would go to Mr Hume Campbell their Council, and prevail with him to attend your Grace with all their Affidavits many of which, I found were sworn after the Day mentioned in the order of Council. I told them I apprehended the latter could not be admitted, but insisted in the strongest terms on their laying the others immediately before your Grace, and they at last promised me they would, nor have I ever seen them since. I have now again ordered my Clerk to go to them to inform them of the last Commands I have received, but as I have no Compulsory Power over them I can not answer for their Behaviour, which indeed I have long disliked, and have therefore long ago declined giving them any Advice, nor would I unless in Obedience to your Grace have anything to say to a set of the most obstinate Fools I ever saw; and who seem to me rather to act from a Spleen against my Lord Mayor, than from any Motive of protecting Innocence, tho' that was certainly their Motive at first. In Truth, if I am not deceived, I suspect they desire that the Gipsey should be pardoned, and then to convince the World that she was guilty in order to cast the greater Reflection on him who was principally instrumental in obtaining such Pardon. I conclude with assuring your Grace that I have acted in this Affair, as I shall on all Occasions with the most dutiful Regard to your Commands, and that if my Life had been at Stake, as many know, I could have done no more.

I am, with the highest Respect,

My Lord Duke

Y^r Grace's most obedient,

and most humble servant,

HENRY FFIELDING.

Ealing
April 27, 1753.
His Grace the Duke of
    Newcastle.''*

Whether the affidavits were secured the correspondence does not show; but the report of the law-officers of the Crown and the decision of the cabinet council were favourable to Mary Squires, who was forthwith pardoned by the

---

* These two letters were discovered and first published by Miss Godden, pp. 273-275.—Record Office. ''State Papers, Domestic,'' Geo. II, 127, No. 24.

King. Then grand juries began to wrestle with the evidence against Elizabeth Canning for wilful and corrupt perjury. At length she was indicted and brought to trial at the Old Bailey before a bench of seventeen judges, including the Lord Chief Justice, with the most eminent counsel on both sides. After listening to conflicting evidence for seven days, the bewildered jury, aided by the instructions of the court, pronounced her guilty of the charge, though two of them had grave doubts and all recommended her to mercy. By a divided court, nine to eight, she was sentenced on May 30, 1754, to imprisonment in Newgate for one month and to transportation for seven years to one of his Majesty's American colonies. At the request of her friends, who made up a purse for her, she was sent to New England. She came to Wethersfield, in Connecticut, where she was befriended by Elisha Williams, sometime Rector of Yale College, until her marriage on November 24, 1756, to a young man of her own age, John Treat, to whom she bore five children. Her husband, though of a good family, being a grand-nephew of Governor Robert Treat, was "a scatter-brain young fellow," who, owing to the improvidence of himself and wife, had to sell their farm. Once Mrs. Treat visited England to receive a legacy. She died on June 22, 1773. Except that she was not a good manager and helped her husband to spend a comfortable fortune, nothing is recorded against her character after she came to America.*

Through all the legal transactions culminating in the trial of Elizabeth Canning, the excitement of the public was intense. Her story as related in the information given before Fielding awakened pity for a demure, innocent-appearing girl who had borne a good reputation and had resisted to the point of starvation endeavours to force her

* H. R. Stiles, "A History of Ancient Wethersfield," New York, 1904, II, 716.

into the ways of a Virtue Hall. The instincts of a pure woman had triumphed, and the hag who sought to entrap her had been condemned to the gallows. Such was the general view at the time Mary Squires received sentence; nor did Elizabeth Canning ever lose the sympathy of her friends. But after the gypsy's trial others besides Sir Crisp Gascoyne, who studied the testimony as published in the newspapers, doubted the truth of Canning's strange narrative and were impressed by Squires's insistence that she and her children were far away from Enfield through all the early part of January. While the Lord Mayor was quietly seeking evidence for the gypsy's alibi, Dr. John Hill broke the momentary calm by assailing the verdict in several articles which he contributed to ''The London Daily Advertiser'' under the name of ''The Inspector.'' Not that this disreputable writer had any sincere regard for truth or justice; but he found here a theme likely to be replete with scandal. The effect of the attack was to put on the defensive the partisans of Canning; for whom Fielding, nettled by Hill's censure of the way in which Virtue Hall had been induced to confess, made ''the retort courteous'' in ''A Clear State of the Case of Elizabeth Canning.''

The pamphlet, completed on March 15, 1753, except for a postscript which was added the following Sunday, the eighteenth, was published the next week, while passions were beginning to run high between ''the Canningites'' and ''the Egyptians,'' as the two parties were called. Fielding, who would concede nothing, rehearsed his entire connection with the case from the first visit of Mr. Salt down to a recent examination of Canning since her trial, in the light of the affidavits which, it was rumoured, had been obtained by the Lord Mayor. By every means in his power, he had tried, he said, to bring the girl to a confession, if she were guilty of perjury; but she had always persisted in the truth of her original accusation with an air of perfect innocence which persuaded all who were present of the justice of her cause. He was forced, he declared, by all the rules of evidence, to accept her story, however improbable in some details, as in the main true. He nevertheless admitted that though she bore all the evident marks of simplicity in her face and bearing, she might have imposed upon him as well as upon the judges and jury at the trial of Mary Squires, for no one can lay claim to infallibility. In this spirit Fielding closed with the hope that the Lord Mayor and the Government would probe the case to the very bottom. As for himself, he had no desire to be found in the right and should not be the least displeased were he mistaken, for he was concerned with nothing but the discovery of the truth in an affair involving the administration of national justice.

Within a few days, Fielding's pamphlet, which was bought up by "the Canningites," passed into a second edition. Hill immediately replied for "the Egyptians" in "The Story of Elizabeth Canning Considered. With Remarks on what has been called, *A Clear State of Her Case,* by Mr. Fielding; and Answers to the several Arguments and Suppositions of that Writer." The effect of this public debate, though it won over some to the side of Hill, was to incense the friends of Canning and to rouse them to renewed activity in her behalf. Hitherto an object of pity, the girl became the heroine of the town. Subscriptions were opened for her at the fashionable coffee-houses, where she made her appearance at appointed hours, to receive handsome purses from gentlemen, to be looked at, to be admired. At White's, she was presented with thirty guineas. At the same time, numerous sixpenny prints of her and the gypsy were put into circulation—authentic portraits, wherein the unfortunate girl looks modest and innocent, while the gypsy is rendered as abhorrent as possible. A particularly fine etching by Thomas Worlidge, "the celebrated painter over the Little Piazza, Covent-Garden," cost a shilling and sixpence. One plate, having five distinct engravings, presents "a true draught of Elizabeth Canning," with the house she was confined in, the flight of the gypsies, and "The Inspector General of Great Britain" conversing with them. Of most interest is a group called "The Conjurers, drawn from life by the Right Honourable the Lady Fa-y K-w"; for it contains a full-length portrait of Fielding as he appeared in March, 1753. The scene is a stage, with pictures of the Mansion House and the Royal College of Physicians on the wall in the rear. In front rests a conjurer's bottle labelled "Another Bottle"; behind which stand within a magic circle three conjurers—Sir Crisp Gascoyne between Hill and Fielding. Hill is introducing with a gesture the hideous gypsy, while Fielding is speaking earnestly in favour of Canning, who is gently supported at his side, as if she might else collapse, by another woman. His legs swollen with the gout are swathed to the knees; a sword—the emblem of justice—serves him for a cane; and the scales of Astraea hang in full view from a pocket near a hand held out in protection of his fair client. Sir Crisp looks thoughtful and puzzled—uncertain, I daresay, where the truth lies. Some rude verses beneath the sketch say that when a cause cannot be understood by one wise head, it is necessary to call in the conjurers.*

The controversy spread into all the newspapers and magazines. There was a ballad entitled "The Devil Outdone," in which several disputants appear and quarrel; and a wit wrote a poem called "The Day of Doom," to

---

* This print was reproduced by Miss Godden in "Henry Fielding," p. 272, from the copy in the British Museum, "Social Satires," No. 3213. "A True Draught" is numbered 3211. For the reproduction of other prints, and lists, and accounts of the Canning pamphlets, see "The Gentleman's Magazine" and "The London Magazine," for 1753 and 1754. The trial of Canning is given in Howell's "State Trials," 1813, XIX, 262-275, 285-691, and 1418. The prints are described by Stephens and Hawkins in "Catalogue of Prints and Drawings in the British Museum: Political and Personal Satires," III, pt. II.

prevent, he said, further talk about Elizabeth Canning. Pamphlets, once started by Fielding and Hill, flew about, at the rate of five or six a month until they numbered a score or two. The questions whether life can be sustained for four weeks on a small loaf of bread and a piece of mince pie, and whether, assuming an affirmative, a person so nourished would be able to walk ten miles immediately thereafter, were raised by Fielding in his pamphlet, but he left the answer to the physicians. Dr. James Solas Dodd, who had published the year before an essay on the natural history of the herring, collected, in "A Physical Account of Elizabeth Canning," several instances of great authority to prove that one may live much longer than a month without any food at all. Daniel Cox, M.D., a member of the Royal College of Physicians, followed with "An Appeal to the Public, in Behalf of Elizabeth Canning." By permission of her friends, he repeatedly examined the girl—that is, looked into her mouth and questioned her about her habits of body—and came to the conclusion that all suspicions of her immorality were baseless. In the endless stream of pamphlets, Fielding was sometimes censured for acting in the double capacity of advocate and magistrate. This was the view taken, for example, in the anonymous "Canning's Magazine: or, A Review of the Whole Evidence that has been hitherto offered for, or against Elizabeth Canning and Mary Squires." True, Fielding accepted a fee from Salt and afterwards examined the witnesses of the prosecution; but the fee was for his advice on the proper procedure against the suspected offenders; it had no connection with his hearing of the case. Still, a justice of the peace to-day who had received a fee from either party would be disqualified for performing the judicial function. In the eighteenth century, however, this precaution against prejudice was not felt to be necessary. The attempt of Fielding's enemies to turn the public against him on this score met with no success. Indeed, his frank statement of his conduct, in the opinion of "The Gentleman's Magazine," completely exonerated his character.

Fielding's sympathy with distress, not a paltry fee, warped his vision. This was made clear by Allan Ramsay the painter, who, taking the pseudonym of "a clergyman," entered the fray with "A Letter to the Right Honourable the Earl of —— Concerning the Affair of Elizabeth Canning." Ramsay had the highest regard for Fielding; no one in his day paid a more just tribute to "Tom Jones," written by a man "who has succeeded so well in every subject he has undertaken, either of business or pleasantry." And he adds of Fielding's pamphlet: "Perhaps there are none of his performances that more discover the ingenuity of the man of wit, the distinctness of the lawyer, or the politeness and candour of the gentleman." Nevertheless, he was surprised to find on what slight grounds Fielding based his belief in the veracity of Canning; to put it bluntly, she misled him by her simple manner. Moreover, Ramsay hints that Salt also deceived the justice. On this point, Sir Crisp Gascoyne spoke more boldly in "An Address to the Liverymen of the City of London," justifying the part he had taken in the celebrated case. The integrity of Fielding the Lord Mayor did not question; he put the blame mostly upon Salt. "If Virtue Hall's examination had been taken," he declares, "as she would have freely given it; if no threats had been used to frighten her; if Mr. Fielding himself had prepared her information, or perhaps had only been present when it was prepared, the troubles, which ensued, could not have happened." Probably Salt was not a scamp; but he was surely led into a questionable act by his zeal. Fielding, who looked upon him as an honest man, let him write out the information of Canning as well as of Hall in private. This explains why the statements of the two women agree in all essential details and wherein lay Fielding's mistake.

It is not known whether Fielding ever lost faith in the innocence of Canning; but after Squires's pardon he became, as we have seen in one of the letters to the Duke of Newcastle, disgusted with the conduct of the girl's friends because they tried to withhold certain affidavits which threw doubt on her story. Subsequently, when a true bill was found by the grand jury against Canning for perjury, they kept her in hiding, and surrendered her only after a proclamation was made on a Sunday at her parish church commanding her to appear for trial at the next Sessions of the Old Bailey. She never quite confessed the crime with which she was charged; throughout the trial she maintained her composure and could not be swerved from her original story; but before the sentence was pronounced, she addressed the court in a low voice, saying that she had no intent of swearing the gypsy's life away, that what had been done was only in self-defence, that she desired to be considered as unfortunate. Where she was during the month's absence from home still remains a mystery. On the assumption of her being an impostor, it may be surmised that she was with a midwife and that she fabricated the robbery to save her reputation. No one, however, has a right to say this, for it accords neither with what is known of her previous life nor with her life in America. The case may be forever argued, with the weight of the legal evidence rather against her.

No other incident in Fielding's career as justice of the peace brings out so clearly his human side. If he erred, it was because like Parson Adams he put too great trust in the outward word and action. "To be placed above the reach of deceit," they are his own words, "is to be placed above the rank of a human being; sure I am that I make no pretension to be of that rank; indeed I have been often

299

deceived in my opinion of men, and have served and recommended to others those persons whom I have afterwards discovered to be totally worthless. I shall, in short, be very well contented with the character which Cicero gives of Epicurus. *Quis illum neget et bonum virum et comem et humanum fuisse!* And whoever will allow me this, which I must own I think I deserve, shall have my leave to add, *tamen, si haec vera sunt non satis acutus fuit.*" In these words we have a summary of Fielding. Great as was his intellect, he was above all else a man.

CHAPTER XXII

THE STORY OF AMELIA

The more the business at the Bow Street court, the less became Fielding's income. Those long investigations into riots and robberies, which kept the justice up all night, yielded him in each instance but a few shillings; and the habit grew upon him of composing petty quarrels, out of which he received nothing but thanks. If a wife or a husband accused the other of an assault, he advised them to overlook the grievance, to keep the peace, and, if possible, to live happily thereafter. One morning he was perplexed when Mary Macculloch and Jane Macculloch were arraigned before him for beating Elizabeth Macculloch, all of whom claimed the same man for husband. As none of the three wives had any evidence of her marriage, he decided that Elizabeth, who seemed to have known the man first, possessed the best right to him. The second and third wives, by consenting to the compromise, escaped Bridewell. Again, one evening a boy only twelve years old was brought in and charged with theft. What occurred in the court room was told by Fielding's clerk who reported the case: "The parents of the child (both of whom had an extreme good character) appeared; and the mother fell into agonies scarce to be conceived. In compassion to her, and to the tender years of the child, the justice, instead of sending him to prison, which would have probably ended in the death of the mother, and in the destruction of the son, recommended to his father to give him an immediate private correction with a birchen rod. This was executed with

301

proper severity, in the presence of the constable; and the parents, overwhelmed with joy, returned home with their child."* So humane an administration of justice may have been for the good of society; but when there was no commitment there was no fee. Had Fielding had an eye to his pocket he would have first sent quarrelsome husbands and wives, apprentices and urchins, to jail; and then bailed them out, thereby collecting a fee for each act.

His family expenses increased somewhat though not largely. Illness made it more and more necessary for him to retire to Fordhook and to leave the business of his court with his brother John. A daughter Louisa was baptized at St. Paul's, Covent Garden, on December 3, 1752, and was buried at Hammersmith on May 10, 1753. Before this time, his sister Sarah must have become mainly dependent upon him and his brother. But the trouble lay not so much in the maintenance of members of his family. "When in the latter end of his days," says Arthur Murphy, who associated with him at this time, "he had an income of four or five hundred a-year, he knew no use of money, but to keep his table open to those who had been his friends when young, and had impaired their own fortunes." That Fielding's table was free to anyone who wanted to dine or sup with him is most certain, though few names of these good-natured parasites are known. There was William Young, whom he probably employed on his newspapers and with whom he collaborated in different kinds of hack-work; there was Edward Moore, who took, whenever he liked, his friends to pass an evening with the justice; there were Walpole's "three Irishmen," typical of the lower grade; and there were Jane and Margaret Collier, whose brother had mulcted him out of a handsome sum.

Fielding's charities also exceeded his means. One day Mr. Welch told him that a baker in Bloomsbury, "an honest

* "Covent-Garden Journal," Feb. 4, 1752.

man" named Pierce, whose family he knew, was burned out
on the previous night. The next week Fielding opened a
subscription for them, which amounted to seventy-five
pounds, himself contributing a guinea, or as much as
Lyttelton and twice as much as Warburton. On another
occasion he collected a smaller purse for a Mr. Redman,
presumably a shopkeeper in distress like the baker of
Bloomsbury. His name also appears among "the perpetual
governors" of a lying-in hospital for married women, over
which the Duke of Portland presided. That honour, unless
he held it by virtue of his position as a justice of the peace,
cost him thirty guineas.* How often Fielding repeated
gifts like these, nobody knows; but they point to a habit
in perfect accord with his generous nature, with his benefit
nights, for example, in aid of unfortunate men and women
when he was manager of the Little Theatre in the Haymarket. To this mode of life, his dwindling income, despite
his pension and his shares in the Universal Register Office,
was quite inadequate. Once more he turned to literature,
which he henceforth carried on with the duties of his court
just as in earlier days he had written novels and newspapers while practising law.

For some time the public had been expecting another
novel from Fielding. He could not fail, it was thought, to
attempt an immediate repetition of the success gained by
"Tom Jones," as if a man could put out a work of that
character every year or two. The consequence was that
various novels in the facetious vein, often divided into
books in the epic manner, were set down to the credit or
the discredit of the great master in this style. Lady Mary
Wortley Montagu, for instance, who did not read Smollett's

* "An Account of the Rise and Progress of the Lying-in Hospital for
Married Women, in Brownlow-Street, Long Acre," 1751. See also a similar
pamphlet published by the hospital the next year, and a notice in "The Covent-
Garden Journal," Jan. 28, 1752.

"Roderick Random" until long after its publication, "guessed" it to be her cousin's; and it was translated into French "de l'Anglais de M. Fielding." Likewise, when Francis Coventry in the spring of 1751 published without his name "Pompey the Little, or the Adventures of a Lapdog," Lady Luxborough, speaking the opinion of herself and her friends in the country, declared it to be beyond doubt Fielding's.* The genuine novel, "Amelia. By Henry Fielding Esq;" made its appearance on December 18, 1751,† though the title-page bears the numerals of the new year. A dedication "to Ralph Allen, Esq," is dated "Bow Street, Dec. 12. 1751." The work, consisting of twelve books, was brought out in four duodecimo volumes and sold fully bound at twelve shillings a set.

Several stories concerning its publication early found their way into print; which, though they all contain inaccuracies, are now known to be in part true. "Amelia," Dr. Johnson told Mrs. Piozzi in 1776, was "perhaps the only book, which being printed off betimes one morning, a new edition was called for before night." The first and third volumes of the novel were set up for Millar the publisher by William Strahan, a well-known printer in New Street, who made the following entries in his ledger:

Dec. 1751. Amelia, vols. I. and III., 26½ sheets, no. 5000. Extraordinary corrections in do. £1 5s. 0d.

Jan. 1752. Amelia, 2nd ed. [?] sheets, no. 3000.

It has not yet been discovered who set up the second and third volumes. All told 8,000 copies, we see, were printed; and what Dr. Johnson called "a new edition" was really a second impression without alterations. In the same loose way the second impression was described not only by Strahan but by Fielding's friend, Dr. John Kennedy, as a "second edition." The first impression may have been

* "Letters to Shenstone," 1775, p. 265.
† "Whitehall Evening Post," Dec. 17-19, 1751.

sold out, as Dr. Johnson heard, by the end of the first day. Certainly it did not last beyond a week.*

Other details have come from Sir Walter Scott. "Millar," he wrote in his life of Fielding, "published 'Amelia' in 1751. He had paid a thousand pounds for the copyright; and when he began to suspect that the work would be judged inferior to its predecessor, he employed the following stratagem to push it upon the trade. At a sale made to the booksellers, previous to the publication, Millar offered his friends his other publications on the usual terms of discount; but when he came to 'Amelia,' he laid it aside, as a work expected to be in such demand that he could not afford to deliver it to the trade in the usual manner. The ruse succeeded—the impression was anxiously bought up, and the bookseller relieved from every apprehension of a slow sale." Scott, who seems to have forgotten the source of his information, was perhaps quoting from memory a passage in Wraxall's "Historical Memoirs" (1772), and got it not quite right. "The late Alderman Cadell," the paragraph runs in Wraxall, "who was one of the most intelligent, honourable, and superior men of his profession; told me that his predecessor, Millar, the bookseller, bought Fielding's Amelia of the author; giving him for the copyright, eight hundred pounds; a great sum at that time. After making the purchase, Millar shewed the manuscript to Sir Andrew Mitchell, who subsequently filled the post of British Minister at Berlin; requesting to have his opinion of the work. Sir Andrew observed to him, that it bore the indelible marks of a Fielding's genius, and was a fine performance; but, nevertheless, far beneath 'Tom Jones';

* The Strahan entries were first published by Mr. J. Paul de Castro in "Notes and Queries" (Nov., 1917, p. 466) from excerpts in possession of Mr. R. A. Austen-Leigh. For Dr. Johnson on "Amelia," see G. B. Hill, "Johnsonian Miscellanies," 1897, I, 297; for Dr. Kennedy, see "Some Remarks on the Life and Writings of Dr. J—— H——," as quoted in the next chapter, p. 348.

finally advising him to get rid of it as soon as he could. Millar did not neglect the counsel, though he was too able a man, to divulge the opinion delivered by his friend. On the contrary, at the first sale which he made to the trade, he said, 'Gentlemen, I have several works to put up, for which I shall be glad if you will bid: but, as to Amelia, every copy is already bespoke.' This manoeuvre had its effect. All the booksellers were anxious to get their names put down for copies of it, and the edition, though very large, was immediately sold out.'"*

The interesting story in the form given to it by Wraxall takes us back to the decade following Fielding's death. Thomas Cadell, the elder—who is the one meant in the narrative—became Millar's partner in 1765 and succeeded to the business two years later. It was during his apprenticeship that Millar brought out the collected works of Fielding along with Murphy's biography—an event which gave rise to numerous fresh anecdotes of the novelist. There was, precisely as Wraxall says, "a very large" first edition of "Amelia"; and rumours were current at the time that Millar paid liberally for it, though no one mentioned the amount, and no agreement between publisher and author has come to light to confirm the handsome sum of eight hundred pounds, which, I dare say, the author of "Tom Jones" could easily have commanded for a new novel. It was a shrewd stroke on Millar's part, supposing Wraxall's information correct, to submit the manuscript to Sir Andrew Mitchell, a hardheaded Scot, himself the occasion of many anecdotes, and a wit whom Fielding must have known. He had followed Fielding to Leyden and had been admitted to the bar at the Middle Temple; he remained loyal to the House of Hanover during the Jacobite insurrection, and afterwards gave his active support as a member of Parliament to the Pelham

* Wraxall, ''Memoirs,'' edition of 1836, I, 55-56.

Ministry. In short, he belonged to that class of Scotsmen for whom Fielding had the highest esteem, and whom he numbered among his political friends in the days of "The True Patriot."

So far one follows Wraxall's anecdote with little difficulty. But the "manoeuvre" attributed to Millar is doubtful. It seems incomprehensible that the publisher, a most honourable man, should have tried to impose upon his brethren in the trade. At any rate the supposed ruse did not meet with full success; for, though the first impression "was immediately sold out," the second sufficed for a decade. The novel was indeed soon translated into German and then into French, but no English reprint appeared until 1762. Millar's "manoeuvre" reduced to its lowest terms, becomes, I surmise, only his usual method of puffing a book for which he sought a large sale. When "Tom Jones" appeared, Millar informed readers of the newspapers, it will be remembered, that he could not "get sets bound fast enough to answer the demand for them." In the case of "Amelia" he went somewhat further than this, frightened perhaps by the rather severe judgment which Mitchell had passed upon the novel; for during the first three weeks of December, 1751, he appended to his advertisements of "Amelia" the following paragraph:

"'To satisfy the earnest Demand of the Publick, this Work has been printed at four Presses; but the Proprietor, notwithstanding, finds it impossible to get them bound in Time, without spoiling the Beauty of the Impression, and therefore will sell them sew'd at Half a Guinea.'"*

By the wits this advertisement was ridiculed as an extreme example of the art of puffing a worthless book; and there were several amusing parodies of it, such as the

* See, for instance, "The General Advertiser," Dec. 2; "The Whitehall Evening Post," Dec. 5; and "The London Daily Advertiser," Dec. 21, 1751.

following announcement of the third edition of "An Apology for the Life of Mr. Bampfylde-Moore Carew":

"The great Demand for this Book continuing, it is impossible to get them bound, without spoiling the Beauty of the Impression, it will therefore continue to be sold for 2s. 8d. sewed."*

Thereafter, "Amelia" and "Bampfylde-Moore Carew" were linked together by Grub Street as the two novels of the age which enjoyed the distinction of being put upon "six presses"—the number was thus raised from four to six—at one and the same time.

Notwithstanding this sport at the expense of Fielding, there is no reason to doubt the truth of Millar's statement, which is partially confirmed by the entries in Strahan's ledger. The second and the fourth volumes of the novel, differing from the first and the third in the founts used for title-pages and in several minor details, were entrusted to another printer. The two printers thus engaged upon the book must have possessed at least four presses. Moreover, the date of Fielding's dedication to "Amelia," only a week in advance of publication, is conclusive evidence that the novel was rapidly printed for sale during the Christmas holidays. Quite naturally a press was employed for each of the four volumes; otherwise Millar could not have brought out the novel on time. It was but good business sense for him to lay hand upon all the presses at his disposal, whatever may be said of the bad taste of an announcement so like the confidential information which is supplied by publishers nowadays. Such procedure can hardly be called a ruse, stratagem, or manoeuvre; it is only a means for awakening interest in a forthcoming novel without the intention of deceiving anybody.

Millar did not stop here. It was his custom to give out his most notable books for review in the magazines, two of

* "The London Daily Advertiser," Jan. 15, 1752.

AMELIA.

BY

Henry Fielding, Efq;

Felices ter & amplius
Quos irrupta tenet Copula.

Γυναικὸς οὐδὲν χρῆμ' ἀνὴρ ληίζεται
Ἐσθλῆς ἄμεινον, οὐδὲ ῥίγιον κακῆς.

In FOUR VOLUMES.

VOL. I.

LONDON:
Printed for A. MILLAR, in the *Strand*.
M.DCC.LII.

which he could usually count upon for favourable notices. These two took up "Amelia" in their December numbers, which were published near the first of January. "The Monthly Review" praised the author for his insistence upon the conjugal virtues and the married state as the source of supreme happiness and upon his absolute truth to life in the delineation of character. This commendation on the score of morality came from Ralph Griffiths the editor, a personal friend of Fielding's, and though it was sincere enough, it was lacking in discrimination. It barely served the purpose of saying a good word for the novel; it did not whet the appetite of the reader. "The London Magazine," which had given first place in its pages to "Tom Jones," repeated the compliment to "Amelia," and continued its résumé of the novel, volume by volume, into the appendix of the periodical for the year. It is a good rule never to ask a friend to review your book, for he knows too much about you. "Upon the whole," said this friendly critic with fine condescension, "the story is amusing, the characters kept up, and [there are] many reflections which are useful, if the reader will but take notice of them, which in this unthinking age it is to be feared, very few will." He felt constrained, in his final summary, to point out several "imperfections" in the novel and to take the author to task for his opinions on liberty and his failure to comment upon the most pressing questions in politics. These concluding strictures were worse for the novel than was the silence which "The Gentleman's Magazine" kept for the present. They corroborated all that Sir Andrew Mitchell had said in confidence to the publisher. Somehow the novel was a disappointment; somehow it failed to hit the temper of the times. Why this was so will become apparent in the course of our narrative.

Early in January a copy of "Amelia" reached a group of literary ladies over in Ireland, omnivorous novel readers all, who gyrated around Mrs. Delany, wife of the Dean of Down. She was styled by Madame D'Arblay, who knew her in old age, as "the fairest model of female excellence of the days that were passed." Neither she nor her friends were exactly unbiassed judges, for they placed Mr. Richardson above all other novelists; but they were eager to "peruse" any "frivolous" production of Mr. Fielding and the rest. After reading "Amelia," Mrs. Delany dispatched a letter, giving her impressions, to her sister in England. While admitting that the novel pleased "some few" of her company who had heard it read, she declared as to herself and her husband: "I don't like it at all; D. D. won't listen to it. It has a more moral design than either appears in Joseph Andrews or Tom Jones, but has not so much humour; it neither makes one laugh or cry, though there are some very dismal scenes described."* To say the truth, the public could not understand how so grave a novel had come from Fielding; only those immediately associated with him were aware to what extent illness and his experience as a police magistrate had sobered him. On March 19, 1751, the Rev. Richard Hurd, not yet a bishop, wrote to his friend the Rev. Thomas Balguy after a visit at Prior Park: "I wish you had seen Mr. Allen. He comes up to the notion of my favourites in Queen Elizabeth's reign: good sense in conjunction with the plainest manners— *simplex et nuda veritas.* I dined with him yesterday, where I met Mr. Fielding,—a poor emaciated, worn-out rake, whose gout and infirmities have got the better even of his buffoonery."† This divine of formal morals was as ignorant of Fielding's works as of his life and the vast public services he was then performing. The truth lying behind Hurd's gross expression of what he saw, is that labour and disease were breaking Fielding's constitution, and that in

* "Autobiography and Correspondence of Mrs. Delany," 1861, III, 79.
† F. Kilvert, "Memoirs of Hurd," 1860, p. 45.

consequence there were few of the expected jests on that occasion. The time had arrived when Fielding's temper was not so continuously buoyant as it had been; since the publication of "Tom Jones" he had become in spirit as well as in body a much older man. All this is reflected in "Amelia." Not that there are none of the former flashes of wit. No repartee in Fielding's novels is better known than the one he put into the mouth of Dr. Harrison, the learned Churchman, in the dispute with Colonel Bath over duelling:

"'We are both of the same Church, I hope,' cries the Doctor.

"'I am of the Church of England, Sir,' answered the Colonel, 'and will fight for it to the last drop of my blood.'

"'It is very generous in you, Colonel,' cries the Doctor, 'to fight so zealously for a religion by which you are to be damned.'"

But these wit-combats were less frequent than of old. When he wrote "Amelia," Fielding was in no mood to create another Squire Western and his sister Diana. His imagination was filled with the most serious affairs of life and death.

Such freedom from business as he could gain during the autumn of 1750 Fielding had given to the composition of his "Enquiry into the Increase of Robbers,"—a canvass, as we have seen, of the underlying state of London society whence sprang crime and misery. Immediately after the publication of the pamphlet in January, 1751, he began, I take it, "Amelia," and wrote it rapidly through the year while in actual contact with crime and engrossed with those projects for its restraint which pressed upon him. This opinion, to be frank, is based upon no positive statement by Fielding or his associates. In the literary ana of the period there is no mention of Fielding's being engaged upon "Amelia." If any remark was made about it in the course of the conversation with Hurd, that divine did not think the news worth repeating to his clerical brother. Nor does the novel itself contain a reference or an allusion to a book or incident of the time quite certain enough to fix the date of composition within so narrow limits. In one place the author has in mind a fight between two notorious pugilists, Slack and Broughton, which occurred in April, 1750; and in another place, when ironically recommending "the Apologies with which certain gay ladies have lately been pleased to oblige the world," he may have been thinking not only of "An Apology for the Conduct of Teresia Constantia Phillips," which went into a third edition in 1750, but also of "The Memoirs of a Lady of Quality"—really the scandalous career of Lady Vane,—which Smollett incorporated into "Peregrine Pickle" and published in February, 1751. That Fielding meant to include Lady Vane among his "gay ladies," though probable, is not beyond question. Research really yields nothing definite but Millar's announcement just before publication, and the bare "Bow Street, Dec. 12. 1751." which Fielding appended to the dedication.

And yet there can be no doubt in the mind of a reader that the composition of "Amelia" lies wholly within the year succeeding the "Enquiry." Perhaps it would be too unrestricted a statement to assert that "Amelia" is a criminal pamphlet expanded into a novel. The "Enquiry" is rather the background of "Amelia." In the pamphlet, Fielding proceeds by exposition and argument enforced by examples for illustration. He is there addressing lawyers and legislators. In the novel he proceeds by narrative— by plot and characters—that he may bring home to his readers the moral condition of London within the immediate jurisdiction of his court, and warn the unsuspecting against the lures to vice and crime. He is there addressing the public at large. His aim is expressed in the dedication

312

to Ralph Allen when he says: "The following book is sincerely designed to promote the cause of virtue, and to expose some of the most glaring evils, as well public as private, which at present infest this country." Thus "Amelia" as much as the "Enquiry" was written to lay bare the ills of the social state, with less stress, however, upon the means of reform; for the story must speak for itself. Nobody had ever heard of such a novel.

At the outset, Fielding describes a certain parish within the liberty of Westminster,—St. Martin's in the Fields,—where might be seen a few years back the maladministration of the law in all its shameful glory, through the machinery of decrepit old men called the watch, blundering constables, and a "trading-justice" in whom ignorance and corruption contended for supremacy. Some of the old evil practices have disappeared, it is remarked playfully in a footnote, since 1749, the year after the author was appointed a justice of the peace. In this setting are placed a young lieutenant and his wife Amelia, with their three children of tender age.

The family came from Fielding's old haunts down in Wiltshire. Lieutenant Booth is a fellow of perfect good nature, courteous and frank in manner, with no positive inclination to vice, though not likely to exert any heroic power of resistance against the temptations of the flesh. His bravery has been shown at the siege of Gibraltar, where he was twice wounded for unduly exposing himself to the fire of the enemy. Withal he is well educated, having passed, I should say, through one of the great public schools like Eton. In the course of his reading he once fell in with Mandeville, author of "The Fable of the Bees," whose cynical philosophy of human nature, though he never accepted it, nevertheless greatly influenced him. He grew indifferent to the tenets of the Christian faith in which he had been brought up, and adopted in their stead the doctrine that men act entirely from their passions, however much they may profess to be swayed by the motives of virtue or religion. Among these passions, the young man, reading his own heart, placed love first of all as more potent than Mandeville's base impulses of pride and fear. True to his philosophy, he was exceedingly fond of his wife, whom he won against the prudent opposition of her mother and an elder sister.

Like her husband, Amelia had been well bred in a provincial town. Though she knew no Latin, she read many English plays and poems, and was conversant with "the Divinity of the great and learned Dr. Barrow, and with the histories of the excellent Bishop Burnet." These books developed her native wit, deepened her moral and religious sense, and gave her what outlook she ever gained upon the large affairs of the world. Her father being dead, she placed herself for guidance in the moral crises of girlhood under the direction of Dr. Harrison, an ecclesiastic compounded of all the Christian virtues and all the pagan learning of Greece and Rome. Himself unmarried, he called her his daughter, watched and counselled her; and when he saw where her heart lay, urged on the marriage and performed the ceremony. Amelia's character was cast in the finest mould, and she could lay claim besides to as much beauty as ever fell to the lot of any woman, despite the fact that her nose had been injured by the overturning of a chaise. Perfectly devoted to her husband, she made a voyage to Gibraltar when she heard that he lay ill there of a wound and nursed him into health. On their return to England, the regiment was broken, and the lieutenant was reduced to the usual half pay, then amounting to a scant forty pounds a year. Helped by Dr. Harrison, they retired to the country, where Booth tried his hand at farming. All went well while Dr. Harrison remained in the neighbourhood; but when he was sent abroad as governor to the son of his patron, disaster quickly followed. To escape arrest and certain imprisonment for debt, Booth fled to London for refuge within the verge of the court; and his wife followed him with the children.

The lieutenant took lodgings for his family up two pair of stairs at the house of a Mrs. Ellison in Spring Gardens, on the edge of the fashionable district, where Fielding himself once lived with his wife and children. Near them were the theatres and the opera, masquerades, coffee-houses, and taverns; and within easy reach were Ranelagh and Vauxhall Gardens. None of the temptations of the town as described in the "Enquiry" were absent. There were pleasant walks also in St. James's Park as far west as Constitution Hill, if a duel had to be fought; and it was not a long distance, if the family were in distress, to the Universal Register Office in the Strand, where Mr. John Fielding could recommend to Amelia an honest pawnbroker.

Hovering about Spring Gardens were other army officers home from Gibraltar, some of whom Booth and Amelia knew. There was, for instance, Major Bath, whose sister married Colonel James, a member of Parliament and a libertine. By helping on the marriage, which gave the Colonel a fortnight's pleasure, the Major himself became a Colonel. And there was a nameless young lord, with a special passion for young married women whose husbands could not support them. He was "a sort of cousin" to Mrs. Ellison, at whose house he occupied the best rooms when it was convenient for him to stay there. To him Captain Trent sold his own wife and then exchanged the service of the King for the more lucrative service of his lordship. Trent, who had fought with Booth at Gibraltar, was very generous in gifts to his unfortunate friend. Notwithstanding the real character of these people, all appeared decent and most respectable on the outside. It was a dangerous situation for Booth with few or no guineas in his pocket, and for Amelia who was more beautiful than she knew and whose virtues shut her eyes to vice and deceit. What will happen to Booth when his unsuspecting temper is played upon by wills stronger than his own, may be in part anticipated; but what will happen to Amelia is less certain. Will she go the way of that clergyman's widow, the estimable Mrs. Bennet, whom, in similar circumstances, the unnamed lord won and betrayed? Or will she save herself and her husband? These are the questions that Fielding put to himself and answered without flinching.

While in London, Booth spent a good share of his time in jail. His first experience was before the arrival of Amelia from the country, and within a week of his own. As he was returning to his lodgings one night, he unfortunately rescued a poor wretch from the hands of two gentlemen who were cruelly beating him. The watch came up and conducted all four to the roundhouse; where the assailants, who knew how to deal with a constable, were quickly discharged, while Booth and the man whom he had assisted, neither of them having in his pocket the half-crown necessary to freedom, were held on the charge of assaulting a watchman and breaking his lantern. The next morning Justice Thrasher made short work of committing the culprits to prison; for it was his invariable rule never to let anyone out of his clutches unless he received a wink from his clerk; and these poor fellows did not possess the wherewithal to make that clerk wink. For want of money Booth fared as ill when he reached the prison. As he could not pay "garnish" on his entrance, or the usual fee demanded by the old inmates for punch all round, he was immediately "uncased," or stripped of his coat, and very soon had his pockets picked of all they contained—a penknife and an iron snuff-box.

One Robinson, a freethinker and notorious gambler, shortly became civil and took the new-comer through the prison, relating to him as they went along, like Virgil to Dante in the "Inferno," the history of each prisoner with comment on the injustice of the penal code and the sad condition of the courts. That man lying there almost naked, with two or three scars on his forehead and one leg gone, fought at Gibraltar. Months ago he was arrested on the suspicion of stealing three herrings; and though the court acquitted him of the offence, he must remain here because he cannot pay the justice's fees. That old man and that girl sitting there on the ground and supporting his head in her lap are father and daughter. The girl was sent here for stealing a loaf of bread; and her father for receiving it, knowing it to be stolen. He is now, you see, giving up the ghost; and there is no release for the girl, for theft is a felony punishable by death. On the other hand, that well-dressed man walking surlily by them was indicted the other day for perjury against the life of an innocent gentleman; but he expects to be bailed out in a few hours; for perjury, you know, is only a misdemeanour, punishable at most by transportation and usually not at all.

Scenes so depressing as these were lightened the next day by an encounter with the beautiful and vivacious Miss Mathews, an old friend of Booth's before he courted and won Amelia. She had been sent to prison on a charge of murder, having stabbed with a penknife a lover who deserted her. As she was amply supplied with money by her suitor Colonel James, she had a room apart, where she entertained Booth for a week, not in perfect innocency, while each related to the other the story of their lives subsequent to the days when they used to dance together in the assemblies of a town down in the West. By her aid Booth was released at an expense of nearly eighteen pounds, of which the governor of the prison took five guineas, and the rest went, according to the rules, to Justice Thrasher and his clerk, to Mr. Gotobed the constable, the watchman who had his lantern broken, and the lawyers on both sides. The case against Miss Mathews, whose lover survived the wound from the penknife, was not pressed. Just as they were preparing to leave the prison together, Amelia arrived and took her penitent husband away to their lodgings in Spring Gardens.

Booth, we see, made a mistake in obeying a generous impulse of human nature. Had he possessed ordinary prudence, he would never have interfered with a fray in the street; he would have considered the watch and Justice Thrasher, and have passed nimbly by. In that case, there would have been no renewal of the acquaintance with Miss Mathews whose fascination he could not withstand; there would have been no infidelity to Amelia, no intrigue with a resourceful woman from which he would find it difficult to extricate himself with honour; perhaps there would have been no duel with Colonel Bath, requiring him to run through his adversary. Of his own accord Booth never drank to excess, but he was easily induced by a companion to take more than was good for him; he never suggested play, but he could not decline an offer when it was urged, and he always lost his last shilling; of gentle disposition, he was never quarrelsome, but he would fight if challenged and he would win. In short, anyone by professing an interest in his welfare could direct him at pleasure so long as his own or his wife's honour was not involved. The promises of Colonel James and his lordship to get him into a regiment in active service were prompted, he thought, by sincere friendship; he never suspected that their design was to separate him from Amelia, to send him off to the West Indies where fever would take him forever out of the way. Nor did he understand why they became cool in their desire for his advancement when Amelia declared that she would follow her husband wherever he went. When nothing else was left for them, they schemed to involve him in difficulties at home, to reduce his affairs to extremity, and to keep him in the hands of bailiffs while they set traps for his wife at the masquerade and elsewhere, one or another of which would have been sprung but for the cunning of the experienced Mrs. Bennet who came to her aid. As void of suspicion as her husband, Amelia accepted with delight his lordship's costly presents to her children, played ombre with him at Mrs. Ellison's, and by her charming and affable manners innocently led him on to the point where he expected the usual conquest. Before she knew it, the net was woven as closely about her as about poor Booth.

In the struggle of these captives the wife suffered the most exquisite torture. She had to contend not only with the plots of Colonel James and the young lord against her but also with the mistakes and imprudence of her husband. Whatever that weak man did she paid the penalty for it. The scenes in the novel that awaken the most intense compassion lie not in the prison or the sponging-house; they lie in the poor lodgings of Spring Gardens with Amelia and the children. Tired of half measures, the noble peer at last employed Captain Trent to undo utterly the family. The way was prepared by inducing Booth to play one night at the King's Arms, where he lost all his own money and fifty pounds more which Trent generously lent to him on a note that might be paid whenever it should be convenient. A few days later an unexpected turn in the captain's affairs made it necessary for him to demand immediate payment. There was only one way to obtain this amount, and that was by stripping Amelia "not only of every farthing, but almost of every rag she had in the world." Without hesitation, she packed up all her own and the children's trinkets, the greater part of her clothes even, and deposited them with a pawnbroker for just the fifty pounds. But that money never reached Trent; for Booth did not find the captain, and before he arrived home in the evening he was persuaded by a brother lieutenant to leave the sum with "a great man," who when liberally "touched" always exerted his vast influence with other "great men" in behalf of broken officers seeking advancement. Then Betty the housemaid, concluding that she could find a better place, fled with all the rest of her mistress's clothes and linen, so that Amelia had nothing to wear except what was on her back.

There remained for the immediate support of this family reduced to wretchedness only Amelia's portrait set in a gold locket with three little diamonds. On this last and most precious of her jewels the pawnbroker let her have nine guineas, of which she wished her husband to take eight, keeping only one for herself with which to purchase his supper of fowl and egg sauce and mutton broth with a bottle of wine. In the evening, after the meal had been prepared by Amelia's own hands, he came in, only to tell her that he could not sup with her that night. He could not tell her why; but the reader knows that he had given his honour to visit Miss Mathews. He kept the appointment, and instead of returning as he promised within an hour or two, there arrived towards midnight a note from Colonel James requesting his presence with pistols in Hyde Park precisely at six o'clock the next morning; and upon the heel of this messenger came another, completing Amelia's distress, with the news that her husband had been arrested for the gambling debt to Captain Trent. The bailiff's men had caught him as he was leaving the apartment of Miss Mathews.

On this dreadful midnight, Amelia for once lost faith in her husband. The quarrel between him and Colonel James, she saw from the phrasing of the challenge, was over Miss Mathews. Turning pale as death when she read those words, she threw herself into her chair, and then came the shower of tears as the children ran up in alarm at her strange appearance and asked her what harm had happened to their father.

"Amelia, after a short Silence, looking tenderly at her Children, cry'd out, 'It is too much, too much to bear. Why did I bring these little Wretches into the World! Why were these Innocents born to such a Fate!'—She then threw her Arms round them both, (for they were before embracing her Knees) and cried, 'O my Children! my Children! Forgive me, my Babes—Forgive me that I have brought you into such a World as this. You are undone—my Children are undone.'

"The little Boy answered with great Spirit, 'How undone, Mamma? My Sister and I don't care a Farthing for being undone—Don't cry so upon our Accounts—we are both very well; indeed we are—But do pray tell us. I am sure some Accident hath happened to poor Papa.'

"'Mention him no more,' cries Amelia—'your Papa is—indeed he is a wicked Man—he cares not for any of us—O Heavens, is this the Happiness I promised myself this Evening!'—At which Words she fell into an Agony, holding both her Children in her Arms."

Booth, it is but fair to say, felt keen remorse for his conduct while he lay that night on a miserable bed in the house of Mr. Bondum the bailiff, a short distance away in Gray's Inn Lane. He had been there before, and so knew that this officer of the law held his prisoners as long as he could in the hope of loading them with as many actions as possible and thereby accumulating bail-bonds to the increase of his fees. But this time Booth's sojourn was to be short. Amelia visited him in the morning, when he told her all that had passed between him and Miss Mathews, assuring her that his visit the previous night had been only for the purpose of terminating the intrigue. She listened quietly to his story, which contained nothing which she did not know, for Miss Mathews, in anger at his neglect, had already betrayed him in a letter to his wife. So when Booth asked Amelia to forgive him, she answered in those words which genius put into her mouth: "I firmly believe every word you have said—but I cannot now forgive you the fault you have confessed—and my reason is—because I have forgiven it long ago." Later in the day, Dr. Harrison appeared and found the lieutenant an altered man. Booth had been reading while in the roundhouse, no other book being at hand, a series of sermons by Dr. Barrow, which convinced him of the errors in his own philosophy of conduct. He now saw that wise men are governed by considerations which he had not included in his simple doctrine of impulse, and that the quality of an act, whether good or bad, bears some relation to the motive behind it. This conversion was, of course, welcome news to Dr. Harrison. Without Booth's knowledge he induced Colonel James to keep secret the challenge; and after taking this precaution he bailed out the young gentleman.

Nothing remained now for making a worthy couple supremely happy, except to provide them with an adequate fortune. Amelia had been cheated out of her inheritance by her sister Betty. Their mother, who eventually became reconciled to Amelia's marriage, made a will leaving most of her estate to Mrs. Booth. She suddenly died while her favourite daughter was abroad; and Betty, aided by a skilful attorney, substituted a forged will, which gave the property to herself and cut Amelia off with a trifle. One of the witnesses, then confined in the roundhouse, confessed to Dr. Harrison his part in the transaction; whereupon the rascally attorney was apprehended and conducted, a mob following at his heels, to the house of an honest justice of the peace. In this portrait of an honest justice Fielding half seriously drew himself. It is a curious narrative, reading like a report of the procedure of his court from a contemporary newspaper. Dr. Harrison and his party "found the magistrate just sitting down to his dinner; however, when he was acquainted with the Doctor's profession, he immediately admitted him, and heard his business. Which he no sooner perfectly understood, with all its circumstances, than he resolved, tho' it was then very late, and he had been fatigued all the morning with public business, to postpone all refreshment 'till he had discharged his duty. He accordingly adjourned the prisoner and his cause to the bailiff's house, whither he himself with the Doctor immediately repaired, and whither the attorney was followed by a much larger number of attendants than he had been honoured with before." After hearing the case, the justice committed the forger to Newgate, congratulated Booth on his good luck, and as it was now past six o'clock and none of the gentlemen had dined, he invited them all to go home with him. They had hardly taken their seats at table with the justice and his wife before Amelia, who had just heard of her husband's release and where he was, came running into the room to join them. The magistrate, being in extraordinary good humour that evening, opened his heart and cellars and kept the company in merriment till the clock struck eleven. When the guests had departed, the justice and his wife agreed that they had never seen so charming a creature as Amelia.

"Amelia," said Sir Walter Scott, "may be termed a continuation of 'Tom Jones.'" He did not mean that old characters reappear as they do in the second part of Richardson's "Pamela," but that there are marked family resemblances between the old and the new. Booth is clearly a maturer Tom Jones who has not yet learned the art of life. The temper of each is the same. For all their good qualities, the one as well as the other has weaknesses and must be sobered by a few days in jail. Amelia is likewise a maturer Sophia Western, whose vivacity and strength of will seven years of marriage to an improvident army officer have subdued into patience and endurance. Her sister Betty is a slightly sketched Blifil with altered sex. Dr. Harrison is also a learned brother of Squire Allworthy, conservative in his opinions, bent upon aiding his friends in distress, easily imposed upon by a rogue, and sometimes blinded by his prejudices. This close kinship, I think, extends no further. It certainly does not extend to Mrs. Bennet, that *femme savante* at whom the author laughs, nor to Major Bath whose honest heart is at variance with his notions of dignity. But if we go back to Fielding's first novel, we see that Joseph Andrews has been transformed into a sergeant—Joseph Atkinson, Amelia's foster-brother, who, though in love with her from boyhood, keeps the secret for years, and devotes himself to her happiness with the man she married. But for him, perhaps Amelia and Booth would never have survived their sojourn in London. One more sea-change, and the young sergeant becomes Thackeray's Major Dobbin. Similarly, there are some parallel incidents between Amelia and the earlier novels. Fielding was partial, for example, to mock death-bed scenes. Allworthy, we remember, was brought to the point of death by a cold and took leave of his friends one by one. So Robinson the freethinker in "Amelia," fearing the effects of a blow on the head administered by the bailiff, sends for Dr. Harrison and confesses his sins. A skilful surgeon saves him. Likewise Sergeant Atkinson, suffering from a nervous fever, summons Amelia that he may restore her miniature set in diamonds which he had stolen eighteen years before and worn ever since next his heart. She permits him to kiss her hand and he recovers. Throughout Fielding's three novels, there is in general the same humorous point of view, which, to state it once more, lies in a contrast between the real and the artificial characters of the men and women whom he portrays.

But in "Amelia" more than in its predecessors, Fielding

drew the elements of his plot from the comedies of his youth. "The Justice Caught in his own Trap" had the same criminal background. Justice Squeezum, the watch, the constables, and the roundhouse had not altered much since that time. The main difference is that in the comedy Fielding's aim was farce, whereas in the novel it is the correction of abuses by exposing them. Again, the happy ending of "The Temple Beau" was brought about by the same device as in "Amelia." The father of Veromil died while the young man was travelling on the Continent, and a brother robbed him of his birthright. One of the witnesses to the forged will betrayed the secret and the lawful heir was restored. Even more was taken from "The Modern Husband," which had been damned long ago, ostensibly because it turned upon the traffic of husbands in their wives' beauty. Fielding was never reconciled to the failure of this comedy, which he knew to be true to the fashionable life of the town among men and women living far beyond their means. It was nevertheless a bold venture to submit the same situation to the public once more. Lord Richly of the comedy was transferred with slight change to the novel; he is the unnamed peer. Mr. and Mrs. Modern became Captain Trent and his wife; and Mr. and Mrs. Bellamant passed into Lieutenant Booth and Amelia. Only the last set of characters need detain us. Like Bellamant, Booth can listen to the suggestion that there is only one way to retrieve his fortunes; but being a better man than his predecessor, the idea is utterly abhorrent to him. Moreover, each of the young men is guilty of a single transgression, and each is forgiven by a wife who checkmates every move against her by a libertine. Without going into further details, it may be added that this free use of old plays now seems a very natural procedure for Fielding. The main action of "Amelia" was placed in the spring of a certain year, which, though the author leaves it blank, we know must have been seven years after the siege of Gibraltar, or in the spring of 1734. That was the period of his comedies; to them he turned to refresh his memory for a not too exact historical setting.

In the larger aspects of the novel, Fielding still held to epic analogies. The dramatic action of "Tom Jones," covering but six weeks at the end of 1745, was prepared for, we remember, by a very full account of Tom and Sophia from infancy. We may see them developing year by year among their relatives and neighbours. Everywhere dialogue rises naturally out of the narrative. At that time Fielding's model was the simple and direct method of the Iliad. Similarly, the dramatic action of "Amelia" covers only a few weeks at the end of the London season in 1734; to be more precise, from the first of April on into May; but the preparation for this grave comedy is managed quite differently. The essential facts in the previous history of Booth and Amelia are brought before the reader by means of the long story with which the lieutenant entertains Miss Mathews. This is the indirect method of the Odyssey such as Virgil followed in the Aeneid; particularly it is very like Odysseus relating his adventures to King Alcinous. Little fault can be found with the way in which Fielding follows his model. The trouble lies in the procedure itself when employed in prose fiction; that is, in a novel to be read, not in an epic to be recited. It results in an inordinate amount of narrative. In this case Fielding consumed a whole volume, a fourth of the entire novel, in laying the background of incident for his drama. To his contemporaries, the characters of the piece appeared garrulous; they liked to talk too much, it was said, about themselves.

This monotony Fielding sought to relieve in various ways. While Booth and Miss Mathews in the prison-house tell each other what has happened since they met eight or nine years before, the governor or a lawyer sometimes intrudes to give them and the reader time to breathe; but these interruptions can be only at rare intervals. Moreover, both Booth and Miss Mathews intersperse their narratives with stretches of conversation between the persons of their stories. Booth even reads entire two letters—one from Betty to her sister Amelia, and one from Dr. Harrison to himself and his wife. To these literary conventions the modern imagination does not readily assent. We wonder how the narrators can remember exactly conversations that occurred a long time ago. We wonder how it happened that Booth had those two letters in his pocket. We may ask in what pocket they were carried, for he had been robbed of his coat on entering the prison. Of course he recovered his coat, but the author, I think, fails to say so. Perhaps Fielding did all that could be done in adapting the structure of the Odyssey to a novel, but the form at best remains awkward. When a novelist introduces a story-teller and a listener, or otherwise attempts to explain how he has derived his facts, he falls into all sorts of difficulties, and the critics are certain to annoy him with very disagreeable questions, as we shall see in the next chapter.

CHAPTER XXIII

THE FAILURE OF AMELIA

To Fielding's harm, "Amelia" was taken literally as a self-revelation. The novel contains, indeed, more autobiography than "Tom Jones," as one would surmise were there no contemporary evidence to this effect. The injustice to Fielding arose from a disposition to make no allowance for the novelist's prerogative of dressing fact with fiction. Thus Lady Mary Wortley Montagu, who remembered Fielding as he was in his younger days, wrote from Italy to her daughter, the Countess of Bute: "H. Fielding has given a true picture of himself and his first wife, in the characters of Mr. and Mrs. Booth, some compliments to his own figure excepted; and, I am persuaded, several of the incidents he mentions are real matters of fact. I wonder he does not perceive Tom Jones and Mr. Booth are sorry scoundrels." Lady Mary, who liked her cousin, hardly meant to call him a sorry scoundrel. It was rather that he had depicted himself as such. There is a technical distinction. What compliments Fielding paid to "his own figure" are not obvious. The novel contains but one description of Booth's appearance. When Mrs. James remarks that he is generally allowed to be handsome, her husband retorts: "He handsome? What with a nose like the proboscis of an elephant, with the shoulders of a porter, and the legs of a chairman?"

In her old age, Lady Mary talked much about Fielding to her daughter. Nor was Lady Bute, it is said, a stranger "to that beloved first wife whose picture he drew in his Amelia, where . . . even the glowing language he knew how to employ did not do more than justice to the amiable qualities of the original, or to her beauty, although this had suffered a little from the accident related in the novel—a frightful overturn, which destroyed the gristle of her nose." "He loved her," to quote further, "passionately, and she returned his affection; yet led no happy life, for they were almost always miserably poor, and seldom in a state of quiet and safety. All the world knows what was his imprudence; if ever he possessed a score of pounds, nothing could keep him from lavishing it idly, or make him think of to-morrow. Sometimes they were living in decent lodgings with tolerable comfort; sometimes in a wretched garret without necessaries; not to speak of the spunging-houses and hiding places where he was occasionally to be found."* This was the general view. Wits who were hostile to Fielding for political or other reasons, were quick to seize upon those incidents of the novel most damaging to the character of Booth and apply them directly to the author. In this way a false impression was conveyed of both Lieutenant Booth and Henry Fielding.

The truth is, Fielding followed in "Amelia" his own career but vaguely. It was inevitable that he should become more reminiscent here than in his other novels, for we all in time grow reminiscent. This mood, united with his realistic manner, made the novel read like autobiography despite its rather conventional plot. Incidents in his own life were fused with incidents drawn from the lives of others or from his imagination. So much of himself and his first wife was put into Booth and Amelia as pleased his semi-autobiographic art. Fact and fiction, when one comes to details, can be separated only here and there. Evidence from the outside or antecedent probability are the main guides.

* "Letters and Works of Lady Mary Wortley Montagu," 1861, I, 105; II, 279.

The provincial town where Booth courted Amelia was Salisbury. This we should know even if the author had not let the name slip once or twice in the course of the story. Amelia and Elizabeth, or Betty, Harris correspond to Charlotte and Catherine Cradock. In both cases the father is dead, and the mother dies soon after the marriage of her younger daughter, bequeathing to her the family estate. It is a fair inference from Mrs. Cradock's will that she had become displeased with Catherine, who was cut off with a shilling. Catherine, however, forged no will in her own interest, nor is it to be supposed that she possessed the contemptible character of Betty. There was doubtless jealousy of her sister and opposition to Charlotte's marriage to Fielding. Her interference naturally reacted against her after Mrs. Cradock came to look with more favour upon her son-in-law. When Betty finally flees to France in disgrace, she takes passage at Poole, a seaport where the Cradock sisters used to visit and where their beauty was celebrated by a local poet. In recalling these old scenes, Fielding lived over again his youth when he danced with Charlotte and other Salisbury girls at the assemblies. It is all in "Amelia" as well as in those early verses addressed "To the Nymphs of New Sarum" and in the closing lines of "The Cat and the Fiddle." At one of these assemblies, Booth's gallant conduct won the admiration and love of Miss Mathews. Was Miss Mathews one of the nymphs, we wonder, with whom Harry Fielding sometimes led the dance at Salisbury? Was she betrayed by a handsome Cornet Hebbers? And did Fielding again meet her in London after she had become the mistress of a Colonel James? It may well have been so.

Dr. Harrison, the spiritual adviser of the Harris family, is a typical canon of Salisbury with a parish thirty miles distant. Such an ecclesiastic was the author's grandfather, John Fielding, who held a stall in Salisbury Cathedral and the vicarage of Piddletown, about thirty miles away. This is probably a mere coincidence. One of the cathedral clergy very likely took an interest in the welfare of the Cradock sisters, and may have promoted the marriage of Charlotte to Harry Fielding. But he did not perform the ceremony; nor did he, we may be sure, propose to Fielding the stratagem whereby Booth gained entrance into the Harris house against the mother's will. That trick of concealing a lover in a hamper is an old romantic device which even the genius of Fielding could not make appear probable. Apart from what came from Ralph Allen, the qualities with which Fielding endowed Dr. Harrison were taken, I daresay, from more than one man among Fielding's clerical acquaintance, with special tribute perhaps to the learning of Dr. Hoadly, the Bishop of Salisbury during his courtship of Charlotte Cradock.

Dr. Harrison's parish, which became the scene of the lieutenant's experiments in farming, has always been identified with Fielding's own East Stour. Booth's description of it, though not very definite, fits well enough the Stour valley. The parish lay, he told Miss Mathews, "among meadows washed by a clear trout stream, and flanked on both sides with downs." As his curate was at that time unmarried, Dr. Harrison let the Booths have the parsonage, where they settled down to a delicious life in the cultivation of the doctor's glebe. The earthly paradise, however, was of short duration. At the end of the first prosperous year, Booth rented an adjoining farm, paying for it several times over what it was worth, in the hope of increasing his income; subsequently he purchased an old coach for the convenience of Amelia; and when the curate married an ill-natured wife, they were taken into the parsonage. By these follies the family was ruined. Debts accumulated; the coach excited the envy of neighbours; and the curate's wife was a disturbance to domestic tranquillity. The climax came at the end of the fourth year, when Booth's landlord seized all his stock for rent; and the poor lieutenant was forced to choose between a prison and flight. Preferring freedom, he took the road to London.

This disaster should not be accepted as autobiography. Fielding was married in November, 1734, and disposed of his property at East Stour in 1738. During these scant four years, East Stour was probably his legal home; at least he described himself as of this parish when he entered the Middle Temple in November, 1737. A large part of this time, however, was passed in London. Such farming projects as he undertook may have been unsuccessful; but the cultivation of the soil was never a serious occupation with him. His aim was a London career in law or literature. His farm was only a place for retirement in summer and autumn. As he had been known in the parish ever since he was a boy, it is most improbable that his old friends and former playmates quarrelled with him and cheated him or sought to drive him away. While at East Stour, he lived in a house that had formerly been the parsonage, but it was not shared with a curate's family, for the Rev. William Young resided at Gillingham. When Fielding sold his farm and went to London, his immediate purpose was not to escape debts, but to study law. The curate of the parish, far from disliking him, followed him to London and attached himself to him for life.

My impression from the narrative is that Fielding was thinking of his father's life at East Stour quite as much as of his own. Edmund Fielding, when a colonel without a regiment, was installed by his father-in-law in the parsonage, much as was Booth by Dr. Harrison, and entered upon the career of a gentleman farmer. He purchased other lands, became involved in litigation, and eventually was forced to leave the parish for the more congenial atmosphere of London. If we combine the experiences of father and son, we have a sort of parallel to the misfortunes of Lieutenant Booth.

Still greater caution is needed in the personal application of the distresses that overwhelmed Booth and Amelia while they were living in Spring Gardens. Lady Bute, I fear, relied too much upon the novel for her information concerning Harry and Charlotte. They had indeed a hard life of it; they were called upon to endure even more intense pain and anguish than is recorded of Booth and Amelia; for besides seasons of poverty, they had to face illness and death. Their friend in trouble was Ralph Allen, who, like Dr. Harrison in the novel, perhaps made his appearance at the opportune moment to aid them and to take them to Bath; certainly he gave them a house to live in near his mansion. Like Booth, Fielding contracted debts which he found it difficult to pay; and once, we know, suit was brought against him, while he had lodgings in Spring Gardens, to recover two hundred pounds. At this point the parallel breaks down. Had Fielding ever been imprisoned for debt, we may be sure that the disgrace would have been uncovered by enemies who raked his past for incidents that could be turned to his dishonour. Opposed to duels, he could never have fought one. Nor was he known as a gambler. It is most improbable that he and his wife were ever placed in the situation described in the novel. That situation, as we have seen, was taken from an old comedy. "The illustrious Peer of amorous Memory," whoever he may have been, served equally well for a play before Fielding was married and for a novel afterwards. We may be certain that this nobleman never pursued Mrs. Fielding and that her husband never left her in order to keep an engagement with a mistress.

The military cast given to the novel came, there is some reason for supposing, from the author's memories of army officers who visited his father. There perhaps he saw

Colonel James, Major Bath, and Captain Trent. Did Fielding also take from his father's life the gambling incident? Lieutenant Booth, we recall, was drawn into play at the King's Arms by two sharpers and gave his note to Captain Trent, who was secretly in league with them, for his losses. Similarly Colonel Fielding, raw from the country, had been induced to play a game called faro at St. James's Coffee-House. He likewise lost heavily and left notes with friends of the sharpers. According to English law, gambling debts, known as such, were not collectable; but attempts, as in these two cases, were made to collect them on notes cleverly placed in the hands of apparent outsiders. When suit was threatened against Colonel Fielding, he appealed for protection to the Lord High Chancellor. Lieutenant Booth, less learned in the law, entered no protest, and went to the roundhouse, whence he would have gone to jail but for the intervention of Dr. Harrison.

Without more words, "Amelia" is far from being a clear reflex of the hardships endured by Fielding and his first wife. There is more definite personal history in the story which Booth tells Miss Mathews of himself and Amelia than in the rest of the novel. After the first volume the exigencies of the plot demanded freer use of incident which had no part in the author's own life. True, autobiographic scenes, such as Booth lying along the floor with his children crawling over him, are visible at intervals through the screen, but they are less frequent and they are obscured by the fiction. The same thing is partially true of the two leading characters. Amelia, though always behaving as we may imagine a Charlotte Cradock would have done in the circumstances, nevertheless becomes more and more, as the novel progresses, the typical woman in distress, whose *belle âme* is destined at last to triumph over all attempts to deceive and betray her. Pamela had saved herself and her lover. Amelia saves herself and her husband. At the same time Booth becomes less and less like his prototype; he is transformed into another man whose conduct ill fits Fielding.

It is customary for novelists who indulge in this semi-autobiographic art to idealize themselves. They keep to the front all their good qualities, and either suppress or relate differently those events in their career which they do not care to remember. In harmony with their design, all fictitious incident must move on the same high moral plane. A case in point is "David Copperfield," wherein nothing occurs to dim the character of the hero and consequently of Charles Dickens himself. Fielding reversed the process. He gave to Booth his own prime characteristics, but he allied them with follies and weaknesses which either were not his own or were greatly exaggerated. In a word, he degraded Booth, and consequently himself, by putting him into the atmosphere of "The Modern Husband." For this procedure Fielding had to pay the penalty. The reader asked why Amelia married Booth. And this was much like asking why Charlotte Cradock married Henry Fielding. The hue and cry raised against "Amelia" was a repetition of the hisses and catcalls which drove "The Modern Husband" from the stage. Whether in a novel or in a play, the situation was an offence against the public. Wits pronounced the novel "sad stuff," and parodied its most tender scenes. By way of jest, there was advertised a new novel by the same author to be called "Shamelia." Here it is:

This Day is published,
(In four Volumes Duodecimo, with the help of Dedication, Introductory Chapters, long Digressions, short Repetitions, polite Expletives of Conversation, genteel Dialogues, a wide Margin, and large Letter, Price but 12s.)
SHAMELIA, a Novel.

THE HISTORY OF HENRY FIELDING

Printed for the MAJOR GENERAL,
Where may be had,
The Works of HERCULES VINEGAR Esq;
————————JOHN TROTPLAID, Esq;
The TRUE PATRIOT.
N. B. These are proper to be bound with the
Lucubrations of Sir ALEXANDER DRAWCANSIR.
Likewise,
Several d—mn'd Farces.
A Bundle of Political Pamphlets, by the same
hand, pick and chuse for a Penny.
The Complete JUSTICE OF PEACE.*

The attack on "Amelia" began mildly in newspapers
and magazines with the discovery of "flagrant" inconsistencies in the story. A "notorious" anachronism, for
example, was dwelt upon by the first reviewer of "Amelia"
in "The London Magazine."† According to the chronology
of the novel, Booth was married to Amelia before his departure for Gibraltar, where he fought during the siege, it
must be supposed of 1727, for the fortress had not been
besieged since that date. And yet when Booth came to
London a few years later, the masquerades at Ranelagh
were in full swing. Now, Ranelagh was not opened until
1742, and masquerades were not introduced there until
several years afterwards. How then could Booth and
Amelia still be "young," twenty years or more after their
marriage? How did it happen that their eldest child, born
during the siege of Gibraltar, was still only six years old?
Here is indeed a manifest anachronism. It originated,
just as a similar one in "Tom Jones," when Fielding
passed from his epic narrative into the dramatic action of
the novel. In neither instance were the two styles quite
adjusted to each other.

* "The Drury-Lane Journal," No. I, Jan. 16, 1752.
† Appendix for the year 1751, XX, 596.

336

This anachronism was made worse by involving it with another. Fielding, it has been observed by his biographers, placed at the end of his second volume a very pretentious advertisement of the Universal Register Office:

"ESTATES and Houses, either to be Sold or Lett, in any Part of *Great-Britain;* Lodgings to be Lett, either in Town or Country. Perpetual Advowsons and next Presentations. Offices either civil or military. Money to be lent on all Kinds of Security, from 100 *l.* to 100000*l.* Annuities to be bought and sold. Insurances on Lives, Ships, and Merchandizes, Curiosities, and Animals of all Kinds, &c. &c. &c.

"Masters in all the Arts and Sciences; Apprentices in all Trades; and Servants in all Capacities are registered; and a vast Variety to be heard of at this Office."

It does not seem to be so well known that the invaluable services which this institution could render were illustrated in the first edition of the novel itself. Such, however, is the case. The husband of Mrs. Bennet, a country clergyman, who desired to exchange his living for one more agreeable, heard of the Universal Register Office, where, it was said, "he might probably have his choice of above a hundred curacies." So he preached his farewell sermon and rushed up to London to find that this wonderful office could supply "all the necessities of life." Though he did not get a curacy he was at once equipped with lodgings that pleased him. The courteous treatment he received at this time was remembered when he afterwards wished to make a long journey from town and felt that he could not bear the expense of travelling alone. He applied once more to the office, where he was told of a man who was going the same way. They struck a bargain, each paying his share in the cost of the conveyance. Similarly, when Booth decided that it would be best for his family to leave Mrs. Ellison's, he inquired at the same office for apartments near Dr. Harrison's; and immediately obtained them. There also

Amelia learned of a reputable pawnbroker, with whom she deposited her trinkets and the little picture of herself, receiving on them twice what anyone else would let her have. Finally, we are told by Fielding that but for the assistance of the Universal Register Office, he could never have related many private matters contained in the novel, such as the anecdotes concerning Mrs. Bennet and Miss Mathews. Some of them were communicated to him, he said, by one of the clerks "who, by having a general acquaintance with servants, is master of all the secrets of every family in the kingdom."

For these puffs of an enterprise managed by his brother, Fielding was severely censured, though of course he intended that they should be taken facetiously. Even a very friendly critic, who called himself "Criticulus,"* wished the blot of the Universal Register Office removed from the novel. He would prefer, he assured the author, to take Mr. Fielding's word for the truth of any part of the novel rather than the word of a clerk or of Mr. Booth. Besides this, there was the anachronism. Many people had forgotten when Ranelagh was established or given over to masquerades; but everybody knew that the Universal Register Office was a recent venture. Again it was asked how Amelia could have been with her husband at the siege of Gibraltar and still be "a blooming beauty," say in 1749, when the famous office was opened in the Strand. By that time she must have been above forty, nearly if not quite as old as Henry Fielding himself.

There was a still more unfortunate inconsistency. A remark of Dr. Johnson's about "Amelia," I think, has never been explained. "That vile broken nose never cured," he said, "ruined the sale"† of the book. Though the novel would have failed for other reasons, it was poor

* "The Gentleman's Magazine," XXII, 103 (March, 1752).
† G. B. Hill, "Johnsonian Miscellanies," 1897, I, 297.

THE FAILURE OF AMELIA

Amelia's nose more than all else that did the business. Booth, in relating the accident to Miss Mathews, says that at the beginning of their courtship Amelia's "lovely nose was beat all to pieces" by the overturning of a chaise. Thereupon her suitors all deserted her; and her misfortune became the subject of much mirth among her former girl friends who had envied her beauty. In a company of these girls Booth overhead one of them remark, "She hoped Miss would not hold her head so high for the future." Another answered, "I don't know, Madam, what she may do with her head, but I am convinced she will never more turn up her nose at her betters." And another cried out, "What a very proper match might now be made between Amelia and a certain captain." The captain of course is Booth, who, it appears, had received a slight injury in the same part, "though," Fielding adds, "from no shameful cause." Nettled by these sarcasms, Booth retorted: "Indeed, ladies, you need not express such satisfaction at poor Miss Emily's accident: for without any nose at all, she will be the handsomest woman in England." Though Fielding goes on to say that Amelia underwent "the most painful and dreadful operations of surgery," he nowhere definitely states how successful these operations were. So far as the reader knows, Amelia's face is forever disfigured; and yet she remains a woman of exquisite beauty.

A "noseless heroine" may be impossible at any time; she certainly was impossible in the eighteenth century. Smollett and other wits degraded Amelia to the character of a common wench who had lost her nose in the service of Venus. The approaching death of the unfortunate woman was predicted by "Old England" on December 21, 1751, only a few days after the publication of the novel; and the next month it was announced that poor Amelia had died in the most distressful circumstances. Her obituary,

339

as one may read it in a facetious article of news, ran as follows:

"On *Sunday* last, in the Evening, were privately interred the Remains of Mrs. *Amelia Booth,* who fell a Sacrifice to the poisonous Influence of evil Tongues. A Lady who was possessed of all the domestick Virtues of Life; and so remarkable for her Meekness of Disposition, as to have equalled the Fame of *Patient Grissel.* The Expence of her Funeral was defrayed by his Excellency Sir *Alexander,* who was deeply affected with her Fate, and now begs that no Person will be so cruel and impious as to disturb her Ashes. . . ."*

To his assailants Fielding replied in "The Covent-Garden Journal," a periodical which he began in January, 1752, under the pseudonym of Sir Alexander Drawcansir, by which he was designated in the obituary just quoted. His leader for the eleventh of that month he opened with an epigram of Martial's modernized to read—

> No town can such a gang of critics shew,
> Ev'n boys turn up that nose they cannot blow,—

and from this text proceeded to set forth a few fundamental prerequisites to the office of criticism which would surely reduce the number of those who essayed the trade of vilifying the works of their superiors by uttering at random phrases like "poor stuff," "wretched stuff," "bad stuff," and "sad stuff," such as had been hurled at "Amelia." Of course, Fielding remarks, any person, provided he keep his opinion to himself, is perfectly free to "dislike" on hearsay a book which he is unable to read or understand; but no such liberty can be granted to the professional critic who makes a public proclamation of his censure. Such a man, before being admitted to the order of critics, should be first required to learn the art of reading, other-

* "The Covent-Garden Journal Extraordinary," Jan. 20, 1752.

wise he cannot be called "a reader" either by himself or by others; and even then he should not be permitted to pass "a definitive sentence" on a book before he has read "at least ten pages in it." To this raillery further point was given by inserting in the news-items of the day a protest in behalf of the surgeon who attended Amelia when she was thrown from her carriage. The paragraph in question runs:

"It is currently reported that a famous Surgeon, who absolutely cured one Mrs. Amelia Booth, of a violent Hurt in her Nose, insomuch, that she had scarce a scar left on it, intends to bring Actions against several ill-meaning and slanderous People, who have reported that the said Lady had no Nose, merely because the Author of her History, in a Hurry, forgot to inform his Readers of that Particular, and which, if those Readers had had any Nose themselves, except that which is mentioned in the Motto of this Paper, they would have smelt out."

This frank admission of an oversight due to haste merely offered a new occasion for ridicule. The question was immediately raised by the wits whether the surgeon had good grounds for prosecution, or whether the author's apology was necessary after all. Thus in a rival periodical called "Have at You All: or, The Drury Lane Journal," we read by way of parody on the doctor's threat:

"Whereas it has been reported by the *sharp-nos'd* Gentlemen, the Critics, that AMELIA *has no nose,* because her Biographer has inform'd us, in the beginning of her History, that *her lovely nose was* beat all to pieces; This is to certify that the said Report is malicious, false, and ill grounded; and that the said Author has taken care to obviate it, by telling us, in the said History, when the Cherry Brandy was pour'd over poor Mrs. Atkinson, that AMELIA'S *delicate nose soon smelt it out.*"*

* "Drury Lane Journal," No. III, Jan. 30, 1752.

For variety's sake, the jester, one Bonnell Thornton, an Oxford man, attacked the author's style. Nothing has ever more shocked the formal stylist than the employment of personal pronouns of the third person, such as *he, his,* and *him,* to designate in the same sentence two or more persons. The practice does, indeed, cause confusion in the hands of unskilled writers. But the strenuous attempt of grammarians to avoid it at all costs leads to the awkward and almost unreadable English of legal documents. It is better by far to accept the English language as it is. Fielding so accepted it and acquired a happy use of its pronouns. Writing naturally, just as people talk, he did not stop to consider whether two or three *he's* in a sentence of some complexity referred to the same individual. No reader of common sense, however, could possibly misapply them. Nevertheless, his sentences abounding in pronouns were torn from their context and the reader was asked what he could make out of them. Furthermore, the format of his volumes was sometimes ridiculed. Throughout the novel the paragraphs were short and liberally spaced. The critic, observing this, asked why such a style had been followed; and answered his question by remarking that otherwise there would not have been matter enough to fill four small volumes. After this manner no conceivable point of attack escaped the wits. Nothing was to be left of the novel when they completed their work of destruction.

Fielding delivered one counter stroke and then turned away in silence. For the entertainment of his readers, he set up in "The Covent-Garden Journal," a "Court of Censorial Enquiry," much like the "Court of Criticism" which had been a feature of "The Jacobite's Journal." Before this court were summoned books and authors to make answer in legal fashion to charges brought against them. Amelia's turn came on January 25, but as the examination was very long, it had to be continued through the next sitting of the court. Amelia, having been formally indicted upon the statute of dulness, Counsellor Town opened the case for the prosecution, rehearsing for the enlightenment of Mr. Censor, the judge, most that had been said by the critics against Amelia, combined with the babble of the coffee-houses:

"We shall prove . . . to you, Sir, that the Book now at the Bar, is *very sad Stuff;* that Amelia herself is a *low* Character, *a Fool,* and a *Milksop;* that she is very apt to faint, and apt *to drink Water,* to prevent it. That she once *taps a Bottle of Wine, and drinks two Glasses.* That she *shews too much Kindness for her Children,* and is too apt to *forgive the Faults of her Husband.* That she exerts *no Manner of Spirit,* unless, perhaps, in supporting Afflictions. That *her concealing the* Knowledge of her Husband's Amour, when she knew he had discontinued it, was *low and poor.* That *her not abusing him,* for having lost his Money at Play, when she saw his Heart was already almost broke by it, *was contemptible Meanness.* That she *dresses her Husband's Supper; dresses her Children;* and *submits* to the Thoughts of every servile Office. That she once mentions THE DEVIL, and as often swears BY HER SOUL. Lastly, That she is a Beauty WITHOUT A NOSE, I say again, WITHOUT A NOSE. All this we shall prove by many Witnesses.

"We shall likewise prove that Dr. Harrison is a very *low, dull, unnatural,* Character, and that his arresting Booth, *only because he had all imaginable Reason to think he was a Villain,* is unpardonable.

"That Colonel Bath is a *foolish Character, very low, and ill-drawn.*

"That the Scene of the Goal [*sic*] is *low and unmeaning,* and brought in by Head and Shoulders, without any Reason, or Design.

"That the Abbé is supposed to *wear a Sword;* in short, not to descend to too many Particulars, which you will hear from the Mouths of the Witnesses, that the whole Book is a heap of *sad Stuff, Dulness, and Nonsense;* that it contains no Wit, Humour, Knowledge of human Nature, or of the World; indeed, that the Fable, moral Character, Manners, Sentiments, and Diction, are all alike bad and contemptible.

"All these Matters, Sir, we doubt not to prove to your Satisfaction, and then we doubt not but that you will do exemplary Justice to such intolerable sad Stuff, and, will pass such a Sentence as may be a dreadful Example to all future Books, how they dare stand up in Opposition to the Humour of the Age."

Counsellor Town then called Lady Dilly Dally from a crowd of fashionable ladies to bear witness against the character of Amelia; but as she had never seen the creature before and had formed her opinion solely upon what she had heard her physician Dr. Dosewell say, the judge asked her to step down. In her place "a great number of beaus, rakes, fine ladies, and several formal persons with bushy wigs, and canes at their noses," pushed forward, all eager to speak at once against the frightened woman at the bar in a determination that she should not escape punishment. At this juncture, "a grave man" supposed to be the father of the distressed Amelia, stood up and begged the court that he might be heard. The request being granted, he suggested a peaceful settlement of the case in the following appeal to the judge and the prosecution:

"If you, Mr. Censor, are yourself a Parent, you will view me with Compassion when I declare I am the Father of this poor Girl the Prisoner at the Bar; nay, when I go farther, and avow, that of all my Offspring she is my favourite Child. I can truly say that I bestowed a more than ordinary Pains in her Education; in which I will venture to affirm, I followed the Rules of all those who are acknowledged to have writ best on the Subject; and if her Conduct be fairly examined, she will be found to deviate very little from the strictest Observation of all those Rules; neither Homer nor Virgil pursued them with greater Care than myself, and the candid and learned Reader will see that the latter was the noble model, which I made use of on this Occasion.

"I do not think my Child is entirely free from Faults. I know nothing human that is so; but surely she doth not deserve the Rancour with which she hath been treated by the Public. However, it is not my Intention, at present, to make any Defence; but shall submit to a Compromise, which hath been always allowed in this Court in all Prosecutions for Dulness. I do, therefore, solemnly declare to you, Mr. Censor, that I will trouble the World no more with any Children of mine by the same Muse."

"This Declaration," says the reporter, "was received with a loud Huzza, by the greater Part of the Spectators; and being allowed by the Court, was presently entered of Record. Then Amelia was delivered to her Parent, and a Scene of great Tenderness passed between them, which gave much Satisfaction to many present; some of whom, however, blamed the old Gentleman for putting an End to the Cause, and several very grave and well looking Men, who knew the whole Merits, asserted, that the Lady ought to have been honourably acquitted."

A few of Amelia's friends who had no opportunity to speak in court, expressed themselves elsewhere. "Criticulus," though he lamented Mr. Fielding's anachronisms, gave the novel "a second perusal with great pleasure." "Some of the characters," he said in a letter to "The Gentleman's Magazine," "are handled in so masterly a manner, virtue and vice meet with their due rewards, and it abounds with such noble reflections on the follies and vices, the perfections and imperfections of human nature, that he must be both a bad and ill-natur'd reader, who is not by it agreeably entertain'd, instructed and improved." With reference to the great point in debate, he added justly: "His fair heroine's nose has, in my opinion, been too severely handled by some modern critics, whose writings will never make a sufficient recompence to the world, if Mr. Fielding adheres to what I hope he only said in his warmth and indignation of this injurious treatment, that he will never trouble the public with any more writings of this kind." Similarly the charge in the bill of complaint that Amelia displayed "no manner of spirit," evoked a retort from an anonymous contributor to "The General Advertiser" for January 18, 1752, who thought himself a poet. The verses in part run—

> What hear we now, astonish'd Readers cry,
> No Spirit in the Scenes of *Amely!*
> Where Wit with Sense, Instruction with Delight,
> Keeps pace; where Virtue shines in purest white:
> Where keenest Satire plays the justest Part;
> Stings deep, and only stings the guilty Heart;
> No Spirit there! Quoth Clencher, by my troth,
> He's thinking on his own dear Idol Froth.

Occasional words in approval of "Amelia" also fell from the pens of literary ladies. Mrs. Delany, despite her own antagonism to the novel, conceded, as we have seen, that some of her friends did not share her emotions. Catherine Talbot, who was then living with her mother in the household of Thomas Secker, a future Archbishop of Canterbury, but as yet only Dean of St. Paul's, described for Mrs. Elizabeth Carter quiet afternoons when Martin Benson, the Bishop of Gloucester, came in and read "Amelia" all by himself except for an explosion now and then. "I have not read 'Amelia' yet," she confessed, "but have seen it read and commented upon much to my edification by that good Bishop of Gloucester, who seldom misses spending two or three days of the week at this deanery. . . . I have been particularly delighted with some of our afternoons, when we have sat unmolested by my dressing room fire-side, he reading 'Amelia' (and quarreling excessively at the two first volumes) my mother and I reading or working, or following our own devices as it might happen." To this letter the learned Mrs. Carter replied, with a thrust at the good Bishop and at Hester Mulso, one of Richardson's worshippers, who had flayed Mr. Booth for his treatment of Amelia: "In favour of the Bishop of Gloucester's cold his reading of Amelia in silence may be tolerated, but I am somewhat scandalized that since he did not read it to you, you did not read it yourself. Methinks I long to engage you on the side of this poor unfortunate book, which I am told the fine folks are unanimous in pronouncing to be very sad stuff. The Bishop of Gloucester's excessive sad quarrel with the two first volumes I am determined to conclude proceeded from the effects of his cold. How to account for Miss Mulso's unmerciful severity to Amelia is past my skill, as it does not appear but that she was in very good health when she read the book." Banter of this kind Miss Talbot could not ignore. Three weeks later Mrs. Carter received from her the news: "At last we have begun Amelia, it is very entertaining. I do love Dr. Harrison and the good Serjeant; and Mrs. James's visit to Amelia has extremely diverted me. How many Mrs. James's in that good-for-nothing London! But Mr. Fielding's heroines are always silly loving runaway girls. Amelia makes an excellent wife, but why did she marry Booth?"* More interesting than the prattle of this advance guard of the Blue-Stockings, is the opinion of Dr. Johnson. Twenty-five years later, he told his friends that he "read Fielding's 'Amelia' through without stopping," and pronounced it "the most pleasing of all the romances."† Could Fielding

* For these letters, see "Letters between Mrs. Elizabeth Carter and Miss Catherine Talbot," 1809, II, 69, 71, 75.

† Boswell, "Life of Johnson," edited by G. B. Hill, 1887, III, 43.

have known of this tribute, it would have made full amends for all the abuse with which "Amelia" was deluged.

The most comprehensive view of the novel was taken in a pamphlet called "Some Remarks on the Life and Writings of Dr J[ohn] H[ill]" which appeared at the end of March, 1752, when the heat of the controversy over Fielding's heroine was beginning to subside. According to current rumour, the author, who concealed his name, was Dr. John Kennedy, a well-known collector of Greek and Roman coins. His pamphlet is an exposure of the practices of a notorious quack, who had, as an incident of his career, fallen foul of "Amelia." "You ask me," this scholar writes to an imaginary friend in the country, "for the opinion of the town, and my own of Mr. Fielding's 'Amelia.' I must own to you, they are very different, if we are to form a judgment of the opinion of the town by the sale of the work, which has not as yet gone thro' a second edition. . . . Were I to take it from the circle of my own acquaintance, I should mention 'Amelia' to you as a most finished performance." He then goes on to repeat the praise of "the judicious few" and to attribute the ill repute of "the inestimable Amelia" to a depraved public taste with which Mr. Fielding will not conform. "What you take notice of," he says further, "as to Amelia's nose, was an omission of the author's which has occasioned a vast deal of low wit, and been a standing joke here. I dare say it will be emended in any future edition."

Amelia thus had her partisans. Their number, however, was small when compared with the host of enemies. The novel was as completely damned as any farce whatever. Thereat the happiest man in all England was Samuel Richardson, already meditating his "Sir Charles Grandison" which should give the world a portrait of a perfect gentleman in contrast with that blackguard Tom Jones.

THE FAILURE OF AMELIA

On February 11, 1752, Mrs. Donnellan, who was staying with Mrs. Delany over in Ireland, wrote to him:

"I rejoice to find you proceed in the noble design of shewing the man of virtue in all the different circumstances of social life. But what can you mean by seeming uncertain whether you shall publish it? and how can you be so cruel to your own generation, as to think of leaving it to another? is it that we do not want such a pattern, or that you imagine there are others can give it better? Will you leave us to Capt. Booth and Betty Thoughtless for our examples? As for poor Amelia, she is so great a fool we pity her, but cannot be humble enough to desire to imitate her. But pray, Sir, you that desire women should be learned, what do you say to Mrs. Atkinson? Must we suppose that if a woman knows a little Greek and Latin she must be a drunkard, and virago? Now, perhaps, you have not read this stuff, but I desire you will, and then I think your conscience must make you publish. Poor Fielding, I believe, designed to be good, but did not know how, and in the attempt lost his genius, low humour."

At length the Blue-Stocking had discovered Mrs. Atkinson alias Mrs. Bennet. To her letter Richardson replied on the twenty-second of the same month:

"Will I leave you to Captain Booth? Capt. Booth, Madam, has done his own business. Mr. Fielding has overwritten himself, or rather *under*-written; and in his own journal seems ashamed of his last piece; and has promised that the same Muse shall write no more for him. The piece, in short, is as dead as if it had been published forty years ago, as to sale.

"You guess that I have not read Amelia. Indeed I have read but the first volume. I had intended to go through with it; but I found the characters and situations so wretchedly low and dirty, that I imagined I could not be interested for any one of them; and to read and not to care what became of the hero and heroine, is a task that I thought I would leave to those who had more leisure than I am blessed with.

". . . The best story in the piece, is of himself and his first wife. In his Tom Jones, his hero is made a natural child, because his own first wife was such. Tom Jones is Fielding himself, hardened in some places, softened in others. His Lady Bellaston is an infamous woman of his former acquaintance. His Sophia is again his first wife. Booth, in his last piece, again himself; Amelia, even to her noselessness, is again his first wife. His brawls, his jarrs, his gaols, his spunging-houses, are all drawn from what he has seen and known. As I said (witness also his hamper plot) he has little or no invention: and admirably do you observe, that by several strokes in his Amelia he designed to be good, but knew not how, and lost his genius, low humour in the attempt."

On that very day perhaps, Richardson received a call from Miss Sarah Fielding, for we find him writing on the next morning to Lady Bradshaigh:

"I have not been able to read any more than the first volume of Amelia. Poor Fielding! I could not help telling his sister, that I was equally surprised at and concerned for his continued lowness. Had your brother, said I, been born in a stable, or been a runner at a sponging-house, we should have thought him a genius, and wished he had had the advantage of a liberal education, and of being admitted into good company; but it is beyond my conception, that a man of family, and who had some learning, and who really is a writer, should descend so excessively low, in all his pieces. Who can care for any of his people? A person of honour asked me, the other day, what he could mean, by saying, in his Covent Garden Journal, that he had followed Homer and Virgil, in his Amelia. I answered, that he was justified in saying so, because he must mean Cotton's Virgil

Travestied; where the women are drabs, and the men scoundrels.''*

There was one way by which Fielding might yet save ''Amelia.'' In his younger days, when the audience objected to a particular scene or character or sentiment in any of his comedies, he sometimes made such alterations as the public demanded if the play were to go on. Thus the slaying of the ghost in ''Tom Thumb'' was sacrificed to the hostility of some people who thought the incident either sacrilegious or over-farcical. If, however, the trouble were inherent in the plot, then there could be no recovery. No omissions or readjustments, for example, ever reconciled the audience to ''The Modern Husband.'' ''Amelia'' presented a very interesting problem. It had indeed reminiscences of this old comedy, but the disagreeable situation was less distinct in the novel, being obscured, nay, almost concealed, there by a wealth of other incident. Very few persons could have agreed with Richardson in utterly condemning the book and the author on the score of depraved morals. Moreover, the numerous charges against Amelia formulated in the bill of complaint when the novel was arraigned before Mr. Censor, were intended as a dragnet for everything that could be said in depreciation. No single reader would have subscribed to them all. The one point of agreement was that Fielding, in his haste, had left Amelia without a nose. If that inadvertency and some other technical defects were removed, it seemed probable that the novel might pass muster. Accordingly Fielding decided, as was predicted by Dr. Kennedy, to try the public with a new edition.

The revision to which Fielding subjected ''Amelia'' was most thorough. It extended to minor details of style, all of which I shall pass over, except to remark that Miss

* For the Richardson Letters, see Barbauld, ''Correspondence of Richardson,'' IV, 55, 59; VI, 154.

Mathews had another *t* put into her name. In the first
place, the author went over every reference to Amelia's
accident and brought them into harmony. He made it clear
that her nose was restored by "the surgeon's skill," leaving nothing more than a "little scar," which did not at all
diminish her beauty. He obliterated every vestige of the
Universal Register Office, and so skilfully adjusted the
narrative to the alterations that no one would ever suspect
that the institution had been mentioned in a previous edition. Rather strangely, however, he left "Ranelagh,"
though he might have removed the anachronism by merely
substituting "the Haymarket," where Heidegger's masquerades were in full blast when Booth and Amelia arrived
in London. The probable explanation of Fielding's course
here is that he wished to impress on young men and women
the evils of masquerades. This he could not do so well in
a strict historical background breaking the continuity of
the past with the present. Heidegger was dead and the
fashionable amusement had passed to Ranelagh, with which
place it had become most closely associated by everybody
except here and there a critic endowed with a memory of
unusual excellence. Likewise the prison scenes which
Counsellor Town denounced, were allowed to stand. Nor
was any essential change made in the conduct of Dr. Harrison, for Fielding believed it to be perfectly natural. As
before, Booth was once arrested at the Doctor's suit through
a misunderstanding. On the other hand, Fielding conceded
a slip in arming "Mons. L'Abbé Bagillard" with a sword.
But instead of depriving the French gentleman of his
weapon of defence, as would have been Counsellor Town's
advice, he deprived him of his ecclesiastical title. "Mons.
Bagillard," without disturbing anyone's sense of propriety,
might now draw his sword when Major Bath gave him a
box on the ear. It may be observed that the alteration was
quite unnecessary, for the *abbé galant* of the eighteenth

T. Hudson Pinx.ᵇ   J. Faber Fecit 1754.

Mr. Allen

century wore only a semi-clerical dress which permitted a sword.

Lastly, there were the sentiments which the indictment declared "bad and contemptible." A reader passing from "Tom Jones" to "Amelia" misses the initial chapters which characterize the former novel. Fielding now had no time to write essays so formal as those. In "Amelia" his disquisitions, if we except the exordium, are scattered through the volumes, more as in "Joseph Andrews." For the most part they rise naturally out of a scene or a character. An obvious exception to this general statement is the conversation between Booth and "the very great writer" who fabricated, as Dr. Johnson is said to have done, parliamentary speeches for the magazines. Without any preparation for it the young lieutenant suddenly displays a fund of ancient and modern learning never possessed by a man of his age. It is the mature Fielding who here renders comparative estimates of the writers he read most, criticising by the way the translations of Lucian at a time when he was planning one of his own. More appropriately Dr. Harrison became Fielding's mouthpiece; to this scholar he could transfer his own opinions on the affairs of church and state with perfect consistency. Almost always, whether Fielding spoke through his characters or in his own person, his thought and emotion rose to the highest plane. His little essay on the art of life, with which the novel opens, is as true as it is impressive. The dedication to Ralph Allen is among the finest memorials ever erected to friendship. It is here that Fielding expressed the hope that he might never be so unfortunate as to survive his benefactor.

And yet, Fielding said some things which he wished away, either because they were lacking in good taste or because they were out of keeping with the character who uttered them. Booth he did not disturb; but Dr. Harrison was shorn of two remarks and perhaps more. On one occasion the Doctor, in an irascible mood, cast an unnecessary slur on the army by declaring that officers usually first married their wives for money and then maltreated them. "As little famed," he said, "as the army is for religion, nothing is, I believe, more common than for the officers to make good Christians of their wives, and to teach them true repentance." That observation had to go. Again, the Doctor, when in the country, lived in a very plain house which was furnished with nothing unnecessary, "except books, and the prints of Mr. Hogarth, whom he calls a moral painter, and says no clergyman should be without all his works, in the knowledge of which he would have him instruct his parishioners, as he himself often doth." In his revision Fielding substituted "satirist" for "painter," and clipped off the rest of the sentence, thereby avoiding the absurdity of including instruction in Mr. Hogarth's works among the pastoral duties. Similar extravagant praise was bestowed upon Bishop Burnet of a past age. Speaking directly, the author described him as "almost the only English historian that is likely to be known to posterity, by whom he will be most certainly ranked amongst the greatest writers of antiquity." On sober thought this prophecy appeared too venturesome, and it was removed.

Most curious alterations concern Fielding's eulogies on the physicians whom he counted among his friends. During a severe illness two years before, he had been attended by Dr. Thomas Thompson, who afterwards became his chief medical adviser. Out of gratitude to this man to whom he believed he owed his life, he gave him, perhaps in lieu of a fee, a whole chapter of praise. When one of Booth's children, it is related there, was brought to the point of death by the erroneous treatment of an unnamed physician, the distracted parents summoned Dr. Thompson, who threw all the physic of his predecessor to the dogs, and by simple remedies cured the little patient within three days. Dr. Thompson's medicines also had the same marvellous effect on Sergeant Atkinson after he had been given over by several very great doctors. Happy in the restoration of her husband, Mrs. Atkinson liked to entertain her friends with a humorous account of the sergeant's physicians, always ending, however, "with many vast eulogiums on him who came last." To drop Dr. Thompson, when Major Bath was wounded in the duel with Booth, the victor hurried out to Bond Street to fetch "the most eminent surgeon in the kingdom, or perhaps in the world"; that is, Dr. John Ranby who had dressed the wounds of the father of the Man of the Hill in "Tom Jones." He was too, I suppose, "the eminent surgeon" that mended Amelia's nose. In like manner Dr. Joshua Ward, whom Fielding subsequently consulted, was honoured by a passing notice for his famous pill; while Dr. Robert James's Powder, destined to shorten the life of Laurence Sterne and to kill Oliver Goldsmith, was lauded as "that powder, for the invention of which, my worthy and ingenious friend Dr. James would, in almost any country but this, have received public honours and rewards."

Of these men, Ranby deserved the high repute he bore in his own time; but Thompson, Ward, and James were regarded askance by the medical faculty. Though not exactly quacks, they came near being such. Undue praise of these vain and pretentious men must have been offensive to practitioners jealous of the ethics of the profession. This Fielding implied in a roundabout way. Dr. Dosewell, whom Booth would not summon for consultation over the case of his child, told Lady Dilly Dally that "Amelia" was "a sad stupid book, and that the author had not a bit of wit, or learning, or sense, or any thing else." No doubt Fielding was perfectly sincere in all that he said of the irregular physicians. As other intelligent persons have done in all ages, the sick man in desperation consulted quacks for the relief of disorders which could not be cured, and was buoyed up by the unwarranted hopes which they held out to him. That he put them into his book was due to the generosity of his spirit. But to the outside public, it all appeared as an advertisement of impostors and their nostrums. His impropriety Fielding saw when he undertook the revision of "Amelia." Thompson, whom everybody knew as the physician who let Winnington the politician die of a cold, lost his chapter. Ward and James, though their names were retained, were despoiled of all else. Even the allusion to Ranby nearly disappeared along with a very poor jest of the distinguished surgeon.

And the sequel? No greater disappointment ever overtook Fielding. The public had become absolutely indifferent to his novel. The second impression of the first edition still remained unsold, and nobody cared to see "Amelia" in a new dress. Nothing was now left for Fielding but to appeal to posterity. His copy of "Amelia," revised by his own hand, was carefully preserved by his family (his wife or his brother), who placed it at the disposal of Arthur Murphy for the collected edition of Fielding's works in 1762. It is this revised "Amelia" which has come down to us in popular editions. The author's firm reliance on the great qualities of his last novel has been more than justified. His genius, at its height, it must be admitted, can only be seen in "Tom Jones"; but no single character in that novel has found so many admirers for her perfect womanhood as that Amelia who was derided by the profane wits of her time.

CHAPTER XXIV

THE COVENT–GARDEN JOURNAL

Before "Amelia" was off the press, Fielding was already at the point of launching "The Covent-Garden Journal"— the fourth and last of his ventures in periodical literature. The date first set for the appearance of the initial number seems to have been Saturday, November 23, 1751. According to a notice in "The London Daily Advertiser" three weeks earlier, it was to be "A Paper of Entertainment" under the direction of "Several Eminent Hands." For reasons never announced, publication was delayed. "Amelia" doubtless still demanded the author's attention a month longer than he expected. Many of his graver friends, we know for certain, tried to dissuade him from an undertaking which they thought beneath the dignity of a magistrate; they told him, he says, that he might employ his pen much more to the honour of himself and to the good of the public. Moreover, the declining state of his health had to be considered. He could not free himself from periodic attacks of the gout which lamed him and wore him down fearfully. Nevertheless, in spite of infirmities and all else, he persisted in his design. On a leaf inserted at the end of the second volume of "Amelia," it is announced that the new periodical "will be certainly published on Saturday the 4th of January next," that is, on January 4, 1752. There was no further postponement. On that day the coffee-houses received the first number of "The Covent-Garden Journal," to be continued "every Tuesday and Saturday." The price was threepence a copy.

No one could fail to see who the editor was, though he assumed the name of "Sir Alexander Drawcansir, Knt. Censor of Great Britain." The sobriquet of "Drawcansir," the name which Colley Cibber had contemptuously applied to Fielding in the old theatrical days, was taken from a braggadocio in the Duke of Buckingham's "Rehearsal"—a burlesque of the *miles gloriosus* who goes into battle with the intention of killing everybody about him, whether friend or foe:

> I drink, I huff, I strut, look big and stare;
> And all this I can do because I dare.

When Cibber wrote his "Apology," satirists in the public press as well as on the stage were known as "Drawcansirs of the goose-quill." By assuming the title, Fielding proclaimed himself a free lance who would show no favour to any man or institution or party, or to any vice or folly that deserved reprobation. It was a rôle similar to the one which he had formerly played in the disguise of "Captain Hercules Vinegar, Champion and Censor of Great Britain."

The business secrets of "The Covent-Garden Journal" have never been disclosed; but perhaps the veil may be partially withdrawn. "The Champion," we remember, was owned by a group of booksellers and other men including Fielding, who formed a partnership for the management of its affairs. "The True Patriot" and "The Jacobite's Journal," being political sheets, may have been subsidized by the Government. In their case there seems to have been no partnership. All announcements of the forthcoming "Covent-Garden Journal" were appended to advertisements of the Universal Register Office. To that office in the Strand subscribers were to send in their names and places of abode. When the paper actually appeared, a second distributing point was added—the shop of Mrs. Dodd, the printer of the journal, at the sign of the Peacock, Temple Bar. At either place indifferently, advertisements and letters to the author or editor were taken in. Mrs. Dodd, however, probably assumed none of the financial risks of the undertaking. She appears to have been only the agent of the proprietors of the Universal Register Office, among whom were John and Henry Fielding. "The Covent-Garden Journal," everything goes to show, was a new enterprise of that institution, though the inference is confirmed by no contemporary statement.

The Universal Register Office, which began as an employment bureau, was then extending its business, as we have seen in the chapter on "Amelia," in many directions. There curacies might be exchanged, houses and estates be sold or let, men and ships be insured, and money be borrowed up to a hundred thousand pounds if the security satisfied the lender. Not only was a branch office opened in Bishopsgate, but a similar one, loosely connected with the original, was established in Dublin. At the same time several rival offices were set up in London. By 1751-1752 competition had become exceedingly bitter; and the Universal Register Office had to fight to hold its supremacy. In "The London Daily Advertiser" of November 9, 1751, "one of the proprietors," without doubt John Fielding, protested against the policy of that journal in refusing their advertisements, while cheap and spurious counterfeits were accorded "free admission." On account of the conduct of this and other newspapers he had no adequate means, he declared, of "making the Office known and understood"; and the next day he pleaded with Dr. John Hill, the leading writer on "The London Daily Advertiser," for his assistance in spreading its fame throughout "the polite world."*
In the circumstances, the proprietors of the Universal Register Office evidently decided to have an organ of their own, edited by their own literary man, wherein their varied business could be described at will. Such at least was the

* British Museum, "Stowe MSS.," 155, f. 124.

use they made of "The Covent-Garden Journal." Their advertisements sometimes filled more than a column.

Apart from its sober transactions, the office gained considerable notoriety as the London agency of the Glastonbury waters. It is an interesting story, which recalls for the last time the town near which Fielding passed his early childhood with his grandfather Gould at Sharpham Park. There was living in the neighbourhood an old man, one Matthew Chancellor, who had suffered greatly from asthma or phthisic for more than a quarter-century. After a violent paroxysm on an October night in 1750, he fell asleep from exhaustion, and dreamed that he was at Glastonbury, where One appeared to him in vision and pointed to a spring of clear water which would cure him of his ailments provided he heeded certain specific directions. Before breaking his fast, he must drink a glassful of the water on seven successive Sunday mornings. He followed the instructions and was perfectly healed. The next year the wells at Bath and Bristol were deserted. Ten thousand people, it is said, flocked to Glastonbury to drink from the miraculous spring. It was known as "the blood spring." According to the usual legend, Joseph of Arimathea, when he came to Glastonbury, brought with him the cup from which our Lord drank at the Last Supper, and buried it near the foot of Tor Hill, on the slope of which Squire Allworthy subsequently obtained his extensive view westward to the British Channel. From the spot where the cup lay hidden, gushed forth for centuries a spring of healing waters. The water contains a certain amount of iron, which oxidizes easily on exposure to the atmosphere and leaves a deposit resembling clots of blood. Hence the name given to the spring and an explanation of the miracles wrought on all who stooped to drink. There were then, of course, sceptics and wits to be reckoned with. A physician, who subjected the water to the usual tests, came to the correct conclusion that it was only ordinary spring water, with a little iron in it, such as is in every man's power to obtain with ease and without price. His experiments, which were described in "The General Evening Post," brought forth a sharp retort from a contributor to "The London Daily Advertiser" for August 31, 1751, who called himself "Z. Z." Not only had "Z. Z." seen great numbers of his fellow creatures go to Glastonbury afflicted with asthma and the king's evil and return restored to health and happiness, but he himself had been "relieved from a disorder which baffled the most skilful physicians." This man, according to "The Gentleman's Magazine," was none other than "J——e F——g."*

The identification of Henry Fielding with "Z. Z." is very doubtful. So far as one can judge from the style of the anonymous gentleman, he was the novelist's brother John. But Henry almost equally with John was interested in the waters as a matter of business. A company was formed at Glastonbury for distributing the waters throughout the kingdom. Every week a supply was sent up to the Universal Register Office. It was a question, sometimes debated, whether the curative properties of the waters were not impaired by transportation. Some were of the opinion also that they should be drunk only on Sundays when their specific gravity was noticeably increased. But people who could not afford to visit Glastonbury were forced to take their chances with the water bottled and sold to them at a distance. That Fielding himself had no doubts about the virtues of the waters surviving a journey to London, may be inferred from the fact that he never admitted among the advertisements in his newspapers a panacea which he did not believe in. If one finds Dr. James's Powders there, it is because the editor placed a high value upon the remedy.

* See "The Gentleman's Magazine" for 1751, XXI, 186, 231, 295, 411, 415-416.

So of the Glastonbury waters, which he and the other proprietors of the Universal Register Office commended not only to those desperately ill but to everybody who wished to retain the full vigour of health and spirits. With some variation, the advertisement as printed in "The Covent-Garden Journal" ran:

"GLASTONBURY WATER.

"Last Thursday there came to the Universal Register Office, opposite Cecil-Street, in the Strand, (the only Place where it is to be had in London) a fresh Quantity of Glastonbury Water, so justly valued for its Efficacy in Asthmatic and all scrophulous Disorders. The Quantity to be drank is Half a Pint every Morning fasting, the Price 1s. a Bottle, and the Bottle to be return'd or paid for."

Altogether "The Covent-Garden Journal" was established under conditions most favourable to Fielding. As a shareholder in the Universal Register Office, he profited by an increase in its business due to liberal advertising. As the editor of its organ he received a guinea or more for every leading article that he wrote. Such an opportunity to make some provision, though not large, for his family could not be passed by. Still, powerful as was this motive, it would not alone have prevailed. However hard pressed Fielding may be at any point in his career, we invariably find him actuated also by other considerations than those which promise an addition to his income. At this time, social and legal questions arising out of his office as justice of the peace were uppermost in his mind. Hitherto he had spoken on these subjects through pamphlets; now he had a medium through which he could address the public twice a week if he so desired.

Accordingly, under the head of "Covent Garden" he gave in each number of his journal a résumé of the cases that had come before his court since the last issue, sometimes reproducing in brief the questions and answers in an examination. Whenever he got into his power any members of a desperate gang, he invited people who had been robbed to come and identify them if they could. If he was compelled to let a villain go free because of some defect in the law, he gave the grounds for his decision with pertinent observations on the statute in question. In refusing, for instance, to issue warrants when a young man was discovered with the wife of an industrious labourer, he remarked that he could do nothing else, "adultery being no crime by the laws of England." If he could have his own way, he would put the offence, he said ironically elsewhere, on a par at least with pocket-picking. In discharging a poor woman, the mother of three small children, who was accused of stealing a cap valued at threepence, he asked the legislature to amend the law covering petty larceny which no justice with a heart could enforce. Parliament was then in session and was considering some of the reforms in the penal code which Fielding had advocated in his pamphlets. They were all urged anew in "The Covent-Garden Journal," and several of them, as we have seen, passed into statutes. When measures for the improvement of the poor seemed sure to fail, he argued, taking his cue from Swift's "Modest Proposal," that it would be better to slay the poor outright than to let them die piecemeal of cold and hunger. Other newspapers reported crimes for those who liked to read of them. Here was a newspaper that gave the proceedings of the Bow Street court in order that legislators and the public at large might see how the laws against crime actually worked out in practice. The news from Bow Street was for them a course of instruction in criminal law given by a justice of the peace who knew his business and could enliven the lecture with humour.

Never before was Fielding's journalism quite so free

from external restraint. When managing "The Champion," he had to deal with an associate editor and a group of miscellaneous shareholders, from whom he eventually broke away in disgust. Though he enjoyed a greater degree of independence in "The True Patriot" and "The Jacobite's Journal," even there his main themes were determined for him by the political questions of the day, and his supporters expected him to defend the Ministry—their measures and their characters—against a fierce Opposition. The editor of "The Covent-Garden Journal" was his own man, having no one to please but his brother and a few other gentlemen engaged with him in a common enterprise. All they could ask of him was that the journal should sell. Naturally his general model was set by his previous newspapers. There must always be a leader or a substitute for one, moral and literary disquisitions, the current news with humorous comment, and as much advertising as could be obtained from the publishers of books. Politics in the narrow sense of the word, Fielding announced in his first number, would be left to the other newspapers, though he might at times discuss those questions of real public interest with which his brethren of the quill never concerned themselves. He promised them also that he would not encroach, if he could help it, upon "the Land of Dullness" which had been theirs by right from time immemorial. His was to be a "Paper of Entertainment and News." Of course, he remarked pleasantly, it may be taken for granted that his prime object is to "correct and reform" the age. Still, this aim he did not wish to be regarded too seriously. Seated at his ease, he would luxuriate, wherever whim might lead him, in the fields of literature and life and manners.

It is amusing to see the editor, from whose pen came nearly all the leaders and other literary matter of the journal, trying to keep up the fiction that he was aided by "several eminent hands." In all there were seventy-two numbers of "The Covent-Garden Journal," extending from January 4 to November 25, 1752. The first six leaders were signed A, the initial of Sir Alexander. Thereafter Fielding began to introduce other initials until he had several of them, always returning to A at intervals. Thirty leaders or parts of them have this signature. When he employed A, readers were to understand that the editor was speaking directly on his aims, on the state of the periodical press and of literature generally, and on the lighter follies and vices of the time. When he wished to become more serious, he often chose the letter C, which had been his favourite in "The Champion." C was a writer of sterner morality than A. He put his mark to nineteen leaders. J once appeared with a Socratic dialogue between a philosopher and a fine lady who met at Tunbridge Wells.

There was also M, a sort of literary hack, who on three or four occasions, it is uncertain which, edited and arranged in their proper order letters addressed to Sir Alexander from Tim Buck, Dorothy Single, Peter Grievous, and other persons of fanciful names. P retold a gay story out of Ariosto, and contributed a whimsical essay on the theatrical state in which Garrick then reigned as the benevolent despot. S instructed the public in the qualities necessary to "hearers" who would profit most by the theatre, interspersing his views with anecdotes. Some years since, we are told, two bucks mistook Ben Jonson's "Alchemist" for a low farce that was to follow it, and proceeded to hiss the actors off the stage. "When Mr. Handel," to relate another story, "first exhibited his Allegro and Penseroso, there were two ingenious gentlemen who had bought a book of the words, and thought to divert themselves by reading it before the performance began. *Zounds* (cried one of them) *what damn'd stuff this is!—Damn'd stuff indeed,* replied his friend. *God so!* (replied the other, who then first cast his eyes on the title-page) *the words are Milton's.*"

All the other leaders—fifteen or sixteen of them—were left without any initial at the end to cover the whole. Sometimes it was deliberately omitted; more often, I think, through carelessness or unconcern. The same practice was extended to the news of the day, which the editor printed under the head of "Modern History. Cum Notis Variorum." Of these humorous commentators, the most industrious were C and M. To a notice of Mrs. Clive's benefit in March, C adds a sentence of most liberal praise: "Mrs. Clive in her walk on the stage is the greatest actress the world ever saw; and if as many really understood true humour as pretend to understand it, she would have nothing to wish, but that the house was six times as large as it is." This is the Miss Raftor, the charming Irish girl, whose unusual comic talents Fielding claimed to have been the first to discover, and to whom, after she had become Mrs. Clive, he dedicated "The Intriguing Chambermaid." Similarly, to an account of a charity sermon by the Bishop of Worcester, C appends the comment: "This worthy Prelate is a true labourer in the vineyard. To his great care and diligence, the late Act against spirituous liquors was chiefly owing. A law, which, if it hath not abolished, hath very considerably lessened the pernicious practice of gin-drinking." He was the prelate to whom Fielding a few weeks later dedicated his pamphlet on murder. Two years before had died at Bath, Edmund Castle, the Dean of Hereford and Master of Corpus Christi College, Cambridge. He was a learned man, very quiet and simple in his bearing. A Latin inscription to his memory, placed over his grave in his parish church at Barley in Hertfordshire, Fielding admired for its elegance and for its truth to the character of the Dean. M neatly translates the epitaph into English in order that the sincerity, piety, justice, and charity of the ecclesiastic may be more widely known. The Dean of Hereford must have been among Fielding's acquaintances, else

he could not have written of him as he did. This is one more
indication of the scope of Fielding's friendships, which included the dignitaries of the church as well as London wits
and facetious Irishmen.

Besides C and M, several other commentators intrude
their presence. Politicus and Punicus, abbreviated to
"Pol" and "Pu," shine with special brilliancy in caustic
observations on the state of the town and the state of the
nation. The former, for example, reads in a newspaper:
"Yesterday at noon a man about fifty meanly dressed, was
beat down at the end of Charles Court in the Strand, by a
porter that had on his back three iron-bars; by which
accident he was killed on the spot. The porter was coming
up the Court just as the poor man passed the end of it;
and the irons unluckily met his temple. He was immediately carried to St. Martin's Roundhouse to be own'd."
The accident arouses the indignation of Politicus, who retorts: "Some little enquiry ought likewise to have been
made after the porter: For the worthy body who are called
by that name, by their insolence and carelessness, make one
species of those numerous nusances that infest the public
streets." There was also another pair of newsmongers,
called Gelosophus and Incerti, who favoured the public with
their opinions. If an item of news touched literature, then
the editor might supply the comment without any signature.
When, for example, Garrick was preparing to bring out an
adaptation of "Cenie," one of the newspapers displayed
its ignorance of the work in the following words: "A
comedy, written in French by a lady, called Cenie, and
translated by the Rev. Mr. Francis, author of the translation of the works of Horace, is now in rehearsal at Drury
Lane Theatre, and will soon be acted. This comedy, which
is of the genteel species, without any intermixture of low
characters, met with great success at Paris; and by its fate
on our stage will be seen, whether the English taste can be

pleased with that kind of comedy, which, as it has no drollery, can never excite laughter.'' Thereupon Sir Alexander remarks: ''That kind of comedy which has no drollery, is in truth no comedy at all. And so is the case at present; for this comedy (as I have heard) happens to be a tragedy.''*

Initials at the end of articles became less frequent after the fortieth number, and they dwindled from the news-columns long before that time. The editor, however, maintained to the last the appearance of having many correspondents, whose characters are deftly portrayed in letters bearing tell-tale names. Of these contributors in verse and prose, there are more than fifty. Beneath the fictitious signatures they bear, may or may not be placed also an A or C or M for the further mystification of the reader. ''Why and Wherefore'' protest against Sir Alexander's attack on contemporary scribblers—a set of wretches unworthy of notice. ''P. W.'' runs up a parallel between ''The Covent-Garden Journal'' and the Universal Register Office on the lines of their usefulness. ''Y. Y.'' sends in a few ''bad verses,'' inspired by still worse ones which a gentleman wrote on hearing Belinda recite some lines from ''The Fair Penitent.'' ''Humphry Gubbin,'' a Somerset youth, is shocked by the scant dress of the ladies whom he sees at Ranelagh. ''Every-body'' enters a com-plaint against ''No-body,'' and ''No-body'' replies to him. ''Paul Traffick'' and ''Zara Grandemonde'' take different views of an article on ''people of fashion,'' one approving, the other disapproving the sentiments of the editor. ''Misargurus'' explains how he came to the conclusion that money is the source of all the social and political vices. True to his logic, he converted his estate into money and was proceeding to unload his pockets in the Thames, when he was seized by his heir and conveyed to Bedlam, whence

* ''The Covent-Garden Journal,'' Nos. 1 and 4.

he writes to Sir Alexander, inquiring how long it will be before the rest of mankind regain their senses.

"Humphrey Newmixon," a dry-as-dust historian of the fortieth century, depicts from that distant day the manners of the eighteenth century. His learned work is based upon a few fragments which he luckily discovered of the "Annals or Journals" written by one Sir Alexander Drawcansir, who flourished during the reign of "George the Good." If Sir Alexander, he says, wrote anything else, it has not survived to this fortieth century. "Tom Telltruth," who has wasted the better part of his youth on the classics and other university studies, proves the uselessness of an education derived from books, while "Antigallicus" comments on an advertisement of a Frenchman who professes to teach all the languages and all the sciences without the least effort on the part of the learner. In contrast with these triflers, "Axylus," an old bachelor upwards of sixty, moralizes on the case of Mary Blandy, just convicted at Oxford of poisoning her father. The amiable "Axylus," a cousin to Squire Allworthy or Parson Adams, finds his sole delight in the happiness of others and in reading the works of Dr. Barrow. "Iago" sneers at him as a fool. It was thus impossible for Fielding, essentially a novelist, to conduct a newspaper without projecting himself into a motley group of characters.

All this is not to say that Fielding received no assistance, nor that all his correspondents were imaginary. His clerk Joshua Brogden, it is implied in several places,* selected the most interesting cases of the Bow Street court for the inspection of the justice before their publication. In this work Brogden became so skilled that Fielding, if we are to take soberly a remark in number twenty, sometimes left even the comment to him. Still, instances of this freedom seem to be rare. Most of the comment, advice, and in-

* Nos. 2, 20, 21, 72.

struction bears the certain stamp of the editor-in-chief. Only when the remarks degenerate into commonplace moralizing is there any suspicion of Brogden instead of Fielding. Occasionally, when the justice was engaged in few or no examinations important enough to make public, he would himself fill most of the space usually assigned to his clerk with an address on a more general topic connected with the administration of the law. In number fifty, for example, he discusses, disguising himself and his style in "Humphry Meanwell," the arbitrary conduct of the police and the proper treatment of women suspected of being street-walkers. In this manner the editor and his clerk prepared the reports from Bow Street.

Besides Brogden, there was another assistant, whose name Fielding withholds. It was the business of this second person to forage through the newspapers in search of miscellaneous occurrences and to place them in order for "the notes variorum." At first Fielding himself, he says in the second number, attempted to collect these items, but had to give it up after one trial because the newswriters of his day were so dull that they put him to sleep. "There is," to quote his own facetious language, "a pernicious consequence which attends reading over these several diurnal histories, and which, I am convinced, my readers themselves must have often experienced; this is a certain languor, or stupor, or, to express myself in more plain English, a total dulness, that seizes me whenever I have travelled through two or three of these authors. If indeed, I can preserve myself from sleep so long (which is a difficult matter,) I am always thrown, by such reading, into a state so perfectly lethargic, that I am scarce able to utter a word of common sense for several hours afterwards." Having failed himself, he decided to turn this labour over to "a man of so wakeful a capacity, that he defies the juice of poppy itself to set him asleep. This gentleman hath orders to extract the best intelligence he can find, and to endeavour as seldom as possible at a joke, which is, I find, a very offensive thing to tender years."

This Argus whose eyes no dulness could close was without doubt William Young alias Parson Adams, who since the days of "The True Patriot" and "The Jacobite's Journal" had been known as Mr. Fielding's "quotation-hunter." Just now they were issuing proposals for a joint translation of Lucian from the original Greek, "with Notes Historical, Critical, and Explanatory." There were to be "two large Volumes in Quarto," at the price of two guineas a set. "Every thing which hath the least tendency to the indecent," they assured prospective subscribers, "will be omitted in this translation; and this, as the translators hope to prove, will be little more than rescuing the author's fame from the forgeries of writers of a note very inferior to Lucian." Nothing came of this expurgated Lucian, which was advertised several times in "The Covent-Garden Journal";* and the Rev. Mr. Young had to continue his browsing among "the modern historians" for some months more. It would be unfair to the intelligence of the parson to say that none of the jokes appended to the news which he gathered came from his own brain. But the phrasing, whatever the signature beneath, usually points directly to a greater master of humour.

These three—Fielding, Brogden, and Young—comprised, unless I am mistaken, the permanent editorial staff of "The Covent-Garden Journal." With them was associated, I think, for a time Arthur Murphy, Fielding's first biographer. This young Irishman, just setting out in his career as journalist, fell at the feet of Fielding in admiration. "The inimitable Mr. Fielding," as he knew him, was not a humorist in the usual sense of the word, that is, not a man of whims and oddities; but a gentleman of "exquisite

* Nos. 51, 52, 53, etc.

humour'' in his writings and conversation. Parson Adams
he thought the most ludicrous creature in all literature save
perhaps Don Quixote; and prophesied that Fielding was
sure of a place with the immortals—with Lucian and Cervantes and Swift.* In the first essays which we know
positively as his, he is absorbed with the ideas of Fielding
whom he imitates and appropriates. This discipleship is
most apparent in the ''The Gray's-Inn Journal,'' a weekly
periodical which Murphy began in October, 1752, and wrote,
almost single-handed, for two years. Here we may see him
forming himself on the style and manner of ''The Covent-
Garden Journal.'' That Murphy served a previous apprenticeship with Fielding is most probable, though it is impossible to assign to him definitely any article in ''The
Covent-Garden Journal.'' Obviously there is an M to
lead one on; but if it be followed blindly it will lead one
astray, for nothing is more certain than that Fielding
sometimes employed this initial for his own work. One
of the most humorous character-sketches, for example, in
''The Covent-Garden Journal'' occurs in number thirty-
three. It is of a ''rider, or rideout'' to a London linen-
draper, who while down in Somersetshire assumes the rôle
of a gentleman. ''R. S.,'' who falls in with this commercial
traveller (as we should call him now) at an inn, describes
his outrageous behaviour in a letter to Sir Alexander.
Beneath the initials of this fictitious correspondent there is
also an M. Were his life at stake, Murphy could never have
painted that portrait. It could have come from no hand
except the one which drew the portrait of Didapper in
''Joseph Andrews.'' It must have been taken from the
life by Fielding in his travels through the West. In several
other places, however, M embraces no more than the
editorial work or a contribution safely within the capacity
of an intelligent Irishman. Some months before Murphy

* See ''The Gray's-Inn Journal,'' Nos. 38, 86, 96, 97.

began his own periodical, M dropped out of "The Covent-Garden Journal." It looks as if this initial, first suggested by Murphy's name, was designed especially to perplex the reader. In the early numbers it was often appended to "the notes variorum." A natural conclusion is that Murphy sometimes assisted Parson Young in dishing up the news, and occasionally supervised the editorial columns. Still, where nothing is certain, no certain statement can be made.

The many contributions to "The Covent-Garden Journal," actual and fictitious, seem to form a veritable maze. In the second number, the editor humbly entreated all Ministers of State to favour him with "an account of all their secret transactions, and negotiations," and begged the gentlemen in Opposition to inform him from time to time of "all their private schemes and plans of operation," assuring both the ins and the outs that he would display, with proper discretion, anything which they wished to communicate to an eager public. Likewise the lights of the learned world were invited to illumine his pages; and gentlemen and ladies conversant with the town were requested to relate what occurs at routs, assemblies, and drums. And then, as if he had forgotten the aspirants to poetic fame, he inserted in number five the following notice for their benefit:

"All Gentlemen Poets, and others, who are willing to serve and please their Country, by publishing their Elegies, Songs, Epigrams, and other short Pieces, under the Inspection of Sir Alexander Drawcansir, Knt. are desired to send in their said Pieces to the Universal Register Office, opposite Cecil-Street, in the Strand, where they shall receive all fitting Encouragement."

These invitations, which were in accord with the conception of journalism current in the eighteenth century, furnished Fielding with a cover for miscellaneous pieces which he could not write so well, if at all, in the character of editor. He could now displace, whenever he desired, the set editorial with a group of poems or letters which appeared to represent different correspondents. Under assumed names he could praise or censure opinions expressed in his leading articles, or indite an epistle to Sir Alexander in one number and reply to it in the next. Variety of authorship thus seemed to exist where sometimes there was none whatever. Naturally the guileless, who were not in the editorial secret, submitted their manuscripts, of which most went into the fire, while some were published after being rewritten, and a still smaller number were deemed good enough to print without alteration. The result is that we have in "The Covent-Garden Journal" three classes of "contributions": those entirely Fielding's, those partially his, and those entirely another's except perhaps for slight rephrasing here and there. And all three degrees of authorship may exist within the limits of a single leader when composed of several detached pieces.

To dissociate Fielding's work from the rest is not so difficult a task as one might think. By the time a biographer reaches "The Covent-Garden Journal," he should be familiar with his style and the range of his ideas. He always has at hand Fielding's many favourite expressions and in particular his use of *hath* for *has*. In applying these tests he must, however, consider that Fielding was not quite alone in employing obsolescent forms of the verb and that he may drop them for the sake of disguise. Moreover, pieces in prose and verse will be found where neither *hath* nor *has* appears. Accordingly there are cases of doubtful authorship which will bring one to a stand; but they are not numerous, for Fielding could not easily conceal himself even in a periodical. There is no one but himself in the leaders, letters, paragraphs, and comment marked with A or C. J is an uncertain gentleman who may be James Harris. M is half Fielding and half somebody else. P is Fielding who masks his face on a second appearance. S is P without his masque and consequently Fielding also. Equally clear is the editor's presence in the majority of cases undistinguished by any of these initials; that is, in those contributions where he coins a name in harmony with the views expressed, or where, as in his farewell to the public, he thinks no signature at all necessary.

It is Fielding who speaks through "Every-body" and "No-body" and the other characters which were enumerated in the paragraphs a few pages back, with the possible exception of "Y. Y." In number forty he is three distinct individuals: he is Misotharsus (or the Hater of Pertness) outlining a treatise on "The Art of Swaggering in Print," Peter Upright praising Sir Alexander's essay on charity, and Tom Thoughtless who despises the same essay, though he encloses a guinea for Pierce, the poor baker burned out in Bloomsbury. In number sixty-two, he assumes the name of Tragicomicus in order to write freely upon William Mason's "Elfrida," a dramatic poem modelled on ancient tragedy. This curious production in blank verse is unbroken by acts or scenes and has "a continued chorus" of British maidens, who never leave the stage and thus render impossible any deviation from the unities of time and place as well as of action. It is the kind of tragedy, said Mason in letters prefixed to the piece, which a Greek dramatist would write were he living in the eighteenth century. Indeed, nobody would have ever thought of constructing a drama otherwise, had there been no Shakespeare, who, however elevated his genius, lacked the sober judgment of Racine. Tragicomicus, who feels like doing a mischief to the critic who picks faults in Shakespeare, exposes the absurdity of any attempt to restore the unities and chorus of pseudo-classicism. "Methinks," he remarks, "Mr. Chorus would be a very impertinent fellow if he was to put in his observations on any of Shakespeare's interesting scenes; as for example, what do you think of this same Chorus, if he was to be upon the stage, when, in the play of Othello, Iago is imprinting those exquisite tints of jealousy upon Othello's mind in the third Act; or suppose when Desdemona drops the fatal handkerchief, the Chorus was to call after her to bid her take it up again, or tell the audience what was to happen in case she did not." It is to be understood, he adds in a postscript, that "I have no objection to the Choruses of the immortal Handel."

Tragicomicus then gives way to Philomath—Fielding in his full masque—who inquires of the editor whether a freethinker like himself can live happily with a Christian wife who abhors his philosophy, and believes him destined to eternal punishment because he follows reason as a guide and is unable to put faith in matters he does not comprehend. How far, he begs to know, may a woman meddle with her husband's principles? There once occurred, says Sir Alexander in lieu of a direct reply, a dispute between a certain author and a certain actress concerning the omission of some lines in the former's play. The author persisted in the opinion that they were his best lines and so should be retained; while the actress declared that she did not know what they meant and should not be required to convey an idea to the audience where there was none to convey. The question was at length referred to Quin, a great casuist as well as a great actor, who, after meditating on the lines, gravely returned the actress her part, saying that he must decide against her, for "every gentleman hath a right to be damned in his own way."

Reversing the process, one may eliminate, with different degrees of probability, sometimes with certainty, major and minor pieces with which Fielding had little or nothing to do except to publish them. Though they are few and of little consequence when compared with the rest, some of them are worth considering for the faint light they throw upon Fielding's genuine contributors. If we could actually know the names of these persons, it would add another human interest to "The Covent-Garden Journal." Our old friend Z. Z. writes two letters—one of them on the mis-behaviour of a coxcomb at Mr. Rich's theatre and the other on a gentleman who invents stories about his affairs with other gentlemen and relates them in confidence to his friends in the hope of gaining importance thereby. Neither of these letters—in numbers sixteen and twenty-eight—has any of Fielding's peculiarities of style. Now, though the signature of this correspondent was rather common in eighteenth-century journalism, it was being used the year before, so far as I have observed, only by the man who praised the Glastonbury Waters and the Universal Register Office in "The London Daily Advertiser." He is clearly the same man who once subscribed himself there as "One of the Proprietors of the Universal Register Office." Had he signed his own name, it would have been, there is little doubt, John Fielding. Z. Z.'s letters in "The London Daily Advertiser" are so different in content from those having the same signature in "The Covent-Garden Journal," that a comparison of their styles does not, perhaps, fully estab-lish a common authorship. It is a true maxim that style cannot remain fixed while subject changes. Still, all the letters of Z. Z., in whichever newspaper they appeared, are more or less in the nature of protests from the pen of a very deferential gentleman who "ventures upon" rather than asserts his opinions. This was a characteristic of John Fielding as seen in his various pamphlets.

Two other letters which the editor himself did not write also lead to the Fielding household. They were published in successive numbers—sixty-three and sixty-four—and bear the signature E. R. This correspondent, who has retired from society, now having no business, no relations, nor friends, tells the story of an unfortunate curate, and draws short character-sketches of inconsiderate, vain, and malevolent persons whom he has met in London and in travels through Dorsetshire, the old home alike of E. R. and the Fieldings. The author, without mentioning the Universal Register Office, praises by indirection the efficiency of that institution in procuring faithful servants who will not get drunk and then burn the children or set the house on fire. As described by himself, E. R. is a benevolent gentleman of small income who seeks out worthy people in distress and relieves them to the extent of his means. Here is the hand of the woman who wrote "The Adventures of David Simple" and the "Familiar Letters." The first of E. R.'s two contributions is the only leader in "The Covent-Garden Journal" without a motto printed at the head. Ample space, however, was reserved there for one. It seems as if Fielding were ill or away at the time and left the editorial columns of two numbers to be filled by some of his sister's unpublished character-sketches, for the first group of which no motto was supplied. She may have also written for the journal under other signatures, and her brother John may not have confined himself to Z. Z. Without attempting to determine the full extent of their contributions, it may be safely said that they occasionally came to Henry's aid in emergencies.

Once Fielding takes for a leader the letter of a certain W. W., who styles himself an apothecary though he could not have been one. This man gives in number sixty-five a sketch of his partner, who has frequent silent moods when he lays an embargo on his tongue for a whole week or a fortnight together, and will answer no question put to him except by signs. The unknown author of this amusing letter was an easy writer well-versed in Mr. Fielding's works and an admirer of the theory of humour expounded in "Joseph Andrews." It is hardly more than conjecture to say that W. W. conceals Arthur Murphy. A little before this time,

Fielding became interested in an endeavour to establish a Medical Society of Surgeons of the Royal Navy for the study of diseases peculiar to seamen. "It is with pleasure," he says, "we observe the prodigious improvements which this most noble art of surgery, the elder sister to that of physic, hath lately received in this country, and the much greater which it is in a fair way of receiving; we wish we could say as much of the younger sister." Accordingly he lets Benevolus have the first place in number thirty-eight to set forth in detail the plan of this undertaking, and finds room in number forty-one for a reply to the strictures of a certain Crito who feared an invasion of the province pre-empted by the Royal Society. Again, it would be mere conjecture to identify Benevolus with Dr. Ranby. To please his old friend, James Harris of Salisbury, Fielding inserted in number twenty-one an abstract of "Hermes," a dull treatise on universal grammar which the philosopher had published the previous year. Nobody but Harris knew what the book meant, and consequently nobody but Harris could have been the author of the review. Likewise, when Millar brought out a translation of "The History of the Portuguese during the Reign of Emmanuel . . . written originally in Latin by Jerome Osorio," Sir Alexander published an admirable account—in number twenty-three—of the Portuguese author and his works, far superior to anything a literary hack could have produced. It may have been prepared by the translator himself—James Gibbs, the architect who designed the Radcliffe Library at Oxford.

At intervals occur poems which purport to have been contributed by those gentlemen eager "to serve and please their country." In all there are, I think, nine or ten of these poems. Were they genuine contributions?—or did the editor himself write most of the verse as well as most of the prose that went into his newspaper? Anyone who has read the "Miscellanies" of 1743 has nearly the full measure of Fielding's poetic talent. All the poems in that collection were occasional. Some were serious panegyrics in Popean couplets; but most of them were light and humorous verses—addresses to Salisbury beauties, epigrams, and burlesque paraphrases of the ancients. The same cleverness may be seen also in the mottoes which Fielding placed at the head of his leaders in "The Covent-Garden Journal." He usually chose a few lines from a Latin or Greek poet, making such alterations as he wished in the original, and then gave his translation a modern twist towards the subject in hand. "Odi profanum Vulgus," when rendered "I hate the Mob," serves as an introduction to an essay on the interference of the rabble in the enforcement of the law; when rendered "I hate profane Rascals," it becomes pertinent to a sketch of a young gentleman who utters an oath with every breath. Similarly, "Redeunt Saturnia Regna," if turned by a dash and a pun into "Old Sat—n himself is come to Town," fitly adorns a thesis set up in irony to prove that the present age, abounding in every manner of vice and iniquity, is the worst in the world's history. In line with these trifles we have several short pieces in the body of "The Covent-Garden Journal," none of which, whether signed A. B., Y. Y., C., or M., or left unsigned, is of any importance whatever. The translation of a Latin epigram in number ten, "made by a gentleman of distinction on his third marriage" was definitely acknowledged by Fielding as his own when he appended a C. It is uncertain what he meant by the use of M. But with one or two exceptions all these fugitive verses, which appeared in the early numbers, may be surely ascribed to Fielding.

Real doubt concerning the authorship of poems in "The Covent-Garden Journal" arises only in the later numbers, where the pieces assume a more sustained character. In the case of an essay, excellence creates a presumption in favour of Fielding's being the author; whereas in the case of a poem excellence rather counts against him. A bad poem is more likely to be his than a really good one. The twenty-eighth leader opens with a pastoral elegy on the death of Frederick Prince of Wales, which the editor says he would have published three weeks before had not the manuscript been "unfortunately mislaid." The poem, signed "Cantabrigiensis," is followed by two letters, which, to judge from the style, were not written by Fielding. An M at the end of the series seems to cover in this instance not the authorship but merely the editorial work expended upon three genuine contributions. The poem in question is one of the best imitations then appearing of Gray's famous "Elegy written in a Country Churchyard." Indeed, it compares favourably with the elegies which William Mason of Cambridge composed a little later in memory of his political and personal friends; but it is too uneven in its phrasing to have come from one whose verse, however correct, always runs on a dead level. Most probably, it was the work of another Cambridge man, Fielding's friend Christopher Smart, whose poems often first saw the light in newspapers and periodicals. True, the elegy does not appear in any edition of Smart's poems; but that fact does not militate against his authorship, for a considerable body of his verse has escaped the collector. If Fielding wrote the elegy, he never before rose to the rhetorical height of

> O! how we hail'd him in his mid Career!
> How dawn'd his Morn! Meridian blaz'd how bright!
> 'Till envious Death deform'd the rising Year,
> In Winter's Solstice like the sudden Night!

This appears to be the imagery of a Christopher Smart.

With equal clearness Smart may be seen either in his own person or by way of imitation in number fifty, which contains two poems, the first being six stanzas on "Lovely Jenny Weston" from the pen of "Geoffry Jingle." These lines are in that other manner of Smart's when he easily drops from the grand style into those whimsical love poems which he had been contributing to "The Midwife." One of these poems, bearing the date May 1, 1751, is an elegy "written in a London Churchyard" on "my Lovely Jenny."* Its measure, rhyme scheme, and tone are exactly reproduced in the tribute to Jenny Weston. Not that the latter poem is a mere echo of the former. It reads like a variation on the same theme by Smart himself. Had Fielding written the stanzas on "Lovely Jenny Weston," they would have broken down, I fear, in parody or burlesque. Still the chances are about equal that they are his.

The second poem in number fifty, at any rate, brings us back abruptly to Fielding with "A Plesaunt Balade, or, Advice to the Fayre Maydens: Written by Dan Jeffry Chaucer." Nowhere else, so far as I remember, does Fielding give the slightest evidence of any first-hand acquaintance with the father of English poetry. In the list of the world's great humorists enumerated in "Tom Jones," the name of Chaucer is conspicuous for its absence. It now turns out that Fielding read Chaucer without the aid of a modernized version, though he probably did not place so high an estimate on the poet as we do to-day when his language and the technique of his verse are better understood. In the middle of the eighteenth century, the ability to read Chaucer at all was an accomplishment possessed by but few. Fielding was among those few. His knowledge of Chaucer did not extend far—certainly not beyond parts of "The Canterbury Tales," which he read, one may see from the orthography, in Urry's edition of the poet. In its phrasing, his "balade" is especially reminiscent of the story of the cock and the hen, the sly humour of which he admirably adapts to an expostulation with the ladies on a theme rather common with him; but towards

* "The Midwife," II, 56-57.

the end he elaborates a pun entirely foreign to the spirit of Chaucer, who never exceeded the limits of an occasional play upon words. The curious poem, a mixture of middle and modern English, runs on thus:

> Listhnith, Ladies, to youre oldè Frende:
>   If yee be fayre, be fayre to sum gode Ende.
> For Gallants rath or late must loken out
> For thilk same Yoke, so ese out of Dout,
> *Yclepid Marriage: Yet sootly Weman be,
> *Malum per accidens vel malum per se,*
> As lerned Clerkes saie; this Latin is,
> Ladies, that yee al bene Mannis chefe Blis.
> And as a Wife is Mannis helpe and Comfort,
> His Paradise, his Solace, and Disport;
> So pardie, is Man Woman's chefe Stay,
> Harknith then, Dames, to my moral Lay:
> Ne stand ye *shill I, shall I;* 'tis childis Play:
> Eke dangerous, sings the Saw, is all Delay.
> Now listnith to my Similitude,
> Gode is the Moral, tho' the Rime be rude.
>   Where Medway's Stremes meandring, flowen wyde,
> There many a Sole, and many a †Made abyde:
> (Tho' on the Banks, God wot, few *Mades* doe walk,
> And fewer *Soles,* that think rite wel and talk.)
> Now thilke same Mades, fresh broughten to the ‖Chepe,
> Are rated high; but little can they kepe:
> Downs fals the Price. *Ah! benedicite!*
> Who bies my Mades? Ne one, ne tway, ne three;
> So handled they bene, by my Father's Kin,
> The *Mades* wont sell, they are not worth a Pin.

There remains but one other poem which does credit to Fielding. It is a translation, in number fifty-eight, of the first Elegy of Tibullus, "which," says the unnamed correspondent who is supposed to have sent it in, "you must formerly have got by heart . . . at Eton." The disguise

---

* Called   † A Fish so named   ‖ Market

here is of the thinnest texture. For his version Fielding chose the heroic couplet, which of all kinds of verse he wrote with most ease and grace. How well he succeeded in this instance will become evident by quoting a passage midway in the poem. They are the famous lines in the original:

> To me, no Joy my Father's Wealth affords,
> I envy not the rich Man's ample Hoards.
> Give me a little Field to plant, or sow,
> A little Bed where I my Limbs may throw!
> How pleas'd at Night, when Winds disturb my Rest,
> To clasp my Delia to my panting Breast.
> Or when the drenching Rains around us sweep,
> Lull'd by the Noise prolong our balmy Sleep!
> Be this my Fate, be Wealth his sordid Care,
> Who can Life's varied Toils and Dangers bear.
> Perish all Thoughts of Gold, or Gem, or Stone,
> E'er Delia's Eyes in Tears my Absence moan.

There have been translations of Tibullus in a much simpler style than Fielding's, which is dominated by the influence of Pope. In his own opinion, he did but "tolerable justice to an incomparable elegy." So much the reader can grant him.

Here ends with Fielding himself our journey through the maze of his contributors and assistants. The identity of the persons whom we have met has not been always quite determined; they are uncertain shadows cast by originals whose faces we cannot always completely make out. Some of the forms we have seen stalking through the journal, we did not expect to discover there.* On the other hand, relying too much upon the eyes of those who had already made the journey, we supposed that we should see clearly certain

---

* Mr. Austin Dobson should be credited with the discovery of James Harris under the disguise of J (p. 374). See his "Mr. Harris of Salisbury" in "The National Review," April, 1918, p. 208.

gentlemen who are absent. There is no sign of Fielding's former collaborator on ''The Champion.'' Ralph was primarily a political writer, and politics were excluded from ''The Covent-Garden Journal.'' Nor is there anyone who looks much like Lyttelton. At first sight we may think that we have a glimpse here and there of Garrick; but on closer view he invariably turns out to be Fielding himself in the habit of the actor and theatrical manager.

CHAPTER XXV

BATTLE OF THE WITS

Fielding's reappearance in the rôle of journalist was an event of prime interest to his contemporaries. Since his "failure" (so his enemies said) with "The True Patriot" and "The Jacobite's Journal," he had published "Tom Jones" and had acquired further prestige as the chief police magistrate of the metropolis. The attention which he gained from friends and foes alike was immediate. Beginning with the first number, his articles were generally reprinted, somewhat abridged, not only in the two most substantial monthlies of London but also in "The Scots Magazine" and other periodicals of the North. There was also a queer piracy over in Dublin, called directly "The Covent-Garden Journal." On the title-page stands out in large letters the name of "Henry Fielding Esq." as the alias of Sir Alexander Drawcansir. The publisher was the well-known pirate "James Hoey, at the Sign of the Mercury, in Skinner-Row," who had long been accustomed to lay his hand upon any London book or pamphlet for which he thought there would be a sale in Ireland. He began his periodical, the first number appearing on Thursday, January 23, 1752, as a weekly; but soon afterwards it was turned into a semi-weekly in order to satisfy the demands of the students at Dublin University during term-time. Fielding's leaders and humorous pieces supplied Hoey with most of his material for many months. The Dublin "Covent-Garden Journal," however, was not an exact reprint of the original. Though the robber took such

386

leaders as he wished from Fielding, he frequently re-worked them in part by way of adaptation to Dublin society. As time went on, he pillaged other London periodi-cals, and obtained fresh contributions and news-items from Dublin University. It was a successful enterprise. Long after the gentleman ceased to draw his sustenance from Fielding, the Dublin periodical, under varying titles, lived on for several years. Doubtless Fielding's novels had been sought all along by University students, but this is the only authentic record we have that any of these young men were eager to read and imitate what he had written.

In contrast with Fielding's silent admirers throughout the Kingdom of Great Britain and Ireland, were the noisy gentlemen of the metropolitan press, who made it a business to belittle all his works. "The Covent-Garden Journal" in conjunction with "Amelia" became the literary storm-centre of 1752. Since we last saw Argus Centoculi, he had changed his skin. "Old England" was now conducted by "Jonathan Free, of the Duchy of Cornwall, Esq." Appar-ently the clever scoundrel under these disguises was now William Kenrick, the scurrilous versifier and pamphleteer. Apparently, too, he had appropriated some time since the name of "Porcupine Pelagius," stealing it from one Morgan. As the Porcupine of the Sea, he had drawn in "The 'Piscopade" (1748) a satirical sketch of Fielding as a turncoat politician; and in "The Scandalizade" (1750) he had ridiculed Fielding's praise of Hogarth in "Tom Jones" as that of a jackanapes trying to ingratiate himself into the favour of a lion. It was clearly the same man, also, who had dedicated to Fielding in mockery "The Old Woman's Dunciad" (1751). In turn Fielding had treated him with the utmost contempt in "The Jacobite's Journal."

Whoever the man was, he never abated in his hostility towards Fielding. As Jonathan Free, he crawled out of his lair and began to spit venom as soon as he heard that the impotent author of a bawdy novel intended to take down his old hurdy-gurdy and drone forth once more the sad music of Covent Garden. Kenrick tried hard to make out that the new periodical was being established as an organ of the Pelham Ministry. In "Old England" for January 11, 1752,* he has an essay on "Fame, Lucre, and Poverty" as "the grand Springs of human Actions," and illustrates his text, after turning "fame" into "infamy," by the many transformations of "Harry Foolding, Esq," a discredited novelist and trading-justice, not long ago masquerading as John Trottplaid, and now as a superannuated virago called "Goody Drawcansir." In the career of this man ever ready to alter his face, one may see, Kenrick asserts, lucre, poverty, and infamy in all their colours. To show just how "The Covent-Garden Journal" came into existence he adds the "Fragment of a Farce, not intended for the Press, tho' now acting" on a stage concealed from the people. In the first scene enters alone Harry Peg'em, otherwise Henry Pelham, in great distress over the failure of his foreign policy. Treading upon his heels, comes Littlebones, that is, Lyttelton, who suggests that they again employ the impudent fellow who wrote their "Jacobite's Journal" to distract the attention of the public from the critical state of affairs at home and abroad. Thereupon Harry Foolding appears and learns what his masters want of him. A quid of tobacco somewhat embarrasses his speech, but, after removing it, he succeeds in telling them that as their servant he will obey their commands.

This and all other efforts to lure Fielding into politics were in vain. Nothing was left for "Old England" except general abuse of an idle justice of the peace who turned his office over to a brother and wasted his time in writing dull paragraphs on the news of the day, which nobody could read. Not one coffee-house in four, it was asserted, would

* See also "Old England" for Dec. 21, 1751, and Jan. 18, 1752.

admit the new journal, "celebrated" as it was in the author's own opinion. This nagging evoked no direct reply. The truth is, Fielding had long ago done with "Old England," now in its decline. He had no desire to fight over again, as he was invited to do, the political battles of 1747-1748. They were all dead issues. There was at least live game to be encountered in a passage at arms with "The London Daily Advertiser," whose leaders, written by Dr. John Hill, were the talk of the town.

This man we have already met in the company of Tom Jones and Elizabeth Canning. He was a clergyman's son who, instead of following his father's profession, became an apothecary and eventually obtained a medical degree from the University of St. Andrews, and admission to the Royal Academy of Sciences at Bordeaux. His specialty was the brewing of herbs into various "teas" for the correction of human ills. He discovered, for example, a cure for the gout, the disease of which he himself died. The year before his death he was honoured by the King of Sweden with the Order of Vasa, which entitled him, he thought, to sign himself Sir John Hill; and as early as 1752 he could write after his name, "Doc. Acad. Reg. Scient. Burd. etc. Soc." He was a handsome man about thirty-six years old, and he dressed like a beau. His previous history was known to everybody, for he did not put his light under a bushel; it always burned conspicuously on a candlestick. When Fielding was manager of the Little Theatre in the Haymarket, Hill, who had an apothecary's shop near Covent Garden, was trying to become an actor. Failing in this endeavour to rise in the world, he subsequently wrote a treatise on the actor's art, and submitted a play called "Orpheus, an English Opera," to Rich of the Covent Garden Theatre. Rich not only rejected the piece, but accepted and brought out only a few months later an "Orpheus and Eurydice" by Theobald. Hill, enraged at this treatment, set up the claim that the second Orpheus was stolen from his libretto, and to prove it he published his own opera. Not knowing the real authorship of the second piece, he charged the manager with the theft. The controversy that followed between Rich and Hill, in which each called the other a liar, gave the apothecary the first opportunity he had ever had to display his surpassing talent for vituperation. On a sudden he found himself. There was no doubt about that. Fielding was then writing for "The Champion." Though he was inclined to side with Rich on the merits of the dispute, he thought that Hill excelled in the rhetoric of abuse and invective.* Hill's pen was now worth something, much more than Samuel Johnson's at that time, to the booksellers.

Still, he plodded on for some years with herbs and natural history in the hope of gaining recognition by the Royal Society. That body, however, did not place so high a value on his scientific work as he did himself, and he was unable to persuade its members to admit him as a brother. In retaliation he burlesqued their discoveries and proceedings in three pamphlets, of which the one entitled "Lucina sine Concubitu" is a masterpiece of indecent wit. The man who wrote that was certain of a public. He was accordingly engaged, in March, 1751, to write, at two guineas a week, the leading articles for "The London Daily Advertiser." In order to take this post he discontinued a monthly periodical called "The British Magazine," which he had been editing since 1746. Six days every week, keeping it up for years, Hill contributed the leader to "The London Daily Advertiser" under the name of "The Inspector." His vanity, impudence, and fine disregard for truth amused readers generally, however much his character may have been despised by them. He was an entertaining liar; his newspaper sold; and he prospered beyond imagination.

* "The Champion," Jan. 29, 1739/40.

Somewhat later he let it be known that his income from all sources—from his herbs as well as from his Inspectors and scandalous pamphlets and fictions—amounted to fifteen hundred pounds a year. Though it was probably not yet half that sum, it enabled him, being a bachelor, to live in style. Every day he might be seen "rolling in an emblazoned chariot" from his house in Bloomsbury to his headquarters at the Bedford Coffee-House under the Piazza in Covent Garden. In a room of this rendezvous of wits and actors he set up a large wooden head of a lion, and gilded it all over, for the reception of letters to the Inspector-General of Great Britain. Through its wide and voracious mouth, the contributions fell into a strong-box upon which the animal's paws rested. This "Terrible Leo," it was announced, had formerly been designed by Hogarth for the use of Sir Richard Steele at Button's Coffee-House while the latter gentleman was writing "The Guardian." By appropriating this old lion's head, the quondam apothecary meant to proclaim himself the successor of that rare wit who once ruled at Button's.

Here was promise of finer sport than with that Argus whose hundred eyes had already been put out. As yet, no enmity existed between Hill and Fielding. The two men had doubtless met casually at the Bedford. The year before, Fielding had committed to Newgate one John Smith for robbing Dr. Hill of a gold watch and ring, a picture of his mistress set with diamonds, and twenty shillings in silver.* On the other side, Hill had praised the design of the Universal Register Office, and had given the palm to the author of "Tom Jones" above all the "imitators" of that novel, including Smollett.† To Fielding the Inspector was a delightful impostor whose unmasking would excite merriment. The title which Fielding chose for his journal was

---

* "The London Evening Post," Jan. 9-11, 11-14, 1751.

† "The London Daily Advertiser," March 15 and Oct. 31, 1751.

a sort of challenge to the man who had installed himself at the Bedford and pre-empted the affairs of Covent Garden. Against him, too, was levelled the first leader, wherein Fielding remarks that, though "The Covent-Garden Journal" costs the reader twice as much as "The Daily Advertiser," it contains almost twenty times as much matter, and so should be sold, on the basis of any just comparison, at above two shillings a copy instead of a paltry threepence.

This whimsical computation, which nettled Hill, was introductory to a "Paper War between the Forces under Sir Alexander Drawcansir and the Army of Grub-street," the events of which were related in the first four numbers of "The Covent-Garden Journal." It began as a jocose warfare reminiscent of Swift's "Battle of the Books." One of his designs, Sir Alexander announced, in founding another newspaper, was to free the press from a horde of scribblers who threatened the republic of letters with as complete destruction as that which their ancestors—the Goths, Huns, and Vandals—once brought upon the Empire of Rome. Against this swarm of barbarians under the generalship of "his Lowness the Prince of Billingsgate" (that is, the scurrilous Dr. Hill), Sir Alexander marshals a formidable army of veterans in gilt armour. The Greeks are led by Homer, Aristotle, Thucydides, Demosthenes, Lucian, and Longinus. The Romans are under the command of Virgil, Horace, Cicero, Tacitus, Terence, and Quintilian. In the loyalty of these ancients Sir Alexander can trust absolutely, for not one of the enemy, he says, is able to communicate with them. He also has a few French reserves with Molière and Bossu at their head, but he cannot quite rely upon these troops with whom Grub Street sometimes meddles, though never coming to a perfect understanding with them. Major-General Millar, the bookseller, raises a large body of English veterans under Bacon and Locke, editions of whose works he was then bringing out. These leaders whose faces the enemy has never seen, Sir Alexander counts among his staunchest friends.

The allied army assembles on a morning before the Universal Register Office, the headquarters of the commander-in-chief, to receive directions for the capture of the town. General Millar easily disperses detachments of the enemy sent from Grub Street to guard the most eminent printing-houses. Indeed, the cowards all take to their heels on the approach of his forces, except two small bodies under the command of "Peeragrin Puckle" and "Rodorick Random," who offer some slight resistance until they hear that their flank is in danger from a fresh army led by "a younger brother of General Thomas Jones." Panic-stricken by the rumour, they tumble over one another in precipitate flight. Other bodies of Sir Alexander's troops march to the coffee-houses, at all of which, except the Bedford, the gates fly open to welcome them. David Garrick and James Lacy, Esqs., the managers of Drury Lane, appear at headquarters and humbly present the commander-in-chief with the keys of their theatre; but he returns them into the hands of Mr. Garrick, the best actor the world has ever produced. The generalissimo inquires pleasantly after the different members of the great actor's company, especially after Miss Bellamy, who was, he declares, "not only one of the best actresses, but one of the finest women of her age." In the course of the conversation, Sir Alexander says several kind things of Mr. Rich of Covent Garden, praising his genius in pantomime, and expresses some wonder at his absence. It is explained to him that Mr. Rich would doubtless have made his appearance long before this, had he not been detained by the enemy.

Only the Bedford Coffee-House, where Rich was shut up, was disposed to defy Sir Alexander's army. The general is assured that he has many friends in the garrison of critics there, perhaps a majority over all, who would like to declare themselves openly in his favour, but they are kept in awe by "a strange mixed monster," a sort of chimera, which some take to be a lion, though closer observers report that "his ears are much longer than those of that generous beast." Not yet prepared for a direct assault upon this stronghold, Sir Alexander one evening orders that the said coffee-house be *block-headed* up in order that none of the enemy may escape. Hearing, however, that there is a *Hill* before the door, he orders that it be removed before attempting to force an entrance the next morning. On nearer approach the *Hill* proves to be only a paltry *Dunghill*, which "had long before been levelled with the dirt." Thus, to the disappointment of an expectant town, the great assault never takes place. The leaders of both armies meet, and articles of a "firm peace, amity, and concord" are signed by Sir Alexander Drawcansir, Generalissimo of the Army of Literature, and their Lownesses, the Princes of the Republic of Grub Street. As in the Treaty of Aix-la-Chapelle terminating a decade of useless slaughter, all things are to remain as they were before the war; all parties agree to sit down quietly and take their losses without murmur. Grub Street is to retain its old dominions of Dulness, Billingsgate, Blasphemy, and Indecency; it is to have sole and entire right forever in all the newspapers, except one to be called and known by the name of "The Covent-Garden Journal," whose editor promises to confine himself to matters of interest and never to encroach upon the possessions of the Low and Unmighty Republic.

The excellence of Fielding's burlesque warfare suffers some abatement towards the close where he calls Hill, though by indirection, a blockhead, an ass, and a dunghill. In these passages he was himself guilty of the Billingsgate he professed to despise. Surely he could not complain if his antagonist replied in kind. With considerable humour, Hill held up to derision Fielding's noseless heroine, his puns and misspellings, and gave in the following paragraph—an italicized news-item in "The London Daily Advertiser" for the eighth of January—his own version of the contest with the Lion:

"We hear from the Bedford Coffee-House in Covent-Garden, that an unhappy Gentleman of that Neighbourhood, having Yesterday Morning in Wantonness, thrust his Head into the Mouth of the Lion that resides there, felt the Jaws unexpectedly close upon him: On this, enquiring with a hollow Voice, whether he shook his Tail, and being answered in the Affirmative, he begged the By-Standers to pray for him. A terrible Crash was immediately after heard, and notwithstanding the uncommon Resistance of the Skull, it is credibly reported, that the Teeth had met through it. He was immediately after conveyed Home, but his Surgeons are afraid the Wounds will prove mortal."

It was give and take on each side, within the liberal bounds permitted by eighteenth-century ridicule, until Hill accused Fielding of deception in instituting the newspaper war. In the course of his "Inspector" for the ninth of January, Hill said:

"The Author of Amelia, whom I have only once seen, told me at that accidental Meeting, he held the present set of Writers in the utmost Contempt, and that in his Character of Drawcansir he should treat them in a most unmerciful Manner. He assured me, with great Civility, that he had always excepted me from the general Censure; and after honouring me with some Encomiums which, as I neither desired nor deserved, I shall not repeat, told me he hoped we should always be upon good Terms. He proceeded to mention a Conduct which would be, he said, useful to both: This was the amusing our Readers with a Mock-fight; giving Blows that would not hurt, and sharing the Advantage in Silence.''

This charge of playing fast and loose with the town was followed the next day by an extremely scurrilous portrait of Fielding in his capacity of police magistrate. Here we see ''the worshipful Mr. Justice Feeler'' conducting an examination of a cook-maid brought before him on the complaint of her master ''for lying a-bed in a morning.'' Despicable as the sketch is, it is not without humour; it was reprinted in the succeeding issue of Hill's newspaper ''at the earnest desire of the public.'' By these attacks on his honour Fielding was touched to the quick; and he retorted with unusual bitterness. Hill, he declared, came to him of his own accord to inquire about the rumoured war. ''I told him, with the utmost good humour,'' says Fielding, ''I should attack his Lion; and that he might, if he pleased, in the same manner, defend him.'' This statement of what took place at the meeting is undoubtedly correct; it was so understood by Christopher Smart.* Exasperated by Hill's false report of a private conversation, and by his charge of venality, Fielding denounced his Lowness as not only one of ''the meanest of those who ever drew a pen'' but as ''absolutely the vilest fellow that ever wore a head.''

Greatly to his honour, Fielding tried to put an end to the newspaper war as soon as it degenerated into personal abuse, and immediately apologized to his readers for the part he had played in an ignoble contest with a man who had nothing to lose but much to gain by any sort of notoriety. ''It was not my intention,'' he says in perfect candour, ''to attack the character of any person; and if I have been once provoked to so disagreeable an excess, no provocation shall again hurry me so far.''† Henceforth ''vice and folly, and not particular men,'' were to become

* ''Hilliad,'' 1753, p. viii.
† ''The Covent-Garden Journal,'' Jan. 18, 1752.

the object of his ridicule. Except in one or two instances, he kept his word; but he had no control over his enemies. The floodgates of vituperation, once opened against him, were never closed until he laid aside his labours. Most determined efforts were made to discredit him thoroughly as novelist, journalist, and magistrate.

Fielding's references to Rodorick Random and Peeragrin Puckle were merely in a spirit of fun, without satirical intent. Still, by giving these gentlemen commands in the army of the enemy, he really classed Smollett, if the author wished to take it that way, among the Grub Street writers. Smollett did take it that way; and Fielding was now attacked not by the harmless roarings of a wooden lion, but by a living viper. On January 15, 1752, only a week after Rodorick and Peeragrin had fled in disorder before the forces of Sir Alexander Drawcansir, Smollett shot forth his venom in a sixpenny pamphlet called "A Faithful Narrative of the Base and Inhuman Arts that were lately practised upon the Brain of Habbakkuk Hilding, Justice, Dealer, and Chapman."[*] The said Hilding, it is added on the title-page, "now lies at his House in Covent-Garden, in a deplorable State of Lunacy; a dreadful monument of false Friendship and Delusion." The author, who pretends to be a neighbour and well-wisher of the distempered gentleman, signs himself "Drawcansir Alexander, Fencing-Master and Philomath." His identity is certain. Smollett was still smarting under the imagined wounds which he had received from Lyttelton and Garrick, neither of whom could discover the dramatic merits of his "Regicide," though a decade had lapsed since they had first given the play a perusal. He had accordingly been compelled to publish his tragedy by subscription without its having yet reached the stage. In the meantime, Garrick's company had been performing one or more of Fielding's comedies

[*] "The London Daily Advertiser," Jan. 15, 1752.

every season, while Lyttelton had accepted the dedication of "Tom Jones" besides aiding the author in numerous ways. Smollett could not free himself from the delusion that Fielding was a rival who owed his success mainly to the patronage of friends. He was obsessed with the notion that Fielding had stolen several of his characters from "Roderick Random." Partridge, he believed, was copied from Strap, and Miss Mathews from Miss Williams. God save the mark! The Scot had already pilloried Lyttelton and Garrick as Marmozet and Sheerwit in "Roderick Random," and again with some other "little fellows" in his preface to "The Regicide." More recently, as I have related elsewhere, Lyttelton and Fielding had been defamed in "Peregrine Pickle." The obnoxious passage, however, had since been expunged, and the author had apologized for his unwarranted attack on two gentlemen. It now seemed to Smollett as if Lyttelton and perhaps Fielding were not satisfied with his *amende honorable*. A good-natured smile at his expense, the Scotsman read as a sneer. The newspaper war was aimed, he thought, not at Dr. Hill but at Dr. Smollett. His retort was brilliant and brutal.

The "Faithful Narrative" was partly modelled upon Pope's "Narrative of the Frenzy of John Dennis." Though Hilding had always been subject to fits of madness, the dreadful state of lunacy into which his faculties have now fallen, we are told, was due to a visit from two gentlemen, one of whom is "a long, lean, lank, misshapen spectre," known as Sir Gosling Scrag; that is, Sir George Lyttelton. There was a terrific explosion when Scrag told Hilding that he must once more take up his pen against their common enemies, especially against "that rascal Peregrine Pickle, who hath brought us both to ridicule and shame."—No, sir; shouts Hilding, foaming at the mouth, no more quarrels with that man and with other "soldiers of courage and proof," from whom I am sure to receive "unnumbered drubbings" and by whom I shall be eternally disgraced. Have I not already been "hooted at, beat and battered" as "your Zany or Jack-pudding?" And what has been the reward from you? Bread, you say; but it has come so late that I no longer have any teeth to chew it.

This frenzy, however, is easily turned in a new direction by Scrag, who administers to the patient "a few drops of a salutary elixir" which he always carries in his pocket. The mad man, obedient to his master, now gathers his forces, under the delusion that he is another Alexander and that his troops, really consisting of the tag, rag, and bobtail of the town, are the veterans of Greece and Rome. His Aristotle is but a constable, his Pindar a shoeblack, and his Horace a thief-taker. Mounted upon a jackass, the commander-in-chief sets forth at the head of an army of vagabonds on a march through the Strand. He is so drunk that he reels in his seat, his cheeks are puffed out with tobacco, his face and coat are covered with snuff, and when he speaks it is but to curse his enemies. Directly behind him tramp the noseless Amelia hand in hand with her beloved Booth, one Jones who pretends to be a gentleman, by the side of a hoary sheep-stealer disguised as the Old Man of the Hill, and "a notorious felon and imposter" called Partridge. His blind brother, "the proprietor of a twelve-penny office," brings up the rear. Most of these ragamuffins take to their heels on descrying their betters emerge from the novels of Mr. Smollett. Those unable to escape are all arrested for riot and committed to the house of correction. Hilding, however, is rescued from a police-officer by his neighbours, and taken home to be blooded, blistered, and purged. Smollett closes with a prayer that the unhappy gentleman may likewise be relieved from the "perfidious arts and infernal snares" of "that miscreant Scrag" who had wheedled him into ruin.

For this malicious caricature of himself and his best

friend, Fielding took no vengeance on Smollett. If he ever made any specific allusion to the onslaught, it was in "The Covent-Garden Journal" three days later, where he avowed his own lack of gall, quoting a remark of Pope's to which I have earlier referred: "I can, with great truth, declare, that I do not at this instant, wish ill to any man living. Indeed, if a sentiment which I heard drop from the late Mr. Pope be true, that nature never produced a more venemous animal than a bad author, I am sure that I want, at least, one ingredient in that character." Smollett, also, after firing one shot, retired from the field; and when the heat of battle was over he recorded for posterity his mature estimate of his brother novelist, free from passion. "The genius of Cervantes," he says in his "History of England," "was transfused into the novels of Fielding, who painted the characters and ridiculed the follies of the age with equal strength, humour, and propriety."*

Fielding's calumniators were like the Hydra's heads. The moment one was cut off, at least another immediately shot forth. The morning after Smollett entered and withdrew from the fray, there appeared Bonnell Thornton to take his place. Thornton was the son of a Covent Garden apothecary who sent him to Oxford in the hope of making a physician out of him. Though the young man gave some attention to medicine, such talent as he really possessed tended towards literature of the lighter sort. In the course of time, he became very well known among the minor journalists. Dr. Johnson thought him clever and diverting. A good Latinist, he translated into blank verse several of Plautus's comedies. But his forte was nonsense, jest, and caricature. Since taking his first degree in arts at Oxford in 1747, he had been on the town, with little or nothing to do. By 1750 he had fallen in with Christopher Smart, to whose periodical called "The Student, or, the Oxford and Cam-

* "Continuation of the Complete History of England," 1766, II, 160.

bridge Monthly Miscellany,'' he contributed more or less for two years. In the first number (January 31, 1750), he has, for example, an imitation of Tibullus's first Elegy, which may be compared to its disadvantage with the translation which I have attributed to Fielding; and there is a suspicion that he is the ''Timothy Beck'' who made fun of Fielding's ''Enquiry . . . into the Increase of Robbers.'' At any rate, he appears to have been one of ''the comical fellows'' who frequented ''the Ship and Anchor near Temple-Bar.'' Heavy drinking eventually put an end to him.

When ''The Covent-Garden Journal'' made its appearance, Thornton conceived the idea of following it week by week with a threepenny periodical in parody, burlesque, and abuse of Fielding's style and sentiments. The publication had as title ''Have at You All: or, The Drury-Lane Journal. By Madam Roxana Termagant,'' and was addressed directly to ''Sir Alexander Drawcansir, Author of the Covent-Garden Journal.'' From its first appearance on January 16, 1752, it was published regularly every Thursday down to March 26; then the author skipped a week, and brought his jest to a close on April 9. In all there were twelve issues, though the last one is numbered thirteen. ''The Drury-Lane Journal'' was in no proper sense a newspaper; it was a series of periodical pamphlets, forming when complete a book of two hundred and eighty-six pages. It lived and thrived on ''The Covent-Garden Journal.'' Thornton took up one by one Fielding's leaders, purposely misread them, and ridiculed the ideas which he himself put into them. He burlesqued the news-items and the advertisements in which Fielding was most concerned, drew a character sketch of the shifty author from his début as Pasquin down to his metamorphosis into Sir Alexander and ''Justice Scribble,'' and described ''the rout, progress, and defeat'' of his forces in the war with Hill and Smollett.

He denounced Fielding's style as the most unintelligible
to be found in the English language, sneered at his pretence
to learning, and called upon him to publish, if he wished to
be understood, a new Misspelling Book, a Primer of Puns,
and a Conundrum Grammar. When "The Covent-Garden
Journal" failed to supply the necessary material, he fell
upon the noseless heroine, and rewrote a chapter of
"Amelia" as it should have been written, reducing all the
incidents to the level of a brothel. In short, "The Drury-
Lane Journal" is a continuous flow of abuse and invective
at which a reader stands aghast.

And yet Thornton manifested no personal hatred of
Fielding, nor that jealousy which actuated Smollett. His
Billingsgate appears to have been a matter of business, a
part of the day's work; it was mostly professional. For
this reason it has been conjectured by Dr. Jensen that he
was merely a hireling in the employ of someone who really
nourished a grudge against Fielding. Such undoubtedly
was the case. Thornton's editorial headquarters were at
the Public Register Office, recently established in King
Street, Covent Garden, in the heart of the district whence
Fielding's newspaper received its name, and near the court
over which the justice presided. The manager of this office
was a young Frenchman known as D'Halluin or Dullwin,
who had been a temporary clerk in the Universal Register
Office. He came there mysteriously the preceding year,
and as mysteriously disappeared. When next seen he was
at the head of an employment bureau of his own.

John Fielding, amazed at the conduct of a stranger
he had aided in distress, accused him, in "The London
Daily Advertiser" for November 4, 1751, of stealing the
secrets of the Universal Register Office; and two days later
Dullwin replied with vigour in the same newspaper, declaring that there were no secrets to be learned in that mis-
managed and inefficient institution which took the fees of

its patrons but rendered no services in return. To the hostile registry office in King Street, "The Drury-Lane Journal" was clearly an adjunct; there, says the title-page, it was "printed and sold." This fact helps explain its character. It was designed to ridicule out of existence the Universal Register Office and its organ "The Covent-Garden Journal." The attacks were direct and persistent through continuous burlesque of a registry office which pretended to "universality." From time to time, for example, John Fielding gave in his brother's newspaper a list of curios on sale at his office, beginning with "A Bullfinch that pipes the March in Rinaldo at Command." This kind of notice was a favourite with Thornton for parody. In the first number of his journal, he set out, in rewriting the advertisement on his own lines, with the wonderful bullfinch and then went on to enumerate items like "A Justice's Sword, of base Metal, with a *double* edge, not very sharp, and no *Point*," and "A Pair of Scales, Ditto, to weigh *Puns* in." All circumstances considered, the obvious conclusion is that Thornton, seeking an avenue for the display of his literary talent, suggested the plan of "The Drury-Lane Journal" to Dullwin, and found a ready acceptance of his proposal. By burlesque of Fielding and his business enterprise, Thornton saw a chance to climb into public notice.

Fielding understood Thornton's motives and ignored him. He may have had Thornton in mind with others in his defence of "Amelia" and in a denunciation of "the detestable vice of slander"; he certainly described the species to which Thornton belonged in two essays on the swaggerer in print who strives for notoriety by "diving into, dwelling on, and exaggerating the faults and defects of writers, especially those who are reputed the most excellent of their kind, whether ancient or modern." The satire, however, is most general. Fielding never mentioned Thornton or Dullwin or "The Drury-Lane Journal"; he merely alluded to them in the remark that the quantity of filth brought from Grub Street and emptied into Covent Garden was so great that the master-scavenger could no longer keep the place clean, even if he had treble the number of carts at his disposal. They and their tribe were but summer insects that

Buzz, flutter for a while, then die.

Of these ephemera was "The Covent-Garden Journal Extraordinary. By Sir Alexander Drawcansir, Knt. Censor of Great-Britain"—a threepenny burlesque which "The London Daily Advertiser" of January 20 announced as this day published at noon, and printed for J. Sharp, a bookseller near Temple Bar. Inasmuch as the same title was subsequently used by Thornton for supplements to his "Drury-Lane Journal," it is to be presumed that the skit came either from him or from some companion at the Ship and Anchor. Of this pamphlet, made up as a periodical, only one number was ever issued; and of that number, dated January 20, 1752, the only copy known to exist is now in the library of Yale University. Substance and style point rather definitely, though not certainly, to Thornton as the author. It contains, in its six pages, burlesque items of news, and a facetious account of Smollett's entrance into the newspaper war. Before a permanent peace can be assured, Sir Alexander's forces must yet reduce "a *small Hutt,* built of mud and covered with thistles." An ironical leader has as subject "the transmigration of circumstances, incident to individuals in the course of one mortal peregrination," as illustrated by the career of a vagabond who becomes at last a justice of the peace, and by the good fortune of a cook-maid who succeeds to the honours of her former mistress. Of these mutations the author professes to approve. A magistrate of unblemished character, he says, "may grant a warrant, sign a mittimus, and receive the shilling"; but only a man who is "conversant in all

ADVERTISEMENT.

WHereas I, Sir *Alexander Drawcanfir*, of *Covent-Garden*, Knight, have been of late moſt rancorouſly ſlandered in a virulent Pamphlet, en-tituled, *A Narrative of the baſe and inhuman Arts practiſed upon the Brain of* Habbakkuk Hilding, *Juſtice, Dealer and Chapman*, &c. whereby I am likely to ſuffer greatly both in my Character and Occupation ; in order to vindicate myſelf from the ſcandalous Aſperſions contained in the ſaid Pamphlet, and at the ſame Time to confute the Author of ſuch an infa-mous Libel, I hereby promiſe the Reward of five Pounds, to any Perſon or Perſons, who ſhall prove that I was ever ſeen diſturbing the Peace of his Majeſty on Aſs-back ; or known to blow a Trumpet, Horn, or any other Wind Inſtrument, as Herald to any Beaſt, or Collection of wild Beaſts ; or even to diſtribute printed Bills, or invite Paſſengers at the Door of any Houſe, Barn or Booth, in which any ſuch Spectacles were exhi-bited—excepting, neverthelefs, from this my Promiſe ſuch Tranſactions as I have been concerned in as an Author, Stroller and Puppet-ſhow Man.

Witneſs my Hand

Alexander Drawcanſir.

Articles of N E W S.

ON *Sunday* laſt, in the Evening, were privately interred the Remains of Mrs. *Amelia Booth,* who fell a Sacrifice to the poiſonous Influence of evil Tongues. A Lady who was poſſeſſed of all the domeſtick Virtues of Life ; and ſo remarkable for her Meekneſs of Diſpoſition, as to have equalled the Fame of *Patient Griſſel.* The Expence of her Funeral was de-frayed by his Excellency Sir *Alexander,* who was deeply affected with her Fate, and now begs that no Perſon will be ſo cruel and impious as to di-ſturb her Aſhes. She had for ſome Time paſt been in a conſumptive Way, and as ſhe drew near her latter End, her Friends perceived about her an earthy and mortified Odour, of which, however, ſhe herſelf was not ſen-ſible———*This laſt Circumſtance is not at all to be wondered at ; if we reflect*
that

A PAGE FROM THE COVENT-GARDEN JOURNAL EXTRAORDINARY

those wily frauds which are practised by the children of iniquity" can be depended upon to ferret out the intricate courses of "dissimulation and deceit." In a word, it takes a thief to catch a thief. Likewise a woman in the front of fashion may make a good wife; but a cook-maid has certain advantages over her. She ministers directly to the principal end of life, which is to live well; she is not so expensive a luxury as a fine lady, for she requires less for dress and diversions; she can detect all the devices in the kitchen to rob her household, as she has been a servant herself and knows the dishonesty of the class to which she once belonged; and by imbibing a portion of that fire to which she has been so much exposed, she is likely to possess "a degree of vivacity sufficient not only to enforce her commands, but also to enliven conversation, and give the necessary fillips to the spirits of her lord and husband."

Nine days later, according to Hill's newspaper, appeared a sixpenny pamphlet entitled "The March of the Lion, or the Conclusion of the War between the Dunce and the Dunces, written with all the Blackguardism of Justice Bobbadill, all the Politeness of the Inspector, all the Wit of the Fool, and all the Smartness of Mary Midnight." This piece of irony, printed for Cooper, seems to have been aimed not only against Fielding but against all who had taken part in the warfare. Prospective readers were informed that they would be entertained by "the Progress of the Golden Savage from the Bedford Coffee-house, in search of new Quarters." No copy of this trifle has yet come to light. The same is true of "A Speech made in the Censorial Court of Alex. Drawcansir, Monday, 6th June, 1752, concerning a late Act of Parliament," which was announced in "The General Advertiser" of June 27. The undiscovered address sold at sixpence and was printed for the author, whom the biographers have supposed to be Fielding himself. Again lurks in the background Thornton or one of his associates. Some information about the pamphlet is supplied by "The Monthly Review" for July, whose editor, Ralph Griffiths, there characterized it as "a dirty, loose, idle attempt to ridicule the late Act of Parliament against Bawdy-Houses."[*]

The measure referred to was the one of March 26, for preventing robberies, regulating places of amusement, and punishing persons who keep disorderly houses. Fielding could not have ridiculed that statute, for he was in full sympathy with its provisions; he had fought for it and he may have framed it. In practice, however, that part of the law dealing with prostitution did not work very well. The principals often escaped while their wretched women suffered the full penalty. Too great powers, it was generally thought, were given to constables and their understrappers. Sometimes perfectly sober and virtuous women were arrested, if found on the street at night, and taken by watchmen to the roundhouse. More than once, as may be seen in "The Covent-Garden Journal," Fielding had to reprimand these indiscreet officers of the law. After incidents of this kind, he published in his newspaper for June 23, 1752, a letter from "Humphry Meanwell," probably written by himself, protesting against the rigour and arrogance with which the law was being enforced and suggesting that it would perhaps be better to regulate rather than attempt to suppress a perplexing social evil. In consequence of these observations, Fielding's enemies at once pounced upon him as a friend of rakes and harlots. Such seems to have been the insinuation in the "Speech" which was put, four days later, into the mouth of Alex. Drawcansir. If Fielding had been misunderstood, he set himself right with the public in his leader for the first of August. He there refers to the many letters which he has received praising and condemning the opinions expressed by

[*] "The Monthly Review," VII, 74.

"Humphry Meanwell," and then discusses the subject in a tone which could not have offended the gravest of his readers.

Fielding's personal appearance invited caricature. His long grey coat, worn on the street against the winter's cold, made him look taller than he really was. Gout compelled him to swathe his legs and sometimes to walk on crutches. His prominent nose and protruding chin were rendered more conspicuous by the loss of his front teeth. He liked to orate as well as to tell a whimsical story. There were humorous facial gestures and a humorous play of the eyes which one knows less about. When his physical infirmities were beginning to press upon him, Foote, as we have related, impersonated him for the audience at Covent Garden Theatre; and Fielding, stung by the actor's portrayal of a shabby gentleman haranguing a crowd, denounced the actor as a breaker of God's images. As Sir Alexander Drawcansir he was now brought into two plays; of which one was printed but not acted, and the other was acted but not printed.

The first was called "Fun: A Parodi-tragi-comical Satire." Though the author concealed his name, he did not conceal his style. He was the William Kenrick whom we have already met. His play consists of eight loose scenes, written partly in verse and partly in prose. The parody runs mostly on "Macbeth," though there is an occasional shift to "Hamlet." Sir Alexander takes the place of Macbeth in Shakespeare's tragedy; and Dr. Mountain alias Dr. Hill is adjusted to the rôle of Macduff. Thornton appears as Roxana Termagant, a young woman who masks a passion for Sir Alexander in a seeming hatred. Another character—Sir Nackadil Trunnion—derives his surname but nothing more from the uncle of Peregrine Pickle. The witches brew a hell broth of dulness out of contemporary books and pamphlets. Into the cauldron go

"A Journal Jacobite," the bawdry of "The Wedding Day," "all the sense of Pasquin," "the body of Tom Thumb," and "four ounces of a noseless wench." "Tom Jones" is spared the ignominy, though both "Pamela" and "Clarissa" contribute their "virtue" to the charm. The same inglorious end awaits Smollett's "Random" and "Pickle," Hill's salacious stories of intrigue, and Thornton's lucubrations in the press. Thereupon from the cauldron rise the ghosts of Vinegar, Trottplaid, and a Jacobite to startle Sir Alexander by their gory locks. A fourth ghost deceives him into the belief that he will be victorious in the combat with Grub Street:

> Be vain, be insolent, and take no Care,
> Who writes, who rails, or who the Critics are:
> *Drawcansir* never shall be vanquish'd, 'till
> To fight against him, rise a mighty *Hill;*
> 'Till the fierce *Lion* leaves the *Afric* Shores,
> And in a Coffee-house unregarded roars,
> 'Till Sexes change, and then thy arm oppose.

The equivocation of the witches hardly needs explanation. In the final scene Sir Alexander learns that Dr. Mountain has brought a lion from the jungles of Africa and enthroned him at the Bedford and that Roxana Termagant is a man in petticoats. Unnerved by the disclosure, the champion is easily struck to the ground by the swords—or the fists— of his two antagonists. He rises and makes his exit dying.

Aside from the main plot, there is a parody of Fielding the police magistrate. Dr. Mountain brings one File before Justice Bobadil for assault and robbery; and Mrs. Brindle asks his Worship to commit to Newgate Lord Riot for ravishing her. In both cases the justice decides against the evidence. He orders Dr. Mountain to be detained on a suspicion that his charge is false, and lets Riot go free, though the gentleman admits his guilt. Throughout the examinations, Bobadil is portrayed as a trading justice who truckles to people of power and fortune. It has been pointed out by Dr. Jensen that this scene was based upon the case of one John Smith, whom Fielding once held for the rape of an old woman who proved to be the prisoner's wife; he was the same John Smith that was subsequently sent to jail for robbing Dr. Hill.* Of course Kenrick misrepresents Fielding's conduct on these occasions; but that is the method of satire.

Kenrick advertised the first performance of this "Grand Composition of Fun and Musick" for the thirteenth of February, 1752, at the Castle Tavern in Paternoster Row.† Admission was to be by tickets procurable at various taverns and coffee-houses for two shillings and sixpence. The Castle Tavern was then a rendezvous for the Grub Street wits including our old friend Ben Sedgly. There Christopher Smart as Mrs. Mary Midnight sometimes entertained them with nonsensical orations in banter of Henley's harangues at Clare Market. An excellent burlesque of Smart's wild and whimsical talk is given in the fourth scene of Kenrick's play. He seems to have been assisted by musicians and a small troupe of dogs and monkeys—or rather companions dressed as dogs and monkeys,—who performed tricks and sang songs. Smart's exhibitions were popular all over the town. Had the officers of the law so desired, they could hardly have interfered with these harmless diversions, for Smart was careful to keep within the Licensing Act. An oration, relieved by some music and antics, could not properly be regarded as a play. The case was different with Kenrick's "Fun." Although he attempted to pass it off as a bit of nonsense and music, it was a dramatic performance within the meaning of the law, and as such it could not be presented outside the patent theatres except by a special licence from the

* Mr. G. E. Jensen, "The Covent-Garden Journal," 1915, I, 66.
† "The General Advertiser," Feb. 10, 1752.

Lord Chamberlain. Moreover, its character was offensive. Smart, under the signature of Mary Midnight, protested against the rumour that he was the author of the scandalous piece.* As Fielding's friend he naturally told him what was in the air; and the justice, it is said, took the proper measures to protect himself. Apparently the audience was all assembled on the evening of February 13, when the performance was prohibited by a special order from the Lord Mayor and the court of Aldermen.† The actors—all amateurs made up of Kenrick's friends—were evidently dispersed by a body of constables. Subsequent attempts to bring out the satire having failed, it was published as a shilling pamphlet on the seventh of March, and distributed gratis to the disappointed purchasers of tickets. A preface continues the ridicule of Fielding, complains of the Lord Mayor's hard usage, and hints that Smart was responsible for the miscarriage of an exhibition much like his own.

The second piece—the one performed but never printed —is known by its sub-title "Pasquin turn'd Drawcansir." The author was supposed to be Charles Macklin the actor;‡ and there can be no doubt that he put it together. Fielding and Macklin had been friends for more than twenty years. One of the actor's first parts on coming to London was Porer in "The Coffee-House Politician," and since then he had played many rôles in Fielding's comedies. As he was a hot-tempered Irishman who at one time quarrelled with most if not all of his associates, it is probable that the course of friendship between him and Fielding did not al-

---

* "The General Advertiser," Feb. 12, 1752.

† D. E. Baker, "The Companion to the Play House," 1764, Vol. I, under *Fun.*

‡ "The Inspector in the Shades," p. 15 (July, 1752). See also, G. A. Stevens, "Distress upon Distress," preface dated Dublin, May 1, 1752, pp. xiii-xiv, and xxi (where most of Macklin's playbill is given "for the Benefit of all Theatrical Puffers"). Also Jensen, "The Covent-Garden Journal," I, 71-72.

ways run smooth. Still, this conclusion is not quite justified by any positive evidence. The indications are only of impatience, the one with the other, rather than of any angry dispute. Ten years before, in the prologue to "The Wedding Day," which Macklin wrote and spoke, the actor carried jests at the expense of the playwright as far as they could go without passing into ridicule. He clearly mimicked Fielding there—his reckless speech and facial movements—and prophesied that the play would fail. Long before 1752, Macklin had broken with Garrick at Drury Lane and was then playing in Rich's company at Covent Garden. The rivalry between the two houses was intense, almost bitter. As Garrick's close friend, Fielding sided with him in the theatrical controversies of the year. Among the many players on whom he bestows eloquent praise in "The Covent-Garden Journal," Macklin's name, I think, nowhere occurs. This oversight, coupled with some banter of the Covent Garden Theatre as an adjunct of Grub Street, doubtless nettled the actor who in retaliation now introduced Fielding upon the boards At the same time, it is certain that there was no malice in the presentation, for Fielding published in his newspaper two advertisements of the forthcoming performance. In the first of them, it is announced on March 14, 1752, that Mr. Macklin's benefit at Covent Garden Theatre will take place on Wednesday, the eighth of April, when the actor will appear as Sir Francis Wronghead in "The Provok'd Husband." After this comedy, the playbill as reprinted in "The Covent-Garden Journal" goes on to say, there will be exhibited "A New Dramatic Satire, of two Acts," entitled

Covent-Garden Theatre:
OR,
PASQUIN turn'd *DRAWCANSIR,*
Censor of Great Britain.

THE HISTORY OF HENRY FIELDING

Written on the Model of the Comedies of Aristophanes,
and the Pasquinades of the Italian Theatre in Paris:
With Choruses of the People after the Manner of
the Greek Drama.
The Parts of the Pit, the Boxes, the Galleries, the
Stage, and the Town, to be performed
By THEMSELVES for their Diversion;
The Parts of several dull disorderly Characters, in
and about St. James's, to be performed
By CERTAIN PERSONS, for Example;
And the Part of Pasquin-Drawcansir, to be
performed
By his CENSORIAL HIGHNESS,
For his Interest.
The Satire to be introduced by an Oration, and
to conclude by a Peroration: Both to be spo-
ken from the Rostrum, in the Manner of cer-
tain Orators,
By Signior *PASQUIN.*

The only contemporary account of the performance yet
discovered comes from the pen of Bonnell Thornton. It
confirms the tradition that Macklin failed to please. On
that April night Thornton took a seat in the theatre whence
he could observe the whole house and thus watch the behaviour of pit, box, and gallery. Evidently to his dis-
comfort, he saw the piece completely damned. The next
day he gave in "The Drury-Lane Journal," assuming the
name of "The Town," an odd list of reasons for its failure.
"The medley entertainment" was "too long and too short,
too witty and too dull"; it was too trenchant in its satire
of "fine gentlemen, and fine ladies, and gamesters, and
lords, and maids of honour"; it made the audience applaud
when they wished to hiss; and the orator in his prologue
and epilogue "laugh'd at us to our faces" instead of con-

fessing his own faults and beseeching our indulgence. There is an intimation, too, that the town came with malice prepense to condemn "the new pasquinade," whether it should prove to be good or bad. On just what its character was no certain light is thrown either by Thornton's persiflage or by Macklin's humorous playbill. It may be safely assumed, however, that Macklin made himself up as Drawcansir and taxed the town with its follies in the style of "The Covent-Garden Journal." Other members of the company—Mrs. Cibber and Mr. Barry, excellent mimics both—would be called upon to impersonate the unnamed fine ladies and gentlemen including perhaps Dr. Hill. Macklin of course spoke the oration and peroration, which seem to have been burlesques of Smart's efforts in the same line. The orator doubtless paused in his speeches for laughter or groans as he made his hits. This, I take it, is what was meant by turning the audience into a chorus. So ended the last attempt to make sport of Fielding on the stage. Coming from Macklin, the portrait could not have had the grossness of Foote's indecent caricature.

When Fielding in the name of Sir Alexander Drawcansir concluded a treaty of peace with the Low Republic of Letters, it was stipulated that he might erect a Court of Censorial Enquiry, similar to the courts he had once established in "The Champion" and "The Jacobite's Journal," for the examination of books, plays, and pamphlets by whomsoever written, provided he should lay no claim to jurisdiction over any newspaper except his own, and should refrain from passing judgment upon the character of any author who could prove himself a citizen of Grub Street. It was further agreed that the Theatre Royal in Drury Lane should be under the protection of the Court so long as Mr. Garrick and Mr. Lacy continued to be its managers. Some question arose over the theatre in Covent Garden, for it had remained in a neutral state from time immemorial.

As a compromise, it was decided that each of the two parties possessed equal rights to criticise the plays and entertainments at that house; each was left to decide unmolested whether a given production belonged to the realm of wit or to the realm of Grub Street. Through his court Fielding thus shifted to literature and the stage the warfare which he had begun with ridicule of the newspapers.

The Court of Censorial Enquiry, most memorable for the arraignment of Amelia, was the scene of several other interesting legal transactions. When Millar published for Charlotte Lennox "The Female Quixote," a very clever novel on the lines of the Spanish original, the Censor delivered a long speech in its praise. His conduct on this occasion especially pleased Dr. Johnson who quoted him in the next number of "The Gentleman's Magazine";* and the novelist herself, though of the Richardson faction, henceforth became Fielding's staunch friend to the end. What Fielding said of the new novel has lost much of its interest, for we no longer regard the book as "a most extraordinary, and most excellent performance." That is laudation due to a chivalrous impulse of the moment. The real significance of the encomium, perfect in its kind, lies in the fact that in the course of it Fielding expressed more fully than elsewhere his opinion of the great humorist whose manner he had imitated in "Joseph Andrews." In brief, he thought that Cervantes carried absurdity too far in many of the adventures of Don Quixote, and he gave the palm to Sancho Panza—"perhaps a masterpiece in humour of which we never have [seen], nor ever shall see the like."

Over against "The Female Quixote," the Censor set another novel of the season. In the previous autumn Mrs. Eliza Haywood, the author of many scandalous tales and memoirs, came out with a new novel, better than the rest, entitled "The History of Miss Betsy Thoughtless." In

* March, 1752, XXII, 146.

the old days, Mrs. Haywood had helped turn, it may be recalled, "Tom Thumb" into an opera, and had thus been casually associated with Fielding at the Little Theatre in the Haymarket. In her novel, she says that this house was "then known by the name of F——g's scandal-shop; because he frequently exhibited there certain drolls, or, more properly, invectives against the ministry: in doing which it appears extremely probable that he had two views; the one to get money, which he very much wanted, from such as delighted in low humour, and could not distinguish true satire from scurrility; and the other in the hope of having some post given him by those whom he had abused, in order to silence his dramatic talent." Since that time, she has seen him, she adds, "wriggle himself into favour, by pretending to cajole those he had not the power to intimidate."* In consequence of this attack on a reputable novelist and justice of the peace, "B——T——" was summoned before his Censorial Highness to answer to a charge of dulness. She pleaded against the jurisdiction of the court on the ground that she was a lawful subject of Grub Street. A demurrer being entered, the case was argued by able lawyers on each side. The Court, in a long and amusing address on the history of Grub Street, decided for the defendant. It was proved to his satisfaction that the author of "B——T——" belonged to the kingdom of Grub Street and as such had a right, by the terms of a recent treaty, to be as dull as she pleased; indeed, that she could not be expected ever to deviate into wit. By one of fortune's whims, the novel which Fielding utterly condemned was translated into German in 1754 as a late work from the pen of the man who wrote "Tom Jones."

At the opening of the dramatic season, Garrick took into his company Henry Mossop, a young Irishman endowed with unusual talents, and most generously gave up

* "Betsy Thoughtless," 1751, I, 76-77.

to him several of his own leading parts, all of which Mossop played well. Naturally vain, his success turned his head. He boasted that he was the equal of Garrick, although, as he expressed the gradation, he usually placed himself just below the great actor. Old theatre-goers, though they conceded Mossop's abilities, missed the presence of Garrick, who, perhaps a little piqued at the reception of a rival, kept in the background. They wondered why Garrick let Mossop have his great rôle in Macbeth. Accordingly Mossop was haled before the Censor of Great Britain to show cause why he had assumed the style, title, and dignity of Macbeth, while Mr. Garrick, the only true and lawful Macbeth, was still in full life and health. After some exquisite raillery, seasoned with just praise, the humbled Irishman was discharged by the Court. A few days afterwards Garrick resumed Macbeth, a part in which he was above all others, says Fielding, matchless. Aside from Garrick, the actor at Drury Lane whom Fielding liked best was William Havard, not so much for his art as for his qualities as a man. Havard reminded him of the elder Mills whom he had known in his youth. Both possessed the most amiable qualities, and both for this reason were often given the most amiable rôles, wherein they appeared exactly as they were in life. Havard often played Horatio to Garrick's Hamlet; whereof Fielding quotes Garrick as saying: "Mr. Havard always acts the part of my friend; and whether on the stage, or off, I never desire a better." With the recommendation that everybody attend Mr. Havard's benefit on the eleventh of April, the Censorial Court adjourned *sine die.*

To be exact, the court, whose proceedings were first reported in the fifth number, on January 18, came to an end in the twenty-eighth number, on April 7. It was, however, revived in the last issue of the periodical for a final deadly stroke upon the head of Dr. Hill. During the period of its existence, its sittings were quite irregular—on the average once a fortnight, instead of every Saturday as at first announced. The court often met but to adjourn, or to give sanction to a letter or a book review from a hand other than the Censor's. To say the truth, the jest became a trifle tiresome. Legal phrases perplexed the reader; and legal machinery cramped the author. Very likely, too, Fielding discovered that his health and the time at his disposal would not permit him to report a mock-trial every week in addition to writing two articles. Partly from inclination, partly from necessity, he discontinued his court, and thereafter found in his leaders scope enough for such raillery of Grub Street as he cared to indulge in.

So alluring an object for ridicule as the Robinhood Society, for instance, could not be resisted. This was a debating club composed mainly of tradesmen, mechanics, and lawyers' clerks, who met every Monday evening at the sign of Robinhood in Butcher Row near the Strand, a tavern then kept by a Mr. Hall. Its perpetual president was an oratorical baker named Caleb Jeacocke. In a caricature sketch of the time, he appears sitting at a table in the society's wainscoted room at the Robinhood, with two loaves of bread on his head,—with watch, hammer, and other utensils of his office before him. He is listening to a vehement speech by a man who has a shoemaker's last under one arm. Fielding aptly renamed the president "Mr. Whytebred." Anyone might attend and debate for five minutes the question of the evening on the payment of an admittance fee of sixpence, which covered the cost of all the beer or lemonade he might drink and left something over for charity. The society, which had had a long history under other names,* became notorious if not famous. Macklin, it is said, used to visit the tavern and take part

* "The History of the Robinhood Society," 1764; and Jensen, "The Covent-Garden Journal," I, 128, 182; II, 167-174.

in the debates, and a little later Burke and Goldsmith also. Fielding, too, must have attended as a silent spectator. It was not a bad place for practice in public speaking; but the debates there on questions of church and state awakened great indignation, especially among the clergy. The Robinhood Society was denounced as a club of freethinkers, "a second pandemonium, or assembly of evil spirits," all of whom were certain to be consigned in the end to everlasting punishment.

To the Robinhoodians Fielding devoted two numbers— the eighth and the ninth—of "The Covent-Garden Journal." What struck Fielding was the absurdity of any discussion between uneducated men on subjects which have perplexed moralists and philosophers. Accordingly, he entertained the public with the speeches of a Scotch barber, an Irish solicitor, a weaver, a tailor, a chandler, and other great men whose names and occupations he did not always remember. On the question "whether infinite Power could make the World out of Nothing,"—or rather, in the Latin of the Robinhoodians, "whether," as some wise man had asserted, *"ex nihil O Nothing is fit,"*—"it was urged with great force of wit and eloquence, by Mr. Goose, that the best taylor, and the worst, were alike unable to make a coat without materials. That, in this case, a taylor with infinite power, would be in the same condition with a taylor who had no power at all. And if so small a thing as a coat could not be made out of nothing, how could so large a thing as the world be cut out of the same no materials." On the question "whether Relidgin was of any youse to Sosyaty," James Skotchum found most of the company on his side when he rose and said, "Sir, I ham of upinion, that relidgin can be of no youse to any mortal sole: bycause as why, relidgin is no youse to trayd, and if relidgin be of no youse to trayd, how ist it yousefool to sosyaty. Now no body can deny but that a man maye kary on his trayd very wel without relidgin; nay, and beter two, for then he maye wurk won day in a wik mor than at present; whereof no body can saye but that seven is mor than six: Besides, if we haf no relidgin we shall haf no pairsuns, and that will be a grate savin to the sosyaty; and it is a maksum in trayd, that a peny sav'd is a peny got.'' This fun with the Robinhood society was apparently resented by some of the members, perhaps by Macklin, ''who was particularly celebrated for his harangues on religious subjects.''* Thornton facetiously remarks that at a subsequent meeting the Robinhoodians took as their topic, ''Whether this Society be a proper subject for the Drama,'' and concluded that it would be such, provided ''a stormy hero,'' like Sir Alexander Drawcansir, were introduced to bring about the catastrophe.†

At intervals, Dr. Hill renewed his gibes at Fielding, in the midst of which occurred an incident which set everybody laughing. The Inspector for April 30, 1752, made an insidious attack upon the character of Mountefort Brown, a young gentleman of some parts, well known among people of fashion and pleasure. It was implied that he was a rake, a coxcomb, and a coward. The young man and his friends immediately waited upon Hill and demanded that he retract or fight. The libeller was disposed to do neither. A week later the two men met one evening in the rotunda at Ranelagh Gardens, where Brown pulled off Hill's wig, struck him down with a cane, and kicked him, to the amusement of a group of companions. Hill feared that he was mortally hurt—being smartly kicked, he declared, not in the spot where it was reported, but in the side. Daily bulletins printed in his newspaper informed the public of his serious condition. The kick caused an empyema, as he called it, and he felt his life fast ebbing away. He really

* ''The Pasquinade,'' 1753, p. 21.
† ''The Drury-Lane Journal,'' No. 5, Feb. 13, 1752.

got a good drubbing; that was all. On May 9, three days after the assault, Mr. Brown, "attended by many gentlemen of the first rank and figure," surrendered himself before Justice Fielding.* Here was a very comic situation.

Fielding not only admitted the young buck to bail, being assured by "the affidavit of an eminent physician" that Dr. Hill was in no danger of his life, but went out of his way to declare that nothing appeared in the examination against the honour of Mr. Brown, who had been vilified and misrepresented "in a common news-paper," that is, in the Inspector of "The London Daily Advertiser." As predicted, Hill recovered; and when Brown came up for trial at Hicks's Hall, no prosecutor appeared against him, and he was consequently discharged. The empyema was a source of mirth for months. Squibs and sixpenny pamphlets filled the air. In some of them the aid of Fielding was suspected. There may have been ground for the suspicion; but none of the pamphlets known to me were actually written by him, if style counts for anything. Accordingly they are here all passed by. More entertaining than the pamphlets were two prints immediately put into circulation. "A Night-Scene at Ranelagh" depicts Brown holding Hill by an ear while the doctor is calling for a constable and trying to run away. "Le Malade Imaginaire" shows Hill lying in bed, surrounded by physicians in consultation; one of whom, seated at his head, is feeling his pulse; and others, who stand at the foot, are suggesting facetious methods of treatment, such as "Give de Ass de Milk" or "Raise his Spirits with a Blister."† By the wits who took Brown's side, Fielding was always highly praised for his conduct in the case; by Hill and the

* "The Covent-Garden Journal," May 12, 1752.

† The two prints, copies of which are in the British Museum, are reproduced and described by Jensen, I, 72, 74, 124-127. The best account of the case is a pamphlet entitled "A Narrative of the Affair between Mr. Brown and the Inspector," 1752.

doctor's friends, he was charged with protecting a man guilty of an assault with the intent to kill.

After this fracas, Hill became very bitter towards Fielding. To pass over slurs which contain nothing novel, we come to another incident so preposterous as to be unbelievable. On August 13 appeared a twopenny pamphlet entitled "The Impertinent." It was advertised as a serial —half newspaper, half pamphlet—to appear every Thursday. The periodical never survived the first issue, and no copy of that is known to exist; but an extract from it has been preserved. In it Fielding, Smart, and Hill are all huddled together for abuse. Fielding, though he possessed wit, belongs, it was said, to the monkey type of genius which delights in mischief; Smart is a dull and indefatigable ass, so insensible that he does not feel the thistles that prick his lips; Hill displays the qualities of both species, being as capricious as the monkey and as obstinate as the ass. All are hungry. Against this scurrility, Hill inveighed in his Inspector for August 25, declaring that so infamous a periodical as "The Impertinent" should not be allowed to exist longer. By that time the secret was out. Hill himself wrote "The Impertinent" as well as the violent protest against it. For this deception he was held up to public scorn by Dr. Johnson in "The Gentleman's Magazine" of the same month. The angry reviewer likened Hill's conduct to that of a detected felon, who, when pursued, cries out "stop thief," in the hope of escaping in the crowd that follows him. Johnson's indignation, in which, he says, the public shared, was partly owing to the fact that "The Impertinent" was printed "in the manner of 'The Rambler,'" and that it "cruelly and unjustly attack'd Mr. Smart," a personal friend whom he loved and admired.

Unabashed by the exposure, or rather puffed up by the notoriety gained by it, Hill continued his personal satire with increased violence. Thereby Smart was awakened to fury. In his own name and that of "a particular friend" —of course Fielding—he branded Hill as a liar in "The Daily Gazetteer,"* and set to work on a satirical poem to be called "The Hilliad," addressed to a

Pimp! Poet! Puffer! 'Pothecary! Play'r!

The poem, when it came out, was prefaced by a letter and prolegomena, which included a quotation from "The Impertinent" and a handsome tribute to the genius and character of Mr. Fielding. In the meantime Fielding himself, who had kept quiet since his release of Mountefort Brown, entered the fray with a relentless piece of ridicule and irony. It is all in his leader for August 22, 1752. He there gives a receipt to prevent the ill effects of a raging vanity in an author. He advises him to write a panegyric on himself, claiming for each of his vices the corresponding virtue. If you sprang from a dunghill, boast of your ancestry; if you have been knocked and cuffed about, proclaim your courage and call everybody else a coward; if you are known to be an infamous liar, insist upon your high sense of honour, though you have betrayed all your friends. Then, after you have written your panegyric, give it to the flames, where it will be beyond the reach of malice. Remember the words ascribed to Socrates: "Never speak of yourself: for he who commends himself is vain; and he who abuses himself is absurd."

A still livelier tune was struck up when the theatres opened in the autumn. The undignified rivalry between Garrick of Drury Lane and Rich of Covent Garden then broke out into open war. It had been a sort of tacit understanding between the two houses, that the former should hold rather closely to the regular drama while the latter should have a pre-emption on pantomime. Still, for some time, each manager had been encroaching on the domain of

* Reprinted in "The Gentleman's Magazine," Dec., 1752, XXII, 600.

the other. Two years before, for example, Rich enticed from Garrick two of his best players—Barry and Mrs. Cibber, who pressed him and Mrs. Bellamy hard in the rôles of Romeo and Juliet. At the same time Rich was improving his pantomime. Recently his revival of Theobald's "Harlequin Sorcerer," as I have elsewhere related, met with extraordinary success. For the present season he devised a new entertainment called "The Fair," as an afterpiece to his regular performances. It included, besides the tricks of Harlequin, some expert tight-rope walking by an acrobat named Maddox from Sadler's Wells, and a menagerie of comedians made up as animals. In addition to the rather common lion, bear, cat, dog, and monkey, there were a serpent and an ostrich. The company at Drury Lane also had an excellent Harlequin in Henry Woodward, who had learned his art from Rich. Especially popular was his "Harlequin Ranger," written in conjunction with Garrick. Into this piece Garrick now introduced a scene burlesquing Rich's rope-walker and animals. Rich and his friends were hot at what they denounced as an attempt to draw the audience away from Covent Garden. In truth, it was doubtful which gave the more delight—the original entertainment or the burlesque of it.

On this question the public divided. One of the gentlemen who felt strongly on the subject bore the name of Richard Fitzpatrick. On the evening of the ninth of November the said Fitzpatrick led a party to Drury Lane with the intent of stopping the performance. His purpose he accomplished by throwing an apple from his box at the head of Woodward as soon as Harlequin began his mimicry of Rich. The actor, perhaps hit in the spot aimed at, bowed low and ironically thanked the gentleman for the honour done him. Thereupon ensued a great commotion, amounting almost to a riot; during the next days the town was torn asunder by a dispute over what Woodward actually said when he picked up the apple from the stage. Fitzpatrick declared that the actor then and there challenged him to a duel, thereby affronting him, for no gentleman could fight a low fellow like a player. To set himself right with the public, Woodward appeared before Justice Fielding and swore to an affidavit denying that he ever intended a challenge.* A day or two afterwards Fitzpatrick gave Woodward the lie in a sworn statement before Justice Lediard, another Westminster magistrate.† The case of Woodward *vs.* Fitzpatrick therewith went to the gentlemen of the press for interminable argument without hope or desire of a decision.

Since we last took a survey of these men three new periodicals had sprung up. First, there was Arthur Murphy with "The Gray's-Inn Journal," of which the initial number appeared on October 21. This literary periodical, besides having a Court of Censorial Inquiry in which Dr. Hill received sentence to be transported for a libel on Mr. Christopher Smart of Cambridge, was in general so closely modelled on "The Covent-Garden Journal" as to make it appear that Fielding was conducting two newspapers at one and the same time. In commending Murphy for his imitation, Smart wrote "that 'tis a certain test of true humour to be delighted with the writings of Mr. Fielding."‡ Next came, on November 7, "The Adventurer," with which rumour also connected Fielding as well as his sister Sarah, perhaps because A was used as an initial to some of the articles, and "Benevolus" and "Misargyrus" were signed to a few contributions. Fielding, however, never wrote for this rather sober but excellent periodical; nor probably did his sister. The editor was John Hawkesworth, a friend of Dr. Johnson's. The last

* "The General Advertiser," Nov. 16 and 18, 1752.
† "The London Daily Advertiser," Nov. 17 and 18, 1752.
‡ "The Midwife," Vol. III, 137.

to appear was Thornton, who insulted the public once more with another periodical-pamphlet, "addressed to the writers of the age, but more particularly to Sir Alexander Drawcansir." It was called "The Spring-Garden Journal," written by "Miss Priscilla Termagant, a near Relation of the late Mrs. Roxana." It lasted through four weekly numbers—from Thursday, November 16, to Thursday, December 7, or as long as the author felt there was any occasion for its existence. Thus augmented, the wise men of the press debated the great cause of the theatres.

Hill, under the guise of defending Fitzpatrick, violently assailed Woodward, whom he hated for very personal reasons. In his newspaper he printed Fitzpatrick's affidavit and a long letter giving the gentleman's version of what occurred on the memorable night at Drury Lane. But these were both mild in comparison with the Inspector's own onslaught upon Woodward, whom he denounced as the instigator of the riot and as "the meanest of mankind."* On the other side, Woodward argued his case in "The General Advertiser," until the columns of that newspaper became too restricted to hold his expanding anger. Then he exploded in a sixpenny pamphlet bearing the title "A Letter from Henry Woodward, Comedian, the Meanest of all Characters; to Dr. John Hill, Inspector-General of Great-Britain, the Greatest of all Characters." In a subsequent pamphlet by "Sampson Edwards, the Merry Cobler of the Hay-Market," ironically entitled "A Letter to Mr. Woodward on his Triumph over the Inspector," there is a hint that Fielding had a hand in Woodward's open letter to Hill; and at a somewhat later date, we find it ascribed to Fielding and Garrick jointly. Both surmises are, however, without warrant. The pamphlet in question, of which three editions were sold immediately, has nowhere any traces of aid either from Garrick or Fielding. Wood-

* "The London Daily Advertiser," Nov. 17, 1752.

ward himself, who had been educated at the Merchant Taylors' School, was quite capable of drawing this satirical sketch of the life and character of Dr. Hill. Indeed, probably no outsider knew of those personal relations formerly existing between Hill and Woodward which were therein exposed to the public view.

Already, before the case reached the pamphlet stage, Murphy had commended Garrick for bringing into contempt Rich's dreadful animals; and Hawkesworth had outlined a new pantomime on the labours of Hercules in burlesque of that manager's marvels and monstrosities. Thornton indulged in horse-play at Hill's expense, while "The Gentleman's Magazine" preserved a benevolent neutrality in favour of Garrick, who, to allay the storm, removed the obnoxious scenes from "Harlequin Ranger." At this juncture Fielding, espousing the cause of Garrick, came out in "The Covent-Garden Journal" for November 18, 1752, with a happy burlesque of the quarrel between the two theatres. Much as in the war between Literature and Grub Street, he marshals the forces of Drury Lane under Generals Garrick and Woodward against the forces of Covent Garden under General Rich and his lieutenants. Except for an attack on Hill, it is all in the spirit of banter. The Garrickeans put to rout a company of "ninnies" armed with a small but very dangerous weapon known as a catcall, and capture their trumpeter, who tries to run away but is prevented by an empyema in his side and many bruises. When the prisoner—"the basest and meanest" man that ever blew into a trumpet—was brought before Garrick, "the chief with great disdain turned his back, and ordered the fellow to be dismissed with full power of trumpeting again on what side he pleased." Hill continuing his abuse of Woodward varied by attacks on Smart, Fielding the next week revived his Censorial Court for his final stroke. John Hill alias Jack the Trumpeter is summoned before

Sir Alexander to answer to his infamous conduct. He pleads against the jurisdiction of the court on the ground that he is beneath its notice, and his plea is allowed.

With this parting thrust followed by a farewell to the reader, "The Covent-Garden Journal" came to an end on November 25, 1752. It had run through seventy-two numbers. Its history as an enterprise was much like that of the other two periodicals which Fielding had conducted single-handed save for assistants. One special feature after another dropped away—the Journal of the War, the Censorial Court, and the comment on the news. Moreover, with the fifty-third number, on July 4, "The Covent-Garden Journal" was reduced to a weekly, to appear every Saturday morning; and at the same time an announcement was made that no advertisements, whatever the length, would be received at less than three shillings, with the result that this source of income nearly disappeared. In the leader of that day Sir Alexander says that he has lately given out some hints that he intended to resign his office as Censor of Great Britain on account of his great age, and that he would have done so on that morning had he not been waited upon the day before by the whole town, whose spokesman, Counsellor England, pleaded with him in a most pathetic oration not to withdraw from them their only ray of light. Moved by this affectionate address, Sir Alexander promised to carry on his paper once a week, and dismissed his callers with a gracious smile. Behind these facetious phrases lay hard business considerations. No doubt it was irksome for Fielding to write two leaders every week. There is no doubt also that the periodical did not pay as well as its promoters expected. In a word, "The Covent-Garden Journal" nearly succumbed to the lean months of summer. Thereafter, for lack of adequate support, Fielding's interest waned. Finally, the squabbles that he was forced into if he were to hold his own with a Hill or a

THE HISTORY OF HENRY FIELDING

Thornton, disgusted him. Without warning he threw down his pen, remarking, as he did so, that he had neither desire nor leisure to carry on the paper longer.

And yet, Fielding's resolution was not so sudden as it appeared to be. Among the older newspapers was one known for short as "The General Advertiser,"* which Henry Woodfall, the printer of "Joseph Andrews," had long managed for the proprietors. In anticipation of the demise of "The Covent-Garden Journal," Woodfall's newspaper was reorganized under the title of "The Public Advertiser." Fielding, in the last issue of his journal, recommended it to his subscribers and published an extended announcement, written by himself, of its aim and prospective character. A part of this announcement appeared simultaneously in "The General Advertiser" of the same day. The new journal, in which Garrick, it is said, became a shareholder, was to contain the playbills of both the theatres. Mr. Brogden, by consent of Justice Fielding, was to supply the criminal news; and advertisements might be left with him or at the Universal Register Office as well as with various booksellers. These details make it clear that some of the proprietors of the Universal Register Office—perhaps John and Henry Fielding—were shareholders along with Garrick. As a business enterprise, "The Public Advertiser" was thus the immediate successor of "The Covent-Garden Journal." There were also rumours that Fielding undertook the editorship. As late as February, 1753, this opinion persisted in a satirical pamphlet called "A Scheme for a New Public Advertiser . . . printed for Justice Fail-paper."† To say the truth, "The Public Advertiser," the first number of which appeared on December 1, 1752, was dull enough to give point to the

* It was in full "The London Daily Post and the General Advertiser," which has been earlier quoted under the title of "The London Daily Post."
† "The Monthly Review," Feb., 1753, VIII, 144-145.

wit's suggestion that the time had arrived for the proprietors to make over this newspaper once more, and place its management in abler hands. Fielding, however, never contributed to "The Public Advertiser" anything more than a paragraph expressing his good will, which was run across the page beneath the title of the first number, and subsequent requests that notices of robberies and advertisements of goods lost or stolen be sent to his clerk for inclusion among the items of Bow Street news. His farewell to the reader in "The Covent-Garden Journal" was, so far as is known, his last correspondence with the gay Muse who presided over eighteenth-century journalism.

Sir Alexander's enemies danced a jig over his grave. Hill ironically chose as text for an obituary notice, "De mortuis nil nisi bonum," and professed to be more concerned with the living than with the dead.* "Old England"—presumably Kenrick—took as text "What would have been scandalous in a writer of character was decent in the Censor"; and related the history of "Alec," who was born and "benighted" only to die all within the same year—"a prodigy in nature, and an example hung up in gibbets of ridicule."† Thornton, in addition to various skits such as "An Essay in the true Drawcansirian Stile and Sentiment," described the hero's death and made public his last will and testament.‡ By this instrument "Tom Jones" was bequeathed to the Foundling Hospital, "as a token of gratitude and respect"; "Joseph Andrews" went to Parson Young, the author's "chaplain and quotation-hunter"; Sir Alexander's virtue—all and every part of it—was presented to Dr. John Hill, "as a man needful of the same"; but his honour, "for certain private reasons," was to be compounded with the dust.

* "The London Daily Advertiser," Dec. 6, 1752.
† "Old England," Dec. 2, 1752.
‡ "The Spring-Garden Journal," Dec. 7, 1752.

Apart from the annihilation of Dr. Hill, the satire of "The Covent-Garden Journal" was rarely personal. Fielding drew no malicious portraits like those in Pope's "Dunciad." In a few instances the application, to be sure, was as clear as daylight. There were "Mr. Whytebred" and "Peeragrin Puckle," for example. But in general Fielding described classes; he cut out the coat and let anyone put it on whom it fitted. His ridicule, having good nature behind it, was formed to awaken laughter not to sting or to goad an enemy. For anything Fielding ever wrote in "The Covent-Garden Journal," Thornton had no occasion whatever to brand him as one who bit or snarled at his contemporaries. In most amusing essays, Fielding entertained his readers with a comic history of his own times, explained to them who their "betters" were in the social scale, and what was meant by "people of fashion" in contrast with real ladies and gentlemen. He gave them an account of the great monarchs in the history of English literature; he told them of the devices of unscrupulous booksellers to dispose of worthless wares, and let them see the processes whereby the works of the learned as well as of others are destroyed by pastry-cooks and trunk-makers. At times he became very sober when dealing with grave social evils; and always he united instruction with whim and humour. Nowhere may this be better seen than in his essay—his fourth number—on the complete change in meaning which many words, in perfect accord with a theory of Mr. Locke's, had undergone within a generation or two. Fifty and upwards of these unfortunate victims of fashion he brought together in a list which included:

"ANGEL. The Name of a Woman, commonly of a very bad one.

AUTHOR. A laughing Stock. It means likewise a poor Fellow, and in general an Object of Contempt.

BATTLE OF THE WITS

DEATH. The final End of Man; as well of the *thinking Part of the Body,* as of all the other Parts.

DRESS. The principal Accomplishment of Men and Women.

FINE. An Adjective of a very peculiar Kind, destroying, or, at least, lessening the Force of the Substantive to which it is joined: As *fine* Gentleman, *fine* Lady, *fine* House, *fine* Cloaths, *fine* Taste;—in all which *fine* is to be understood in a Sense somewhat synonymous with useless.

FOOL. A complex Idea, compounded of Poverty, Honesty, Piety, and Simplicity.

GREAT. Applied to a Thing, signifies Bigness; when to a Man, often Littleness, or Meanness.

HAPPINESS. Grandeur.

HONOUR. Duelling.

HUMOUR. Scandalous Lies, Tumbling and Dancing on the Rope.

JUDGE. }
JUSTICE. } An old Woman.

LEARNING. Pedantry.

MODESTY. Aukwardness, Rusticity.

PATRIOT. A Candidate for a Place at Court.

PROMISE. Nothing.

RELIGION. A Word of no Meaning; but which serves as a Bugbear to frighten Children with.

VIRTUE. }
VICE. } Subjects of Discourse.

WIT. Prophaneness, Indecency, Immorality, Scurrility, Mimickry, Buffoonery. Abuse of all good Men, and especially of the Clergy."

This "Modern Glossary," as Fielding called it, was almost a summary of his reflections on the age of George the Second.

Of special interest are several leaders pertaining to his art. His literary career near its end, Fielding reaffirmed

431

or modified certain opinions which he had expressed in his plays and novels, in his prefaces and early essays. He never ceased to ridicule those playwrights and scholars who presumed to improve on Shakespeare. In his youth he exhibited Colley Cibber on the stage, it will be remembered, in the very act of reconstructing "King John." Somewhat later he described a scene in the Elysian Fields where Shakespeare protests against the emendations to the text of his plays such as, the august shade was told, had been made by Theobald. Among critical editions of Shakespeare that had since appeared was one by Warburton, which outdid all others in arrogance. Theobald in the main merely suggested new and often happy readings in difficult passages. Warburton, densely ignorant of Elizabethan English, not only asserted with absolute positiveness that numerous words and phrases, whose meaning is perfectly clear, got into the text by mistake; but, being omniscient, he was able to restore the exact word or phrase that Shakespeare wrote in a given case. In number thirty-one of "The Covent-Garden Journal," Fielding turned the laugh on this school of commentators by a parody of their method, choosing for his purpose the celebrated soliloquy of Hamlet, which he entirely made over in phrasing and punctuation, and then left it without form or sense. Though he avoided any personal reference, Warburton was clearly the man whom he intended to hit. We have seen, too, in the preceding chapter, Fielding's contempt for that pseudo-classicism such as William Mason tried to transplant, which belittled Shakespeare's art and would substitute for it the chorus and the undivided scene; which would remove from a "Hamlet" or a "Lear" all the relics of an ignorant and barbarous age and rewrite those great tragedies as a Racine would have written them. On all these dramatic and textual questions, time has given judgment in favour of Fielding.

432

He enumerated the humorists whom he most prized, and to whom, we may say for him, his genius was most akin. They were Lucian, Cervantes, and Swift. "These authors," he declares in the tenth number, "I shall ever hold in the highest degree of esteem; not indeed for that wit and humour alone which they all so eminently possest, but because they all endeavoured, with the utmost force of their wit and humour, to expose and extirpate those follies and vices which chiefly prevailed in their several countries." With the great triumvirate he joined Shakespeare and Molière, who, though more than humorists, were blessed with the same talents, and who employed them for the same purposes. If this list be compared with the one given in "Tom Jones," it will be noticed that three names have disappeared. Where is Rabelais? Where is Marivaux? Where is Aristophanes, whose comedies Fielding once began to translate with the help of Parson Young? Why Rabelais and Aristophanes are absent Fielding explains at once, as if to allay wonder. They were endowed, he admits, with the very same talents as the rest, but they made a wretched use of them; their design, in Fielding's opinion, was "to ridicule all sobriety, modesty, decency, virtue and religion, out of the world." On Marivaux he is silent. This French novelist, however, was not primarily a humorist, and so the failure to mention him awakens little or no surprise. Fielding's early admiration for Marivaux, which prompted him to uncritical outbursts of praise in "Joseph Andrews" as well as in "Tom Jones," had since naturally waned, with the passing of Marivaux's influence upon him. In "The Covent-Garden Journal" he but corrected an ill-considered estimate of previous years.

His interest in Cervantes, despite the glowing passage on the great triumvirate, had considerably declined also. He now found it difficult to concede that the head of a sensible man could be totally disarranged by reading romances.

433

The adventures to which Don Quixote was subjected, accordingly appeared to him incredible; and he gave the palm to Sancho Panza. Had Fielding written "Joseph Andrews" in 1752, it would have contained none of that horse-play which seems inappropriate as a background to the character of Parson Adams. Certainly the burlesque would have been less unrestrained. The humorists whom Fielding stood by from his boyhood to the end were, then, Lucian and Swift. To him these two writers were the masters of parody, burlesque, and irony; and with all their brilliant endowments of wit and humour, they were men sound and sincere to the core of their being. It was among the last of Fielding's frustrated hopes that he might receive from the public sufficient encouragement to go on with the translation of Lucian projected by himself and Parson Young. It would have been a labour of love. As for himself, he says that "he hath formed his stile upon that very author"; and for his collaborator, that "no man now alive is better versed in that language in which the wit of Lucian lies as yet concealed." That his readers might have an idea of what the result would be, he adds: "To translate Lucian well into English, is to give us another Swift in our own language."*

It has sometimes been said that Fielding in "The Covent-Garden Journal" repudiated the theory of the ridiculous which he had set forth in "The Champion" and the preface to "Joseph Andrews." There is, however, colour rather than full warrant for this conclusion. In several detached essays,† he restates, if I understand him, his former theory in different terms, and at the same time enlarges the scope of it. Following Congreve and Ben Jonson, he defines a humour, in the Elizabethan sense of the word, "as nothing more than a violent bent or disposition of the mind to some

* "The Covent-Garden Journal," No. 52.
† "The Covent-Garden Journal," Nos. 10, 19, 55, 56.

particular point.'' This variation from the normal is really
acquired, though it may be so ingrained as to appear a
natural characteristic or idiosyncrasy. A humour is not
necessarily ridiculous; but it may become ridiculous either
by the degree or the manner of its manifestation. ''Excess,'' says Fielding in a paraphrase of Horace, ''even in
the pursuit of virtue, will lead a wise and good man into
folly and vice.'' Piety, patriotism, and paternal affection,
for example, have all afforded ridiculous characters for the
stage. Likewise, the way in which a humour exerts itself
determines its effect or quality. Ambition in Macbeth
awakens terror. There the humour is tragic. Ambition
in the drunken sailors of ''The Tempest'' awakens mirth.
There the humour is comic. So of pride, avarice, jealousy,
and other ruling passions, the tragic and comic aspects of
which are well known to those who attend the theatre.

A theory of humour which includes Macbeth is rather
startling; the author seems to be a bit pedantic, if indeed
he has not gone astray. Still, all that he says is true
enough; he is aiming at a comprehensive definition preliminary to the statement that the idea of the ridiculous must
be annexed to all the humours with which comedy is concerned. As in ''Joseph Andrews,'' he calls them ''affectations,'' but he does not derive them specifically, as he did
there, from vanity and hypocrisy. Probably experience
had proved to him the narrowness of that formula. In
''The Covent-Garden Journal'' he associates the humours
with ill breeding, showing how the coxcomb and the clown—
those perennial butts of comedy—rise inevitably out of
English life, especially out of the system of education then
prevalent. If everybody were well-bred, there would be a
perfect uniformity of manners throughout the nation, just
as there is now at Court; hence there would be no humours
for the comic writers to ridicule. At the same time would
depart also profanity and indecency and all other spurious

forms of humour such as the practical joke and roasting. As an obvious means of ridding the next generation of those ridiculous characters that haunt the church, the state, and the professions, there is a facetious proposal that the science of good breeding, as well as Greek and Latin, be taught in all the schools and at the two universities. To the public at large, Fielding would recommend a book mentioned in "Joseph Andrews"—the Abbé Bellegarde's "Reflexions on the Ridiculous," wherein are laid down all the rules necessary to their enlightenment. All these observations on humour are in the main a clever adjustment of the old theory to half-serious essays on good behaviour.

Similarly, Fielding ran through the uses of the word wit, in contrast with dulness, for a definition.* As in the case of humour, it is an error, he says, always to unite the idea of levity with wit, and the idea of gravity with dulness. Nothing, in his view, could be duller than the "pert" and "entertaining" essays of some of his contemporaries; whereas in all ages the writers of most wit have often been very grave men. By wit as employed here, Fielding means the neat and felicitous expression of thought in words and phrases that arrest one's attention. In this sense he finds true wit in Plutarch as well as in Lucian, a high degree of it, here and there, in Plato and Aristotle, Cicero and Seneca, and much more of it in the Epistles of St. Paul than in all the writings of "the unjustly celebrated Petronius." At first sight, it is as disconcerting to have St. Paul placed upon the throne of wit as it was to have Macbeth classed with humorous characters. But what Fielding is insisting upon is that there must be seriousness and a fine perceptive sense behind all true wit. Add a certain drollery of style, and the result is Lucian, Cervantes, and Swift. Take away the substance, and nothing remains but the sparkle of a moment—there is left no permanent brilliancy. To give

* See especially No. 18.

point to his conclusion, Fielding declares that the sermons and controversial tracts of Dr. South contain more true wit in union with exquisite drollery than all the comedies of Congreve.

Taken all together, these fragmentary disquisitions on wit and humour do not squarely contradict anything that Fielding had ever written before. His revaluation of the writers whom he most read and his analysis of the humorist's art do, however, point to a man who has come to take a sober view of life and his craft. Congreve, the comic dramatist whom he closely imitated at the outset of his career, he now reads with less pleasure than the sermons of Dr. South. Wit and humour, to interest him, must now be fraught with a high moral purpose. The man who once burlesqued "Pamela" now quotes with approbation a remark of Richardson's to the effect that pleasantry should be only the vehicle of instruction. This opinion, to judge from the entire range of his work, had always been in the rear of Fielding's thought, but he never before expressed himself so outspokenly; nor had his moral aim, though always present, been so clear in his earlier productions. The counterpart to the stress he puts upon morality in the discussion of literary art, is "Amelia." If his procedure in "Amelia" be compared with that in "Tom Jones" or even in "Joseph Andrews," it will be seen that he unmasks the affectations in the old way, but that he brings to the front as never before the motives which led him to write his last novel. He wished to cure society "of some of the most glaring evils, public and private." That, too, he asserts again and again, was the design of those master humorists whom, once having read, he can never forget. It was equally the design of "The Covent-Garden Journal."